The End of the Lake-Dwellings in the Circum-Alpine Region

Edited by

Francesco Menotti

Oxbow Books
Oxford & Philadelphia

Published in the United Kingdom in 2015 by

OXBOW BOOKS
10 Hythe Bridge Street, Oxford OX1 2EW

and in the United States by

OXBOW BOOKS
908 Darby Road, Havertown, PA 19083

© Oxbow Books and the authors 2015

Hardcover Edition: ISBN 978-1-78297-860-2
Digital Edition: ISBN 978-1-78297-861-9

A CIP record for this book is available from the British Library

Library of Congress Cataloging-in-Publication Data

The end of the lake-dwellings in the Circum-Alpine region / edited by Francesco Menotti.
     pages cm
  Summary: "After more than 3500 years of occupation in the Neolithic and Bronze Age, the many lake-dwellings around the
Circum-Alpine region 'suddenly' came to an end. Throughout that period alternating phases of occupation and abandonment
illustrate how resilient lacustrine populations were against change: cultural/environmental factors might have forced them to
relocate temporarily, but they always returned to the lakes. So why were the lake-dwellings finally abandoned and what exactly
happened towards the end of the Late Bronze Age that made the lake-dwellers change their way of life so drastically? The
new research presented here draws upon the results of a four-year-long project dedicated to shedding light on this intriguing
conundrum"--Provided by publisher.
  Includes bibliographical references.
  ISBN 978-1-78297-860-2 (hardcover) -- ISBN (invalid) 978-1-78297-861-9 (digital) 1. Lake-dwellers and lake-dwellings-
-Alps Region--History. 2. Human settlements--Alps Region--History. 3. Bronze age--Alps Region. 4. Iron age--Alps Region.
5. Alps Region--Antiquities. 6. Human ecology--Alps Region--History. 7. Social change--Alps Region--History. 8. Alps
Region--Social conditions. 9. Alps Region--Environmental conditions. I. Menotti, Francesco.
  GN785.E53 2015
  392.3'6093722--dc23
                                        2015016507

Printed in Great Britain by Latimer Trend

For a complete list of Oxbow titles, please contact:

UNITED KINGDOM
Oxbow Books
Telephone (01865) 241249, Fax (01865) 794449
Email: oxbow@oxbowbooks.com
www.oxbowbooks.com

UNITED STATES OF AMERICA
Oxbow Books
Telephone (800) 791-9354, Fax (610) 853-9146
Email: queries@casemateacademic.com
www.casemateacademic.com/oxbow

Oxbow Books is part of the Casemate group

Cover image by Sarah Ommanney

Contents

Acknowledgements

This volume stems from a large international project funded by the Swiss National Science Foundation, in connection to the SNF-Professorship the editor was offered in 2009. Therefore, my sincere gratitude (and that of all the members of the project) goes to the Swiss National Science Foundation (with a special thanks to Inés de la Cuadra for her prompt availability when help was needed) for its invaluable support throughout the duration of the project!

There are also a number of people/colleagues to whom I am particularly grateful for their invaluable help during the writing/editing of this volume. First and foremost a special thank you goes to the project team members: (in alphabetical order) Annekäthi Heitz-Weniger, Benjamin Jennings, Marlu Kühn, Philippe Rentzel, Barbara Stopp, Philipp Wiemann, and most recently also José Granado. The authors of Chapter 3 would also like to thank Joachim Köninger for the stimulating discussions; the authors of Chapter 5 are very grateful to the Archaeological Services of Zurich and Zug, the Laboratory of Dendrochronology and Underwater Archaeology of the City of Zurich, and the Soprintendenza per i Beni Archeologici del Piemonte for their support and generous availability in providing the samples for this study – they would also like to say thank you to Kristin Ismail-Meyer and Christine Pümpin for their kind assistance; and finally, the authors of Chapter 6 are very much indebted to Örni Akeret, Christoph Brombacher, Stefanie Jacomet, Bigna Steiner and Lucia Wick for their help.

The entire IPAS (Integrative Prehistory and Archaeological Science) at the University of Basel has been very supportive throughout the duration of the project and the writing up of this volume; special thanks to Jörg Schibler, Stefanie Jacomet, Angela Schlumbaum, Renate Ebersbach, Kristin Ismail-Meyer, Brigitte Heiz Wyss and Viviane Kolter.

I am also indebted to a number of people not necessarily involved in the project directly, but who have contributed greatly to the development of this volume: Sandy Hämmerle for translating Chapters 5, 6 and 7, and Jamie McIntosh for translating Chapter 2 (all from German); Marc-Antoine Kaeser for the permission to publish two images, Urs Leuzinger for his support and useful insights; and to the people at Oxbow Books (in particular Julie Gardiner, Tara evans and Sarah Ommanney) for their invaluable help.

Last but not least, I am extremely grateful to the Department of Archaeology at the University of Exeter (in particular Robert Van de Noort and Alan Outram) for kindly hosting me as an honorary visiting professor during the writing up and editing of this volume. Very helpful and exceedingly kind was also the support staff Jo Hatt, Lauren Ausden and Phil Robinson. A warm thank you goes in particular to Anthony Harding and his wife Cheryl for their kind friendship and succulent meals at their cottage, and to Bryony and John Coles for the various interesting conversations (over a nice cup of tea) at the Royal Albert Memorial Museum.

List of Contributors

Andre Billamboz
Landesamt für Denkmalpflege
Baden-Württemberg
Hemmenhofen
Germany

Annekäthi Heitz-Weniger
Integrative Prehistory and Archaeological
Science
University of Basel
Switzerland

Benjamin Jennings
School of Archaeological Sciences
University of Bradford
United Kingdom

Joachim Köninger
Janus-Verlag
Freiburg im Breisgau
Germany

Marlu Kühn
Integrative Prehistory and Archaeological
Science
University of Basel
Switzerland

Michel Magny
CNRS
Laboratory de Chrono-Environnement
UFR des Sciences et Techniques
Besançon
France

Nicoletta Martinelli
Dendrodata s.a.s.
Verona
Italy

Francesco Menotti
School of Archaeological Sciences
University of Bradford
United Kingdom

Philippe Rentzel
Integrative Prehistory and Archaeological
Science
University of Basel
Switzerland

Barbara Stopp
Integrative Prehistory and Archaeological
Science
University of Basel
Switzerland

Philipp Wiemann
Archäologischer Dienst Graubünden
Chur
Switzerland

List of Figures

List of Tables

List of Maps

Chapter 1

The lake-dwelling phenomenon: myth, reality and ... archaeology

Francesco Menotti

Introduction

The study of the Circum-Alpine region[1] (Fig. 1.1) lake-dwellings does not only concern archaeological research, but it also encompasses a number of other disciplines as well as a myriad of aspects of our social existence; and that is why we often come across the term 'phenomenon'. In order to understand how the lake-dwelling (phenomenon) research developed, and how we (archaeologists, and scholars of other disciplines) have managed to achieve such an excellent knowledge of those prehistoric lacustrine settlements, it is necessary to go back to the very beginning, and indeed when Mr Aeppli made that fortunate discovery which, in many ways, has changed how people perceive their cultural heritage in central Europe and beyond. The chapter shows how greed and nationalistic propaganda initially prevailed over scientific research, but then common sense won, leading to the development of solid scientific studies, which have revealed all the splendour and fascination of those lakeside villages.

As new research methodology was being developed and knowledge accumulated, we sadly realised that despite their remarkably long tradition (over 3500 years), and their resilience to environmental adversity, the lake-dwellings unexpectedly (or maybe not) 'disappeared' towards the end of the Late Bronze Age, and in some areas even earlier. The Chapter concludes by leaving the question as to why that happened unanswered – it is in fact the task of each of the seven following chapters to provide the reader with crucial clues that will be discussed in the conclusive chapter, when the 'culprit' will be finally revealed.

Ober-Meilen: where it all began

It was a cold winter morning of 1854 when, walking along the eastern shore of Lake Zurich near Ober-Meilen, Mr Johannes Aeppli (a local school teacher) noticed unusual wooden piles sticking out of the shallow water. He took a close look and realised that they were extraordinarily old, perhaps the remains of forgotten bridges, walkways or platforms of some sort. Excited by his discovery, and completely unaware of the immense repercussions that it

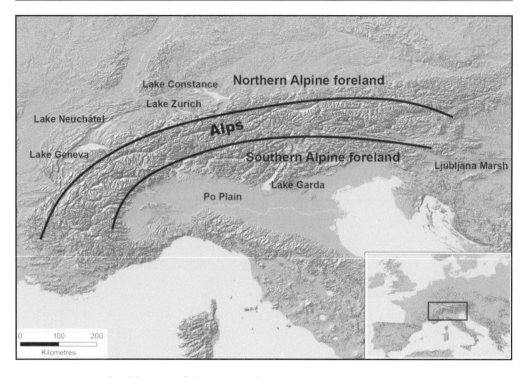

Figure 1.1. Geographical location of the Circum-Alpine region (graphic: Ben Jennings. Base map created using STRM data and ArcWorld River and Lake Overlay).

would have on archaeological research, and on Switzerland in general, in the years to come, he promptly contacted the Antiquarian Society in Zurich to report his finding. It did not take too long for the president of the society, Ferdinand Keller, to visit the site and to grasp that what had just come to light was something major, and which would revolutionise the way we (archaeologists) study our past, and, in a way, also how Switzerland would shape its future (Menotti 2004; 2012: 2–9).

Keller did not waste his time, and started to study straightaway what turned out to be the remains of an ancient lacustrine settlement. His hard work paid off, and he managed to publish a detailed report, namely *die keltische Pfahlbauten in den Schweizersee* (Keller 1854), by the end of the same year. Keller kept his enthusiasm for the Swiss *Pfahlbauten* (Lake-dwellings) for the next two and a half decades, producing seven more reports for the Antiquarian Society in Zurich; six as a single author (Keller 1858, 1860, 1861, 1863, 1866b, 1879), and one with V. Gross, F. A. Forel and E. von Fellemberg (Keller *et al.* 1876). The first six reports were so successful that they reached international reputation – they were even translated into English by John Lee and published as a book: *The Lake-Dwellings of Switzerland and Other Parts of Europe* in 1866 (Keller 1866a), with a second revised and updated edition in 1878 (Keller 1878). The series of the Antiquarian Society reports continued even after Keller's death in 1881; first was Jacob Heierli who wrote the ninth *Bericht* (Heierli 1888), and then, after a long pause of

36 years, the reports started again with David Viollier, who published the last three ones (10th, 11th and 12th) from 1924 to 1930 (Viollier 1924; Viollier *et al.* 1930; Viollier 1930). From the 1930s onwards, the Antiquarian Society reports ceased being published; it is difficult to say whether this was due to a diminished interest in the Swiss lake-dwellings, or because they were, at that time, right in the middle of one of the longest disputes in archaeology, namely the *Pfahlbauproblem* (see below).

The remarkable popularity (national and international) reached by the Swiss, and indeed the entire Circum-Alpine region, lacustrine settlements was not, unfortunately, reflected in academia. In fact, despite the above-mentioned publications, people and 'scholar' alike, were initially more interested in the lucrative side of that rare material culture. Instead of being eager to find out more about who those mysterious lake-dwellers were, it was more like 'how much money they could make'. Everyone wanted a 'piece of the action', and that resulted in the outbreak of what is known as the *Pfahlbaufieber*, an unprecedented 'lake-dwelling artefact rush' that seriously endangered our cultural heritage.

Fishing objects: a lucrative enterprise

In the first couple of decades that followed the Ober-Meilen discovery, the immense popularity gained by the lake-dwellings triggered a feverish quest for prehistoric lacustrine artefacts. Every single lake (regardless of its size) within the Circum-Alpine region was literally assaulted in search of those precious objects. The 'demand' created a unique trade and exchange network within Switzerland first, expanding to the other lacustrine regions of the Alpine foreland later, and finally stretching all over continental Europe, the British Isles, and as far as the United States. The hierarchical structure of this lucrative 'net' started with wealthy collectors on top, followed by improvised antiquarians and/or greedy scholars in the middle, and, at the base of the pyramid, the fishermen. It was indeed the latter category that mercilessly scavenged the lake shores in the hope of finding those quite-different 'fish'. Even their fishing gear underwent a radical transformation; from traditional rods/nets to peculiar tools (see Fig. 1.2) suitable for the collection of any sort of object that resembled a lake-dwelling artefact lying on the bottom of the lake (Desor 1865).

This disgraceful exploitation of ancient artefacts grew exponentially within less than a decade. By then, improvised antiquarians from Switzerland and beyond had made their fortune collecting and selling those objects to private collectors; and those 'commercial' exchanges are still traceable today thanks to the surviving letters of correspondence. Some of the best known examples include the correspondence between F. Keller and J. Messikommer,[2] F. Keller and F. Schwab,[3] and F. Keller and V. Gross[4] to mention but a few – some of the exchanged letters explicitly stated buying and selling lake-dwelling artefacts (Altorfer 2004b; Kauz 2004). This lucrative trade of lake-dwelling material culture was carried out not only nationally, but it stretched well over the Swiss geographical borders, as proven for instance by the correspondence between V. Gross and John Evans[5] (see the John Evans' lake-dwelling collection, Ashmolean Museum[6]), or between Carl Rau[7] and J. Messikommer (Arnold 2013).

What is even more discreditable concerning the above-mentioned infamous artefact trade

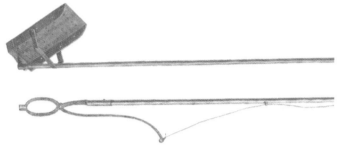

Figure 1.2. Particular 'utensils' used to collect lake-dwelling artefacts from the lake shores during the 19th century's lake-dwelling 'fever' (after: Desor 1865).

is that also important museums (*i.e.* Peabody Museum, the Field Museum in Chicago, Milwaukee Public Museum and many more) from all over the world were involved in that eager acquisition of 'precious' lake-dwelling materials (Arnold 2013). The result of this 'business' was catastrophic, especially for Switzerland where the authorities eventually started to take some measures to protect the Swiss cultural heritage. The Swiss Confederation managed, for example, to acquire V. Gross's enormous collection of ancient lacustrine artefacts (8227) for the incredible (at the time – 1884) sum of 60,000 Swiss francs (Altorfer 2004b: 121–22), before it was nearly sold to an anonymous collector in the United States. The same did not unfortunately happen with G. A.-E. Clément's collection (made of lacustrine artefacts from around Saint-Aubin, Lake Neuchâtel), which was indeed sold to a Boston broker – the collection is currently at the Peabody Museum at Harvard (Arnold 2013: 882).

Amongst the various above-mentioned negative associations, the lake-dwelling 'rush' brought forward also positive aspects for Switzerland; it, for instance, made the Confederation a popular holiday destination (and not only as far as skiing was concerned) in Europe. In fact, famous lake-dwelling sites such as Robenhausen on Lake Pfäffikon were often preferred to more popular destinations (*i.e.* Davos or St Moritz), and the visitor's book kept by Messikommer is the undisputable proof of it (Altorfer 2004a: 94). Another positive outcome of the frenetic lake-dwelling sensation was that it laid the foundations of wetland and scientific archaeological research; although, alas, we had to wait more than a century to see the first results (see below).

Lake-dwelling: history, politics, nationalism and much more

The 19th century lake-dwelling phenomenon in Switzerland was not restricted to lucrative commercial (and/or 'academic') activities, but it also encompassed a number of other spheres of the Swiss society, such as education, politics, art, architecture and literature in general (Kaeser 2004; Menotti 2012: 5). The artificially constructed *Pfahlbaukultur* (lake-dwelling culture) found particularly fertile soil in the Swiss education system; it became, in fact, clear that children were the most vulnerable to be indoctrinated into a, at the time, needed nationalism. Descriptions of how 'important' the life of the *Pfahlbauer/lacustres* (lake-dwellers) was, occupied a large portion of the pupils' school books (one of the most popular being *la Patrie*, published [in various editions] by C.-W. Jeanneret); even the popular literature (*i.e.* novels, poetry, etc.) started to 'exploit' this 'trendy' topic. It is believed that even Le Corbusier,[8] who certainly studied on one of the *La Patrie* editions, developed his fascination for the pile dwellings at a very early age, and that appeal would, later on, be reflected in a large number of his architectural expressions (for example the house on stilts at the Côte d'Azur, France [1922]; Villa La Roche, Paris [1923–4]; Villa Savoye, Poissy [1927–30]; Unité d'Habitation, Marseille [1947–52]; and even a number of buildings in Moscow, to mention but a few) (Vogt 2004, 1998). Artists, in particular painters, also started to use the 'village on stilts' motive for their work; the number of paintings which, in one way or another, represented the idyllic life on the lake are countless, but the most famous one is certainly the 'Neolithic lake village at a Swiss lake' (1867) by Rodolphe Auguste Bachelin.[9] The painting was exhibited (as part of the Swiss contribution) at the *exposition universelle de Paris* (World Exhibition in Paris) in 1867 (Rückert 2004: 170–1, fig. 2). By the turn of the century, the Swiss pile dwellings had gained such popularity that also firms and factories used their image to advertise their products (Fig. 1.3).

Amongst the myriad of ways in which the lake-dwelling image and their constructed historical significance was exploited by the Swiss society, the most obvious (and dangerous) one was the promotion of the Swiss identity and nationalism. The Ober-Meilen discovery (see above), occurred during a delicate moment in Swiss history, when the Confederation had just come out of a civil war, the *Sonderbundskrieg* (separate alliance) (1847), and, as people were searching for stability and a strong Swiss identity, Keller's 'platform' happened to be the best expression of the *Helvetia Sonderfall* (the Swiss exception) (Kaeser 2006). The propaganda worked, and the shaking wooden platform was transformed into a solid rock (with the Swiss Federal Palace on top) representing an idyllic island of solidity surrounded by stormy waters (see fig. 7 in Kaeser 2006). As biased and unsubstantiated as it might have been, this brainwashing process would have faded away with no harm, if it had not transformed into shameful racial statement (allegedly based on 'scientific' anthropological research carried out by the anthropologist Julius Kollmann) on the existence of a *Homo alpinus* race (Helbling-Gloor 2004: 190). It was such a nonsense that eventually led to a growing interest in biologically based notions of ethnicity, which developed further into dangerous eugenic movements in the first half of the 20th century.

Figure 1.3. The lake-dwellings as advertising means to promote commercial products (photograph: courtesy of Marc-Antoine Kaeser, Laténium Museum, Neuchâtel, Switzerland).

Myth meets science: the *Pfahlbauproblem*

Despite being based upon ephemeral ethnographic studies with no scientific evidence, Keller's notion of lacustrine villages built on a 'communal' wooden platform consolidated and perpetuated undisputed throughout the second half of the 19th century. The above-mentioned artificially constructed *Pfahlbaukultur*, its involvement in various aspects of society with a special emphasis placed on nationalistic views refrained any 'attack' (certainly from within Switzerland) to Keller's theory – to contrast it, meant, to a certain extent, lack of patriotism, and as a result, the 'dogma' remained valid for over 70 years. It was in fact not until the mid-1920s that Reinerth (working on a 'different' kind of lake settlements on Lake Feder [Federsee], Germany) suggested that those prehistoric lacustrine settlements might have not stood in the water permanently. The new idea was initially rejected (especially by Swiss scholars); but then, with more evidence, and this time coming from 'proper' pile dwellings on Lake Constance, it was slowly taken into consideration. By building a 22×22m double-walled cofferdam (located in the water at more than 50 metres from the lake shore), Reinerth was able to prove that despite the fact that the village had been constructed on stilts, it was inundated by water only periodically as a result of seasonal/climatic variations (Reinerth 1932) (see Fig. 1.4). This was the first sign of 'thawing', and it was also noticed (though feebly) in the last two *Berichte* of the Antiquarian Society in Zurich (Viollier 1930; Viollier *et al.* 1930) – the *Pfahlbauproblem* (the lake-dwelling dispute) had just begun (Menotti 2001). A second 'attack' to Keller's dogma was launched by O. Paret some 20 years later; Paret (1958, 1942) dared even more than Reinerth, arguing that the lake-dwellings (but only very few of them) could have been built on stilts, but far from the lake shore, and they were never influenced by the lake's fluctuating waters, regardless of how high they were (Fig. 1.4). Paret's theory was strongly disputed initially (see for instance Keller-Tarnuzzer 1945), but then the irrefutable evidence from the Wauwil peat moor (near Lucerne, Switzerland) provided by E. Vogt (1951) managed to convince also the staunchest sceptics. Alas, Keller seemed to be defeated (or at least temporarily), the lake-dwellings became 'lakeside-dwellings' (no longer on stilts and surrounded by water), and the 100th jubilee of their discovery in 1954 was celebrated by sadly denying their existence.

The lake-dwellings, or what was left of them, were forgotten until the economic boom brought to light a substantial number of new lacustrine settlements, as a result of land development and the construction of new roads/highways. In the meantime, the advent of 'New Archaeology' (Binford 1962; Binford and Binford 1968) along with the development of new and more reliable scientific analyses allowed a more careful appraisal of those well-preserved remains – the outcome was astonishing: Keller, Reinerth and Paret were all right. It was in fact realised that there were settlements built on stilts (and even on platforms as Keller imagined) and permanently surrounded by water, others (still on stilts but as individual structures) were flooded only seasonally, and some were located near the shore but never influenced by the lake level fluctuations, no matter how high the water level was (see Fig. 1.4). Most importantly however, they were all classified as 'true' lake-dwellings, regardless of their architectural differences – the *Pfahlbauproblem* was finally over, and the 150th anniversary of their discovery in 2004 was a proper celebration of their existence (Menotti 2004). From

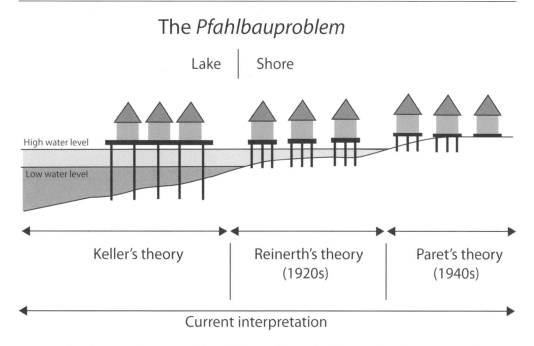

Figure 1.4. Schematic depiction of the Pfahlbauproblem (the lake-dwelling dispute) (modified from Menotti 2001).

then onwards, the lake-dwellings (and their research) experienced a positive revival, becoming part of the UNESCO World Heritage list in June 2011 (Menotti 2012: 353).

Multidisciplinary research: new directions ahead

With the end of the lake-dwelling dispute, research was then able to focus on other more important issues such as patterns of occupation and chronology (see below), environmental and cultural transformations, climate change, and, last but not least, people (how the lake-dwellers lived, in what they believed, *etc.*). The study of this myriad of topics was facilitated by the development of a number of sub-disciplines within archaeology that allowed a better understanding of the various aspect of people's life. Thanks to the advent of radiocarbon dating first, and dendrochronology later, calendar dates could finally be given to those lacustrine villages. The latter technique in particular, allowed the reconstruction of precise development sequences of settlements from their construction to their abandonment (Billamboz 2013, 2004). Dendrochronology has recently moved one step further with the development of dendrotypology, which not only takes into account the chronological aspect of occupation, but also other important factors such as environmental change and forest management (see Billamboz and Martinelli, Chapter 3 this volume). Major contributions to the lake-dwelling research were also made by archaeobotany, archaeozoology and geoarchaeology. Thanks to the pristine preservation of plant remains in waterlogged conditions, the remarkable results achieved by archaeobotanical analyses in the past forty years are second to none. These have helped shed light not only on the various aspect of the lake-dwellers' everyday life such as economy, trade/exchange, diet and social interaction, but they have also contributed to the reconstruction of palaeoenvironments and vegetation history around the lakes (Jacomet 2004, 2007, 2013 – see also Kühn and Heitz-Weniger, Chapter 6 this volume). All this could not have been done alone; significant contributions were also made by archaeozoology and geoarchaeology. The former has for instance improved our knowledge on people's carnivorous diet and how meat was procured, *i.e.* via animal husbandry or game hunting (Schibler 2004, 2013 – see also Stopp, Chapter 7 this volume). In some cases it has even been possible to link special events (such as overexploitation of wild species) to change of climatic conditions (Schibler and Jacomet 2005). Finally, similar fundamental results in the lake-dwelling research have been obtained by geoarchaeology. Let us not forget that archaeological remains are, after all, found in the soil; thorough pedological analyses of archaeological terrains (the matrix within which the artefacts are buried) are therefore germane to our understanding of site formation processes, which may hold the secret of the settlement biographical development and, with it, the possible causes of its abandonment (Goldberg and Macphail 2006; French 2013 – see also Wiemann and Rentzel, Chapter 5 this volume). An area of research within lake-dwelling studies that does not, alas, have a long tradition, is the study of people's social structure, organisation, and beliefs. The simple fact that social hierarchy and organisation is not readily evident in the lake-dwellers' material culture should not be an excuse for avoiding the topic. Systematic studies of artefacts, inhabited spaces and their relationship to the surrounding environment may reveal what the naked eye (or perhaps even a biased one) has not as yet spotted. Research is catching up quickly though, and new approaches to fill in this gap have already been advanced in the study of households, beliefs, contact and cultural change (Doppler *et al.* 2010; Ebersbach 2010; Jennings 2012a, 2012b, 2014; see also Jennings, Chapter 8, this volume).

Although all of the above-mentioned sub-disciplines have obtained remarkable results in solo studies, their real potential lies in their synergetic collaboration with one another (Wiemann *et al.* 2013). This is indeed the multi-disciplinary approach to research adopted with the SNF project[10] upon which the current volume is based. The single sub-disciplines have worked on different topics alone, obtaining a number of results; where possible though, these results have been subsequently compared with, and tested against, the results obtained on similar topics, but by other sub-disciplines. Only when the results were corroborated by two or more sub-disciplines, were they accepted as valid. For instance, lake-level fluctuations can easily be spotted in the soil stratigraphy where lake marl has been identified between, or within, the anthropogenic layers. At the same time though, these water transgressions should produce evidence of aquatic plant remains or pollen to confirm an increase of waterlogged conditions and/or humidity in and around the site. In ideal cases, all this could also be supported by dendrochrological/dendrotypological studies showing growth impediment (*e.g.* narrow rings) within the tree-ring sequence caused by the excess of water, as happened at the Early Bronze Age lake-settlement of Siedlung-Forschner at the Federsee, Germany (Billamboz 2003, 2009; see also fig. 6.4 in Menotti 2012: 263). Finally, if the suspected climatic variations are confirmed by palaeoclimatological studies, the results cannot be disputed, and therefore regarded as valid. Environmental/climatic evidence is of course not the only evidence taken into consideration; the remarkable level of preservation on lacustrine sites also allows cultural factors to be studied. For example, the ratio of wild : domestic animals can also give us clues as to whether, due to environmental change, one or the other varies considerably (Schibler and Jacomet 2005; Schibler *et al.* 1997; Menotti 2009). Last but not least, also material culture/artefacts play a crucial role; for instance, identifying their locations (*e.g.* displacement from their original location), provenience, spatial distribution and function is all part of the germane process of 'reconstructing' the site/settlement, with the final goal of shedding light on whoever built, inhabited, and eventually abandoned that settlement.

Chronology and occupational patterns: a discontinuous continuity

The solid development of the above-mentioned science-oriented disciplines within lake-dwelling studies has not only improved our understanding of the lake-dwellers' way of living and their material culture, but also the chronology of their settlements, including the various occupational patterns. It is for instance incredible how chronological charts (especially concerning the lake-dwelling areas of northern Switzerland and southern Germany) have changed since some of the first attempts of Vogt (1967) to place the various lake-dwelling archaeological cultures in (relative) chronological order in the early and mid-1960s. Although some radiocarbon dates had already been obtained from the rich organic materials found at the lake-dwelling sites, it was not until the 1970s that the chronologies were given the first calendric years (Stöckli 1986: 14). It was however in the 1980s, thanks to the development of the first dendrochronology series, that the lake-dwelling chronology was revealed in all its splendour (Becker *et al.* 1985). It was, for instance, established that the lacustrine settlement tradition in the northern Circum-Alpine region started around the 42nd century BC and terminated towards the end of the 7th century BC. Despite a myriad of advantages though, the precision of dendrochronology brought some 'disappointment', revealing that the over-3500-year-long lake-dwelling occupation was far from continuous; there were in fact periods of occupation alternating with periods of abandonment. Each time that a new discovery was made, there was of course the hope that occupational gaps would be filled, but, even some thirty years later, some of those hiatuses are still there (*e.g.* in the middle Neolithic [*c.* 3540–3410 BC]; in the transitional period late Neolithic/Early Bronze Age [*c.* 2400–2100 BC] and in the Middle Bronze Age [*c.* 1500–1100 BC]; and various other regional ones) (see Fig. 1.5). In the southern slopes of the Alpine range (Slovenia, northern Italy and part of the Po Plain), the less-reliable tree-ring chronologies (see Billamboz and Martinelli, Chapter 3 this volume) do not allow for precise chronologies; it is however quite clear that there the prehistoric lacustrine villages (including the *terramare*) ceased to be built much earlier than in the north. In fact, by the 12th century BC, despite no major climatic oscillations, all lake-dwellings had been abandoned, with the sporadic occupation (not confirmed by dendrochronology) at Viverone in the late 11th century BC (Rubat Borel 2006: 440; 2009) being the only exception (see also Köninger, Chapter 2, this volume).

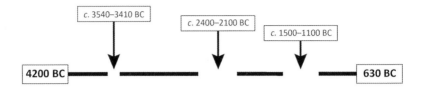

Figure 1.5. Chronology of the three main lake-dwelling occupational hiatuses in the Circum-Alpine region (graphic: Ben Jennings).

From a zoomed-out standpoint, the Circum-Alpine region lake-dwelling tradition is therefore seen as a continuous one, but as we zoom in to different areas or different lakes, the picture changes drastically. In some regions, occupational patterns seem to follow the various climatic variations, whereas in other zones the apparently symbiotic climate-lacustrine settlements relationship is not so obvious. In fact, in some periods, there is an apparent contradiction, namely a complete lack of occupation during favourable climatic conditions (see Chapters 4 and 9, this volume). It is therefore clear that occupational patterns are (or could be) dictated by much more complex factors than simply climatic variations. What is apparent though, is that regardless of what caused the numerous hiatuses, the lake-dwellers always returned to the lake shore after they were abandoned, except at the very end of the Late Bronze age/beginning of the Iron Age, when, for some reason (see Chapter 9, this volume), the lake-dwelling tradition ceased.

Conclusions

It is almost unimaginable that a nice stroll along the Ober-Meilen shore of Lake Zurich in that cold winter of 1854 would have triggered a phenomenon that spanned through a myriad of aspects of our social life; from economy, to politics, cultural heritage education, arts, and, last but not least, archaeological research. The novelty of ancient lacustrine material culture prompted curiosity, which initially degenerated into disgraceful greed for money and disrespect for our cultural past, transforming, later on, into political drive and dangerous processes of nationalistic propaganda. It then took a turn to more creative orientations such as art, literature and architecture, neglecting, alas, the scientific aspect of archaeological research. The potential was however there, and it eventually came out; first with the so-called *Pfahlbauproblem* initiated to determine whether those ancient lake villages were built on stilts or directly on the ground, and then with the establishment of what is now known as wetland archaeology. It was thanks to the development of a number of sub-discipline within archaeology (*e.g.* archaeobotany, archaeozoology, geoarchaeology and dendrochronology) that the immaculately preserved organic artefacts showed all their potential. This, however, amongst the many advances in the research, brought about also a slight disappointment; the lake-dwelling tradition was not a continuous event, and, most importantly, did not last forever. In fact, the 7th century BC shows the last evidence for a way of life that perpetuated for more than three and a half millennia, and then 'suddenly' disappeared. At this point we cannot help but wonder: what is it that really happened?

Notes

1. By 'Circum-Alpine region' is meant the geographical area encompassing not only the Alps, but especially their surrounding regions also known as 'Alpine foreland' or 'pre-Alpine region'. It is indeed within this area that the lakes [and lake-dwellings] are located. The Circum-Alpine region stretches across six countries, namely Switzerland, southern Germany, eastern France, Austria, Slovenia and northern Italy (see Fig. 1.1).
2. Jakob Messikommer (1828–1917) Farmer and lake-dwelling research pioneer – he was the discoverer of the famous lake-dwelling site of Robenhausen, on Lake Pfäffikon, Switzerland.
3. Colonel Friedrich Schwab (1803–1869), hunter and collector of antiquities.
4. Victor Gross (1845–1920), medical doctor and collector of antiquities.
5. Sir John Evans (1823–1908), British antiquarian, archaeologist and geologist.
6. The author worked on John Evans Lake-dwelling collection at the Ashmolean Museum Oxford in 2004/5, developing the following webpage: http://www.ashmolean.org/ash/amps/jevans/. The correspondence between Evans and Gross is mentioned in various letters, which are part of Evans' collection in the archives of the Ashmolean Museum.
7. Carl Rau (1826–1887) German school teacher, and eventually curator of the Department of Antiquity at the Smithsonian.
8. Charles-Édouard Jeanneret, alias Le Corbusier (1887–1965), was a Swiss-French architect known as one of the pioneers of modern architecture.
9. Rodolphe Auguste Bachelin (1830–1890), Swiss painter.
10. SNF project is entitled: 'The end of the lake-dwelling phenomenon: cultural *vs* environmental change'.

References

Altorfer, K. R. (2004a) Pfahlbautourismus und Pfahlbauentdeckungen im Ausland. In Antiquarische Gesellschaft in Zürich (ed.) *Pfahlbaufieber: Von Antiquaren, Pfahlbaufischern, Altertümerhändlern und Pfahlbaumythen*: 91–101. Zürich: Chronos Verlag.

Altorfer, K. R. (2004b) Von Pfahlbaufischern und Alterthümerhändlern. In Antiquarische Gesellschaft in Zürich (ed.) *Pfahlbaufieber: Von Antiquaren, Pfahlbaufischern, Altertümerhändlern und Pfahlbaumythen*: 103–24. Zürich: Chronos Verlag.

Arnold, B. (2013) The Lake-dwelling diaspora: museums, private collectors, and the evolution of ethics in archaeology. In F. Menotti and A. O'Sullivan (eds) *The Oxford Handbook of Wetland Archaeology*: 875–91. Oxford: Oxford University Press.

Becker, B., Billamboz, A., Egger, H., Gassmann, P., Orcel, C. and Ruoff, U. (eds) (1985) *Dendrochronologie in der Ur- und Frühgeschichte: die absolute Datierung von Pfahlbausiedlungen nördlich der Alpen im Jahrringkalender Mitteleuropas*. Basel: Schweizerische Gesellschaft für Ur- und Frühgeschichte.

Billamboz, A. (2003) Tree rings and wetland occupation in southwest Germany between 2000 and 500 BC: Dendroarchaeology beyond dating. *Tree-Ring Research* 59: 37–49.

Billamboz, A. (2004) Dendrochronology in lake-dwelling research. In F. Menotti (ed.) *Living on the lake in prehistoric Europe: 150 years of lake-dwelling research*: 117–31. London: Routledge.

Billamboz, A. (2009) Jahrringuntersuchungen in der Siedlung-Forschner und weiteren bronze- und eisenzeitlichen Feuchtbodensiedlungen Südwestdeutschlands. Aussagen der angewandten

Dendrochronologie in der Feuchtbodenarchäologie. In Landesamt für Denkmalpflege (ed.) *Siedlungsarchäologie im Alpenvorland XI*: 399–556. Stuttgart: Konrad Theiss Verlag.

Billamboz, A. (2013) Dendrochronology in wetland archaeology. In F. Menotti and A. O'Sullivan (eds) *The Oxford Handbook of Wetland Archaeology*: 617–31. Oxford: Oxford University Press.

Binford, L. R. (1962) Archaeology as Anthropology. *American Antiquity* 28(2): 217–25.

Binford, S. R. and Binford, L. R. (eds) (1968) *New perspectives in archaeology*. Chicago: Aldine.

Desor, E. (1865) *Les palafittes ou constructions lacustres du lac de Neuchâtel*. Paris: Libraire Éditeur.

Doppler, T., Pichler, S., Jacomet, S., Schibler, J. and Röder, B. (2010) Archäobiologie als sozialgeschichtliche Informationsquelle: ein bisland vernachlässigtes Forschungspotential. In E. Classen, T. Doppler and B. Ramminger (eds) *Familie – Verwandtschaft – Sozialstrukturen. Sozialarchäologische Forschungen zu neolithischen Befunden*: 119–39. Kerpen-Loogh: Welt und Erde Verlag.

Ebersbach, R. (2010) Soziale Einheiten zwischen 'Haus' und 'Dorf' – neue Erkenntnisse aus den Seeufersiedlungen. In E. Classen, T. Doppler and B. Ramminger (eds) *Familie – Verwandtschaft – Sozialstrukturen. Sozialarchäologische Forschungen zu neolithischen Befunden*: 141–56. Kerpen-Loogh: Welt und Erde Verlag.

French, C. (2013) Geoarchaeological and soil micromorphological studies in wetland archaeology. In F. Menotti and A. O'Sullivan (eds) *The Oxford Handbook of Wetland Archaeology*: 555–68. Oxford: Oxford University Press.

Goldberg, P. and Macphail, R. I. (2006) *Practical and theoretical geoarchaeology*. Oxford: Blackwell

Heierli, J. (1888) Pfahlbauten – Neunter Bericht. *Mitteilungen der Antiquarischen Gesellschaft in Zürich* 22(2): 1–66.

Helbling-Gloor, B. (2004) Die Pfahlbauer in Schulbuch und Jugendliteratur. In Antiquarische Gesellschaft in Zürich (ed.) *Pfahlbaufieber: Von Antiquaren, Pfahlbaufischern, Altertümerhändlern und Pfahlbaumythen*: 187–201. Zürich: Chronos Verlag.

Jacomet, S. (2004) Archaeobotany: a vital tool in the investigation of lake-dwellings. In F. Menotti (ed.) *Living on the lake in prehistoric Europe: 150 years of lake-dwelling research*: 162–77. London: Routledge.

Jacomet, S. (2007) Plant macrofossil methods and studies: use in environmental archaeology. In S. A. Elias (ed.) *Encyclopedia of Quaternary Science*: 2384–412. Oxford: Elsevier.

Jacomet, S. (2013) Archaebotany: the potential of analyses of plant remains from waterlogged archaeological sites. In F. Menotti and A. O'Sullivan (eds) *The Oxford Handbook of Wetland Archaeology*: 497–514. Oxford: Oxford University Press.

Jennings, B. (2012a) Settling and moving: a biographical approach to interpreting patterns of occupation in LBA Circum-Alpine lake-dwellings. *Journal of Wetland Archaeology* 12: 1–21.

Jennings, B. (2012b) When the Going Gets Tough…? Climatic or Cultural Influences for the LBA Abandonment of Circum-Alpine Lake-Dwellings. In J. Kniesel, W. Kirleis, M. Dal Corso, N. Taylor and V. Tiedtke (eds) *Collapse or Continuity? Environment and Development of Bronze Age Human Landscapes. Proceedings of the International Workshop 'Socio-Environmental Dynamics over the Last 12,000 Years: The Creation of Landscapes II'*: 85–99. Kiel: Rudolf Habelt.

Jennings, B. (2014) *Travelling Objects : Changing Values. The role of northern Alpine lake-dwelling communities in exchange and communication networks during the Late Bronze Age*. Oxford: Archaeopress.

Kaeser, M.-A. (2004) *Les Lacustres: Archéologie et mythe national*. Lausanne: Presses Poyltechniques et Universitaires Romandes.

Kaeser, M.-A. (2006) Des fantasmes d'une Suisse insulaire. Le mythe de la civilisation lacustre. *Perspective – Actualités de la recherche en histoire de l'art* 1/2: 178–86.

Kauz, D. (2004) Zur Praxis antiquarisch-prähistorischer Forschung: Die Zirkulation von Artefakten,

Wissen und Geld. In Antiquarische Gesellschaft in Zürich (ed.) *Pfahlbaufieber: Von Antiquaren, Pfahlbaufischern, Altertümerhändlern und Pfahlbaumythen*: 147–67. Zürich: Chronos Verlag.

Keller-Tarnuzzer, K. (1945) Pfahlbauten Arbon-Bleiche. *Jahrbuch der Schweizerischen Gesellschaft für Ur- und Frühgeschichte* 36: 19–26.

Keller, F. (1854) Die keltische Pfahlbauten in den Schweizerseen – Erster Bericht. *Mitteilungen der Antiquarischen Gesellschaft in Zürich* 9(3): 65–100.

Keller, F. (1858) Pfahlbauten – Zweiter Bericht. *Mitteilungen der Antiquarischen Gesellschaft in Zürich* 12(3): 111–55.

Keller, F. (1860) Pfahlbauten – Dritter Bericht. *Mitteilungen der Antiquarischen Gesellschaft in Zürich* 13(3): 73–116.

Keller, F. (1861) Pfahlbauten – Vierter Bericht. *Mitteilungen der Antiquarischen Gesellschaft in Zürich* 14(1): 1–34.

Keller, F. (1863) Pfahlbauten – Fünfter Bericht. *Mitteilungen der Antiquarischen Gesellschaft in Zürich* 14(6): 129–88.

Keller, F. (1866a) *The lake-dwellings of Switzerland and other parts of Europe.* (Translated and arranged by John Lee). London: Longmans Green & Co.

Keller, F. (1866b) Pfahlbauten – Sechster Bericht. *Mitteilungen der Antiquarischen Gesellschaft in Zürich* 15(7): 245–320.

Keller, F. (1878) *The lake-dwellings of Switzerland and other parts of Europe.* (Translated and arranged by John Lee. 2nd edn). London: Longmans Green & Co.

Keller, F. (1879) Pfahlbauten – Achter Bericht. *Mitteilungen der Antiquarischen Gesellschaft in Zürich* 20(3): 1–58.

Keller, F., Gross, V., Forel, F. A. and Von Fellenberg, E. (1876) Etablissements lacustres: résultats des recherches exécutées dans les lacs de la Suisse occidentale – Siebter Bericht. *Mitteilungen der Antiquarischen Gesellschaft in Zürich* 19(3): 1–69.

Menotti, F. (2001) The 'Pfahlbauproblem' and the history of the lake-dwelling research in the Alps. *Oxford Journal of Archaeology* 2 (4): 319–28.

Menotti, F. (ed.) (2004) *Living on the lake in prehistoric Europe.* London: Routledge.

Menotti, F. (2009) Climate variations in the Circum-Alpine region and their influence on the Neolithic – Bronze Age lacustrine communities: displacement and/or cultural adaptation. *Documenta Praehistorica* 36: 61–66.

Menotti, F. (2012) *Wetland Archaeology and Beyond: Theory and Practice.* Oxford: Oxford University Press.

Paret, O. (1942) Die Pfahlbauten. Ein Nachruf. *Schriften des Verein für Geschichte des Bodensees und seiner Umgebung* 68: 75–84.

Paret, O. (1958) *Le mythe des cités lacustres et les problèmes de la construction néolithique.* Paris: Dunod, (La nature et l'homme; 2).

Reinerth, H. (1932) *Das Pfahlbaudorf Sipplingen. Ergebnisse der Ausgrabungen des Bodenseegeschichtsvereins 1929–30.* Leipzig: Curt Kabitsch.

Rubat Borel, F. (2006) Il Bronzo Finale nell'estremo Nord-Ovest italiano: il gruppo Pont-Valperga. *Rivista di Scienze Preistoriche* LVI: 429–82.

Rubat Borel, F. (2009) Entre Italie et Gaule: la transition âge du Bronze / âge du Fer dans le Piémont nord-occidental et la Vallée d'Aoste. In M. J. Roulière-Lambert, A. Daubigney, P.-Y. Milcent, M. Talon and J. Vital (eds) *De l'âge du Bronze à l'âge du Fer en France et en Europe occidentale (Xe-VIIe siècle av. J.-C.). Actes du XXXe colloque international de l'A.F.E.A.F., thème spécialisé co-organisé avec l'A.P.R.A.B (Saint-Romain-en-Gal, 26–28 mai 2006)*: 237–52. Dijon: Revue Archéologique de l'Est, supplément 27.

Rückert, A. M. (2004) Pfahlbauten aut Reisen: Darstellungen der Pfahlbauzeit an Welt- und Landesaustellungen (1867–1939). In Antiquarische Gesellschaft in Zürich (ed.) *Pfahlbaufieber:*

Von Antiquaren, Pfahlbaufischern, Altertümerhändlern und Pfahlbaumythen: 169–86. Zurich: Chronos Verlag.

Schibler, J. (2004) Bones as a key for reconstructing the environment, nutrition and economy of the lake-dwelling societies. In F. Menotti (ed.) *Living on the lake in prehistoric Europe: 150 years of lake-dwelling research*: 144–61. London: Routledge.

Schibler, J. (2013) Bone and antler artefacts in wetland sites. In F. Menotti and A. O'Sullivan (eds) *The Oxford Handbook of Wetland Archaeology*: 339–55. Oxford: Oxford University Press.

Schibler, J. and Jacomet, S. (2005) Fair-weather archaeology? A possible relationship between climate and the quality of archaeological sources. In D. Gronenborn (ed.) *Climate variability and Culture change in Neolithic societies of Central Europe 6700–2200 cal BC*: 27–39. Mainz: Römisch-Germanisches Zentralmuseum.

Schibler, J., Jacomet, S., Hüster-Plogmann, H. and Brombacher, C. (1997) Economic crash in the 37th and 36th century BC cal in Neolithic lake shore sites in Switzerland. *Anthropozoologica* 25–26: 553–70.

Stöckli, W. E. (1986) Einleitung. In C. Osterwalder and P. A. Schwarz (eds) *Chronologie*: 8–18. Basel: Schweizerische Gesellschaft für Ur-und Frügeschichte.

Viollier, D. (1924) Pfahlbauten – Zehnter Bericht. *Mitteilungen der Antiquarischen Gesellschaft in Zürich* 29(4): 150–252.

Viollier, D. (1930) Pfahlbauten – Zwölfter Bericht. *Mitteilungen der Antiquarischen Gesellschaft in Zürich* 30(7): 1–89.

Viollier, D., Ischer, T. and Tschumi, O. (1930) Pfahlbauten – Elfter Bericht. *Mitteilungen der Antiquarischen Gesellschaft in Zürich* 30(6): 1–57.

Vogt, A. M. (1998) *Le Corbusier, le noble savage: toward an archaeology of modernism*. Cambridge, MA: Massachusetts Institute of Technology.

Vogt, A. M. (2004) Le Corbusier im Bann des 'Pfahlbau-Fiebers'. In Antiquarische Gesellschaft in Zürich (ed.) *Pfahlbaufieber: Von Antiquaren, Pfahlbaufischern, Altertümerhändlern und Pfahlbaumythen*: 203–11. Zürich: Chronos Verlag.

Vogt, E. (1951) Das steinzeitliche Uferdorf Egolzwil 3 (Kt. Luzern). Bericht über die Ausgrabung 1950. *Zuschrift für Schweizerische Archäologie und Kunstgeschichte* 12: 193–219.

Vogt, E. (1967) Ein Schema des Schweizerischen Neolithikums. *Germania* 45: 1–20.

Wiemann, P., Kühn, M., Heitz-Weniger, A., Stopp, B., Jennings, B., Rentzel, P. and Menotti, F. (2013) Zurich-Alpenquai: A Multidisciplinary Approach to the Chronological Development of a Late Bronze Age Lakeside Settlement in the Northern Circum-Alpine Region. *Journal of Wetland Archaeology* 12: 58–85.

Chapter 2

Bronze Age lacustrine settlements in the Circum-Alpine region: chronology, architectural styles, occupational patterns, and much more

Joachim Köninger

Introduction

In 1980, the lectures (subsequently published by Kimmig *et al.* 1981: 1–63) held by the Bronze Age study group as part of the annual conference of the West and South German Association of Archaeology in Baden (Canton Aargau, Switzerland), summarised the state of research, up until that time, in Bronze Age (lake-) pile-dwellings around the Circum-Alpine region. In south-western Germany, the project Bodensee-Oberschwaben (Lake Constance-Upper Swabia) had just started, but some of the spectacular results (similar to those achieved up until then in western Switzerland and the southern slopes of the Alps) were already available. The highlights included aerial photography able to identify Late Bronze Age constructions on the shores of the Swiss Plateau lakes, as well as the discovery of a peat bog containing complex wooden architecture of an Early and Middle Bronze Age settlement at Fiavè, south of the Alps. Kimmig *et al.*'s (1981: 11) research report – essentially a topographical atlas and corpus of finds from wetland settlements – also showed the positive outcomes of systematic research of Bronze Age settlements around the Alpine region. Research increased throughout the 1980s, with the addition of emergency/rescue excavations and the reappraisal of older find inventories in museum collections and *Kantonsarchäologie* achieves. Discoveries diminished slightly in the 1990s and 2000s, but lake-dwelling studies are still very active today (*e.g.* Degen 1981; Kimmig *et al.* 1981; Schlichtherle 1981; Ruoff 1981; Aspes *et al.* 1982; Köninger *et al.* 1982; Köninger 1986; Becker *et al.* 1982; Gross *et al.* 1987; Perini 1987, 1988; Bernatzky-Goetze 1987; Rychner 1987; Arnold 1986, 1990; Bericht RGK 1990; Hochuli 1994; Hafner 1995; Balista and Leonardi 1996; Billamboz and Martinelli 1996; Schöbel 1996; Bernabò Brea 1997; Schlichtherle 1997; Ruoff 1998; Billaud and Marguet 1999, 2005; De Marinis 1997, 2002, 2007a, 2007b; Wolf 1998; Wolf *et al.* 1999; Spring 2000; Conscience and Eberschweiler 2001; Menotti 2001, 2004; Bertone and Fozzati 2004; Eberschweiler 2004; De Marinis *et al.* 2005; Köninger 2006a; Rubat Borel 2006; Eberschweiler *et al.* 2007; Martinelli 2007; Pillonel 2007; Gaspari 2008; Scherer and Wiemann 2008; Billamboz *et al.* 2009; Arnold 2009; Winiger and Burri-Wyser 2012; Köninger and Schöbel 2010; Rubat Borel 2010; Arnold and Langenegger 2012; Bleicher *et al.* 2013; Gut 2013; Rapi 2013).

The comprehensive dendro-dating of numerous lacustrine settlements, which nowadays is taken for granted, seemed rather unimaginable in the early 1980s. The dendrochronology studies that started in Switzerland with Ulrich Ruoff and in southern Germany with Becker and Billamboz (Becker *et al.* 1985) spread to Italy and Slovenia, allowing outstanding accomplishments in the past 30 years (see Billamboz and Martinelli, Chapter 3 this volume). In addition to a network of sustainable dendro-data, research fields oriented towards forestry and the history of the climate stared to develop, and dendrochronology became a science in its own right (see Bleicher 2013). Increasing interest in environmental archaeology allowed thorough investigations of the various socio-economic aspects of Bronze Age settlements.

That Neolithic and Bronze Age lake-dwellings of the Circum-Alpine region would, one day, become part of the UNESCO World Heritage Project seemed only a dream in the 1980s (note that Kimmig (1981) proposed an 'Atlas of Stone and Bronze Age wetland settlements' in the Circum-Alpine region), but all the efforts undertaken by the various academic and non-academic institutions eventually paid off in 2011, when the dream became reality (see Ch. 1).

This chapter highlights the various chronological and cultural contexts of the Bronze Age (BA) lacustrine settlements in the Circum-Alpine region, focusing in particular on settlement structure, house construction, and individual settlement dynamics. Special emphasis will also be placed upon the BA settlement network, differentiating (where possible) the connective aspects of the north and south of the Alps – especially as far as the early Early Bronze Age lake-dwellings are concerned.

The Circum-Alpine Bronze Age

The Circum-Alpine region was subject to a great variety of cultural zones of influence during the Bronze Age; as a result, it cannot be regarded as a homogenous cultural area (cf. Schlichtherle 1997: 13). A uniform pile-dwelling culture that spread across space and time (*e.g.* the Circum-Alpine region; the Neolithic and the Bronze Age) never existed; rather, there were a series of cultural groups that changed according to specific areas and specific periods. Like other earlier or later periods, the Bronze Age was no exception (Fig. 2.1).

The Early Bronze Age (EBA) north of the Alps was generally divided as follows: the Rhône culture to the west (cf. Hafner 1995; Winiger and Burri-Wyser 2012), the Singen and Arbon cultures linking central and eastern Switzerland and south-western Germany to the east (Köninger 2006a), and the Straubing culture and their various ceramic groups in Bavaria (Möslein 1997: 37ff.). Pile-dwelling settlements farther east on the periphery of the Alps in the Austrian cultural groups of Veterov, Unterwölbling, Litzen ceramics, and Wieselburg-Gata are unknown. In these cultural groups, only influences of the ceramic spectrum of lacustrine dwellings of the Lago di Garda (Lake Garda) region can be found (Rapi 2013: 542).

Generally, on the northern rim of the Alps, there were some differences between the north-western Alpine groups and the Danube groups (David-Elbiali and David 2010: 300).

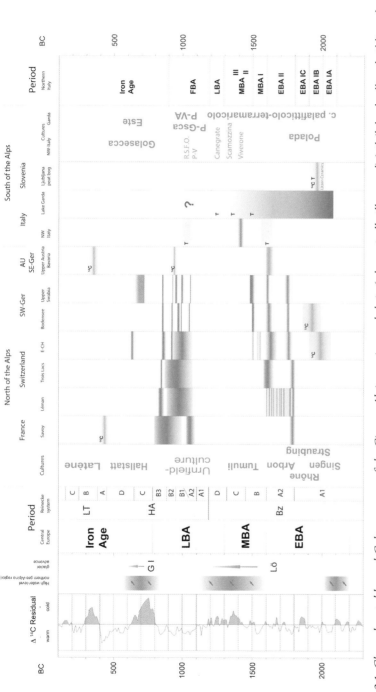

Figure 2.1. Chronology tables and Culture groups of the Circum-Alpine region and their (schematically illustrated) 'pilellake-dwelling building phases'. Generally based on dendrodata, compiled with reconstructed high lake-levels on pre-Alpine lakes and Δ¹⁴C-residual curve (the Δ¹⁴C-Residual curve, glacier advance and lake-level data are from: Maier and Vogt 2007, fig. [Abb.] 70). Key: Lö = 'Löbbenschwankung' cold phase; G I = 'Göschenen I' cold phase; ¹⁴C = based on radiocarbon dates; T = based on typological analyses; EBA = Early Bronze Age; MBA = Middle Bronze Age; LBA = Late Bronze Age; HA = Hallstatt; LT = La Tène; Bz = Bronze; Ger = Germany; CH = Switzerland (data from: Becker et al. 1985; Arnold 1990; Beer et al. 1994; Hafner 1995; Seifert 1996; Billamboz and Schöbel 1996; Marguet 1997; Wolf et al. 1999; Köninger 2001; Conscience and Eberschweiler 2001; Marguet 2005; Billaud and Marguet 2005; Köninger 2006a; Rubat Borel 2006; Martinelli 2006, 2007, 2013; Gaspari 2008; Corboud and Pugin 2008; Billamboz 2009; Müller and Lohrke 2009; Bleicher 2011; Winiger and Burri-Wyser 2012; Gut 2013). Key (northern Italy): EBA= Bronzo Antico; MBA = Bronzo Medio = LBA = Bronzo Recente; FBA = Bronzo Finale; R.S.F.O = Rhin-Swiss-France-Oriental group; P-V= Pont Valperga group; P-Gsca = Proto Golasecca group; P-VA = Proto Villanova group (data from: De Marinis 2002: 23ff; 2009: 535ff.).

The south-western German group; the Swiss and French groups; and the Singen, Arbon, and Rhône cultures; belong to the western areas, whereas the Straubing, Unterwölbling, Veterov, and Wieselburg-Gata groups and the Litzen ceramics belong to the eastern zone. On the eastern side of the southern Alpine slopes, the Deschmann pile-dwellings in the Ljubljana Marsh show traces of Early Bronze Age occupations of the Ljubljana culture, with the most recent finds (according to the Litzen ceramics) seen as coming from the Early Bronze Age (Parzinger and Dular 1997: 74f.; Dular 1999; Gaspari 2008: 71ff.). The Early Bronze Age lake-dwellings to the south of the Alps with a clear centre around Lake Garda are ascribed to the Polada culture. In this region and in the adjoining Po Plain, the pile-dwelling culture is referred to as 'ciclo culturale palafitticolo-terramaricolo' (pile-dwelling-*terramare* culture) (De Marinis 1997; Rapi 2013: 542). To a certain extent, this is justifiable, as the archaeological cultures of the Early and even Middle Bronze Age here were significantly linked to the pile-dwellings and the *terramare*.

The spatial structuring of the Middle Bronze Age (MBA) was somewhat more extensive. North of the Alps, the few lacustrine settlements that can be definitely identified as belonging to the early Tumulus culture are only found, according to Innerhofer (2000: 447), in the south-west (*Nadeltrachtkreis*). The prevalent MBA cultural groups south of the Alps were: the Viverone culture (De Marinis 2009: 538ff.), also called 'the north-western Italian facies of the Middle Bronze Age', according to Rubat Borel (2010: 28f.), in north-western Italy; and the already-mentioned 'ciclo culturale palafitticolo-terramaricolo' in the east (De Marinis 1997, 2006: 539).

There were hardly any representatives of Late Bronze Age (LBA) cultural groups on the lake shores south of the Alps (cf. De Marinis 2009: 542), with only one example on Lake Viverone in the second half of the 11th century BC (attributed to the R.S.F.O, HaB1) (see Fig. 2.1; cf. Rubat Borel 2006: 240ff.). In contrast, Late Bronze Age lake-shore settlements in the northern pre-Alpine region became re-established (after the MBA hiatus) between Lake Geneva and Lake Starnberg from the middle of the 11th century BC and continued until the end of the 9th century BC (and in very isolated cases even later – see below).

Iron Age pile structures were very scarce, but they did exist (at least in the northern part of the Circum-Alpine region) (cf. Gollnisch-Moos 1999; Billaud 2005: 14f.; Schlitzer 2005: 53ff.). The fish-trap complex from Oggelshausen-Bruckgraben, although certainly not a regular lake settlement, is one such case (and not the only one – see below). The settlement-like features and the early Iron Age find materials of this site in the Federsee (Lake Feder) of south-western Germany (Köninger 2002: 34ff.) substantiate the attraction and also the economic significance that the pre-Alpine lakes had for the settlers of the pre-Alpine region even in later prehistory (7th and 5th/4th centuries BC).

Locations of Bronze Age sites

Bronze Age lake-shore settlements are mostly located on the large Alpine lakes, but there are also some notable examples on smaller lakes. The choice of settlement sites followed the patterns already established in the Neolithic. Repeatedly, preferred sites for Bronze Age complexes were shallow-water morainic shoals near the lake shores and island-like (or peninsula) locations that were geographically favourable for protection or communication. Lake-shore settlements are also often found near inlets/outlets of rivers, for example Seefelder Aach (Unteruhldingen on the Bodensee), or the various tributaries of Lake Geneva, *e.g.* La Venoge and Morges, on which the Early Bronze Age lake-shore settlements of Preverenges, Morges, and Tolochenaz were situated (cf. Schlichthlerle 1990: 227ff.). In Upper Swabia, the BA settlements Wasserburg-Buchau and Siedlung-Forschner on the Federsee are situated at a central position in the northern section of the trans-Alpine communication axis Lake Garda – Lake Constance (going over the Reschen Pass, Lenzerheide, following the northern gateway to the central Alps, and following the Alpine-Rhine valley via Lake Constance), which leads, via the Schussen, to the Danube: one of the major communication routes to the east. Generally the number of LBA lake-shore settlements on the large pre-Alpine lakes was larger than the number of EBA ones.

Particularly dense settlement areas were sited at narrow parts of the lakes or at lake outlets, such as 'Konstanzer Trichter' and 'Stiegener Enge' on the Bodensee (cf. Schlichtherle 1990; Köninger and Schöbel 2010), the 'Hurdener Enge' on upper Lake Zurich, the outlet of the River Limmat on lower Lake Zurich (cf. Ruoff 1981; Gut 2013), and also on the outlet of the River Rhône on Lake Geneva.

Bronze Age lake-settlements south of the Alps are found in similar locations (cf. Balista and Leonardi 1996: 223f.; Rapi 2013: 532f.). Important regional as well as long-distance communication routes are also noticeable, and this applies in particular to a number of BA lake-shore settlements in the Lake Garda region, on Lake Varese and on Lake Viverone, the latter situated near the Aosta Valley (the gateway of the western Alps).

In addition to simple clusters of settlements (see Köninger 2006a: 224; Billaud 2012: 354f.; Gut 2013: 82, 142, fig. [Abb.] 86), the Early and Late Bronze Age lake-dwellings were also constructed in chains of settlements along the lake shores (see Marguet 1997: 136; Conscience 2005: 63; Köninger and Schöbel 2010; Burri-Wyser 2012) or, as in the case of the Lake Garda region, on geological morainic amphitheatres near the lakes (*e.g.* the *Amfiteatro morenico*) (Rapi 2013, 527). Peninsulas projecting into the lakes indicate that a considerable number of the complexes were deliberately erected at places where the landward sides of the settlements were difficult to access, thus offering some form of security. South of the Alps, security and protection evidently played a major role in the choice of site, as exemplified by the landside enclosures and palisades at Lake Viverone (Bertone and Fozzatti 2004), Lake Monate (Martinelli 2013), and Lake Garda (Rapi 2013).

The distribution of Bronze Age lacustrine settlements around the Circum-Alpine region

Bronze Age lake-dwellings are scattered all over the Circum-Alpine region, but the vast majority are, however, located in the north-western Alpine foreland. The most populated areas were the Swiss Plateau lakes and Lake Zurich in Switzerland, Lake Bourget in Savoy (France), and in the German-Swiss border area of the Bodensee (see Billamboz and Schöbel 1996: 203ff.; Billaud and Marguet 1999, 2005; Köninger 2006a; Hafner 2006: 110ff; Pillonel, 2007; Billamboz *et al.* 2009: 532f.; Gut 2013: 46ff.) (see Map 2.1 at the end of this chapter).

Off-site features such as pathways, logboats, and other isolated finds are also part of the rich lake-dwelling archaeological assemblage (Eberschweiler 2004; Billamboz 2009).

South of the Alps, another distinct concentration of Bronze Age lake-dwellings is found in the Lake Garda region (see Map 2.1 at the end of this chapter). Other important settlement sites lie to the west between Lake Como and the Aosta Valley, for example at Lake Varese (Martinelli 2013: 117ff.) and Lake Viverone (Menotti *et al.* 2012). A few more settlements are also located in the Ljubljana Marsh in Slovenia (cf. Parzinger and Dular 1997; Gaspari 2008; Dular 1999).

In the north-eastern Circum-Alpine region, Bronze Age lake settlements are primarily represented by old finds of the late 19th/early 20th centuries. In fact, apart from the pile dwellings of Roseninsel on Lake Starnberg (cf. Schmid *et al.* 2000), there has been hardly any research in the region. The reasons for this scarcity of sites (only four – see Map 2.1 at the end of this chapter) could be linked to specific factors (Dworsky and Reitmaier 2003: 51ff.). For instance, it might be the result of peculiar cultural-historical issues, which are difficult to identify. This is somewhat strange, as quite a few lakes in the areas are indeed suitable for lacustrine settlements.

Chronology of lacustrine settlements

Dendro-dating and radiocarbon dating (¹⁴C)

The way the Bronze Age lake-settlements have been dated using the two main dating techniques (*i.e.* dendrochronology and ¹⁴C) varies considerable throughout the Circum-Alpine region. The majority of Bronze Age dendro-data comes from Switzerland (Becker *et al.* 1985; Arnold 1990; Seifert 1996; Wolf *et al.* 1999; Eberschweiler 2004; Bleicher 2011; Arnold and Langenegger 2012; Winiger and Burri-Wyser 2012; Gut 2013), south-western Germany (Bodensee-Upper Swabia) (Billamboz 2009; see also Chapter 3, this volume), and Savoy in eastern France (Billaud and Marguet 1999: 16ff.; Billaud 2012: 350ff.). A further key area is northern Italy, where floating sequences (mostly in Lake Garda) have been developing since the late 1980s (cf. Billamboz and Martinelli 1996: 91ff.; Martinelli 2007; see also Chapter 3, this volume).

The tree-ring sequence north of the Alps correlates well with the regional standard chronology, and the dates are as accurate as ±1 year (in some cases, they are accurate to within six months), whereas south of the Alps only a series of floating regional curves exist; most settlements are dated by ¹⁴C with the help of wiggle-matching, reaching an accuracy of ±10–30 years. It is also important to notice that the absolute dating of lacustrine settlements of the early Early Bronze Age in northern Switzerland and south-western Germany is mostly based on radiocarbon data. This is mainly due to the use of quick-growing timbers (possibly coppice shoots) from open areas for the construction of the lacustrine settlements. As a result, the wood samples have few annual rings and cannot be dated dendrochronologically (cf. Conscience 2001: 147ff.; Köninger 2006a: 237ff.). Finally, attempts to date Bronze Age lake-settlements with dendrochronology in Slovenia and especially in Austria have not been very successful (cf. Veluscek and Cufar 2010: 352f.; see also Chapter 3, this volume).

Sample numbers and dating density

The number of dated timbers per settlement site varies significantly, but in the northern parts of the Alps, a reasonably high number of dated samples would be more than *c.* 1,000 per site. At the Siedlung-Forschner settlement in the Federsee moor, for example, from a total of 7,818 timbers, sorted by type, 1,759 were used for tree-ring analyses (Billamboz 2009: 422, Tab. 1, DC-Statistik für Bodensee-Oberschwaben; Billamboz 2009: 418, fig. 9). By contrast, in Concise (Lake Neuchâtel), thanks to the high proportion of oaks, of the 1,760 wood samples from Bronze Age constructions, 1,709 were dated (Winiger and Burri-Wyser 2012: 22, fig. 18). From the considerably smaller lake-settlement at Bodman-Schachen I, on the other hand, there are all in all fewer than 100 dated wood samples (Köninger 2006a: 244ff.). In some felling phases, such as the Late Bronze Age constructions at Zurich-Alpenquai, very few woods were omitted (cf. Gut 2013: 138, fig. [Abb.] 75). The possible targets of dendrochronology range from simply dating (*e.g.* giving calendar years to the settlements) to establishing a detailed history of the construction of the entire site (site biography), including the reconstruction of the forest management of individual settlements (*e.g.* Langenegger 2012).

The existing remains of Bronze Age settlement phases on the lake shores of the northern pre-Alpine region – Switzerland and south-western Germany – have been systematically recorded, forming a close-knit data network of dendro-data and radiocarbon data. For almost all the archaeologically established settlement phases, sufficient numbers of sites have been dated and placed in their proper chronological context. However, this is not to say that all the settlement phases are represented in an absolute chronological grid. The use of young woods with few annual rings, or non-oak constructions, may still hinder the smooth development of the chronological sequence. The Early Bronze Age settlements of the lakes in Savoy (France) have not been so lucky as their Swiss/German counterparts; in fact, only one settlement (Sevrier Les Mongets, Lake D'Annecy, France) has, up to now, been dated at 1800 BC (see Billaud 1993: 114f.).

The dendro-data series from the lake-settlements south of the Alps are less comprehensive – they cover, in fact, fewer than 50 samples (cf. Martinelli 2007), and they belong to the Early (mostly the first part) and Middle Bronze Age of northern Italy. Questions about the history of the construction and the inner structure of Bronze Age lake-settlements, as well as the dynamics of the settlers, of the southern Circum-Alpine region can thus, at least on the basis of dendrochronology, be pursued only to a limited extent for the time being.

Cultural context and chronology of Bronze Age lacustrine settlements

Early Bronze Age

After a long hiatus in occupation at the very beginning of the Bronze Age, lake-settlements of the northern Circum-Alpine region started reappearing (according to ^{14}C) between the 21st and 19th centuries BC (see Fig. 2.2). The first sites are from Zurich-Mozartstrasse on Lake Zurich (Bleicher 2011: 59ff.); Greifensee-Böschen and Greifensee-Starkstromkabel on Lake Greifen (Greifensee) (Conscience and Eberschweiler 2001: 136ff.); and Bodman-Schachen IA, Ludwigshafen-Seehalde (layer 10), Arbon-Bleiche 2, Bodman-Weiler I, and

Eschenz/Öhningen-Orkopf on Lake Constance (see Map 2.2 at the end of this chapter) (Köninger 2006a; cf. Benguerel *et al.* 2011: 84ff.).

The Bodman beakers (Fig. 2.3A) could be viewed as the 'ceramic index fossil' that is consistently present at the lake-settlements. On the other hand, the metal objects make it even more difficult to link the sites to the typical Bronze Age chronology of metal finds. As a result, their chrono-cultural context relies almost fully on their ^{14}C dates. The ^{14}C dates from the lake-settlements with Bodman facies overlap the earlier ^{14}C dates from the Singen burial ground (Fig. 2.2) near Hegau on the Bodensee. The grave inventory at Hegau contains paddle pins (*Ruderkopfnadeln*), a Horkheim pin, and a small disc-headed pin (*kleine Scheibennadel*) – all typical examples of the early southern German Early Bronze Age, which, according to Ruckdeschel, dates to BzA1a and A1b (Ruckdeschel 1978: 297f.; Krause 1988: 75f, 78). The Bodman facies can thus be included in the early Early Bronze Age of the Singen culture (BzA1) (Köninger 2006a). Furthermore, a rim shard of a handled beaker from grave 63 of the Singen burial ground (Krause 1988: 46 f.; Table [Taf.] 6.D5) compares well with the Bodman beakers. Further proof of the cultural classification of the Bodman beakers is provided by ceramics found at Singen Nordstadtterrasse, an Early Bronze Age settlement site that Krause believes to be the remains of a farmstead, which he places in the chronological context of the neighbouring burial ground (Krause 2001: 71f.). Here, there are beaker shards similar to those of Bodman-Schachen I and to those of layer 10 at the lake-dwelling of Ludwigshafen-Seehalde (Köninger 2006a). The dating of the Bodman beakers to the early Early Bronze Age is almost certain, but it cannot be ruled out completely that such beakers were still in use in the BzA2a stage. However, concluding a definite place in the BzA2a chronology, as recently proposed by David and David-Elbiali (2010: 302ff.) in a typological study that included finds from Concise-sous-Colachoz (Burri-Wyser 2012: 173), does not seem to be feasible.

Dendro-dates (although wiggle-matched) in the southern slopes of the Alps (mainly northern Italy) come from the oldest Bronze Age lake-settlements in the Lake Garda region. The cultural layers from settlement phases Lavagnone 2 and 3 have yielded dates between 2080 and 1991 BC (Lavagnone 2) and between 1984 and 1916 BC (Lavagnone 3) (De Marinis, 2007b: 9f.). The period corresponds to the local early Early Bronze Age (BA IA-B) (Rapi 2013: 538ff.), which includes the cultural context of Polada (cf. De Marinis 2002; Martinelli 2007; David-Elbiali and David 2010).

The relationship between the two aforementioned regions (Bodensee/Zürichsee and Lake Garda) is tangible via the ceramic inventory. Amongst the settlement ceramics from Singen (Krause 2001: 67ff.), there is a fragment of a handle with a simple knob-like attachment (Fig. 2.3.A7a), as found in the inventory of Lavagnone 2 and dating to the BA IA phase (Bermond Montanari *et al.* 1996: 60f.; Rapi 2013: 540f.). Furthermore, in the stratified early Early Bronze Age settlement ceramics from Lavagnone (sector B), there are double lugs (see below) and bellied pots with circumferential double bands, which are best compared to vessel ceramics from Greifensee-Böschen (Conscience and Eberschweiler 2001: 143, fig. 7.5; Rapi 2007: figs 35 and 175) and Greifensee-Starkstromkabel (Conscience and Eberschweiler, 2001: 145, fig. 8). Additional similarities are also noticeable between the beaker from Starkstromkabel (which shows an extended attached handle and a wide

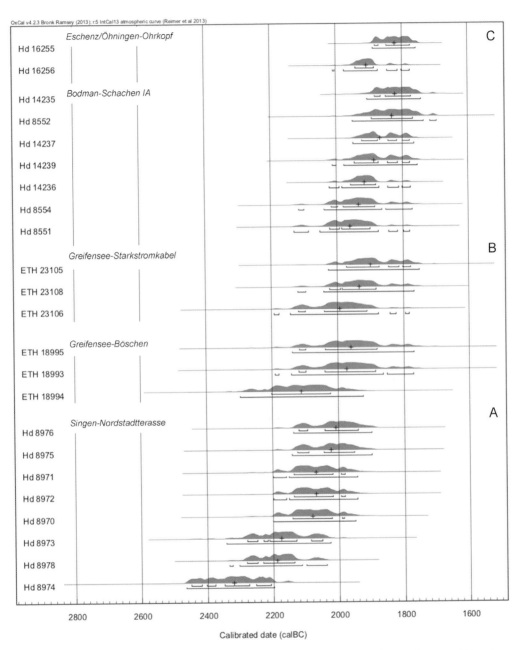

Figure 2.2. ¹⁴C dates of the early EBA from the Bodensee region and the lake-shore settlements of Zürichsee. A = grave fields Singen; B = lake-settlements Greifensee; C = lake-settlements Bodensee (¹⁴C Data after Krause 1988: 169ff.; Conscience and Eberschweiler 2001: 138f.; Köninger 2001: 97; 2006a: 237ff.).

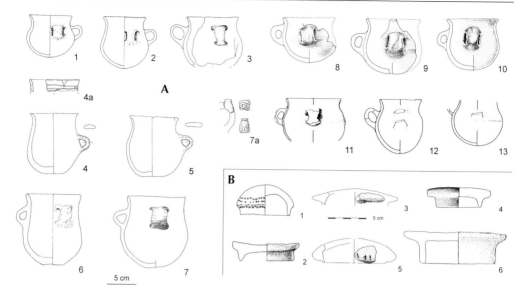

Figure 2.3. (A: 1–13) Bodman beaker from early EBA lake-shore settlements and knob at handle from settlement on mineral soil at Singen 'Nordstadtterrasse'; and (B) ceramic lids from Bell-Beaker culture sites (3–6), and early EBA sites (1–2). A: 1–3. Ludwigshafen-Seehalde, layer 10; 4–7. Bodman-Schachen I, layer A; 7a. Singen 'Nordstadtterrasse' (find-complex B, Sn 273); 8–10. Zürich Mozartstrasse (8 layer 1u, 9 Phase A, 10 Phase A and B); 11. Greifensee-Böschen; 12–13. (surface finds) Greifensee-Starkstromkabel (after: Conscience and Eberschweiler 2001: 141, fig. [Abb.] 5.1, p. 142 fig. [Abb.] 6.1.9; Köninger 2006a, table [Taf.] 1, pp. 212f.; Schmidheiny 2012, tables [Taf.] 2.17, 7.66, 11.133). B: 1. Early find at Bodman 'am Schachenhorn' (probably also Bodman-Schachen I); 2. Zürich-Mozartstrasse; 3. Chevenez-combe En Vaillard; 4. Ornaisans 'Médor'; 5. Chevenez-combe Varu; 6. Heilbronn-Böckingen (after: 1. Köninger 2006c: 79ff.; 2. Schmidheiny 2011: table [Taf.]. 11.157; 3. and 5. Deslex Sheik et al., 2006: 51ff.; 4. Guilaine et al., 1989: fig. [Abb.] 1.11; 6. Sangmeister 1959: table [Taf.] 19.8).

grip – Fig. 2.3.A12 – Conscience and Eberschweiler 2001: 142, fig. 7.1) and those from Lavagnone (BA I A), which, themselves, are stylistically and chronologically linked to the Greifensee settlements (Rapi 2007).

More intra-regional connections are to be found south and east of the Lake Garda region, with the small Early Bronze Age burial grounds of Sorbara di Asola 'Campagnotti' (Mantova) and Arano di Cellore di Illasi (Verona) (Map. 2.2) showing typological similarities to the Polada culture; in the case of Arano, objects are also supported by ^{14}C dates (Valzolgher 2013: 555ff.). It is worth noticing, though, that the find spectrum from both burial grounds is less rich in metals than Singen is. The lugged neck ring and a dagger blade from Arano, as well as the stratified flanged axe of Torbole type, are made of Lavagnone 2 copper, which is produced from fahlore (*Fahlerz*) ore. The same type of ore was used for all metal objects from Singen, showing that the production of tin bronze was not yet established in either region (cf. dazu Kienlin 2007: 6ff.). The similarity between the two regions is also stressed by De Marinis and Valzolgher (2013: 555f.), who refer to the Singen metal as '*metallo tipo Polada-Singen*'.

The Singen cemetery contains gender-specific burials, as identifiable from the Bell Beaker pottery type. At the same time, vessel forms, V-buttons, and arm guards in the finds allow, within the context of the older Polada culture, clear lines to be drawn with the traditions of the Bell Beaker culture (cf. De Marinis and Valzolgher 2013; Rapi 2013) – connections can also be drawn between the Bell Beaker culture and the lacustrine settlements of the Bodensee, as well as those of the Lake Zurich regions. Layer A of Bodman-Schachen I contains a shard of a line-decorated 'bell beaker', which was found together with ceramics of the Bodman facies (Köninger 2006a: 128f, 211); in the old find inventory of Bodman-Schachen, there is also a lid (Fig. 2.3, B1) which almost certainly belongs to the Bell Beaker culture. A similar lid was found in layer 1 of Zurich-Mozartstrasse on Lake Zurich (Fig. 2.3.B2; Schmidheiny 2011: 119, tables [Taf.] 11 and 157), but this shows fewer similarities to other Bodman beakers in the Zürichsee and Bodensee region. All this points to the slight inaccuracy of Schmidheiny's (2011: 125) categorisation of spherical and Bodman beakers.

Cereal cultivation also points in the same direction, as large amounts of spelt wheat (*Triticum spelta* L.) were found in Bodman-Schachen I (layer A), confirming that the earliest certain evidence in the Bodensee region indeed comes from the sites of the Bell Beaker culture (Rösch and Sillmann 2007: 100f.; cf. Jacomet 2008: 364). The final piece of proof is the v-perforated button from grave 7 in the Singen cemetery (Krause 1988: 98). We can therefore conclude that the cultural roots of the early Early Bronze Age in the Lake Garda, Bodensee, and Lake Zurich regions could be placed in the context of the Bell Beaker culture. As a result, there were quite a lot of similarities between these regions in this period (21st–20th centuries BC); this is confirmed by burial practices, artefact assemblages, and also metallurgy. What is even more interesting is that up until that period, the lake-dwellings were exclusively confined to these regions. Admittedly, this does not explain why in other areas of Switzerland, France, and northern Italy with similar early Early Bronze Age characteristics the lake-settlements of the 21st–20th centuries BC are missing.

The second dendro-dated period is the 19th century BC, and it is more evident south of the Alps (Map 2.3, at the end of this chapter), where it is part of the later Polada culture (De Marinis 2002, 2007a; Rapi 2013: 540f.). It is interesting to notice that in the stratigraphy of Lavagnone (sector B – phase BA IC), there are apparent stylistic features linked to the '*Barche di Solferino*'-type ceramics. One slight shortcoming of this area is that the correlations between the stratified material and the dendro-data of this period are less reliable – unfortunately, the same could be said for later (Early and Middle Bronze Age) lake-settlements of the southern Circum-Alpine region.

Reliable dendro-dates for lake-settlements are available north of the Alps, but only from the 18th century BC onwards. Most of these settlements are located in Switzerland; a few are located in Savoy (France) and on the Federsee in Germany; and, according to more recent investigations, some can be found at Unteruhldingen-Stollenwiesen on the Bodensee (Billaud 1993; Billamboz 2009: 499, fig. 110 – Phase E 2; Corboud and Pugin 2008: 52; Burri-Wyser 2012: 172ff.; see also Chapter 3, this volume). This new occupation is chronologically placed after a short climatic depression in the 19th century BC, as far as indicated by the ^{14}C-residual curve (cf. Fig. 2.1).

Cultural layers have not survived in the Bodensee and Federsee settlements of this phase;

therefore, the cultural context of the dated structures is unclear (see Burri-Wyser 2012: 172, fig. 167). In western Switzerland, on the other hand, the stratified material from these structures is reliably linked to the Aare-Rhône groups of the Rhône culture (cf. Burri-Wyser 2012: 172ff.). We do not know exactly why dated settlement phases from the middle of the 18th century BC are missing on Lake Zurich, are scarce on the Bodensee, and absent in northern Italy. This is partially due to the difficulty of dating the wooden material available and due to the climate (cf. Fig. 2.1). In fact, most of the evidence from the 18th century BC comes from Lake Geneva located further to the south (Map 2.3), possibly due to the more moderate climate (also see below).

South of the Alps, however, the settlement gap does not seem to be climate related but more linked to the difficulty of dating the wooden samples. Interestingly, the ceramics of this period belong to the '*Barche di Solferino*' type (Rapi 2013: 540; Cazzanelli 2002: 187ff.), but this typological classification, according to Cazzanelli (2007: 189, fig. 17), lies in the 17th century BC. As a result, it cannot be ruled out that lake shores in the 18th century BC were temporarily avoided as being a terrain that was unfavourable for settling, maybe because the natural lakeside resources had been depleted by previous settlement phases.

Regarding the 17th century BC, most of the Early Bronze Age lake-shore settlements north of the Alps date to the second half of the century (Fig. 2.1). The majority of the data comes from the lake-settlements of north-eastern Switzerland and the Bodensee, which culturally belong to the Arbon culture. Less common is the evidence from the lakes of the Swiss Plateau and Lake Geneva; the lake-dwellings (such as those of Concise-sous-Colachoz) there are part of the later Aare-Rhône groups of the Rhône culture. The generally prospering settlement activities probably point to the resumption of the dominating favourable climatic conditions together with assumed low water levels on the great pre-Alpine lakes (Billamboz 2009: 499). These favourable conditions ceased once again (at least north of the Alps) between 1600 and 1590 BC. As pointed out above, dendro-dates from the 17th century BC in the southern part of the pre-Alpine region are scarce. The few dated lacustrine villages are those of Frassino I (dated between 1709 and 1637 ±12 BC) and Bosca di Pacengo (1639 and 1611 ±10 BC S-Data [sapwood without the last three rings]) in the Lake Garda area and that of Sabbione on Lake Monate. The material culture of these sites belongs to the transition from Early to Middle Bronze Age (Martinelli 2007: 105) or, according to De Marinis (2002: 23ff.), to the Horizon '*Barche di Solferino*' of the late Early Bronze Age.

Middle Bronze Age

According to dendro-data, the Middle Bronze Age lake-settlements north of the Alps span from the 16th century BC to around 1500 BC. It should be pointed out though that none of the complexes produced stratified find materials that could be linked to the dendro-data. It is therefore assumed that the lake-dwelling Middle Bronze Age period started in the 16th century BC or, at the latest, at around 1500 BC. This supposition was developed from the study of the Siedlung-Forschner settlement material culture, especially its last dendro-dated occupational phase (Forschner 3), which ended around 1480 BC. Evidence for an early start of the Middle Bronze Age chronology in the northern Circum-Alpine region is found in layer C at Bodman-Schachen I; the site in fact shows that MBA pottery was already in the Bodensee region around 1600 BC. Along similar lines, a ^{14}C series consisting of 12 datasets from tumuli graves in south Germany (Müller and Lohrke 2009: 25ff.) indicates a setting for the Middle Bronze Age already deep in the 16th century BC. According to Reinecke's chronology correlated to all ^{14}C data, the period occupied a time span of 1550–1300 BC (Müller and Lohrke 2009: 28ff.), and the ^{14}C data range for the middle Danube Tumuli culture Mährens (dating between 1650/1600 and 1300/1255 BC) (Peska 2013: 391f.) matches these dates quite well. As far as the aforementioned beginning of the Middle Bronze Age in northern Italy is concerned, from the viewpoint of the central European chronology of the Middle Bronze Age, the balance is tipping slightly towards the higher chronology (slightly older), particularly as no real Early Bronze Age B inventory has been dated there (cf. Vanzettin 2013: 276ff.).

North of the Alps, 16th-century MBA lake-dwellings are scarcely found on smaller lakes (*e.g.* the size of Lake Nussbaum), as well as on larger ones such as Lake Biel (Nidau BKW) (cf. Billamboz 2009: 532f.) and Lake Neuchâtel (Concise) (Winiger 2012: 119ff.) (Map 2.4). The dendro-dates of the 16th century BC lake-village of Zurich-Mozartstrasse could be added to the list, but they are currently under revision (cf. Bleicher 2011: 54 ff., 65). The only recorded evidence of the 16th century BC from the lake shores south of the Alps is Il Sabbione (1583 and 1563 ±30 BC) on Lake Monate (Martinelli 2013: 118ff.).

The second (and last) phase of Middle Bronze Age lake-settlement occurred between Lake Zurich and Upper Swabia at the very end of the 16th century BC. Subsequently, the lake-shore settlements stop here, with the latest felling phases at around 1480 BC. Dendro-dates (from the lakes) between 1480 and 1050 BC are generally not available north of the Alps (Menotti 2001). In general, this is explained by a cold phase (the '*Löbbenschwankung*' –Löbben Glacier Advance Period [LAP]) and the connected glacial thrusts in the Alps and high lake water levels (Billamboz 2009: 501). The lacustrine sites shifted inland on mineral ground (Schlichtherle 1994: 64f.; Menotti, 2003). Also, on Federsee, the rising water levels seem to have had an effect on the relinquishment of the Siedlung-Forschner settlement at around 1500 BC (Köninger 2009: 276). The few dendro-dates available from the 15th and 14th centuries BC are only attributed to non-settlement sites, for example from pathways or from finds washed away from unidentified settlements, such as those of Chollerpark on Lake Zug (Billamboz 2009: 532f.).

The only certain evidence of lake-settlements at the end of the 15th century BC comes from south of the Alps; more precisely, it comes from Viverone I (Emissario) on Lake Viverone (Piedmont). A floating wiggle-matched dendrochronological sequence from oak piles of an inner dwelling, in association with two further ^{14}C dates from alder palisades, suggests a building phase around 1420 BC (see Chapter 3). Despite the MBA complexes of the Lake Garda region being thought of as having been occupied until the 15th century BC (cf. De Marinis 2002, 2009; David-Elbiali and David 2010) and displaying some Late Bronze Age artefacts, they were probably settled until the *Bronzo Recente* (well into the 13th century BC – Nicoletta Martinelli pers. comm. 2013). However, all these sites still remain without dendro-dates (see above).

Late Bronze Age

Although there are some isolated dendro-dates from the first half of the 11th century BC, properly recorded data for the Late Bronze Age lake-dwellings between the Savoyan Alps and the Federsee begins again in the middle of the 11th century BC (Map 2.5) and ends with the felling phases of 805 BC (Eberschweiler 2004: 14; Billaud, 2012: 351) – this period mainly covers the later phase of the Bronze Age (HaA2/B1–B3). In Upper Swabia and the Swiss Plateau, there was a short gap in occupation between *c.* 920 and 870 BC (Fig. 2.1). On the other hand, on Lake Geneva and in the Savoyan Alps, the preconditions for settling the lake shores were evidently more favourable during this period (cf. Billamboz 2009: 502), and they were occupied until 805 BC. Over-exploitation of the natural resources is an important issue, and it is believed to have played a crucial role in some of the abandonments of the lake shores (especially as far as short-lasting settlement phases are concerned) (see Chapter 3).

South of the Alps, we have a totally different scenario. Here, the settlement density on the lakes drastically decreased within the 12th century BC. Apart from stray LBA lacustrine objects, the Late Bronze Age (*Bronzo Finale*) in the Lake Garda region seems to be completely absent. In the north-western part of Italy, on the other hand, settlements can still be found (cf. De Marinis 2009: 539ff.), as clearly shown by the pile-dwelling on Lake Viverone (cf. Rubat Borel 2006: 241).

Iron Age pile-dwellings

According to environmentally deterministic views, the *Göschenen I* cold phase is to blame for the final disappearance of the lake-dwellings of the Circum-Alpine region at the end of the Late Bronze Age (cf. Gut 2013; Billamboz 2009). Although they were not used as settlement areas, the lakes (with their natural resources) held their attractiveness even after they had been deserted. A good example of the continuous link to the lake shores is the fish-trapping complex of Oggelhausen-Bruckgraben, which was in operation between 720 and 620 BC (cf. Köninger 2002). The pile structure of the complex consisted of a number of v-shaped angular units stretching for a couple of hundred metres along the former creek (the Federbach). At the end of the weir-like structures, small pile houses were erected (possibly where the fish were collected). The dimensions and the long-lasting use suggest a commercial character of the complex. The small pile houses were located above the funnel-shaped converging ends of the unit, where probably fish traps (weirs) were installed to intercept the fish that had been channelled there – according to archaeozoological analyses of fish remains, the complex served solely to trap pike probably on their way to spawn in the shallow lake areas. The extensive vessel ceramics available and further exceptional find materials are astonishing. The ceramics are tempered by materials (*e.g.* hematite) non-endemic to Federsee but to the Swabian Alb (15 km away). Amongst the metal finds, there is also a Billendorf pin and an iron fibula, including undulating clasp and an iron key. Briefly summarised, the users of this complex were certainly not local to the area; they probably belonged to a high social status community from the Swabian Alb, who owned the fishing rights at the Federsee (cf. Köninger 2002:

34ff.). This complex is certainly not a regular settlement built on the lake, although the find spectrum is typically found in settlements.

More in line with regular lake-settlement remains are the Iron Age timbers from Ürschhausen-Horn on the Nussbaumersee (Lake Nussbaum) in northern Switzerland, dating between 633 and 635 BC, (cf. Gollnisch-Moos 1999: 155ff.), the Early La Tène constructions at Roseninsel on the Starnbergersee (Lake Starnberg) in south-eastern Germany (Schlitzer 2005: 53ff.), and at Tresserve/Le Saut on Lake Bourget in France (Billaud 2005: 14 ff.). The building structures from Lake Bourget and from Lake Starnberg date (according to ^{14}C) from the 5th to 4th century BC (Fig. 2.4). This evidence, along with other scattered evidence, shows that there was yet another feeble attempt to settle wetland environments, but a series of unexpected cultural changes prevented this from happening (see Chapters 8 and 9). Of course, one should not forget the erosion issue, as quite a few LBA lacustrine settlements show. However, although a good argument, it has little to do with the final demise of the lake-dwelling tradition in the Circum-Alpine region.

Settlement structures and ground plans north of the Alps

The settlement structures of some 26 lake-settlements (about 10% of the total number known) in the northern Circum-Alpine region have been studied in detail (Figs 2.5–2.7). Their construction pattern, thus, can hardly be considered representative of individual regions – they can only indicate tendencies. House outlines and settlement plans can be considered to be sufficiently well documented by charting dendro-dated piles and ground-level wooden construction elements such as perforated plates (*Flecklinge* or *Pfahlschuhe*), sleeper-beam constructions (*Schwellbalken*), and log/block constructions (*Blockbau*) (Pillonel 2007: 126ff.) – the latter were exclusively found in Late Bronze Age contexts.

Single- and two-aisled sleeper-beam constructions are proof of the earlier occupation (A and B) during the Early Bronze Age in Zurich-Mozartstrasse lake-dwellings (Schmidheiny 2011: 71ff.). They are also proof of occupation during the Late Bronze Age in Zug-Sumpf, Lake Zug (Seifert 1996). In the case of Zurich-Mozartstrasse, the arrangement of buildings is reminiscent of the structure of the Alpine settlements of Cresta Cazis and Savognin Padnal (cf. Köninger 2009). The majority of the mostly 25–40 m² buildings were two-aisled constructions in the Early Bronze Age; however, in the Middle Bronze Age, three-aisled buildings appeared for the first time in Bronze Age contexts, reaching surface areas of *c.* 50 m² (Köninger 2006a). These three-aisled buildings, however, were already known from the Corded Ware lacustrine settlements on the Bodensee (cf. Billamboz and Köninger 2008: 328f.; Köninger and Billamboz in print).

In the Late Bronze Age, apart from a few two-aisled buildings (*e.g.* Unteruhldingen-Stollenwiesen Uu1 and 3; and Zug-Sumpf, earlier settlement – cf. Schöbel 1996; Seifert 1996; Köninger in print), the majority of the buildings were three aisled (cf. Billamboz and Schöbel 1996; Arnold and Langenegger 2012). In the case of Bevaix Sud, the base areas of these buildings are between 90 and 120 m², being roughly 6 m wide and 15–18 m long – the largest building, which includes the extension of a fourth aisle, is 17 m long and 9 m wide, thus having a base area of 150 m² (cf. Arnold and Langenegger 2012).

As previously mentioned, log/block constructions (*Blockbau* or *Blockgevierte*) are only

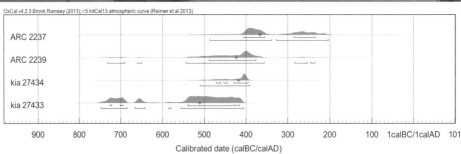

Figure 2.4. Iron Age pile-dwellings. Top: Oggelshausen-Bruckgraben, scaled reconstruction of the Iron Age fishing complex (© LAD, Photo: M. Erne); bottom: Iron Age ^{14}C-dates from pile-settlements. Ro: Roseninsel-Starnbergersee (Germany); Tr: Tresserve/Le Saut-Lac de Bourget (France) (data from: Billaud 2005; Schlitzer 2005).

found in the Late Bronze Age lake-settlements. Their possible function as foundations of elevated/semi-elevated house floors has now been advanced following the discovery of the Greifensee-Böschen lake-dwelling (Fig. 2.5.B1, a, b, c; Eberschweiler *et al.*, 2007). Complete block-construction buildings (*Blockhäuser*), such as those of Zug-Sumpf on Lake Zug (Seifert 1996), Ürschhausen-Horn on the Nussbaumersee (Gollnisch-Moos 1999), and Wasserburg-Buchau on the Federsee (Reinerth 1928; Kimmig 1992: 31ff.), are now open

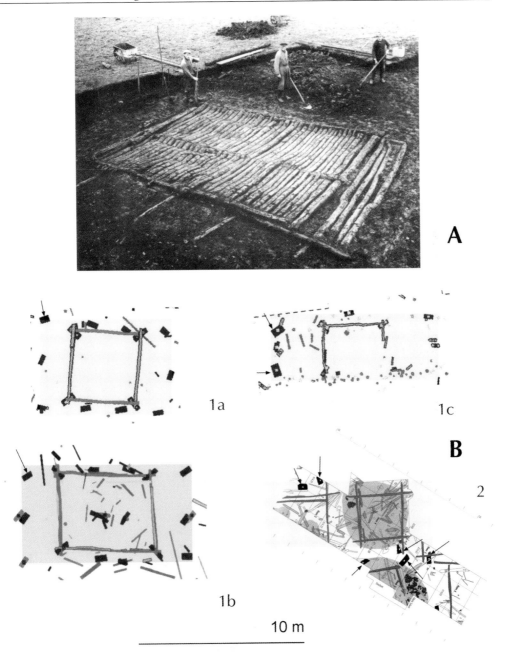

Figure 2.5. Foundation timbers (log [block-] construction) from LBA lake-settlements. A: Wasserburg-Buchau, House 9, 'ältere Siedlung'; B: 1. a–c Greifensee-Böschen; 2. Zug-Sumpf. Grey shading: supposed area of building, reconstructed on the basis of the support boards (arrows) strewn around the foundation timbers (after: Schöbel 2000: fig. 12; Seifert 1996; Eberschweiler et al. 2007).

to question. For instance, the *Blockgevierte* raised house floors were used in conjunction with perforated planks (*Flecklinge*), such as at the Zug-Sumpf '*jüngere*' settlement (Fig. 2.5B2). Beams clearly project over the *Blockgeviert*; floor boards placed on top of the base beams were recorded at House 9 at Wasserburg-Buchau (Fig. 2.5.A) (Schöbel 2000: 95, fig. [Abb.] 12; cf. Eberschweiler *et al.* 2007: 271). As far as can be read from the published plan documents, if we take into account the dimensions of some of the well-known *Blockgevierte*, we can calculate the areas of the buildings: for example, 6 and 11 m^2 at Zug-Sumpf (Seifert 1996: 134) and 7 to 15 m^2 (in some cases up to 20 m^2) at Wasserburg-Buchau. In Ürschhausen-Horn, they vary between 7 and 23 m^2 (cf. Gollnisch-Moos 1999: 74), but the majority are around 10 m^2. This limited area makes it improbable that they were all houses (note that most of them were categorised as such on account of fireplaces). In contrast, more plausibly sized houses with base areas of 25 to 30 m^2 are found when the *Blockgevierte* are complemented by *Fleckling* constructions, as in Zug-Sumpf for instance (Fig. 2.5.B2). House floors directly constructed at ground level, a little raised above it (*e.g.* Zurich-Mozartstrasse Village A and B), or with *Blockbaugevierte* (as in Wasserburg-Buchau or Ürschhausen-Horn) have rarely been substantiated. The great majority are believed to have had raised house floors.

Features that indicate the functions of individual buildings are extremely rare, if available at all, and only in exceptional cases have they been extensively studied (*e.g.* Eberschweiler *et al.* 2007). One such study focused on the central building at Greifensee-Böschen, whose exceptional ceramic inventory implies a community house; a further building at the same settlement served as a supply centre (Eberschweiler *et al.* 2007). The special structures at the EBA settlement A at Zurich-Mozartstrasse (Schmidheiny, 2011: 72) are considered to have been buildings of an economic nature (*i.e.* storage and supplies). Storage buildings were also documented at the LBA complex at Ürschhausen-Horn on Nussbaumersee (Gollnisch-Moos 1999: 87f. and 150). Specialised buildings are even believed to have been part of fortifications (see below), and this is particularly evident in the case of the bridge building at the MBA settlement of Siedlung-Forschner 3 (Billamboz *et al.* 2009: 252ff.). Other examples can be found at Concise-sous-Colachoz, village 11 (Winiger 2012: 76f.) (in this case linked to the planigraphy of the piles), and at the buildings enclosed by a lateral course of palisades at the LBA complex of Unteruhldingen-Stollenwiesen (settlement 1) on Lake Constance (Fig. 2.6; Köninger in print).

The majority of Bronze Age buildings at lacustrine settlements were houses. There are, however, some structures, such as those of Baldegg (Spring 2001: 135) and Zurich-Mozartstrasse (Schmidheiny 2011) (*e.g.* Fig. 2.7.B3), which were clearly different from other buildings and probably had particular functions. Apart from Greifensee-Böschen, where some of the constructions could have been used as storage buildings, specific-use buildings (or even animal stables) are not easy to identify. Therefore, questions as to whether cattle were kept in the settlement or not still remain unanswered in most cases.

Settlement sizes differ considerably (Figs 2.7–2.9). In the Early Bronze Age, exceptionally small settlements such as Bodman-Schachen I or Zurich-Mozartstrasse with built-up interior areas of 1,000 m^2 (rarely 1,500 m^2) and with up to ten buildings were followed by medium-sized complexes of 2,000–3,000 m^2 with 15 to 20 buildings. Large lake villages,

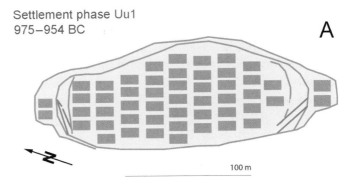

Settlement phase Uu1
975–954 BC

A

100 m

Figure 2.6. Unteruhldingen-Stollenwiesen, Uu1, (975–954 BC). A: Sketch of hypothetical reconstruction with interior containing systematic house rows and lateral bastion-like outer house ground plan between sections of palisades; B: Course of palisades G and C on the north extremity of complex with house locations in between (H). Palisades in northern section of the complex and house ground plans are dendrochronologically concurrent – pile samples from southern section as yet undated (after: Köninger in print; Dendrochronological dates: courtesy of André Billamboz).

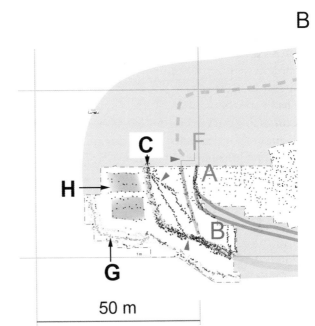

B

50 m

in contrast, covered surface areas up to 5,000 m² with 20 to 30 buildings in the Early and Middle Bronze Age (cf. Köninger 2006a), expanding to 20,000 m² with more than 30 buildings in the Late Bronze Age (cf. Arnold 1990). Additionally, at Lake Bienne/Biel and at Lake Zurich, there is evidence of solitary buildings in the Late Bronze Age (Altdorfer and Conscience 2005: 43). Starting in the Early Bronze Age, a trend can be seen towards an increase in the size of the lacustrine settlements, and the large LBA complexes are fairly different from those of the Early and Middle Bronze Age.

Bronze Age lake-shore settlements were mostly constructed in tightly packed rows (facades to the 'street') and lines (gables to the 'street') of houses (Figs 2.7–2.9). In terms of the Early Bronze Age, most of the construction patterns are difficult to group regionally or chronologically. There are, however, some differences; on the Bodensee, in central and eastern Switzerland, and on Lake Geneva, for instance, the patterns consist mostly of lengthwise lines of houses with gables pointing towards the lake shores (Fig. 2.7A.B5; Fig. 2.8.1–3 and .6). The access to the settlements leads to the centre of the residential agglomerate without the buildings being oriented towards it (Fig. 2.8.3 and .6). On the other hand, complexes in western Switzerland, especially in the Early Bronze Age (Fig. 2.7.B5; Fig. 2.8.10) and also partly in the Late Bronze Age (Fig. 2.9.4), were arranged as linear villages. The same can be said of the EBA complex at Sévrier-Les Mongets, Savoy, Lake Annecy (Billaud 1993) (Fig. 2.7.B7).

The two Bronze Age settlements of the Federsee (Siedlung-Forschner (Fig. 2.7.B1) and Wasserburg-Buchau (Fig. 2.9.3)) differ from those with tightly packed lines or rows of houses (cf. Köninger 2006a; Köninger and Schlichtherle 2009). The complexes are obviously divided into quarters and built according to a loose arrangement of groups of buildings. One would not be too wrong to claim that these building patterns follow the Danubian layout (Fig. 2.12.B), which is also reflected in the buildings of the Middle Bronze Age hill settlement on neighbouring Heuneburg (cf. Gersbach 2006). There, building patterns are different from those in south-western Germany, Switzerland, and even in the lake-settlements south of the Alps (Fig. 2.10.1 and .3; Fig. 2.12.B), including the *terramare* of the Po Plain (cf. Vanzetti 2013: 271). The social structure of the lake-dwelling inhabitants is difficult to identify from the settlement layout. However, in the case of Siedlung-Forschner a sort of clan-like organisation can be spotted, as there are recognisable different building traditions within the various quarters, with each of them having a large(r) building (Fig. 2.11.B; Köninger and Schlichtherle 2009). Conversely, it can hardly be claimed that the compactly built lake-settlements had an egalitarian social structure.

Many of the Bronze Age lake-settlements were surrounded by simple palisades or enclosed by fence-like structures (cf. Hafner 2010; Köninger and Schöbel 2010). It is particularly interesting that, especially in the context of the Early Bronze Age, fortified or even heavily fortified complexes appear continuously in a diachronic manner (see below).

Proper fortifications are indeed more unusual but do feature in many settlement phases of Bronze Age lake-shore settlements. They range from the simple curvilinear palisades to the fascine-like reinforcements that were pinned between the piles or horizontal board walls.

There is evidence of heavily fortified complexes on the Bodensee and in Upper Swabia, consisting of regular wooden walls, which, depending on the foundation sub-soils, can have different designs. For instance, the settlement of Siedlung-Forschner 1 has a wall of overlapping horizontal planks (Bohlen), whereas the wooden walls at Unteruhldingen-Stollenweisen consist of tightly set ash, maple, and beech timbers (Fig. 2.7.B2; Köninger 2006b: 68ff.). In the Middle Bronze Age, some sections of the wooden walls at Siedlung-Forschner 3 (Billamboz *et al.* 2009) were made of tightly set piles and horizontal wooden planks, whereas Egg-Ober Güll I has a simple wooden wall made of vertical oak planks (Fig. 2.8.3; Köninger 1997: 29ff., 2006; Billamboz 2009). All the aforementioned complexes had parapet walks lying on transverse treaders that were linked to the wall planks by rear-facing anchor posts. Because of the parapet walks and the horizontal reinforcement to the front walls (particularly in the walls made of vertical posts), these constructions were built with angular settings, which differ greatly from the curvilinear pile-row style of the lake-shore villages. In this respect, some form of the fortifying function can be attached to the rather loosely placed pile rows that have an angular setting and thus to the horizontal reinforcements in front of the walls.

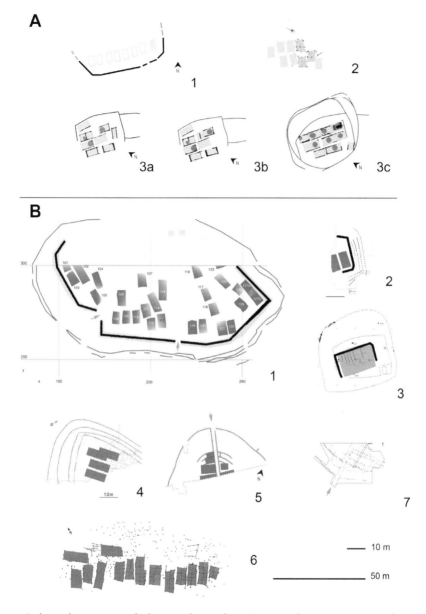

Figure 2.7. Lake-settlement ground plans in the northern Circum-Alpine region. A: early EBA 21/20th (19th) century BC); B: later EBA (18th century BC). A: 1. Eschenz/Öhningen-Orkopf; 2. Bodman-Schachen 1A; 3a. Zürich-Mozartstrasse settlement AA; 3b. Zürich-Mozartstrasse settlement AB; 3c. Zürich-Mozartstrasse settlement B; B: 1. Siedlung-Forschner (Sf 1); 2. Unteruhldingen-Stollenwiesen; 3. Zürich-Mozartstrasse C1A; 4. Sutz-Lattrigen 'Buchstation'; 5. Concise (E11); 6. Préverenges I A; 7. Sévrier-Les Mongets (after: Billaud 1993: 114f.; Hafner 2006: 110ff.; Köninger 2006a; Corboud and Pugin 2008: 39ff.; Köninger and Schlichtherle 2009; Schmidheiny 2011; Winiger 2012; Unteruhldingen: Köninger unpublished report; Eschenz/Öhningen-Orkopf: redrawn from an aerial photograph – M. Mainberger pers. comm. 2013).

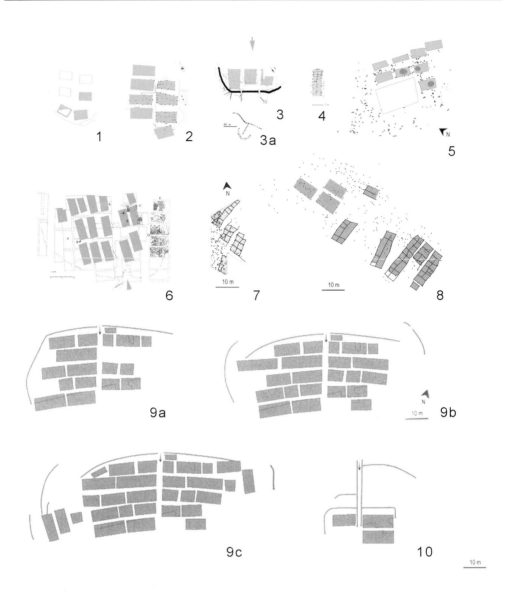

Figure 2.8. Late EBA (c. 17th century BC) lake-settlement ground plans in the northern Circum-Alpine region. 1. Bodman-Schachen I, building phase 2; 2. Bodman-Schachen I, building phase 4; 3. Egg-Obere Güll I; 3a. Egg-Obere Güll – sketched plans from 1898; 4. Meilen-Schellen; 5. Zürich-Mozartstrasse, C2; 6. Hochdorf-Baldegg; 7. Tolochenaz-La-Poudrière; 8. Préverenges IB; 9–11. Concise (E12); 12. Concise (E13). Settlement entrance is marked by arrows (after: Spring 2001; Köninger 2006a; Corboud and Pugin 2008: 39ff.; Schmidheiny 2011; Winiger 2012).

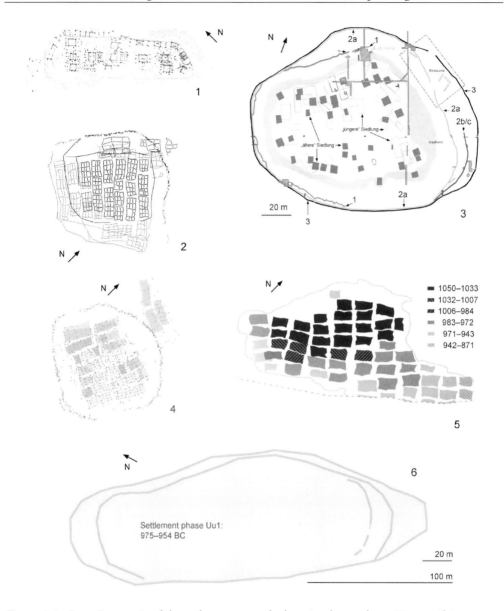

Figure 2.9. Late Bronze Age lake-settlement ground plans in the northern Circum-Alpine region. 1. Greifensee-Böschen; 2. Cortaillod-Est; 3. Wasserburg-Buchau – Settlement plan with dendrodated palisade sections: 1–3. = Wb DC-periods (1: 1058–1054 BC; 2a: 1006–988 BC; 2b: 964–945 BC; 2c: 932–926 BC; 3: 867–852 BC (Billamboz 2005: 98ff.)). Dark shading for timber foundations regarded (according to Reinerth 1928) as log (block-) constructions 'ältere Siedlung'; 4. Bevaix-Sud; 5. Hauterive-Champreveyres; 6. Unteruhldingen-Stollenwiesen, settlement phase Uu1 (after: Arnold 1990; Billamboz 2005; Eberschweiler et al. 2007; Pillonel 2007; Arnold and Langenegger 2012; Köninger in print).

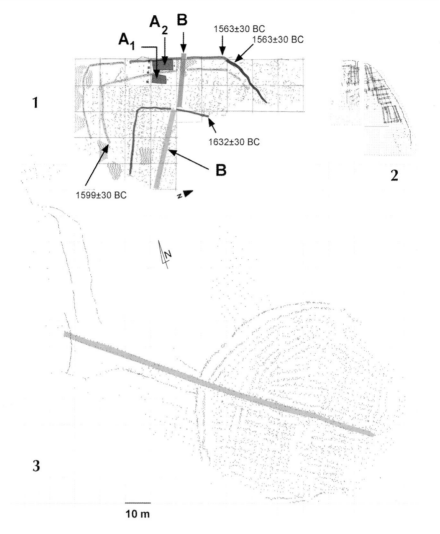

Figure 2.10. Settlement plans of the lake-shore settlements in northern Italy. 1. Cadrezzate 'Il Sabbione' (A1, A2 = guardian houses (A1 1591±30 BC, A2 1583±30 BC); B central access with pile free corridor behind); 2. Fiavè-Carera; 3. Viverone Emissario. Scale adjusted (after: Perini 1987; Martinelli 2013: 119; Viverone pile plan drafted from copies of original pile recordings).

Evidence that this form of fortification already existed in the 20th/19th century BC can be found at the complex of Orkopf on the Bodensee and possibly also at Zurich-Mozartstrasse settlement A and B (Fig. 2.7.A) on Lake Zurich, where it becomes more evident in settlement C1A from the 18th century BC (Schmidheiny 2011: 86ff.). Similar fortifications can also be found at Sutz-Lattrigen 'Buchtstation' on Lake Biel (Hafner 2006: 110ff.) (Fig. 2.7.B3 and .4) and at Rapperswil-Technikum on Lake Zurich (Hügi 2006: 56f.). Parapet walks for this form of fortification cannot be reconstructed, as the wooden structures on the inner side of the pile rows are missing. Interestingly, regular wooden walls – with or without palisades – are

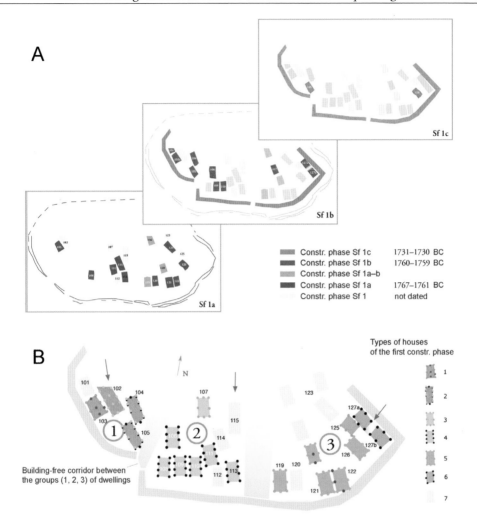

Figure 2.11. Siedlung-Forschner 1. A: Building sequences of the various construction phases Sf 1a–c (dendrochronologically dated construction units). B: Distribution of house types in the three defined groups of buildings: 1. Twin-aisled alder/willow building (Sf 1a); 2. Single-aisled oak/ash double-pile-construction with first posts at the gable; 3. Single-aisled 8-pile-ash-building with first posts at the gable; 4. Single-aisled 8-post-oak building; 5. Twin-aisled 9-post-ash/(elm) building; 6. Single-aisled 6-(12)-post-oak building, or single-aisled 6-post-alder building. 7. Uncertain house types. Note: the red arrows mark possible large houses (after: Köninger 2009: 272f. fig. [Abb.] 158).

limited on the Bodensee and in Upper Swabia. Angular elbow palisades are found from the Bodensee (only in the early phase of EBA settlements) to the Lake Biel area.

In contrast, the complexes further to the south-west are different. On Lake Neuchâtel, as in the Savoy (Fig 2.7.B7), there are multiple curvilinear palisades – in the case of Concise (E11), (Fig. 2.7.B5) these were possibly used in combination with a 'watchtower' between the palisades. The fortifications possibly follow a regional subdivision (Fig. 2.12.B):

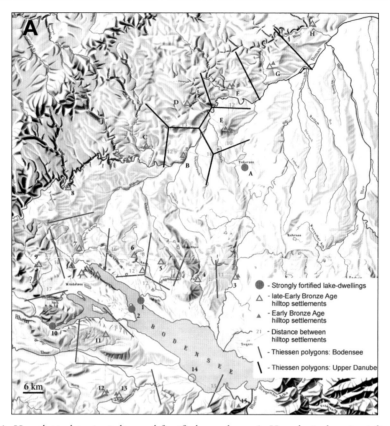

Figure 2.12A. Hypothetical territoriality and fortified complexes. A: Hypothetical territoriality of possible central sites on hilltops and fortified lake-shore settlements of the Bodensee basin and the neighbouring regions (modified from Köninger and Schlichtherle 2009: 378 and fig. 8). 1. Unteruhldingen-Stollenwiesen; 2. Egg-Obere Güll I; 3. Veitsberg Ravensburg; 4. Horgenzell Kappel; 5. Frickingen 'Altheiligenberg'; 6. Owingen Häusern 'Kaplinz'; 7. Hindelwangen 'Nellenburg'; 8. Fridingen a.d. Donau 'Lehenbühl'; 9. Hilzingen-Duchtingen 'Hohenkrähen'; 10. Öhningen-Orkopf; 11. Wäldi-Höhenrain (Thurgau, Switzerland); 12. Toos Waldi (Thurgau, Switzerland); 13. Schweizersholz 'Ruine Heuberg' (Thurgau, Switzerland); 14. Arbon-Bleiche 2 (Thurgau, Switzerland); 15. Rorschacher Berg (St Gallen, Switzerland). A. Bad Buchau Siedlung-Forschner; B. Herbertingen-Hundersingen 'Heuneburg'; C. Bingen 'Burgstelle Bittelschieß'; D. Zwiefalten 'Upflamör'; E. Uttenweiler-Offingen 'Bussen'; F. Lauterach 'Rotenau'; G. Allmendingen-Schwörzkirch; H. Ehrenstein 'Schlossberg' (data from: Köninger and Schöbel 2010: 385 and 420ff.).

- Wooden walls in the Bodensee-Upper Swabia region, probably reflecting Danubian traditions
- Elbow palisades from central Switzerland to the Lake Biel region
- Enclosures with multiple palisades in the Lake Neuchâtel and Savoy regions

Strikingly, the majority of the heavily fortified (wooden walls) and fortified complexes (angular arrangement of pile rows) have been dated to the 18th century BC (Fig. 2.7.B). The only open complex (no fortifications) of the 18th century BC seems to be that of Préverenges on Lake

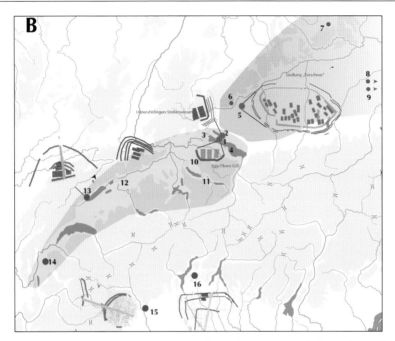

Figure 2.12B. Hypothetical territoriality and fortified complexes. B: Fortified complexes of the Early and Middle Bronze Age. Numbers 1, 2, and 5 are verified fortifications with regular wooden walls. Red: groups of houses built to an irregular pattern; purple: wooden walls; yellow: interior buildings in tightly packed rows or lines of houses, fortified by elbow palisades; green: interior buildings in tightly packed rows or lines of houses, fortified/enclosed on their landward side by palisades. Sites: 1. Egg-Obere Güll; 2. Unteruhldingen-Stollenwiesen; 3. Eschenz/Öhningen-Orkopf; 4. Arbon-Bleiche 2; 5. Bad Buchau Siedlung-Forschner 1; 6. Hundersingen 'Heuneburg'; 7. Freystadt 'Thannhausen'; 8. Blucina-Cezavy; 9. Nitriansky-Hradok-Zamecek; 10. Zürich-Mozartstrasse C1A; 11. Rapperswil 'Technikum'; 12. Sutz-Lattrigen 'Buchtstation'; 13. Concise-sous-Colachoz (E11); 14. Sévrier Les Mongets; 15. Viverone 'Emissario'; 16. Cadrezzate 'Sabbione' (after: Köninger and Schöbel 2010: 419 – plus elaboration. Settlement plans after: Bertone and Fozzati 2004; Hafner 2006; Köninger 2006a; Billamboz et al. 2009; Burri-Wyser and Winiger 2012; Martinelli 2013).

Geneva (Fig. 2.7.B6), but only visible piles on the lake bed have been charted and analysed – evidence of fortification could therefore be missing (cf. Corboud and Pugin 2008). The number of fortified complexes is certainly not representative, but those types of settlements seem not to have been too numerous. However, the 18th century BC in south-western Germany/Switzerland was a time of increasing Únětice contact (cf. Hafner 1995: 176ff.; Krause 1996: 188). As a result, it might not be a coincidence that Únětice metal forms, and thus bronzes with high proportions of tin alloy, even if unstratified), have been recorded at the heavily fortified complexes of Unteruhldingen (Köninger 2006a: table [Taf.] 71: 1119) and Zurich-Mozartstrasse (Schmidheiny 2011: 132, table [Taf.] 20: 373). Is it therefore possible that unsettled times accompanied the emergence of tin alloy bronzes?

In the 17th century BC, most of the complexes – except Egg-Obere Güll I (Egg I) – were open or encompassed by simple enclosures (Fig. 2.8) that, as in Concise (E12), covered only a part of the settlement (the landward side) – instead of protective palisades, they most likely marked the village boundaries. Interestingly, in the case of the Bodensee, the heavily defended settlement of Egg-Obere Güll I came into existence at the same time as the lake villages of Schachenhorn Bs I (building phases 3 and 4). Thus, its fortification could have been the expression of a local hierarchical settlement structure. This seems plausible as, especially in the Bodensee area (around 1620 BC), a number of open complexes (Bs I) were contemporaneous to heavily fortified ones (*e.g.* Egg I).

Late Bronze Age lacustrine settlements have been recorded exclusively north of the Alps, and they were mostly tightly built as typical pile-dwellings (Fig. 2.9.2, .4 and .5; *e.g.* Arnold 1990). There are examples (*e.g.* Unteruhldingen) of houses being built both in rows with the facades parallel to the shore and with gables pointing towards the shore. In addition to the previously mentioned Wasserburg-Buchau in the Federsee (Fig. 2.9.3), the buildings in the complexes at Greifensee-Böschen (Fig. 2.9.1) and Zug-Sumpf (cf. Seifert 1996) are also arranged in a loose and irregular fashion. Open (no palisades) complexes, such as Hauterive-Champréveyres on Lake Neuchâtel (Fig. 2.9.5), are the exception; in fact, most of the Late Bronze Age lake villages are enclosed by pile lines, although the lines are often not continuous. In addition to these enclosed compounds, there are isolated, solitary buildings, such as those found on Lake Biel and Lake Zurich (Altdorfer and Conscience 2005: 43). A special feature of the western Swiss and Savoyan complexes is isolated buildings in close proximity to enclosed settlements (see below).

Properly fortified lake villages were rare in the Late Bronze Age, pile lines with an angular course were lacking, and parapet walks probably did not exist. One exception is the complex of Unteruhldingen-Stollenwiesen, where the complex of the earliest settlement phase (Uu1: 975–954 BC) had a lateral palisade system fanning out with bastion-like projections. Here, further buildings were found to be separated (by palisades) from the main settlement interior (Fig. 2.6), but both the palisades and the buildings are of the same age and clearly belong together. Unlike Unteruhldingen-Stollenwiesen, the earliest settlement of Wasserburg-Buchau in the Federsee region cannot be considered as fortified, as the palisades only enclose half of the settlement (Fig. 2.9.3; cf. Billamboz 2005: 97ff.). On the other hand, the later occupation of Wasserburg shows that the complex was surrounded by one-metre-wide strips of piles, which could be considered as a proper fortification. The same goes for the settlements of Muntelier-Steinberg (Blumer and Wolf 2009: 278) and Nidau-Neue Station on Lake Biel (Hafner 1999: 41ff.).

Individual settlement dynamics

Dendrochronology allows us to achieve a fairly ample understanding of the construction history of the single settlement (settlement biography) – even if it is only of a few complexes. Below are some well-documented case studies.

Early Bronze Age

The earliest felling dates from the Concise E11 complex (dated between 1801 and 1774 BC) are from the palisades and the access way, whereas the earliest evidence for interior constructions dates to 1799 BC (Winiger 2012: 40ff.). As a result, the innermost palisades predate the erection of houses. Due to limited dendrochronological analyses, the precise chronological order in which the houses were erected cannot as yet be determined. As far as the later (1646–1620 BC) settlement of Concise (E12) is concerned, the fence was erected only in the second year of occupation (*e.g.* only after six houses had already been built in 1645 BC). The settlement was later expanded, firstly away from the shore and then laterally – extensions came to an end in 1635 BC. From this date to 1620 BC, only repairs and rebuilding of already existing structures can be identified. The systematic expansion of the village shows gaps in the layout, which, in part, are filled with new buildings in later years. In the most recent settlement at Concise (E13), buildings, access ways, and interior palisades were built at the same time in 1618 BC. The subsequent felling dates up to 1583 BC document repair measures, as do two further sections of palisades in 1607 BC. There are no signs of an expansion to the village (Winiger 2012: 122ff.).

A similar situation occurred at the Préverenges I A complex dated between 1780 and 1758 BC, whose buildings were mainly built in a row (cf. Corboud Pugin 2008: 44ff.). There are also unoccupied spaces in the rows in which buildings were subsequently added up to five years after the construction of the first house. Particularly interesting is the construction of a pioneer building in 1780 BC and the subsequent addition of six further buildings between 1778 and 1776 BC, with the final completion of the row of houses by 1775 BC – all later felling dates indicate reconstructions and repairs. A similar building scheme seems to apply to the lake-settlement of Préverenges I B, which was established between 1625 (maybe even 1630) and 1621 BC (Corboud and Pugin 2008: 46ff.).

The Siedlung-Forschner 1 settlement at the Federsee with felling dates between 1767 and 1739 BC is an impressive example of settlement development (Köninger 2009: 262ff.). At the same time as the first buildings, or shortly before, a palisade system was erected (Fig. 2.11A). The uniform dating of the piles at 1766 BC suggests that the complex was enclosed by palisades within a short period of time. The construction of dwellings carried on until 1759 BC; however, at the same time, a corridor was left free between the palisades and the buildings. A wooden wall was built here in 1759 BC, while the building of houses continued. Some 30 years later, the wooden wall was renewed by placing a new one in front of the old one and repositioning all individual buildings in the interior of the village. The palisade system was neglected; it was left in place only to protect the houses until the proper fortification (*i.e.* the wooden wall) had been completed.

The following can be recognised from the Early Bronze Age case studies:

- Felling dates cover 25–30 years; the complexes existed for one to two generations
- Settlement sites were secured by palisades before, or at the same time as, the first buildings of the interior were erected – no pioneer buildings had been erected before
- The open complex of Préverenge I A started with a pioneer building; two years later, the complex was extended
- The building of settlements followed a specific plan, which is apparent from the very beginning
- The sizes of the heavily fortified complexes and the types of fortification seem to have been pre-arranged

Late Bronze Age

One of the most fascinating LBA lake-settlements in terms of structure and chronology is that of Greifensee-Böschen on Lake Greifen, Switzerland. The settlement was developed within nine years between 1051 and 1042 BC, and it was abandoned after the village was partially destroyed by a fire – interestingly enough, there is no evidence of attempts to repair the damage of the conflagration. It is worth noting that the village was initially centred around two buildings, whose special status can be seen by the large number of drinking vessels found in them. The fence around the village was only built in 1047 BC (five years after the first house was erected) (Eberschweiler *et al.* 2007: 262ff.).

The building remains from the lake-settlement of Bevaix Sud on Lake Neuchâtel (Fig. 2.9, 4; Arnold and Langenegger 2012) are equally well documented. Beginning with a pioneer building in 1009 BC, the village was then expanded to ten houses (in two rows along a main alley) two years later. The majority of the buildings were replaced or extended while others were repaired; this took place in two subsequent phases of renovation in 977/76–973 BC and in 967/963 BC (Arnold and Langenegger 2012: 244ff.). Later on, and directly outside the enclosure of the so-called '*quartier nord*', three new buildings were erected between 957 and 954 BC. The settlement area was well defined from the very beginning, and Langenegger (2012: 158ff.) even believes that some piles found far away from the complex were used as fixed points for surveying purposes.

The development of the village at Hauterive-Champréveyres covers the timespan between 1050 and 871 BC (Pillonel 2007). According to Pillonel (2007), expansion occurred in six phases, from the centre of the settlement towards the lake. The arrangement of the buildings in rows was planned, but a parcelling out of the settlement site and its enclosure (as in the case of the EBA complex E12 of Concise) cannot be deduced from the finds. Deviating from usual practices, the village had no enclosure. Judging from the amount of land available around the site, the village was an 'open' settlement community whose total size and development was not planned in advance.

The building development of smaller villages with shorter times of existence differs from that of the larger western Swiss complexes with a longer-term existence. Small and large Late Bronze Age settlements can be categorised as follows:

Smaller complexes
- Their occupation in western Switzerland is considerably longer than in other regions
- Settlement started with pioneer buildings followed by rapid settlement expansion two or three years later
- Settlement expansion was pre-arranged – 'parcelling out of the settlement area'
- Repairs were carried out after 10–15 years
- The enclosure was erected four or five years after the foundation of the village – it is therefore questionable that the enclosure had the purpose of fortification

Large complexes
- Only one example in western Switzerland: Hauterive-Champréveyres
- Successive rows of houses were built starting landside from the centre of the village
- Apart from the building of rows of houses, no other planning seems to have occurred

Heavily fortified complexes
  • Evidence of the development of buildings within heavily fortified LBA complexes is lacking

As a conclusive remark of the two previous sub-sections, we can ascertain that, north of the Alps, the Early Bronze Age lake-settlements were occupied only for a short time (for one generation, or a maximum of two generations), they were relatively quickly expanded, proper fortifications were made before (or at the same time as) the first buildings were erected (*e.g.* Fig. 2.11), and, in most cases, the sizes of the settlements and the building plans were known prior to construction. Pioneer buildings are known only in one case: Préverenges on Lake Geneva.

Concerning smaller complexes of the LBA in western Switzerland, the houses within the settlement were planned, the environment was prepared (*e.g.* forest clearance, creating of agricultural land, *etc.*), and land claims were possibly made, as shown by the construction of pioneer buildings. It is interesting to note that the proper preparation of the site before the settlement was built is not a peculiarity of the Bronze Age; traces of such practices from the Neolithic are noticeable (see Torwiesen II on Federsee – 33rd century BC) (cf. Schlichtherle 2011: 17ff.).

Settlement structures and ground plans south of the Alps

Settlement structures that allow a deep understanding of the organisation of lacustrine settlements are more seldom south of the Alps. However, the impressive wood architecture of the Fiavè 6 lake-dwellings (former Lake Carera) (Fig. 2.10.2) and of the lacustrine village of Ledro are exceptions south of the Alps, displaying construction designs that match the topography. Fiavè (Perini 1987, 1988) and Ledro (Rageth 1974) were extensively researched in the 1940s and 1970s, when dendrochronology was in its initial stages. Although some dendrochronological analyses were carried out (especially for Fiavè), resulting in floating dendro-data, the links between building phases and ground plan developments have yet to be identified. The building characteristics are, however, known, consisting of combined piles, various board constructions, perforated posts, so-called *Bonifica layers* (see Notes in Chapter 3 for definition), and ground-level constructions (cf. Balista and Leonardi 1996: 203ff.).

The dendrochronological data for the early Early Bronze Age lake-shore settlement of Lavagnone is, without a doubt, much more detailed. The various sections of the excavation allow a hypothetical reconstruction of the oldest complex (cf. Rapi 2013: 532f.), which consists of a corduroy street leading to the 4–5 houses built along the lines of a linear village enclosed by a palisade fence on the landward side (Rapi 2013: 532, fig. 6). More dendrochronologically supported ground plans come from Sabbione (Lake Monate) in north-western Italy. The two-aisled building (dating to the first half of the 16th century BC) is situated outside the palisade area (Martinelli 2013: 119, fig. 3), but this is related to palisade access – behind the building itself, there is a corridor that leads to the interior of the settlement. The building is comparable to the houses ('watch towers') of Concise E11 (cf. Winiger 2012) and Siedlung-Forschner 3 (Billamboz *et al.* 2009), and it is regarded as a form of fortification that served to control access to the settlement. The complex is multi-phased, and each phase has an elbow palisade encompassing the landward side of the settlement. The settlement interiors grew, at intervals of 30 odd years, from 900–1,000 m² to 2,000 m² and finally to 2,500 m². A wooden wall or parapet walk cannot be recognized from the plan of the piles. The structure of the piles in the rest of the interior forms a series of tightly packed buildings, which are similar to those north of the Alps, as well as the MBA *terramare* (cf. Vanzetti 2013: 270).

The pile field of the lacustrine settlement at Viverone-Emissario (Piedmont) in northern Italy has been recorded almost completely, and it is the only lake-settlement that stretches to the end of the 15th century BC (concerning dating, see Chapter 3) and possibly also to the 11th century BC (although not proven by dendrochronology). The pile plan shows, as at Cadrezzate-Il Sabbione (Fig. 2.10.1), a complex enclosed (on the landward side) by palisades with central access. The layout of the palisades, however, differs from that of Il Sabbione in that they are curvilinear. The total area consists of some 5,000 m² with an interior area with buildings covering around 3,500 m² – the buildings are tightly packed together (Fig. 2.10.3).

The find materials from Viverone range from the late Early Bronze Age to the Late Bronze Age, with the majority of the finds belonging to the Middle Bronze Age (cf. Rubat Borel 2006, 2010). The lack of dendro-dates hinders the possibility of finding out whether the settlement developed in various phases or whether there was more than one occupation. For instance, it may be possible that the multiple palisades are not contemporaneous and that the impression of a heavy fortification is just the result of different palisades, which accumulated through time.

From the above statements, we can finally conclude that the lacustrine settlements south of the Alps tend to go from small to medium size from the early Early Bronze Age to the Middle Bronze Age (cf. Köninger and Schlichtherle 2009: 364). What the village complexes have in common is that they are all enclosed on the landward side by palisades. Settlement dynamics are not properly understood, although some useful clues can be gathered from the dendro-dated palisades of Sabbione, which show an increase in the settlement area within 70 years at intervals of 33 and 36 years – a generational rhythm that is similar to that in the northern Alpine foreland (Fig. 2.10.1). Judging by the charted but not dated piles, we can assume (although this is not as yet proven) that the buildings in the interior followed the palisade expansion.

Settlement dynamics

The Early and Middle Bronze Age lake-settlements north of the Alps were, according to dendro-data, consistently occupied for a relatively short period of 20–30 years. As the settlement dynamics of individual complexes demonstrate, the villages were established and abandoned after roughly one generation (Billamboz 2009). Regular waves of settlement at the end of the 17th century BC and around 1500 BC can be observed (cf. Köninger 2006a; Billamboz 2009; Winiger and Burri-Wyser 2012: 127ff.; see also Chapter 3, this volume). Where the inhabitants moved to – the hinterland or other sites along the lake shore – between the 20th and 17th centuries BC remains an open issue. Settlement sites in the direct hinterland of the Bodensee show that, at least in this region, the areas around the lake were settled (see Rigert, 2001). A somewhat self-evident precondition to the establishment of lake-shore settlements is the necessity of mobile human populations within the lake-shore margin. Regarding the period after 1500 BC, however, it is generally presumed that the zones of settlement shifted away from the lake shore and further inland; this placed the settlements outside the shallow-water areas. Due to the gradual rising of the lake water level, it was no longer possible to establish settlements in those regions until the final stages of the second millennium BC (cf. Schlichtherle 1994: 61ff.).

The reasons behind this high-frequency settlement dynamic are unclear. It is possible that settlements were abandoned as soon as the natural resources in the vicinity had been exhausted. Alternatively, new settlement sites may have been sought before the old buildings had to be completely rebuilt; from cultural experience, social memory, and tradition, this would be after about 30 years or one generation. Settlement gaps between *c.* 1900 and 1800 BC and between 1730 and 1660 BC probably correspond to a climatic depression, as indicated by the ^{14}C-residual curve (Fig. 2.1). In contrast, there is no coincidence between the occurrence of lake-settlement and the ^{14}C-curve during the 16th century BC. After 1500 BC, the lack of settlements on the lake shores was caused by the '*Löbbenschwankung*' (the Löbben Glacier Advance Period [LAP]) and was therefore climate related (cf. Magny *et al.* 1998: 137ff.; Nicolussi and Patzelt 2000: 72ff.; Billamboz 2009: 501).

In the Lake Garda region (northern Italy), an entirely different settlement dynamic is evident (cf. De Marinis 2009: 535). The dendro-data from individual settlements spans a number of decades, despite the relatively limited range of the data series. For Lavagnone 2 and 3, the dendro-data ranges from 2077 to 1916 BC (cf. Rapi 2013: 532ff.), with typically 10–15 years (sometimes even 20) between the felling dates (cf. Martinelli 2007: 109ff.). In association with the rich and complex stratigraphies, this data suggests that settlements were occupied for a longer period of time in the first part of the Early Bronze Age, as opposed to settlements that were repeatedly occupied for much shorter periods (cf. De Marinis 2007: 10). Furthermore, and contrary to stratigraphies north of the Alps, the layer sequences in the Lake Garda region at individual settlement sites such as Fiavè-Carera (Perini 1988) and Lavagnone (De Marinis 2007a) extend from the end of the Neolithic to the Middle Bronze Age (*Bronzo Medio* BM IIB), *i.e.* from the 21st to the 17th (perhaps even the 16th) centuries BC (cf. De Marinis 2009: 535f.). In the Lake Garda region, Bronze Age pile dwellings are to be found only up to 1200 BC. (cf. De Marinis 2009: 535f.).

The dendro-data from the lacustrine settlements of Sabbione I at Lake Monate in Lombardy (Martinelli 2013: 118ff.) and from the Emissario site at Lake Viverone (see Chapter 3) shows that the pre-Alpine lakes south of the Alps were amenable to settlement even during unfavourable climatic phases. Thus, climate-related interruptions to the occupancy of the lake shores south of the Alps cannot be ascertained – possibly, as Magny *et al.* (2009: 575ff.) assume, 'palaeoenvironmental and archaeological data collected at Lake Ledro may suggest, as a working hypothesis, a relative emancipation of protohistoric societies from climatic conditions'. Regardless of the factors influencing the abandonment, the settlement cycles around the northern Italian lakes seem to be of longer duration, and they point to a different strategy of natural resource exploitation in comparison to those in the northern Circum-Alpine region. As far as it is understood from the respective dendro-data, the main difference between the Early Bronze Age settlements north and south of the Alps lies in the duration of the individual complexes and the economic strategies employed.

Such comparisons between northern and southern Alpine regions are not possible for the Late Bronze Age, primarily because lake-settlements, with a few exceptions (*e.g.* Viverone, according to artefact typology), are not evident in northern Italy for this period. In fact, in the Lake Garda region, they even ceased to be constructed or occupied before the appearance of Late Bronze Age lake-settlements north of the Alps (cf. Rubat Borel 2006; De Marinis 2009; see also Chapter 3, this volume).

Regarding the Late Bronze Age, north of the Alps there are striking differences in the settlement dynamics evident in the individual pile-dwelling regions. The still rather short-term occupancy of the lake-settlements on the Bodensee and in Upper Swabia (cf. Schöbel 1996; Billamboz 2005), and possibly also at Zürichsee-Untersee (cf. Gut 2013: 77, 82ff.) and Zugersee (cf. Seifert 1996: 122f.), is in opposition to the long-lasting settlements, with possible occupations of over 150 years, in western Switzerland. The reasons for such divergence could be the availability and accessibility of wood resources for use in the building and maintenance of the complexes, as well as woodland management strategies to secure those timber resources. There was evidently an abundance of oak available in the Three Lakes (Lake Neuchâtel, Lake Biel, and Lake Murten) region, as the houses were almost exclusively built using this timber (Pillonel 2007; Langenegger 2012: 240f.). The shift to inferior wood species, as seen at the Federsee for instance (Billamboz 2009: 501f.), did not occur in western Switzerland. On the basis of the varying duration of the Late Bronze Age settlements that have been dendrochronologically identified, varying settlement models are favoured. In western Switzerland, the long-term occupation complexes are seen as founding settlements from which, in the course of demographic developments, subordinate satellite settlements and quarters with shorter-term usage became established in suitable areas nearby. Simultaneous building activities in neighbouring bays suggest the possibility that communities acted collaboratively to construct new settlements (cf. Arnold 1990; Billamboz and Schöbel 1996; Arnold and Langenegger 2012). In addition, isolated (but continuously occupied) central settlements such as Hauterive-Champréveyres and Bevaix L'Abbaye 2 do exist (cf. Arnold and Langenegger 2012: 174 ff.). It is assumed that Late Bronze Age settlement systems comparable to those in western Switzerland also existed in Savoy (Billaud 2012: 355).

In contrast, it is thought that the Late Bronze Age settlements around the Bodensee, and also around Lake Zurich, relocated to more or less neighbouring zones along the lake shore or hinterland after a relatively short period of occupation (cf. Schöbel 1996: 128ff.; Gut 2013: 83). The reason for this occupation system could be shortages in the economic fundaments necessary for continued residence in a lake-settlement, as can be observed through palynological analysis of settlements around Lake Bourget (eastern France), which dates to the middle of the 10th century BC (Billaud 2012: 354ff.).

It remains clear that the settlements in the Bodensee-Upper Swabia region only lasted some 30 years throughout the whole of the Bronze Age. In central and eastern Switzerland, the evidence is not quite so conclusive. Despite the shorter settlement phases in the Bodensee-Upper Swabia region, it cannot be discounted that Late Bronze Age lacustrine settlements lasting 50–60 years (cf. Seifert 1996: 119ff.) and settlements with continuous occupancy over an even longer period of time (cf. Gut 2013: 83) were present in the region. In western Switzerland, on the other hand, it is apparent that between the Early and Late Bronze Age, a switch from short settlement phases to long-term continuous settlement occurred. Consequently, it is possible to speak of a switch in the settlement system between the Early and Late Bronze Age in western Switzerland and possibly also in Savoy. Thus, we can infer that there were also changes in economic strategies, which were evidently not replicated in the Bodensee-Upper Swabia region.

Functions of the lake-dwellings

The functions of the settlement complexes can seldom be defined without entering into speculation. It appears that they were primarily based around farming (see Frank 2006; Rösch 1996). However, certain specializations for individual cases can be deduced from the finds.

On the basis of bone remains, it can be suggested that the sites Bodman-Schachen I B-C focused on deer hunting, with the ratio of wild animals, especially red deer, rather high compared to other contemporary settlements (Köninger 2006a: 197f.). Furthermore, on account of archaeological finds, it can be considered that the site at Lake Ledro specialized in metal extraction and processing (cf. Rageth 1974).

The role of the heavily fortified sites is, on the other hand, far less certain. What can be stated is that they are geographically sited at shore sections that were important for communication and so could have performed some form of territorial function (see below; cf. Köninger and Schöbel 2010). The Bronze Age settlements of the Federsee seem to have dominated the region, but, strikingly, only one settlement per period existed – a situation that also applies to the MBA Viverone settlement south of the Alps.

At least during the 17th century BC, contemporaneous open and heavily fortified settlements were developed within proximity to one another, indicating a potential hierarchy amongst settlements. Such a situation is, however, uncertain for the earlier settlement phases in the Early Bronze Age on the lake shores of the 20th to 18th centuries BC. During the Late Bronze Age, it seems that not all the complexes were equal as far as fortifications were concerned. Fence-like enclosures such as those at Bevaix Sud can be contrasted with fortifications similar to those at Unteruhldingen-Stollenwiesen (Fig. 2.9).

Between the Danube and the Bodensee, the heavily fortified lake settlements of the Bronze Age are connected with a network of hill settlements (Fig. 2.12A) that between them seem to divide up the landscape (cf. Köninger and Schöbel 2010). Similar to the hilltop settlements, the fortified lake-shore sites performed territorial functions and, accordingly, can be counted amongst the privileged central settlements. The special position amongst Late Bronze Age complexes is emphasised by rich hoards of metal (western Switzerland) and numerous metal finds, particularly pins (cf. Fischer 2009; Baumeister 2011: 32f.). According to Baumeister (2011), these metal objects were not accidentally lost but were deliberately deposited/sacrificed. The Late Bronze Age settlement sites were thus holy places where, previously, during the earlier Urnfield culture, religious practices were carried out.

Without a doubt, the Bronze Age lake-shore settlements were part of a settlement pattern that not only included lake settlements but also dry ground sites in direct proximity to the lakes and also the surrounding landscapes, as can be clearly seen in the Bodensee-Hegau region (cf. Dieckmann 1997, 1998; Köninger and Schöbel 2010: 418ff.). These contemporary sites included hilltop settlements, small villages, and solitary farms, which probably provided the populations residing in the lake-settlements with local produce when water levels favoured such construction. During periods of unfavourable conditions, the lake dwellers retreated from the shallow-water zones to higher altitudes for extended durations, as settlement sites in the direct hinterland of the great pre-Alpine lakes between Lake Geneva and the Bodensee indicate (see Schlichtherle 1988, 1994; Köninger and Schöbel 2010: 418f.; Néré and Isnard 2012: 327ff.).

To the south of the Alps, the distribution of Early and Middle Bronze Age settlements in the Lake Garda region and also in Piedmont around Lake Viverone indicates that the lake settlements were part of the local settlement dynamic (see Di Gennaro and Tecchiati 1996: 230ff.; Rubat Borel 2006; De Marinis 2009: 535f.; Rapi 2013: 536ff.). The varying size of individual settlements, from single buildings and small villages to fortified complexes, indicates that different roles were performed depending on the type and size of those settlements. The sizes of settlements and artefactual evidence have so far, however, not provided a classification of site functions; it must be assumed that farming communities erected and inhabited lake-shore villages as a form of subsistence in a wider economic setting.

Conclusions

Despite the fact that the Bronze Age is the least represented archaeological period within the Circum-Alpine region's lake-dwelling tradition (this is due to a number of factors: long(er) hiatuses in occupation, preservation, site disruption, *etc.*), the amount of information available is still quite remarkable. One of the main advantages is the availability of timber, which allowed the analysis of reliable tree-ring sequences, enabling archaeologists to give the lake-dwellings accurate calendar years. Reliable chronology is, however, not the only advantage; the ubiquity of dendro-analysis has allowed a myriad of other research areas to be developed, such as climate/environmental change, forestry management, and settlement dynamics, to mention but a few. It is in fact all of the aforementioned elements (combined with painstaking material culture studies) that have promoted the thorough archaeological reasoning that surrounds the lake-dwelling research. As detailed throughout this chapter, we are now able to give the settlements accurate calendric chronologies, classify them into local/regional groups, understand their biography (from construction to abandonment), and even understand their dynamics within the surrounding landscapes (occupational patterns, settlement rotation, *etc.*). Of course, there are in fact still a large number of lacunae in the research/data availability (some of which will perhaps never be filled), but, as demonstrated by this volume, the potential for achieving great results definitely exists.

Maps

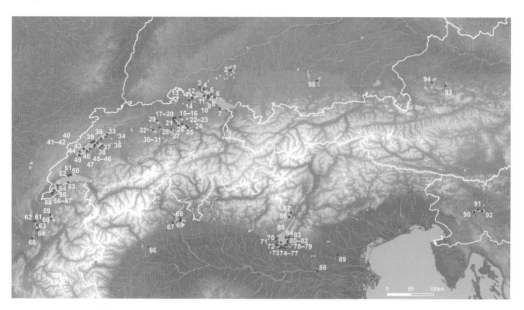

Map 2.1. Map of the distribution of Circum-Alpine pile dwellings. Pile dwelling stations (yellow) and scientifically significant Bronze Age pile dwelling stations (red). (Basic map © Bundesamt für Kultur/ Gestaltung: Emphase GmbH Lausanne, Suisse).

1. Siedlung-Forschner; 2. Wasserburg-Buchau; 3. Bodman-Schachen I; 4. Ludwigshafen-Seehalde; 5. Unteruhldingen-Stollenwiesen; 6. Hagnau-Burg; 7. Arbon-Bleiche II; 8. Konstanz Staad-Hörlepark; 9. Konstanz-Rauenegg and Konstanz-Frauenpfahl; 10. Egg-Obere Güll I; 11. Wollmatingen-Langenrain; 12. Eschenz/Öhningen-Ohrkopf; 13. Eschenz-Insel Werd; 14. Nussbaumersee; 15. Greifensee-Starkstromkabel; 16. Greifensee-Böschen; 17. Zürich-Grosser Hafner; 18. Zürich-Mozartstrasse; 19. Zürich-Bauschanze; 20. Zürich-Alpenquai; 21. Zürich-Wollishofen-Haumesser; 22. Meilen-Schellen; 23. Meilen-Rorenhaab; 24. Hombrechtikon-Feldbach West/Rapperswil-Jona-Feldbach Ost; 25. Rapperswil-Technikum; 26. Wädenswil-Vorder Au; 27. Horgen-Scheller; 28. Zug-Sumpf; 29. Seengen-Riesi; 30. Hitzkirch-Moos; 31. Hochdorf-Baldegg; 32. Sursee Gammainseli; 33. Sutz Lattrigen-Buchtstation; 34. Mörigen; 35. Vinelz; 36. Witzwil; 37. Muntelier-Steinberg; 38. Greng; 39. Hauterive-Champreveyres; 40. Auvernier; 41. Cortaillod; 42. Bevaix; 43. Concise; 44. Grandson-Corcelettes; 45. Chabrey-Montbec; 46. Delley-Portalban; 47. Chevroux; 48. Estavayer; 49. Yverdon; 50. Préverenges; 51. Morges; 52. Tolochenaz-La Poudrière; 53. Thonon-les-Bains; 54. Chens-sur-Lèman; 55. Corsier-Port; 56. Colonge-Bellerive-La Pointe-à-la-Bise; 57. Cologny-La Belotte; 58. Genève-Eaux Vives; 59. Annecy; 60. Sévrier; 61. Chindrieux; 62. Conjux; 63. Brison-Saint-Innocent; 64. Tresserve; 65. Saint-Alban-de Montbel; 66. Viverone; 67. Mercurago; 68. Isolino Virginia; 69. Cadrezzate-Il Sabbione; 70. Lucone di Polpenazze; 71. Padenghe del Garda; 72. Polada; 73. Lavagnone; 74. Barche di Solferino; 75. Bande di Cavriana; 76. Catellaro Lagusello; 77. Isolone del Mincio; 78. Peschiera; 79. Ronchi del Garda; 80. Pacengo; 81. Villa Bagatta; 82. La Quercia di Lazise; 83. Cisano; 84. Cavaion Veronese; 85. San Francesco di Sirmione; 86. Ledro; 87. Fiavè-Carera; 88. Canar di San Pietro; 89. Arquà; 90. Mali Otavnik; 91. Notranje Gorice; 92. Ig; 93. Traunkirchen; 94. Abtsdorf; 95. Feldafing Roseninsel (data after: Arnold 1990: 124f.; Beer et al. 1994: 79ff.; Hafner 1995; Balista and Leonardi 1996: 200ff.; Schöbel 1996: 14, 126, 152ff.; Seifert 1996: 157ff.; Köninger 1997: 29ff.; Hügi 2000; Conscience and Eberschweiler 2001: 136ff.; Eberli 2002: 216ff.; Eberschweiler 2002: 216, 222ff.; Billaud and Marguet 2005: 170 and fig. 1; Conscience 2005; Poggiani et al. 2005; Köninger 2006a; Martinelli 2006, 2007: 103ff.; Corboud and Pugin 2008: 42ff.; Fischer 2008: 37ff.; Schmidheyni 2011; Gaspari 2008; Billaud 2012: 345ff.; Gut 2013; author's own investigations).

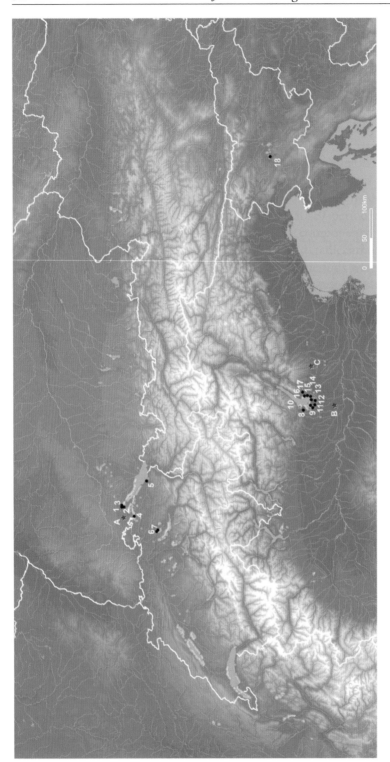

Map 2.2. _Early Early Bronze Age lake-settlements of the Circum-Alpine region (21st–20/19th centuries BC). (Basic map © Bundesamt für Kultur/ Gestaltung: Emphase GmbH Lausanne, Suisse)._

1. Bodman-Schachen IA; 2. Bodman-Weiler I; 3. Ludwigshafen-Seehalde; 4. Eschenz/Öhningen-Orkopf; 5. Arbon-Bleiche 2; 6. Greifensee-Starkstromkabel; 7. Greifensee-Böschen; 8. Lucone di Polpenazze; 9. Lavagnone; 10. San Francesco di Sirmione; 11. Barche di Solferino; 12. Bande di Cavriana; 13. Belvedere di Peschiera; 14. Ronchi del Garda; 15. La Quercia di Lazise; 16. Cisano Porto; 17. Ca' Nova di Cavaion; 18. Mali Otavnik. A = Singen 'Nordstadtterrasse'; B = Asola 'Campagnotti'; C = Arano. Dating: 1, 2, 4, 6, 7 and 18 ¹⁴C data; 8–17 dendrodatalwiggle-matching (cal ±10); 3 and 5 typology (Köninger 2001: 97f., 2006a; Conscience and Eberschweiler 2001: 138f; Martinelli 2007: 103ff; Gaspari 2008: 62 and 72; Bleicher 2011: 49ff. and 65).

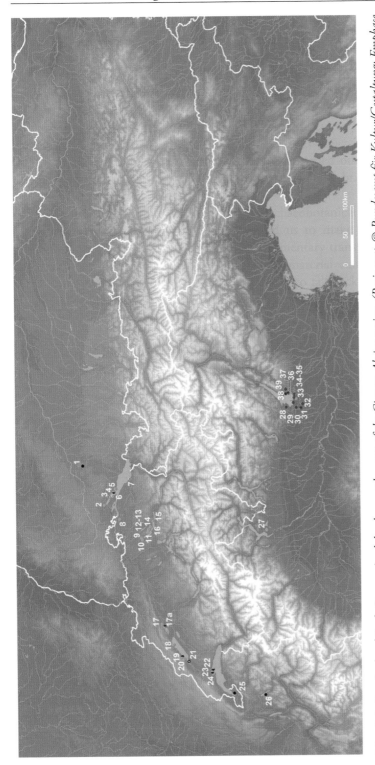

Map 2.3. Dendrodated Early Bronze Age lake-shore settlements of the Circum-Alpine region. (Basic map © Bundesamt für Kultur/Gestaltung: Emphase GmbH Lausanne, Suisse). Red = 21st–20th centuries BC; violet = 19th century BC; blue = 18th century BC; orange = 17th century BC (empty dots = heartwood (earliest possible date).

1. Siedlung-Forschner; 2. Bodman-Schachen I; 3. Nußdorf-Seehalde; 4. Unteruhldingen-Stollenweisen; 5. Haltnau-Oberhof; 6. Egg-Obere Güll I; 7. Arbon-Bleiche 2; 8. Nussbaumersee; 9. Zürich-Mozartstrasse; 10. Zürich-Bauschanze; 11. Feldmeilen-Vorderfeld; 12. Meilen-Schellen; 13. Meilen-Rörenhaab; 14. Uetikon-Schifflände; 15. Rapperswil-Technikum; 16. Wädenswil-Vorder; 17. Nidau-BKW; 17a. Sutz-Lattrigen-Buchstation; 18. Auvernier-Tranchée du Tram; 19. Concise-sous-Colachoz; 20. Onnens-Gare; 21. Yverdon-Garage Martin; 22. Préverenges I; 23. Morges-Les Roseaux; 24. Tolochenaz-La Poudrière; 25. Cologny-La Belotte; 26. Sévrier-Les Mongets; 27. Cadrezzate-Il Sabbione; 28. Polpenazze del Garda, Lucone D; 29. San Francesco di Sirmione; 30. Lavagnone; 31. Barche di Solferino; 32. Bande di Cavriana; 33. Frassino I; 34. Belvedere di Peschiera; 35. Ronchi del Garda; 36. Bosca di Pacengo; 37. La Quercia di Lazise; 38. Cisano-Porto; 39. Ca' Nova di Cavaion (data after: Wolf et al. 1999: 20ff.; Billaud and Marguet 2005: 173f.; Martinelli 2006: 82ff.; Hafner 2006: 110ff.; Corboud and Pugin 2008: 39ff.; Billamboz 2009: 497ff.).

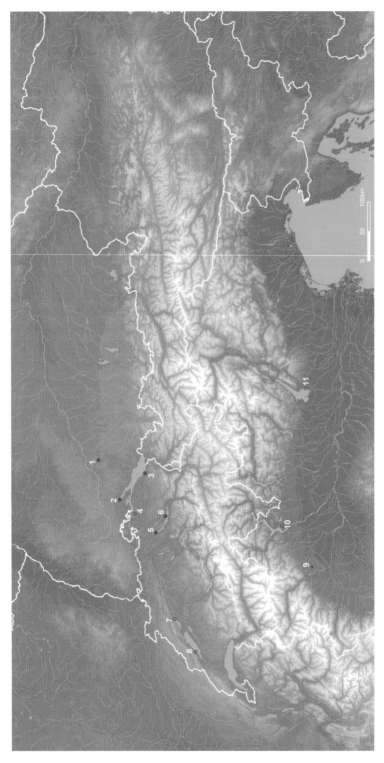

Map 2.4. Dendrodated Middle Bronze Age lake-settlements in the Circum-Alpine region. (Basic map © Bundesamt für Kultur/Gestaltung: Emphase GmbH Lausanne, Suisse). Blue (full dot) = c. 1500 BC; blue (empty dot) = c. 1580–1550 BC; red = end of 15th century BC.
1. Siedlung-Forschner; 2. Bodman-Schachen I; 3. Arbon-Bleiche II; 4. Nussbaumersee; 5. Zürich-Mozartstrasse; 6. Rapperswil Jona-Feldbach Ost; 7. Nidau-BKW; 8. Concise-sous-Colachoz; 9. Viverone (Vi 1) Emissario; 10. Cadrezzate-Il Sabbione; 11. Lazise-La Quercia III (Hochuli 1994; Amt für Städtebau der Stadt Zürich 2004: 355; Köninger 2006; Billamboz 2009; Schmidheiny 2011; Martinelli 2006: 78ff., 2013: 118f.; Winiger 2012: 119ff.; Billamboz and Martinelli this volume).

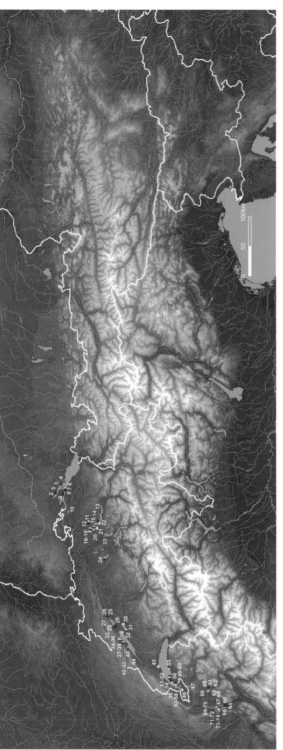

Map 2.5. Dendrodates from the Late Bronze Age lake-shore settlements in the Circum-Alpine region. (Basic map © Bundesamt für Kultur/Gestaltung: Emphase GmbH Lausanne, Suisse). Yellow = 11th century BC; green = 10th century BC; turquoise = 9th century BC; red = 11–9th centuries BC. 1. Wasserburg-Buchau; 2. Sipplingen-Osthafen; 3. Unteruhldingen-Stollenwiesen; 4. Hagnau-Burg; 5. Mainau-Nordstrand; 6. Staad-Hörlepark; 7. Konstanz-Rauenegg; 8. Konstanz-Frauenpfahl; 9. Wollmatingen-Langenrain; 10. Ürschhausen-Horn; 11. Greifensee-Böschen; 12. Fällanden-Rietspitz; 13. Uetikon-Schifflände; 14. Meilen-Schellen; 15. Feldmeilen-Vorderfeld; 16. Zürich-Grosser Hafner; 17. Zürich-Mozartstrasse; 18. Zürich-Kleiner Hafner; 19. Zürich-Alpenquai; 20. Wollishofen-Haumesser; 21. Horgen-Scheller; 22. Wädenswil-Hinter; 23. Zug-Sumpf; 24. Sursee; 25. Nidau-Steinberg; 26. Nidau-Neue Station; 27. Vingelz-Hafen; 28. Le Landeron; 29. Vinelz-Ländti; 30. Muntelier-Steinberg; 31. Avenches-Eau noir; 32. Cudrefin-Les Chavannes III; 33. Hauterive-Champreveyres 3; 34. Auvernier-Brena; 35. Auvernier-Nord; 36. Auvernier-Graviers; 37. Cortaillod Est; 38. Cortaillod-Plage; 39. Cortaillod-Les Esserts; 40. Bevaix-L'Abbay II; 41. Bevaix-Le Desert; 42. Bevaix-Sud/Quartier Nord; 43. Bevaix-Le Moulin; 44. Grandson-Corcelettes-les-Violes; 45. Morges-Grande Cité; 46. Genève-Pâquis A and B; 47. Genève-Plonjon; 48. Corsier-Port; 49. Cologne-Bellerive/Bellerive 1; 50. Thonon-les-bain/Rives 2; 51. Nernier-La Tire (Nernier 2); 52. Messery-Parteyi-Est; 53. Messery-Grand Bois; 54. Chens-sur-Léman/ La Vorgue Ouest; 55. Chens-sur-Léman/La Beauregard 2; 56. Chens-sur-Léman/Touges; 57. Chens-sur-Léman/Fabrique Nord; 58. Chens-sur-Léman/Sous-le-Moulin; 59. Annecy-Le Port II; 60. Veyrier-du-Lac/Sous les Guerres; 61. Sévier-Le Crêt de Chatillon; 62. Duingt-Le Roselet; 63. Duingt-Ruphy; 64. Tresserve-Les Fiollets; 65. Tresserve-Le Saut; 66. Brison St. Innocent-Meimart 2; 67. Brison St. Innocent-Grésine-Est; 68. Brison St. Innocent-Grésine-Ouest; 69. Chindrieux-Châtillon Port; 70. Chindrieux-Châtillon; 71. Conjux-Le Port 3; 72. Conjux-Pré Nuaz; 73. Conjux I; 74. Conjux II (after: Schöbel 1996; Marquet 1997: 12 ff.; Billaud and Marquet 1999: 14ff.; Gollnisch-Moos 1999; Hafner 1999: 38ff.; 2010: 369f.; Eberschweiler 2002: 222; Mainberger and Müller 2004; Altdorfer and Conscience 2005: 39; Archäologischer Dienst Bern 2006: 231; Eberschweiler et al. 2007; Billamboz 2009; Billaud 2012: 35ff.; Gut 2013).

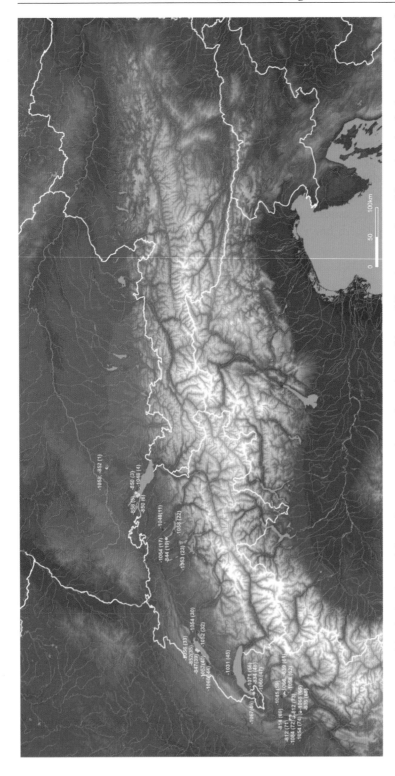

Map 2.6. Age span of dendrodated LBA lake-settlements. In each case the earliest and latest felling dates are charted for each individual region. Marginal sapwood dating and single early wane data – believed to be mature timber of derivative use – are not taken into account. Site numbers are in brackets – for site names see Map 2.5 (after Billamboz 2009; Fischer 2009; Arnold 2009; Billaud 2012; Arnold and Langenegger 2012; Gut 2013). (Basic map © Bundesamt für Kultur/Gestaltung: Emphase GmbH Lausanne, Suisse).

References

Achour-Uster, C., Eberli, U., Ebersbach, R. and Favre, P. (2002) *Die Seeufersiedlungen in Horgen. Die neolithischen und bronzezeitlichen Fundstellen Dampfschiffsteg und Scheller*. Zürich and Egg: FO Publishing. Monographien der Kantonsarchäologie Zürich 36.

Altorfer, K. and Conscience, A.-C. (2005) *Meilen-Schellen. Die neolithischen und spätbronzezeitlichen Funde und Befunde der Untersuchungen 1934–1996*. Zürich and Egg: FO Publishing. Zürcher Archäologie 18.

Amt für Städtebau der Stadt Zürich, Unterwasserarchäologie, (2004) Fundbericht 2003. Jona SG, Feldbach Ost. *Jahrbuch der schweizerischen Gesellschaft für Ur- und Frühgeschichte*, 87: 355.

Archäologischer Dienst Bern, Abteilung Ur- und Frühgeschichte, (2006) Fundbericht 2005. Bronzezeit. Vinelz BE, Ländti. *Jahrbuch Archäologie Schweiz*, 89: 231.

Arnold, B. (1986) Cortaillod-Est, un village du Bronze final *1: Fouille subaquatique et photographie aérienne*. Saint-Blaise: Editions du Ruau. Archéologie neuchâteloise 1.

Arnold, B. (1990) *Cortaillod-Est 6: Cortaillod-Est et les villages du lac de Neuchâtel au Bronze final. Structure de l'habitat et proto-urbanisme*. Saint-Blaise: Editions du Ruau. Archéologie neuchâteloise 6.

Arnold, B. (2009) *À la poursuite des villages lacustres neuchâtelois: un siècle et demi de cartographie et de recherche*. Hauterive: Office et musée cantonal d'archéologie de Neuchâtel. Archéologie neuchâteloise 45.

Arnold, B. (2012) Reliefs actuels et reliefs anciens. In B. Arnold and F. Langenegger (eds) *Plateaux de Bevaix 8: Bevaix-Sud: plongé dans le passé, fouille subaquatique d'un village du Bronze final*: 31–41. Hauterive: Office et musée cantonal d'archéologie de Neuchâtel. Archéologie neuchâteloise 50.

Arnold, B. and Langenegger, F. (eds) *Plateaux de Bevaix 8: Bevaix-Sud: plongé dans le passé, fouille subaquatique d'un village du Bronze final*. Hauterive: Office et musée cantonal d'archéologie de Neuchâtel. Archéologie neuchâteloise 50.

Aspes, A., Fasani L. and Gaggia, F. (1982) *Palafitte: Mito e Realtà*. Verona: Museo civico di storia naturale.

Balista, C. and Leonardi, G. (1996) Insediamenti, strutture subsitstive, ambiente, economia. Gli abitati di ambiente umido del Bronzo Antico dell'Italia settentrionale. In D. Cocchi Genick (ed.) *L'antica età del bronzo, Atti del Congresso di Viareggio, 9–12 Gennaio 1995*: 199–228. Firenze: Octavo.

Baumeister, R. (2011) Nadeln im Moor. In R. Baumeister (ed.) *Glaubenssachen. Kult und Kunst der Bronzezeit. Begleitband zur Sonderausstellung 15. Mai bis 1. November 2011*: 32–33. Bad Buchau: Verein für Altertumskunde und Heimatpflege with Federseemuseum.

Becker, B., BillambozA., Egger, H., Gassmann, P., Orcel, A., Orcel, C. and Ruoff, U. (1985) *Dendrochronologie in der Ur- und Frühgeschichte. Die absolute Datierung von Pfahlbausiedlungen nördlich der Alpen im Jahrringkalender Mitteleuropas*. Basel: Verlag Schweizerische Gesellschaft für Ur- und Frühgeschichte. Antiqua 11.

Beer, H., Meyer, R. A. and Schmid, W. (1994) Taucharchäologische Sondagen an der Roseninsel. *Das archäologische Jahr in Bayern* 1994: 79–82.

Benguerel, S., Dieckmann, B., Mainberger, M. and Schnyder, M. (2011) Siedlungen im Ausfluss des Bodensees – Fortsetzung der Untersuchungen in der ‚Stiegener Enge'. *Archäologische Ausgrabungen in Baden-Württemberg* 2011: 83–87.

Bericht RGK (1990) Bericht der Römisch-Germanischen Komission (ed.) (1990) *Siedlungsarchäologische Untersuchungen im Alpenvorlad. 5. Kolloquium der Deutschen Forschungsgemeinschaft vom 29.–30. März 1990 in Gaienhofen-Hemmenhofen*. Sonderdruck aus Bericht der Römisch-Germanischen Komission 71. 26–406. Mainz: Philipp von Zabern.

Bermond Montanari, G., Frontini, P., Gambari, F. M., Kaufmann, G., Marzatico, F., Montagnari, E.,

Nicolis, F., Pedrotti, A. and Venturino Gambari, M. (1996) Articolazioni culturali e cronologiche: l'Italia settentrionale. In D. Cocchi Genick (ed.) *L'antica età del bronzo, Atti del Congresso di Viareggio, 9–12 Gennaio 1995*: 57–78. Firenze: Octavo.

Bernabò Brea, M. (1997) Die Terramaren in der Poebene. In H. Schlichtherle (ed.) *Pfahlbauten rund um die Alpen*: 63–70. Stuttgart: Theiss.

Bernatzky-Goetze, M. (1987) *Mörigen : die spätbronzezeitlichen Funde*. Basel: Verlag Schweizerische Gesellschaft für Ur- und Frühgeschichte. Antiqua 16.

Bertone, A. and Forzzatti, L. (eds) (2004) *La Civiltà di Viverone. La conqista di una nuova frontiera nell'Europa del II Millennio a. C*. Biella: Eventi & Progetti Editore.

Billamboz, A. (2005) Die Wasserburg Buchau im Jahrringkalender. *Plattform* 13/14: 97–105.

Billamboz, A. (2009) Jahrringuntersuchungen in der Siedlung Forschner und weiterer bronze- und eisenzeitlichen Feuchtbodensiedlungen Südwestdeutschlands. Aussagen der angewandten Dendrochronologie in der Feuchtbodenarchäologie. In A. Billamboz, J. Köninger, H. Schlichtherle and W. Torke (eds) *Die Früh- und Mittelbronzezeitliche Siedlung 'Forschner' im Federseemoor. Befunde und Dendrochonologie*: 399–555. Stuttgart: Konrad Theiss. Siedlungsarchäologie im Alpenvorland XI.

Billamboz, A. and Martinelli, N. (1996) La recherche dendrochronologique en Europe pour l'âge du Bronze ancien. In C. Mordant and O. Gaiffe (eds) *Cultures et sociétés du Bronze en Europe. Actes du colloque 'Fondament culturels, techiques, économiques et sociaux des débuts de l'âge du Bronze'. 117e Congrès national des sociétés savantes, Clermont-Ferrand 1992*: 85–96. Paris: Éditions du Comité des Travaux historiques et scientifiques.

Billamboz, A. and Schöbel, G. (1996) *Dendrochronologische Untersuchungen in den spätbronzezeitlichen Pfahlbausiedlungen am nördlichen Ufer des Bodensees*. 203–221. Stuttgart: Konrad Theiss. Siedlungsarchäologie im Alpenvorland IV.

Billamboz, A. and Köninger, J. (2008) Dendroarchäologische Untersuchungen zur Besiedlungsdynamik und Landschaftsentwicklung im Neolithikum des westlichen Bodenseegebietes. In W. Dörfler and J. Müller (eds) *Umwelt – Wirtschaft – Siedlungen im dritten vorchristlichen Jahrtausend Mitteleuropas und Südskandinaviens. Internat. Tagung Kiel 2005*: 317–334. Neumünster: Wachholtz. Offa-Bücher 84.

Billamboz, A., Köninger, J., Schlichtherle, H. and Torke, W. (eds) (2009) *Die Früh- und Mittelbronzezeitliche Siedlung 'Forschner' im Federseemoor. Befunde und Dendrochonologie*. Stuttgart: Konrad Theiss. Siedlungsarchäologie im Alpenvorland XI.

Billaud, Y. (1995) *Sévrier les Mongets, Haute-Savoie*. Bilan scientifique des centres nationaux 1993. 114–115.

Billaud, Y. (2005) Une structure de La Tène ancienne à Tresserve / Le Saut (Lac de Bourget, Savoie, France). *Nachrichtenblatt Arbeitskreis Unterwasserarchäologie* 11/12, 2005: 11–16.

Billaud, Y. (2012) Le lac du Bourget à la fin de l'âge du Bronze. Premiers éléments pour une reconstruction de l'occupation des zones littorales. In M. Honegger and C. Mordant (eds.) *L'Homme au bord de l'eau. Archéologie des zones littorales du Néolithique à la Protohistoire. Actes du 135e congrès national des sociétés historiques et scientifiques du CTHS 'Paysages'. Neuchâtel 6–11 avril 2010*: 345–361. Paris and Lausanne: CTHS. Cahiers d'Archéologie. Romande 132.

Billaud, Y. and Marguet, A. (1999) L'archéologie dans les lacs alpins francais: l'étude des habitats lacustres de la Préhistoire récente. *Nachrichtenblatt Arbeitskreis Unterwasserarchäologie* 6: 7–20.

Billaud, Y. and Marguet, A. (2005) Habitats lacustres du Néolithique et de l'âge du Bronze dans les lacs alpins francais: bilan des connaissances et perspectives. In P. Della Casa and M. Trachsel (eds.) *WES'04 – Wetland Economies and societies. Proceedings of the International Conference in Zurich, 10–13 March 2004*: 169–178. Zürich: Chronos. Collectio archaeologica 3.

Bleicher, N. (2011) Absolutdatierung. In M. Schmidheiny *Zürich 'Mozartstrasse' 4: Die frühbronzezeitliche Besiedlung*: 49–67. Zürich and Egg: FO Publishing. Monographien der Kantonsarchäologie Zürich 42.

Bleicher, N. (2013) Der richtige Weg: André Billamboz und die frühe archäologische Dendrochronologie. In N. Bleicher, H. Schlichtherle, P. Gassmann and N. Martinelli (eds) *DENDRO ... -Chronologie, -Typologie, -Ökologie. Festschrift für André Billamboz zum 65. Geburtstag*: 27–34. Freiburg im Breisgau: Janus Verlag.

Bleicher, N., Bolliger, M. and Gut, U. (2013) Ein erster dendrotypologischer Überblicksversuch über die Bauholzserien der Ufersiedlungen am Zürichsee. In N. Bleicher, H. Schlichtherle, P. Gassmann and N. Martinelli (eds) *DENDRO ... -Chronologie, -Typologie, -Ökologie. Festschrift für André Billamboz zum 65. Geburtstag*: 51–57. Freiburg im Breisgau: Janus Verlag.

Bleicher, N., Schlichtherle, H., Gassmann, P. and Martinelli, N. (eds) (2013) *DENDRO ... -Chronologie, -Typologie, -Ökologie. Festschrift für André Billamboz zum 65. Geburtstag*. Freiburg im Breisgau: Janus Verlag.

Blumer, R. and Wolf, C. (2009) Fundbericht 2008. Bronzezeit. Muntelier FR, Steinberg. *Jahrbuch Archäologie Schweiz* 92: 278–279.

Burri-Wyser, E. (2012) La céramique. In A. Winiger and E. Burri-Wyser. *Les villages du Bronze ancien: architecture et mobilier. La station lacustre de Concise 5*: 153–213. Lausanne: Cahiers Archéologie Romande 135.

Cazzanelli, F. (2007) La fase del Bronzo Antico II nel settore B. In R. C. De Marinis (ed.) *Studi sull'abitato dell'età del Bronzo del Lavagnone, Desenzano del Garda*: 187–211. Notizie archeologiche bergomensi 10: Comune, Assessorato alla Cultura.

Conscience, A. C. (2001) Frühbronzezeitliche Uferdörfer aus Zürich-Mozartstrasse – eine folgenreiche Neudatierung. Ein kritischer Blick zurück. *Jahrbuch der Schweizerischen Gesellschaft für Ur- und Frühgeschichte* 84: 147–157.

Conscience, A. C. (2005) Wädenswil-Vorder A. Eine Seeufersiedlung am Übergang vom 17. zum 16. Jh. v. Chr. im Rahmen der Frühbronzezeit am Zürichsee. Unter besonderer Berücksichtigung der frühbronzezeitlichen Funde und Befunde von Meilen-Schellen. Zürich and Egg: FO Publishing. *Zürcher Archäologie Heft 19. Seeufersiedlungen.*

Conscience, A. C. and Eberschweiler, B. (2001) Zwei bemerkenswerte Fundplätze der frühen Bronzezeit im Greifensee. *Jahrbuch der Schweizerischen Gesellschaft für Ur- und Frühgeschichte* 84: 136–146.

Corboud, P. and Pugin, C. (2008) L'organisation spatiale d'un village littoral du Bronze ancien lémanique: Préverenges I VD. *Jahrbuch Archäologie Schweiz* 91: 39–58.

David-Elbiali, M. and David, W. (2010) À la suite de Jacques-Pierre Millotte, l'actualité des recherches en typologie sur l'âge du Bronze, le Bronze ancien et le début du Bronze moyen : cadre chronologique et liens culturels entre l'Europe nord-alpine occidentale, le monde danubien et l'Italie du Nord. In A. Richard, P. Barral, A. Daubigney, G. Kaenel, C. Mordant and J.-F. Piningre (eds) *L'isthme européen Rhin-Saône-Rhône dans la Protohistoire. Approches nouvelles en hommage à Jacques-Pierre Millotte (Besançon, 16–18 octobre 2006)*: 295–324. Besançon: Annales Littéraires de l'Université de Besançon 860.

Della Casa, P. and Trachsel, M. (eds) (2005) *WES'04 – Wetland Economies and societies. Proceedings of the International Conference in Zurich, 10–13 March 2004*. Zürich: Chronos. Collectio archaeologica 3.

De Marinis R. C. (1997) L'età del bronzo nella regione benacense e nella pianura padana a nord del Po. In M. Bernabò Brea, A. Cardarelli and M. Cremaschi (eds) *Le terramare. La più antica civiltà padana*: 405–419. Milano: Electa.

De Marinis, R. C. (2002) Towards a relative and absolute chronology of the Bronze Age in Northern Italy. *Notizie archeologiche bergomensi* 7: 23–100.

De Marinis, R. C. (ed.) (2007a). *Studi sull'abitato dell'età del Bronzo del Lavagnone, Desenzano del Garda*. Bergamo: Notizie archeologiche bergomensi 10. Comune, Assessorato alla Cultura.

De Marinis, R. C. (2007b) Il significato delle ricerche archeologiche al Lavagnone. In De Marinis, R. C. (ed.) *Studi sull'abitato dell'età del Bronzo del Lavagnone, Desenzano del Garda*: 1–17. Bergamo: Notizie archeologiche bergomensi 10. Comune, Assessorato alla Cultura.

De Marinis, R. C. (2009) Continuity and Discontinuity in Northern Italy from the Recent to the Final Bronze Age: a View from North-western Italy. *Scienze dell'antichità Storia Archeologia Antropologia* 15: 535–545.

De Marinis, R. C. (ed.) (2013) *L'età del Rame. La pianura padane e le Alpi al tempo di Ötzi*. Brescia: Compagnia della Stampa Massetti Rodella editori.

De Marinis, R. C., Rapi, M., Ravazzi, C., Arpenti, E., Deaddis, M. and Perego, R. (2005) Lavagnone (Desenzano del Garda): new excavations and paleoecology of a Bronze Age pile dwelling site in northern Italy. In P. Della Casa and M. Trachsel (eds) *WES'04 – Wetland Economies and societies. Proceedings of the International Conference in Zurich, 10–13 March 2004*: 221–232. Zürich: Chronos. Collectio archaeologica 3.

De Marinis, R. C. and Valzolgher, E. (2013) Riti funerari dell'antica età del Bronzo in area padana. In R. C. De Marinis (ed.) *L'età del Rame. La pianura padane e le Alpi al tempo di Ötzi* : 545–559. Brescia: Compagnia della Stampa Massetti Rodella editori.

Degen, R. (ed.) (1981) Zürcher Seeufersiedlungen. Von der Pfahlbau-Romantik zur modernen archäologischen Forschung. *Helvetia Archaeologica / Archäologie. in der Schweiz* 12: 45–48.

Deslex Sheik, C., Saltel, S., Braillard, L. and Detrey, J. (2006) Le Campaniforme des vallées sèches d'Ajoie JU. Les sites de la combe En Vaillard et de la combe Varu à Chevenez. *Jahrbuch Archäologie Schweiz* 89: 51–86.

Dieckmann, B. (1997) Mittelbronzezeitliche Siedlungen im Hegau. In Archäologischen Landesmuseum Baden-Württemberg (ed.) *Goldene Jahrhunderte. Die Bronzezeit in Südwestdeutschland*: 67–17. Stuttgart: Konrad Theiss. ALManach 2.

Dieckmann, B. (1998) Siedlungen und Umwelt am Federsee und im westlichen Bodenseegebiet. In B. Hänsel (ed.) *Die Bronzezeit: das erste goldene Zeitalter Europas. Mensch und Umwelt in der Bronzezeit Europas*: 373–394. Kiel: Oetkar Voges.

Di Gennaro, F. and Tecchiati, V. (1996) Insediamenti su Rilievi. In D. Cocchi Genick (ed.) *L'antica età del bronzo, Atti del Congresso di Viareggio, 9–12 Gennaio 1995*: 229–245. Firenze: Octavo.

Dular, J. (1999) Ältere, mittlere und jüngere Bronzezeit in Slowenien – Forschungsstand und Probleme. *Arheološki Vestnik* 50: 81–96.

Dworsky, C. and Reitmaier, T. (2003) 'Salzkammergut reloaded'. Ein Arbeitsbericht zur Kurzinventarisation der prähistorischen Seeufersiedlungen in Mond- und Attersee 2003. *Nachrichtenblatt Arbeitskreis Unterwasserarchäologie* 10: 51–56.

Eberli, U. (2002) Frühbronzezeit. In C. Achour-Uster, U. Eberli, R. Ebersbach, R. and P. Favre *Die Seeufersiedlungen in Horgen. Die neolithischen und bronzezeitlichen Fundstellen Dampfschiffsteg und Scheller*: 216–221. Zürich and Egg: FO Publishing. Monographien der Kantonsarchäologie Zürich 36.

Eberschweiler, B. (2002) Bronzezeitliche Besiedlung. Befund. Spätbronzezeit. In C. Achour-Uster, U. Eberli, R. Ebersbach and P. Favre *Die Seeufersiedlungen in Horgen. Die neolithischen und bronzezeitlichen Fundstellen Dampfschiffsteg und Scheller*: 216, 222–223. Zürich and Egg: FO Publishing. Monographien der Kantonsarchäologie Zürich 36.

Eberschweiler, B. (2004) *Bronzezeitliches Schwemmgut vom 'Chollerpark' in Steinhausen (Kanton Zug)*. Basel: Verlag Schweizerische Gesellschaft für Ur- und Frühgeschichte Antiqua 37.

Eberschweiler, B., Köninger, J., Schlichtherle, H. and Strahm, C. (eds) (2001) *Aktuelles zur Frühbronzezeit und frühen Mittelbronzezeit im nördlichen Alpenvorland*. Freiburg im Breisgau: Janus Verlag. Hemmenhofener Skripte 2.

Eberschweiler, B., Riethmann, P. and Ruoff, U. (2007) *Das spätbronzezeitliche Dorf von Greifensee-Böschen : Dorfgeschichte, Hausstrukturen und Fundmaterial.* Zürich and Egg: FO Publishing. Monographien der Kantonsarchäologie Zürich 38.

Fischer, V. (2008) La Station de Grandson-Corcelettes (canton de Vaud, Suisse) et les accumulations debronzes palafittiques de Suisse occidental. *Nachrichtenblatt Arbeitskreis Unterwasserarchäologie* 14: 37–38.

Fischer, V. (2009) Le phénomène des bronzes palafittiques en Suisse occidentale. In S. Bonnardin, C. Hamon, M. Lauwers and B. Quilliec (eds), *Du matériel au spirituel. Réalitésarchéologiques et historiques des 'dépôts' de la Préhistoire à nos jour:* 159–169. Antibes: Editions APDCA.

Frank, K (2006) Botanische Makroreste aus Tauchgrabungen in den frühbronzezeitlichen Seeufersiedlungen Bodman-Schachen I am nordwestlichen Bodensee unter besonderer Berücksichtigung der Morphologie und Anatomie der Wildpflanzenfunde. Aussagemöglichkeiten zu Nutzpflanzen, Vegetationsverhältnissen und zur Lage des Siedlungsareals. *Forschungen und Berichte zur Vor- und Fruhgeschichte in Baden-Wurttemberg* 85: 431–599. Siedlungsarchäologie im Alpenvorland VIII.

Gaspari, A. (2008) Bronze Age pile-dwelling site at Mali Otavnik near Bistra in the Ljubljansko barje. *Arheološki vestnik* 59: 57–89.

Gersbach, E. (2006) *Die Heuneburg bei Hundersingen, Gemeinde Herbertingen. Eine Wehrsiedlung / Burg der Bronze- und frühen Urnenfelderzeit und ihre Stellung im Siedlungsgefüge an der oberen Donau.* Stuttgart: Konrad Theiss. Forschungen und Berichte zur Vor- und Frühgeschichte in Baden-Württemberg 96.

Gollnisch-Moos, H. (1999) *Forschungen im Seebachtal 3: Ürschhausen-Horn, Haus- und Siedlungsstrukturen der spätestbronzezeitlichen Siedlung.* Frauenfeld: Department für Erziehung und Kultur des Kantons Thurgau. Archäologie im Thurgau 7.

Gross, E., Brombacher, C., Dick, M., Diggelmann, K., Hardmeyer, B., Jagher, R., Ritzmann, C., Ruckstuhl, B., Ruoff, U., Schibler, J., Vaughan, P. C. and K. Wyprächtiger, K. (1987) *Zürich 'Mozartstrasse' 1: Neolithische und bronzezeitliche Ufersiedlungen.* Zürich and Egg. FO Publishing. Monographien der Kantonsarchäologie Zürich 4.

Guilaine, J., Vaquer, J., Coularou, J. and Treiner-Claustre, F. (1989) *Archéologie et Écologie d'une site de l'Âge du Cuivre, de l'Âge du Bronze final et de l'Antiquité.* Toulouse: Centre d'anthropologie des sociétés rurales.

Gut, U. (2013) *Spätbronzezeitliche Besiedlungsdynamik und Waldwirtschaft am untersten Zürichsee. Eine dendroarchäologische Perspektive zur Frage der Besiedlung der Strandplatten am untersten Seebecken und der Bewirtschaftung des angrenzenden Hinterlandes.* Unpublished Thesis submitted to the Lizentiatsarbeit Abteilung für Ur- und Frühgeschichte, Historisches Seminar der Universität Zürich in fullfillment of a Masters Degree in Archaeology.

Hafner, A. (1995) *Die frühe Bronzezeit in der Westschweiz. Funde und Befunde aus Siedlungen, Gräbern und Horten der entwickelten Frühbronzezeit.* Bern: Staatlicher Lehrmittelverl. Ufersiedlungen am Bielersee 5.

Hafner, A. (1999) Sondierungen und Rettungsgrabungen 1998–99 im unteren Bielersee (Westschweiz). *Nachrichtenblatt Arbeitskreis Unterwasserarchäologie* 6: 38–43.

Hafner, A. (2006) Sutz-Lattrigen, Buchtstation. Rettungsgrabung 2004/2005: frühbronzezeitliche Ufersiedlungen. *Archäologie Kanton Bern* 2006: 110–113.

Hafner, A. (2010) Ufersiedlungen mit Palisaden am Bielersee – Hinweise auf Verteidigungssysteme in neolithischen und bronzezeitlichen Pfahlbauten. In I. Matuschik, C. Strahm, B. Eberschweiler, G. Fingerlin, A. Hafner, M. Kinsky, M. Mainberger and G. Schöbel (eds) *Vernetzungen : Aspekte siedlungsarchäologischer Forschung. Festschrift für Helmut Schlichtherle zum 60. Geburtstag:* 357–376. Freiburg im Breisgau: Lavori Verlag.

Hochuli, S. (1994) *Arbon-Bleiche. Die neolithischen und bronzezeitlichen Seeufersiedlungen.* Frauenfeld:

Department für Erziehung und Kultur des Kantons Thurgau. Archäologie im Thurgau 2.

Hochuli, S., Niffeler, U. and Rychner, V. (eds) (1998) *Die Schweiz vom Palaolithikum bis zum frühen Mittelalter: SPM III Bronzezeit*. Basel: Schweizerische Gesellschaft fur Ur- und Fruhgeschichte.

Hügi, U. (2000) *Seeufersiedlungen. Meilen Rorenhaab*. Zürich and Egg: FO Publishing. Zürcher Archäologie 1.

Hügi, U. (2006) Prähistorische Dörfer, alte Brücken: gut erhalten, beinahe verschwunden ... Die Arbeiten der Züricher Tauchequipe in den Jahren 2005/2006, Bericht VIII. *Nachrichtenblatt Arbeitskreis Unterwasserarchäologie* 13: 53–57.

Innerhofer, F. (2013) Von der frühen zur mittleren Bronzezeit in Süddeutschland – Wandel oder Zäsur? In H. Meller, F. Bertemes, H. R. Bork and R. Risch (eds) *1600 – Kultureller Umbruch im Schatten des Thera-Ausbruchs? Tagungen des Landesmuseums für Vorgeschichte Halle 9*: 443–451. Halle: Landesmuseum für Vorgeschichte.

Jacomet, S. (2008) Subsistenz und Landnutzung während des 3. Jahrtausends v. Chr. aufgrund von archäologischen Daten aus dem südwestlichen Mitteleuropa. In W. Dörfler and J. Müller (eds) *Umwelt – Wirtschaft – Siedlungen im dritten vorchristlichen Jahrtausend Mitteleuropas und Südskandinaviens. Internat. Tagung Kiel 2005*: 355–377. Neumünster: Wachholtz. Offa-Bücher 84.

Kienlin, T. L. (2007) Von den Schmieden der Beile: Zu Verbreitung und Angleichung metallurgischen Wissens im Verlauf der Frühbronzezeit. *Prähistorische Zeitschrift*. 82: 1–22.

Kimmig, W. (1981) Feuchtbodensiedlungen in Mitteleuropa. Ein forschungsgeschichtlicher Überblick. *Archäologisches Korrespondenzblatt* 11.1: 1–14.

Kimmig, W. (1992) *Die 'Wasserburg Buchau' – eine spätbronzezeitliche Siedlung. Forschungsgeschichte – Kleinfunde*. Stuttgart: Theiss. Materialhefte zur Vor- und Frühgeschichte in Baden Württemberg 16.

Kimmig, W., Smolla, G., Schlichtherle, H., Perini, R., Arnold, B., Borello, M. A., and Egloff, M. (1981) Bronzezeitliche Feuchtbodensiedlungen im circumalpinen Raum. Vorträge im Rahmen der Arbeitsgemeinschaf 'Bronzezeit' bei der Jahrestagung des West- und Süddeutschen Verbandes für Altertumsforschung. *Sonderdruck aus: Archäologisches Korrespondenzblatt* 11.

Köninger, J. (1986) Abschluß der Unterwassergrabungen in Bodman-Schachen, Kreis Konstanz. *Archäologische Ausgrabungen in Baden-Württemberg* 1986: 52–54.

Köninger, J. (1997) Ufersiedlungen der frühen Bronzezeit am Bodensee. In: H. Schlichtherle (ed.) *Pfahlbauten rund um die Alpen*: 29–35. Stuttgart: Theiss.

Köninger, J. (2001) Frühbronzezeitliche Ufersiedlungen am Bodensee. Neue Funde und Befunde aus Tauchsondagen und Nachforschungen in neuen und alten Sammlungsbeständen. In B. Eberschweiler, J. Köninger, H. Schlichtherle and C. Strahm (eds) *Aktuelles zur Frühbronzezeit und frühen Mittelbronzezeit im nördlichen Alpenvorland*: 93–116. Freiburg im Breisgau: Janus-Verlag. Hemmenhofener Skripte.

Köninger, J. (2002) Oggelshausen- Bruckgraben – Funde und Befunde aus einer eisenzeitlichen Fischfanganlage im südlichen Federseeried, Gde. Oggelshausen, Kr. Biberach. *Heimat- und Altertumsverein Heidenheim an der Brenz* 9: 33–56.

Köninger, J. (2006a) Die frühbronzezeitlichen Ufersiedlungen von Bodman-Schachen I – Befunde und Funde aus den Tauchsondagen 1982–84 und 1986. *Forschungen und Berichte zur Vor- und Frühgeschichte in Baden-Württemberg* 85: 17–430. Siedlungsarchäologie im Alpenvorland VIII. Stuttgart: Theiss.

Köninger, J. (2006b) Unterwasserarchäologie am Überlinger See im Zeichen extremer Niedrigwasserstände. *Nachrichtenblatt Arbeitskreis Unterwasserarchäologie* 13: 64–73.

Köninger, J. (2006c) Deckel, Töpfe und gemusterte Tonobjekte. Anmerkungen zu Funden der älteren Frühbronzezeit aus dem westlichen Bodenseegebiet. *Nachrichtenblatt Arbeitskreis Unterwasserarchäologie* 13: 79–82.

Köninger, J. (2009) Die Baustrukturen der Siedlung Forschner. In A. Billamboz, J. Köninger, H.

Schlichtherle and W. Torke *Die früh- und mittelbronzezeitliche 'Siedlung Forschner' im Federseemoor. Befunde und Dendrochronologie*: 262–276. Stuttgart: Theiss. Siedlungsarchäologie im Alpenvorland XI.

Köninger, J. (in print) Spätbronzezeitliche Ufersiedlungen am Bodensee – Siedlungsstrukturen und Neufunde aus den Ufersiedlungen Hagnau-Burg und Unteruhldingen-Stollenwiesen. Hommage en l'honneur d'André Marguet. *Revue Archéologique de l'Est. supplément.*

Köninger, J., Kolb, M. and Schöbel, G. (1982) Taucharchäologie am Bodensee (Kr. Konstanz und Bodenseekreis). *Archäologische Ausgrabungen in Banden-Württemberg* 1982: 45–50.

Köninger, J. and Billamboz, A. (in print) Schnurkeramik am Bodensee. *Proceedings of the International Conference Corded Days in Krakow, 1st–2nd December 2011.*

Köninger, J. and Schlichtherle, H. (1999) Foreign Elements in South-West German Lake-Dwellings. Transalpine Relations in the Late Neolithic and Early Bronze Ages. *Preistoria Alpina* 35: 43–53.

Köninger, J. and Schlichtherle, H. (2009) Die Siedlung Forschner im siedlungsarchäologischen Kontext des nördlichen Alpenvorland. In A. Billamboz, J. Köninger, H. Schlichtherle and W. Torke *Die früh- und mittelbronzezeitliche 'Siedlung Forschner' im Federseemoor. Befunde und Dendrochronologie*: 361–397. Stuttgart: Theiss. Siedlungsarchäologie im Alpenvorland XI.

Köninger, J. and Schöbel, G. (2010) Bronzezeitliche Fundstellen zwischen Bodensee und Oberschwaben. In I. Matuschik, C. Strahm, B. Eberschweiler, G. Fingerlin, A. Hafner, M. Kinsky, M. Mainberger and G. Schöbel (eds) *Vernetzungen : Aspekte siedlungsarchäologischer Forschung. Festschrift für Helmut Schlichtherle zum 60. Geburtstag*: 81–96. Freiburg im Breisgau: Lavori Verlag.

Krause, R. (1988) *Die endneolithischen und frühbronzezeitlichen Gräber der Nordstadtterrasse von Singen am Hohentwiel. Forschungen und Berichte zur Vor- und Frühgeschichte in Baden-Württemberg 32.* Stuttgart: Theiss.

Krause, R. (1996) Zur Chronologie der frühen und mittleren Bronzezeit Süddeutschlands, der Schweiz und Österreichs. In K. Randsborg (ed.) *Absolute Chronology. Archaeological Europe 2500–500 BC. Acta Archaeologica 67, Supplementa Vol. 1*: 73–86. Kopenhagen: Munksgaard.

Krause, R. (2001) Siedlungskeramik der älteren Frühbronzezeit von Singen am Hohentwiel (Baden-Württemberg). In B. Eberschweiler, J. Köninger, H. Schlichtherle and C. Strahm (eds) *Aktuelles zur Frühbronzezeit und frühen Mittelbronzezeit im nördlichen Alpenvorland*: 67–74. Freiburg im Breisgau: Janus Verlag. Hemmenhofener Skripte 2.

Langenegger, F. (2012) Étude dendro-archéologique. In B. Arnold and F. Langenegger (eds) *Plateaux de Bevaix 8: Bevaix-Sud: plongé dans le passé, fouille subaquatique d'un village du Bronze final*: 133–169. Hauterive: Office et musée cantonal d'archéologie de Neuchâtel. Archéologie neuchâteloise 50.

Magny, M. (2004) Holocene climate variability as reflected by mid-European lake-level fluctuations and its probable impact on prehistoric human settlements. *Quarternary Internatonal* 111: 65–79.

Magny, M., Maise, C., Jacomet, S. and Burga, C. A. (1998) Klimaschwankungen im Verlauf der Bronzezeit. In S. Hochuli, U. Niffeler and V. Rychner (eds) *Die Schweiz vom Paläolithikum bis zum frühen Mittelalter: Bronzezeit (SPM III)*: 137–140. Basel: Schweizerische Gesellschaft für Ur- und Frühgeschichte.

Magny, M., Galop, D., Bellintani, P., Desmet, D., Haas, J. N., Martinelli, N., Pedrotti, A., Scandolari, R., Stock, A. and Vannière, B. (2009) Late-Holocene climatic variability south of the Alps as recorded by lake-level fluctuations at Lake Ledro (Trentino, Italy). *The Holocene* 19: 575–589.

Magny, M., Joannin, S., Galop, D., Vannière, B., Haas, J. N., Bassetti, M., Bellintani, P., Scandolari, R., Desmet, M. (2012) Holocene palaeohydrological changes in the northern Mediterranean borderlands as reflected by the lake-level-record of Lake Ledro, northeastern Italy. *Quaternary Research* 77: 382–396.

Maier, U. and Vogt, R. (2007) *Pedologische und moorkundliche Untersuchungen zur Landschafts- und Besiedlungsgeschichte des Federseegebiets.* Stuttgart: Institut für Geographie der Universität Stuttgart. Stuttgarter Geographische Studien 138.

Marguet, A. (2001) Haute Savoie. Carte archéologique de la rive francaise du lac Léman. *Bilan scientifique du département des recherches archéologiques subaquatiques et sous-marines 1997*: 128–136.

Marguet, A. (2007) Lac de Bourget: Marais de la Chatière, Les Côtes. *Bilan scientifique du département des recherches archéologiques subaquatiques et sous-marines 2005*: 149–151.

Martinelli, N. (2006) Underwater archaeology and prehistoric settlement in a great alpine lake: the case study of Lake Garda. In A. Hafner, U. Niffeler and U. Ruoff (eds) *Die neue Sicht: Unterwasserarchäologie und Geschichtsbild. Akten des 2. Internationalen Kongresses für Unterwasserarchäologie, Rüschlikon bei Zürich, 21.–24. Oktober 2004*: 78–87. Basel: Archäologie Schweiz. Antiqua 40.

Martinelli, N. (2007) Dendrocronologia delle palafitte dell'area gardesana: situazione delle ricerche e prospettive. *Annali Benacensi* 13–14: 103–120.

Martinelli, N. (2013) Dendro-typology in Italy: The case studies of the pile-dwelling villages Lucone D (Brescia) and Sabbione (Varese). In N. Bleicher, H. Schlichtherle, P. Gassmann and N. Martinelli (eds) *DENDRO -Chronologie, -Typologie, -Ökologie. Festschrift für André Billamboz zum 65. Geburtstag*: 117–124. Freiburg im Breisgau: Janus-Verlag.

Meller, H., Bertemes, F., Bork, H. R. and Risch, R. (eds) (2013) *1600 – Kultureller Umbruch im Schatten des Thera-Ausbruchs? Tagungen des Landesmuseums für Vorgeschichte Halle 9.* Halle: Landesmuseum für Vorgeschichte.

Menotti, F. (2001) *'The Missing Period': Middle Bronze Age Lake-Dwellings in the Alps.* Oxford: Archaeopress. BAR International Series 986.

Menotti, F. (2003) Cultural response to environmental change in the Alpine lacustrine regions: the displacement model. *Oxford Journal of Archaeology* 22(4): 375–96.

Menotti, F. (ed.) (2004) *Living on the lake in prehistoric Europe: 150 years of lake-dwelling research.* London: Routledge.

Menotti, F., Borel, F. R., Köninger, J. and Martinelli, N. (2012) Viverone (BI) – Azeglio (TO). Sito palafitticolo Vi1–Emissario. Indagini subacquee e campionamento dendrocronologico. *Quaderni della Soprintendenza Archeologica del Piemonte* 27: 196–201.

Möslein, S. (1997) Die Straubinger Gruppe der donauländischen Frühbronzezeit – frühbronzezeitliche Keramik aus Südostbayern und regionale Gliederung der frühen Bronzezeit in Südbayern. *Bericht der Bayerischen Bodendenkmalpflege* 38: 37–106.

Mottes, E., Nicolis, F. and Schlichtherle, H. (2002) Kulturelle Beziehungen zwischen den Regionen nördlich und südlich der Zentralalpen während des Neolithikums und der Kupferzeit. In G. Schneckenburger (ed.) *Über die Alpen – Menschen, Wege, Waren*: 119–135. Stuttgart: Archäologisches Landesmuseum. ALManach 7/8.

Müller, J. and Lohrke, B. (2009) Neue absolutchronologische Daten für die süddeutsche Hügelgräberbronzezeit. *Germania* 87: 25–39.

Néré, E. and Isnard, F. (2012) L'occupation humaine au Bronze final sur les berges du Léman: deux exemples d'habitats à Chens-sur Léman, 'Rue de Charnage' et 'Véreître'. In M. Honegger and C. Mordant (eds) *L'homme au bord de l'eau. Archéologie des zones littorales du Néolithique à la Protohistoire*: 327–344. Lausanne et Paris: Comité des travaux historiques et scientifiques.

Nicolussi, K. and Patzelt, G. (2000) Untersuchungen zur holozänen Gletscherentwicklung von Pasterze und Gepatschferner (Ostalpen). *Zeitschrift für Gletscherkunde und Glazialgeologie* 36: 1–87.

Parzinger, H. and Dular, J. (1997): Die Pfahlbauten des Laibacher Moors (Ljubljansko barje). In H. Schlichtherle (ed.) *Pfahlbauten rund um die Alpen*: 71–75. Stuttgart: Theiss.

Perini, R. (1987) *Scavi archeologici nella zona palafitticola di Fiavé-Carera 2.* Trento: Servizio Beni culturali della Provincia di Trento.

Perini, R. (1988) Gli scavi nel Lavagnone. Sequenza e tipologia degli abitati dell'Età del Bronzo. In Annali Benacensi (ed.) *Atti del simposio internazionale sui modelli insediativi dell'Età del Bronzo*: 109–154. Cavriana: Annali Benacens 9.

Peška, J. (2013) Das Besiedlungsbild in der Blütezeit der Frühbronzezeit im Gebiet des mittleren Donauraumes. In H. Meller, F. Bertemes, H. R. Bork and R. Risch (eds) *1600 – Kultureller Umbruch im Schatten des Thera-Ausbruchs? Tagungen des Landesmuseums für Vorgeschichte Halle 9*: 387–409. Halle: Landesmuseum für Vorgeschichte.

Pillonel, D. (2007) *Hauterive-Champréveyres 14:Technologie et usage du bois au Bronze final.* Hauterive: Office et musée cantonal d'archéologie de Neuchâtel. Archéologie neuchâteloise 37.

Poggiani Keller, R., Binaghi Leva, M. A., Menotti, E. M., Roffia, E., Pacchieni, T., Baioni, M., Martinelli, N., Ruggiero, M. G. and Bocchio G. (2005) Siti d'ambiente umido della Lombardia: rilettura di vecchi dati e nuove ricerche. In P. Della Casa and M. Trachsel (eds) *WES'04, Wetland Economies and Societies. Proceedings of the International Conference in Zurich, 10–13 March 2004*: 233–250. Zürich: Chronos. Collectio Archaeologica 3.

Primas, M. (1982) Lago di Garda – Lago di Constanza; Rapporti interregionali di etàneolitica superiore ed eneolitica. In Società Archeologica Comense (ed.) *Studi in onore di Ferrante Rittatore Vonwiller*, parte I, volume 2: 571–584. Como: Società Archeologica Comense.

Primas, M. (2009) Nicht nur Kupfer und Salz: Die Alpen im wirtschaftlichen und sozialen Umfeld des 2. Jahrtausends. In M. Bartelheim and H. Stäuble (eds) *Die wirtschaftlichen Grundlagen der Bronzezeit Europas*: 189–211. Rhaden/Westfahlen: Verlag Marie Leidorf. Forschungen zur Archäometrie und Altertumswissenschaft 4.

Rageth, J. (1974) Der Lago di Ledro im Trentino. *Bericht der Römisch-Germanischen Kommission* 55: 73–259.

Rapi, M. (2007) Lavagnone di Desenzano del Garda (BS), settore B: la ceramica del Bronzo Antico I. *Notizie Archeologiche Bergomensi* 15: 109–186.

Rapi, M. (2013) Dall'età del Rame all'età del Bronzo. I primi villaggi palafitticoli e la cultura di Polada. In R. C. De Marinis (ed.) *L'età del Rame. La Pianura Padana e le Alpi al tempo di Ötzi*: 525–544. Brescia: Museo Diocesano.

Reinerth, H. (1928) *Die Wasserburg Buchau. Eine befestigte Inselsiedlung aus der Zeit 1100–800 v. Chr..* Augsburg: Filser. Führer zur Urgeschichte 6.

Rigert, E., Brem, H. and Bürgi, J. (2001) *A7 – Ausfahrt Archäologie. Prospektion und Grabungen im Abschnitt Schwaderloh-Landesgrenze.* Frauenfeld: Departement für Erziehung und Kultur des Kantons Thurgau. Archäologie im Thurgau 10.

Rösch, M. (1996) *Archäobotanische Untersuchungen in der spätbronzezeotlichen Ufersiedlung Hagnau-Burg (Bodenseekreis).* Stuttgart: Theiss. Siedlungsarchäologie im Alpenvorland IV: 239–312.

Rösch, M. and Sillmann, M. (2008) Pflanzenreste aus einer Grube der Glockenbecherkultur in Engen-Welschingen, Kreis Konstanz. *Archäologische Ausgrabungen in Baden-Württemberg 2007*: 98–101.

Rubat Borel, F. (2006) Il Bronzo Finale nell'estremo Nord-Ovest italiano: il gruppo Pont-Valperga. *Rivista di Scienze Preistoriche* LVI: 429–82.

Rubat-Borel, F. (2009) Entre Italie et Gaule: la transition âge du Bronze / âge du Fer dans le Piémont nord-occidental et la Vallée d'Aoste. In M.-J. Roulière-Lambert, A. Daubigney, P.-Y. Milcent, M. Talon and J. Vital (eds) *De l'âge du Bronze à l'âge du Fer en France et en Europe occidentale (Xe–VIIe siècle av. J.-C.). Actes du XXXe colloque international de l'A.F.E.A.F., thème spécialisé co-organisé avec l'A.P.R.A.B (Saint-Romain-en-Gal, 26–28 mai 2006)*: 237–252. Dijon: Revue Archéologique de l'Est, supplément 27.

Rubat-Borel, F. (2010) Testimonianze del potere nella Media età del Bronzo a Viverone: le armi del guerriero e gli ornamenti femminili. In D. Daudry (ed.) *Les manifestations du pouvoir dans les Alpes de la Préhistoire au Moyen-Age. Actes du XIIe Colloque sur les Alpes dans l'Antiquité (Yenne, 2–4 ottobre 2009)*: 377–402. Aoste: Bulletin d'études préhistoriques et archéologiques alpines 21.

Ruckdeschel, W. (1978) *Die frühbronzezeitlichen Gräber Südbayerns: ein Beitrag zur Kenntnis der Straubinger Kultur.* Antiquitas: Reihe 2; 11. Bonn: Habelt.

Ruoff, U. (1981) Die Ufersiedlungen an Zürich- und Greifensee. *Helvetia Archaeologica* 45–48: 19–61.

Ruoff, U. (1998) Greifensee-Böschen, Kanton Zürich. Die Unterwasser-Rettungsgrabung. *Helvetia Archaeologica* 29: 2–20.

Rychner, V. (1987) *Auvernier 6: Auvernier 1968 à 1975 : le mobilier métallique du Bronze final; formes et techniques.* Lausanne: Bibliothèque Historique Vaudoise. Cahiers d'Archéologie Romande 37.

Sangmeister, E. (1959) Endneolithische Siedlungsgrube bei Heilbronn-Böckingen. *Fundberichte aus Schwaben* NF 15: 42–46.

Scherer, T. and Wiemann, P. (2008) Freienbach SZ-Hurden Rosshorn: Ur- und Frühgeschichtliche Wege und Brücken über den Zürichsee. *Jahrbuch Archäologie Schweiz* 91: 7–38.

Schlichtherle, H. (1981) Bronzezeitliche Feuchtbodensiedlungen in Südwestdeutschland. Erste Schritte einer systematischen Bestandsaufnahme. *Archäologisches Korrespondenzblatt* 11: 21–27.

Schlichtherle, H. (1988) Bemerkungen zur vorgeschichtlichen Besiedlung des Klosterplatzes. In S. A. Zettler (ed.) *Die frühen Klosterbauten der Reichenau. Ausgrabungen – Schriftquellen – St Galler Klosterplan. Archäologie und Geschichte*: 317–324 Sigmaringen: Jan Thorbecke. Freiburger Forschungen zum ersten Jahrtausend in Südwestdeutschland 3.

Schlichtherle, H. (1994) Eine Mineralbodensiedlung der Mittelbronzezeit in Bodman, Gde. Bodman-Ludwigshafen, Kreis Konstanz. *Archäologische Ausgrabungen in Baden-Württemberg* 1994: 61–65.

Schlichtherle, H. (1997) Pfahlbauten rund um die Alpen. In H. Schlichtherle (ed.) *Pfahlbauten rund um die Alpen*: 7–14. Stuttgart: Theiss.

Schlichtherle, H. (2011) Die Ausgrabungen in der endneolithischen Moorsiedlung Bad Buchau-Torwiesen II. Eine Einführung in die Befunde und Fundverteilungen. In H. Schlichtherle, R. Vogt, U. Maier. *Die endneolithische Moorsiedlung Bad Buchau-Torwiesen II am Federsee 1: Naturwissenschaftliche Untersuchungen*: 11–28. Freiburg im Breisgau: Janus Verlag. Hemmenhofener Skripte 9.

Schlitzer, U. (2005) Taucharchäologische Untersuchungen an der Nordostspitze der Roseninsel. *Das archäologische Jahr in Bayern 2005*: 53–55.

Schmid, W., Beer, H. and Sommer, B. (2000) *Inseln in der Archäologie. Vorgeschichte, klassische Antike, Mittelalter, Neuzeit.* München: Bayerische Gesellschaft für Unterwasserarchäologie. Archäologie unter Wasser 3.

Schmidheiny, M. (2011) *Zürich 'Mozartstrasse' 4: Die frühbronzezeitliche Besiedlung.* Zürich and Egg: FO Publishing. Monographien der Kantonsarchäologie Zürich 42.

Schöbel, G. (1996) *Die Spätbronzezeit am nordwestlichen Bodensee. Taucharchäologische Untersuchungen in Hagnau und Unteruhldingen 1982–1989.* Stuttgart: Theiss. Siedlungsarchäologie im Alpenvorland IV.

Schöbel, G. (2000) Die spätbronzezeitliche Ufersiedlung Wasserburg Buchau, Kreis Biberach. In W. Schmid, H. Beer and B. Sommer *Inseln in der Archäologie. Vorgeschichte, klassische Antike, Mittelalter, Neuzeit*: 85–100. München: Bayerische Gesellschaft für Unterwasserarchäologie. Archäologie unter Wasser 3.

Seifert, M. (1996) Der archäologische Befund von Zug-Sumpf. In M. Seifert, S. Jacomet, S. Karg, J. Schibler and B. Kaufmann (eds) *Die spätbronzezeitlichen Ufersiedlungen von Zug-Sumpf 1: Die Dorfgeschichte*: 1–197. Zug: Amt für Denkmalpflege und Archäologie Zug.

Spring, M. (2000) *Die frühbronzezeitliche Seeufersiedlung von Hochdorf-Baldegg (LU)*. Unpublished Thesis submitted to the Lizentiatsarbeit Abteilung für Ur- und Frühgeschichte, Historisches Seminar der Universität Zürich in fullfillment of a Masters Degree in Archaeology.

Spring, M. (2001) Die frühbronzezeitlichen Baubefunde von Hochdorf-Baldegg (LU) neu interpretiert. In B. Eberschweiler, J. Köninger, H. Schlichtherle and C. Strahm (eds) *Aktuelles zur Frühbronzezeit und frühen Mittelbronzezeit im nördlichen Alpenvorland*: 133–136. Freiburg im Breisgau: Janus Verlag. Hemmenhofener Skripte 2.

Valzolgher, E. (2013) La necropoli dell'antica età del Bronzo di Arano di Cellore di Illasi (Verona). In R. C. De Marinis (ed.) *L'età del Rame. La Pianura Padana e le Alpi al tempo di Ötzi*: 553–559. Brescia: Museo Diocesano.

Vanzetti, A. (2013) 1600? The rise of the Terramare system (Northern Italy). In H. Meller, F. Bertemes, H. R. Bork and R. Risch (eds) *1600 – Kultureller Umbruch im Schatten des Thera-Ausbruchs? Tagungen des Landesmuseums für Vorgeschichte Halle 9*: 267–282. Halle: Landesmuseum für Vorgeschichte.

Velušček, A. and Čufar K. (2010) Dating of the pile dwellings at the Ljubljanko barje, Slovenia – the situation in 2008. In I. Matuschik, C. Strahm, B. Eberschweiler, G. Fingerlin, A. Hafner, M. Kinsky, M. Mainberger and G. Schöbel (eds) *Vernetzungen : Aspekte siedlungsarchäologischer Forschung. Festschrift für Helmut Schlichtherle zum 60. Geburtstag*: 345–355. Freiburg im Breisgau: Lavori Verlag.

Winiger, A. 2012: Architecture des villages. In A. Winiger and E. Burri-Wyser. *La station lacustre de Concise 5: Les villages du Bronze ancien: architecture et mobilier*: 35–152. Lausanne: Cahiers Archéologie Romande 135.

Winiger, A. and Burri-Wyser, E. (2012) *La station lacustre de Concise 5: Les villages du Bronze ancien: architecture et mobilier*. Lausanne: Cahiers Archéologie Romande.

Wolf, C. (1998) Neue Befunde zur Siedlungsstruktur der westschweizerischen Frühbronzezeit: erste Ergebnisse der Ausgrabungen in den neolithischen und bronzezeitlichen Seeufersiedlungen von Concise-sous Colachoz (VD). In B. Hänsel (ed.) *Mensch und Umwelt in der Bronzezeit Europas. Die Bronzezeit: Das Erste Goldene Zeitalter Europas*: 541–556. Kiel: Oetker-Voges.

Wolf, C., Burri, E., Hering, P., Kurz, M., Maute-Wolf, M., Quinn, D. S. and Winiger, A (1999) Les sites lacustres néolithiques et bronzes de Concise VD-sous-Colachoz: premiers résultats et implications sur le Bronze ancien régional. *Jahrbuch der Schweizerischen Gesellschaft für Ur- und Frühgeschichte 82*: 7–38.

Chapter 3

Dendrochronology and Bronze Age pile-dwellings on both sides of the Alps: from chronology to dendrotypology, highlighting settlement developments and structural woodland changes

André Billamboz and Nicoletta Martinelli

Introduction

Thanks to the dendrochronological network based on southern Germany's oak master tree-ring chronology established in Hohenheim from the 1970s onwards (Becker *et al.* 1985), we can now understand important aspects of the Bronze Age lake-dwelling development, especially north of the Alps. Regarding the early period (the Early Bronze Age), some of the most relevant sites that have contributed to systematic tree-ring investigations include Zurich-Mozartstrasse (Schmidheiny 2011) and Meilen-Schellen on Lake Zurich (Ruoff 1987); Bodman-Schachen 1 on Lake Constance (Köninger 2006); Siedlung-Forschner in the southern Federsee bog (Billamboz 2009); Concise-sous Colachoz on Lake Neuchâtel (Winiger 2008); and Préverenges on Lake Geneva (Corboud and Pugin 2011). Such a dendrochronological frame is still under development south of the Alps, where, nevertheless, cross-dating site chronologies (with the support of radiocarbon wiggle-matching techniques) already offer quite accurate dates for sequencing the development of wetland occupation.

A preliminary study has already highlighted asynchronous trends in settling in wetland environments on both sides of the Alps (Billamboz and Martinelli 1996). At first glance, the lake-dwelling development in northern Italy coincides with two major hiatuses in wetland occupation in the northern Alpine foreland: from the 22nd to the 19th century BC, and from the 15th to the 12th century BC. The latter hiatus (Middle Bronze Age, MBA) is more strongly linked to climate changes and lake-level fluctuations (Menotti 2001; Magny 2013; see also Chapter 4, this volume). It is generally believed that climate deterioration led to the abandonment of lake shores, while their occupation usually occurred in periods of favourable climatic conditions (although this was not always the case – see Pétrequin *et al.* 2004). However, recent palaeoenvironmental research (Magny *et al.* 2009) has led to the hypothesis that climate change had significantly less influence on the northern Italian Bronze Age communities. Thus, by allowing a parallel consideration of settlement adaptations and structural woodland changes (Billamboz 2011), analysing the features of dendro-typology should lead to a more detailed depiction of the socio-ecological context of wetland occupation in the defined domains both north and south of the Alps (N-domain = south-western Germany; S-domain = northern Italy), providing better balance in weighing the factors that may have influenced these environmental and cultural developments differently, in both space and time.

Dendrochronology for the northern Italian Bronze Age

Dendrochronological research in the southern part of the Alpine region has developed quite considerably recently (Martinelli *et al.* in press). Due to the lack of long tree-ring chronologies[1] and trans-Alpine teleconnections, the chronological development for the period considered has to be supported by wiggle-matching (wm) techniques, based on the combination of radiocarbon and dendrochronology, which generally allows dating precision with an error spanning from ±4 to ±29 years (1σ). Considering the pile-dwelling settlements[2] distributed along the southern slopes of the Alps from the Piedmont region in the west to the Friuli region in the east, the major concentration of dendrochronological data concerns the region around Lake Garda (the so-called *area benacense*). This region was one of the most densely inhabited areas in the Bronze Age (BA), with more than 40 lake-dwelling sites, either submerged along the southern shores of the main lake or buried in peat basins of former small lakes in the morainic amphitheatre and/or in depressions along river beds. To date, the respective mean tree-ring series from different settlements in the region have been cross-dated, enabling the construction of two main oak regional chronologies: GARDA 1 (22nd–19th centuries cal BC, 11 settlements) and GARDA 3 (19th–17th centuries cal BC, four settlements). In comparison to previously published series (see Martinelli 2005, 2007), the data presented in Figure 3.2 have been improved by the re-elaboration of all the wiggle-matches according to the new calibration curve IntCal13 (Reimer *et al.* 2013) and the new version of the software OxCal (v4.2) (Bronk Ramsey 2009).

Concerning GARDA 1 (Fig. 3.2, data older than 1800 BC), the results of this revision are only slightly different from previous elaborated ones, and, as before, they represent a turning point for the Early Bronze Age (EBA) absolute chronology not only in northern Italy but also in central Europe (Fasani and Martinelli 1996; Martinelli 1996). Hereby, the settlements of Bande di Cavriana, Barche di Solferino, Lavagnone, and Lucone di Polpenazze, all established in the 21st century cal BC, are considered to be the oldest EBA lake dwellings within the Alpine foreland. Other EBA local, independently wm-dated dendro-sequences can be found in Canàr di San Pietro Polesine (Rovigo) (Martinelli *et al.* 1998) and in Fiavè-Carera, Trento (a 242-year-long single oak series – Martinelli 1996).

As far as the regional chronology GARDA 3 (1830–1611 cal BC) is concerned, in contrast, this new wm revision takes into account more relevant differences for the absolute dating, revising it to be about 70 years older than previously considered (Martinelli and Valzolgher in preparation[3]). The same applies to the independent wm of the sequence of Sabbione – now considered older by about 50 years (Martinelli unpublished). Due to the lack of synchronisation between the few local dendro-sequences available for the MBA and Late

Bronze Age (LBA) periods, further wm has also been calculated separately for the following sites: Castellaro del Vhò (Cremona, MBA), Lazise-La Quercia 2 (Verona, MBA), Tombola di Cerea (MBA–LBA), 'Viverone Vil' on Lake Viverone (Biella-Turin),[4] and Iseo (Brescia, LBA) (Martinelli 2005; Poggiani-Keller *et al.* 2005).

Further developments in dendrochronological research could lead to the establishment of a long, gapless oak master chronology for the Bronze Age in northern Italy. Within this scope, particular attention should be paid to the connections between chronology and stratigraphy, as is currently being done in Lucone D (Baioni *et al.* 2007). From this perspective, major sites with a long history of occupation (*e.g.* Lavagnone and Fiavè) are considered to be key sites for such an approach, with the aim of providing a more precise definition of the BA chrono-typology and a better understanding of the settlement development. This last aspect, already tested in 'Il Sabbione' (Martinelli 2003; Poggiani-Keller *et al.* 2005), can be particularly well addressed by dendro-typology.

Dendro-typology: a newcomer in Bronze Age lake-dwelling research

The potential of dendro-typological analyses was first realized at the site of Siedlung-Forschner on the Federsee (Billamboz 2009), where such studies offered new insights into complex issues regarding the interaction between people and nature. This allowed a better understanding of the various aspects of woodland development that were interwoven with human history. From the beginning of the period and throughout the entire Bronze Age, stronger climate variations on the one side and socio-economic changes related to metallurgy and agriculture on the other side shaped the development of a contrasted settlement history, accompanied by deep changes in the structures of woodlands. This period is therefore particularly suitable for dendro-typological applications, offering further possibilities for trans-disciplinary research in settlement and environmental archaeology. In the northern Alpine foreland, dendro-typology has even highlighted the various stages of development of Early Bronze Age wetland settlements, identifying a balance between natural forces and changes, which were due to long-lasting traditions of land use (Billamboz 2013). In the same way, this chapter is a first attempt to extend the dendro-typological application to the southern pre-Alpine region, namely northern Italy, where the viability of the method has recently been proven (Martinelli 2013). However, due to the lack of long and well-replicated tree-ring sequences from the LBA lake-dwellings, the discussion on northern Italy's Bronze Age is restricted to the EBA and MBA (*i.e. c.* 2200 to 1300 BC).

Dendro-typology is also an attempt to sort and categorise timber in relation to the choice of wood species, the tree-growth patterns and trends, and the degree of stem conversion (Billamboz 2011). Within systematic investigations applied to large sample series, the consequent grouping of tree-ring series according to cambial age and growth trend allows better control in chronology building and in tentative dating of young wood, which is frequently found in wetland archaeology. In the same way, dendro-typology is an excellent tool for the detection of archaeological wooden building structures. Moreover, dendro-typological seriations provide insights into the age structure of the exploited stands with reference to dendro-typological models of woodland management derived from historical

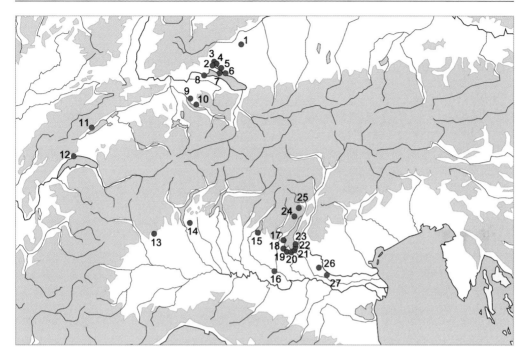

Figure 3.1. Map of the sites mentioned in the paper. North of the Alps: 1: Siedlung-Forschner; 2: Bodman-Schachen I; 3: Ludwigshafen-Holzplatz; 4: Ludwigshafen-Seehalde; 5: Nussdorf-Seehalde; 6: Unteruhldingen-Stollenwiesen; 7: Egg-Obere Güll; 8: Öhningen-Orkopf; 9: Zurich-Mozartstrasse; 10: Meilen-Schellen; 11: Concise-sous-Colachoz; 12: Préverenges. South of the Alps: 13: Viverone Vi1; 14: Sabbione; 15: Iseo; 16: Castellaro del Vho; 17: Lucone di Polpenazze; 18: Lavagnone; 19: Barche di Solferino; 20: Bande di Cavriana; 21: Frassino I; 22: Ronchi del Garda; 23: Bosca di Pacengo; 24: Lago di Ledro; 25: Fiavé-Carera; 26: Tombola di Cerea; 27: Canàr di S. Pietro Polesine.

practices (Billamboz 2011). Finally, dendro-groups are considered as basic units of a multiple approach, addressing the technological, social, economic, and ecological aspects of settlement development and woodland use. From this perspective, and in connection with dendro-ecology and historical ecology, dendro-typology can be seen as an interesting approach for reconstructing the history of woodland use, especially for periods not documented by written sources.

Dendro-typology: highlighting regional patterns of settlement and woodland development north and south of the Alps during the EBA to MBA (2200–1300 BC)

Taking into account the data from selected sites indicated in Fig. 3.1, Fig. 3.2 presents the dendro-typological framework defined for the regions of Upper Swabia, Lake Constance, and northern Italy. For the sake of comparison across the whole period considered here, site chronologies have been added to the first DG-assemblages[5] already performed on a few sites, especially at Lake Garda.[6] The relative typo-chronological background of the study is not homogeneous throughout the Circum-Alpine region; it takes the northern and southern foreland parts into account separately. The northern zone is based on the post-Reinecke typology (Ruckdeschel 1978, with minor adaptations after David-Elbiali and David 2009; see also Köninger, Chapter 2 this volume), while the southern region is referenced to De Marinis (2002) and, specifically for the transition EBA–MBA, to Vanzetti (2013). Sequential observations can be made with consideration for climatic development derived from the curve of radiocarbon production with indications of temperature extremes, as per Usoskin (2008). In the same way, focusing on the specific periods of increased radiocarbon production allows a better comparison of short- and middle-term developments than that given by the overall periodicity obtained from environmental studies supported by radiocarbon dating.

Occasionally, reference will be made to three different wetland-settlement models developed for the Neolithic lake-dwellings (Billamboz 2014b): A) pioneering settlements coupled with clearing activities in natural environments; B) settlement expansion in a period of high demography connected with coppicing practices; and C) contraction in crisis situations linked to woodland degradation. Equally, particular attention will be paid to the relevance of the main characteristics of wetland dwellings, our knowledge of which has been enhanced by the ethno-archaeological surveys of Pétrequin and Pétrequin (2013), and linked to socio-economic factors, namely territorial defence strategies and fishing activities. Considering the region of Lake Garda specifically, a provisional model of settlement dynamics based on archaeological data and dendrochronological sequencing (Fozzati *et al.* 2006; Martinelli 2007) will also be integrated into the comparison. Finally, as documented regarding the LBA lake-shore occupation near Neuchâtel (Arnold and Langenegger 2012), a hierarchical structure pattern based on the pioneer foundations of villages of greater importance, as well as on the addition of smaller satellite entities of shorter durations, will be kept in mind as a suitable model of Bronze Age communities settling in wetlands and their surroundings.

Following the evidence from Fig. 3.2, the aforementioned time window (2200–1300 BC) will be discussed in three separate sections:

Section 1 (2100–1900 BC)

In the reference area north of the Alps, dendrochronological evidence from this period is generally poor. This is due to either taphonomic factors (erosion or a lack of sedimentation in bogs and on lake shores) or the absence of wetland settlements, resulting in the limited availability of wood suitable for dendro-dating. Nevertheless, in some areas (*e.g.* the Federsee basin), several logboat finds act as indications of occupation and possible settlement activities. At Lake Constance, the cluster of radiocarbon dates around 1900 BC indicates the first presence of lake-shore occupation with characteristic pile constructions (Bodman-Schachen 1A, posts fastened to the ground with ligature – Köninger 2006). Similar occupation patterns and dates are replicated at a few other locations around the same lake (Öhningen-Orkopf and Ludwigshafen-Seehalde). An interesting feature seen in the timber

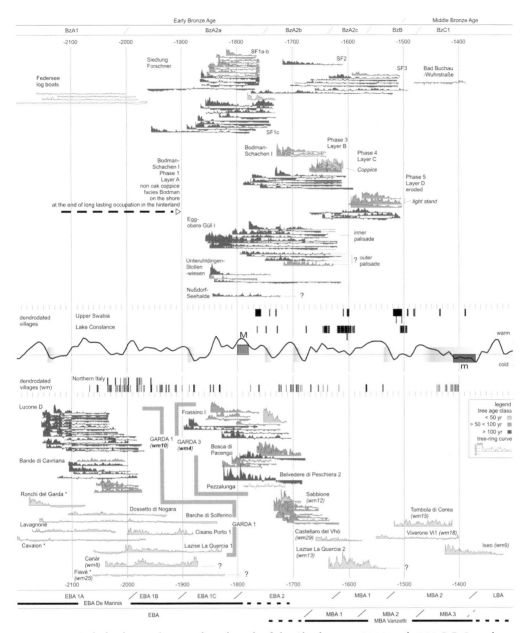

Figure 3.2. Oak dendro-typology north and south of the Alps between 2200 and 1300 BC. In order to highlight parallel settlement developments and woodland structure changes, site tree-ring chronologies (grey colour) and dendro-groups (filled curves, green colour scale according to three main classes of tree age) are presented in synchronous position to the dendrodates indicating the main phases of building activities in wetlands. Above, the data of the northern domain of study (Upper Swabia and Lake Constance) refer to a calendric scale. In the middle part, the dendrodates are projected on the ^{14}C residual curve as climate-proxy temperature reconstruction (M and m are grand temperature maxima and minima after Usoskin 2008). For northern Italy, dendrodating supported by radiocarbon wm techniques is of less precision. In the lower part, dendrogroups and chronologies are presented on the same basis (with indication of the range of the wm precision, e.g. wm10 = wiggle matching with a precision of ±10 years at 68.2% probability). In Garda1, site chronologies indicated with an asterisk are not integrated in the averaged tree-ring chronology. For the sake of simplicity, Roman numbers used by De Marinis have been changed into Arabic ones.

records of these sites is the use of young coppice oak (especially at Bodman-Schachen 1) and various tree species from the zonal and azonal vegetation in Öhningen-Orkopf. For the latter site, located on a sand bank at the outlet of the lake, the combined tree species are the results of intensive timber procurement and exhaustive building activities. Were the inhabitants developing defence strategies in response to a critical situation? An analogy with settlement model C (contraction in crisis situations – see above) is likely, with the 'Bodmaner Fazies' (Köninger 2006) showing a short period of lake-shore occupation at a defensive position established at the end of a long-lasting settlement development in the hinterland, particularly in the Hegau region (Köninger and Schöbel 2010).

In contrast, the dendro-typological assemblage of Lucone D shows very homogenous DG-series reflecting the exploitation of nearly natural and dense mixed oak stands at Lake Garda. Before further interpretation, one should first consider the more or less synchronous starting points of these averaged growth series, which reveal the regeneration of woodland after episodic clearing activities. Thus, a first occupation before 2150 BC can be deduced. At the end of the same series, clearing effects can be identified as abrupt positive growth reactions subsequent to thinning operations in dense stands. Such woodland practices were not based on systematic cutting (clear cutting) but probably more on gap cutting, indicating 'on demand' timber extraction and woodland exploitation. For instance, it appears that, at the beginning of the occupation around the middle of the 21st century BC, reference can be made to model A (pioneering settlement). This interpretation is supported by the palynological records of offshore positions near the site (Badino *et al.* 2011), which show strong clearing activities in the first building phase (2035–2031 cal BC ±10 years), followed by reforestation during a second phase of minor settlement some decades later. A similar clearing pattern is probably to be expected also on the opposite lake side, as shown by the first series measured from piles from Ronchi del Garda, which present a strong negative growth trend as a result of high levels of competition between trees in the exploited stand. This particular, nearly natural, forest development in the hilly vegetation belt all around the Garda basin is not comparable to the one in the lower southern morainic region. In the geological amphitheatre benacense, the assemblage of Bande di Cavriana presents higher variability in tree ages and growth trends, illustrating a greater differentiation of timber sources and also deeper changes in the woodland structure. The same impression is supported by the consideration of further site chronologies in the lower part of the graph of Fig. 3.2. Thus, the observed slight discrepancies reflect, without a doubt, the local or micro-regional character of human impact on the woodland cover between 2100 and 1900 BC.

Section 2 (1900–1500 BC)

In both regions (north and south of the Alps), this period seems to have begun with a phase of afforestation, probably due to a recession of settlement activities, as indicated by the reduced occurrence of dendro-dates for the 19th century BC, with an almost complete absence between 1850 and 1750 BC in northern Italy. This period could correspond to the progressive drying out of wetland environments and the activation of peat formation in the small basins in the morainic area around Lake Garda (Balista and Leonardi 1996). Particular attention should be given to the possible influence of the climate on this phenomenon, without neglecting the eventual impacts of local factors (*e.g.* the geomorphology), which might have influenced the water balance in such small basins.

In the south-western German Alpine foreland, a wave-like development of bog and lake-shore settlements is more evident. As indicated by dendro-typological series, the transition between sections 1 and 2 (see above) corresponds to the regeneration and extension of the forest, implying a decrease in settlement development during the 19th century BC. This was followed by a first wave of occupation in the middle of the subsequent century, probably with environmental impacts confined to a small regional scale (see the example of Siedlung-Forschner, illustrating changes in the surrounding woodland during the course of the building phases 1a to 1c – Billamboz 2009). A similar situation has been recorded in western Switzerland at Concise-sous-Colachoz, Lake Neuchâtel (Winiger 2008), and Préverenges, Lake Geneva (Corboud and Pugin 2011), and it is likely to have also occurred at Lake Constance. In fact, the first dendro-dates at Unteruhldingen-Stollenwiesen, a site famous because of its repeated occupation during the LBA, suggest such a situation.

Two main features of woodland development can be inferred from the dendro-typology: first, preliminary general woodland regeneration, allowing the exploitation of old-aged and slowly grown oaks more than 100 years later; and second, strong, localised settlement impacts on woodland, as recorded at the head of the Überlingersee (the northern part of Lake Constance). This development was amplified through a second, probably larger, wave of occupation that has been well documented in Bodman-Schachen 1 (Köninger 2006, building phases 3 and 4). In the sub-regions of the Federsee (building phase SF3 at Siedlung-Forschner) and the Überlingersee (Bodman-Schachen 1, building phase 5), a third and final period of occupation took place around 1500 BC, during a phase of woodland thinning and landscape opening. If we link these patterns of occupation to the wetland-settling models (see above), we find here again the logical sequence A-B-C, illustrating a long woodland exploitation cycle during the course of this wave-like settlement development.

In northern Italy, significant changes in the woodland structure can already be observed in the first dendro-typological assemblages of Frassino I and Bosca di Pacengo in the Garda region, as well as at Sabbione on Lake Monate. As in the regions north of the Alps, increasing settlement activities are reflected here by asynchronous cutting and regeneration phases as markers of disturbance in the more continuous, natural development of the forest. From this perspective, it appears that the wetland occupation during the last phase of EBA 2 (according to De Marinis) or at the beginning of MBA 1 (according to Vanzetti, 2013) (see Fig. 3.2) probably took place within a larger settlement development, implying a stronger environmental impact on the forest than before. The presence of Turkey oak (*Quercus cerris*) at Frassino (Martinelli and Kromer 1999) could also indicate the requirement of a more differentiated timber supply at that time. The exploitation of various tree species for the outer palisade of Sabbione towards the end of the period could be interpreted in the same manner, as the result of an intensive timber supply in an impoverished environment (Martinelli 2013).

Section 3 (1500–1300 BC)

This period entailed a major climatic depression, with the lowest temperatures around 1400 BC (Usoskin 2008). Climate changes can induce a reorientation of the subsistence strategy with settlement relocation and the development of mining and pastoral activities at low and middle-altitudes in the mountains (Billamboz 2013). At the Federsee, repeated constructions of trackways around the 'Insel Bad Buchau' illustrate adaptations in the settlement system and the decline in the significance of Siedlung-Forschner in the southern part of the bog basin. At Lake Constance, there is no dendro-archaeological evidence for this period. However, it is possible that, during this time, the forests regenerated, achieving maturity for a new phase of lake-shore settlement at the beginning of the LBA.

In northern Italy, the evidence comprises only three rather short and geographically widespread site chronologies: Viverone Vi1 (MBA 2), Tombola di Cerea (MBA 3), and Iseo (*Bronzo Recente*). At Lake Garda, settlement development and activities seem to have decreased, with the presence of lake-dwellings being inferred from archaeological context alone. Therefore, closer comparison between the N-domain and the S-domain is not possible at the moment. This is also the case for the *terramare* settlements in the Po Plain. Based on the evidence of peripheral banks and ditches, this settlement system expanded markedly during the MBA and the first phase of the LBA (*Bronzo Recente*), consequently influencing the deforestation of the lower Po Plain. Hydromorphological studies (Cremaschi *et al.* 2006) have enhanced our understanding of the role, and importance, of water in the defence and subsistence strategies of this settlement type, which lost its importance during the following warmer period of the LBA, probably as a result of issues of water availability. The comparison between the development of *terramare* settlements on the one hand and bog and lake-shore sites on the other hand remains a topic of interest for future research.

Considering the settlement development in the wetlands north and south of the Alps at a multi-centennial scale, it may be assumed that lake-dwellings were mainly represented in the aforementioned sections 1 and 2 (2100–1900 and 1900–1500 BC, respectively). As far as the former is concerned, two distinct models emerge from both domains. At all sites on Lake Constance, the shore occupation occurred at the end of a longer settlement phase in the hinterland; pile-dwellings there should probably be considered as a retreat position with a likely defensive character. Taking into account earlier evidence from the surroundings (*e.g.* Fiavè) of Lake Garda, it is clear that the wetland occupation in this region covered at least the entire span of EBA 1. As suggested by dendro-typology from Lucone D, the discrepancy between the northern and southern domains can be explained by different degrees of settlement intensity during the Eneolithic occupation (stronger in the northern Alpine forelands during the corded ware / Bell Beaker cultural phases, and weaker in the northern Italian wetlands during the *età del Rame*). Similar developments also emerge from the dendro-typological comparison in section 2, but with a model sequence: exploration in natural-like woodlands → expansion in the context of secondary forests → recession parallel to woodland degradation. This shows a better, more tangible, profile in the northern domain than in the southern one.

As already derived from the archaeological evidence at Bodman-Schachen 1 and Siedlung-

Forschner, the micro-regional character of settlement structures and development dynamics is also assumed in northern Italy, particularly in the Lake Garda region (Aspes *et al.* 1998; Fozzati *et al.* 2006). More recently, under the 'freemen' concept, Vanzetti (2013) enhanced this image, underlining the patchy and unstable settlement distribution, as well as a rather egalitarian social system with stronger organisational and hierarchical developments only in phases of demographic expansions (*e.g.* in the MBA *terramare*). Palynological records give the same impression of regional patterns, with strong human impact on vegetation at the local scale, as shown during the course of Lucone D in the EBA 1 occupation (Badino *et al.* 2011). Generally, the land was still largely covered by the forest, and progressive landscape opening is found principally in the context of pioneer settlements with successive phases of occupation, for example the case of Lavagnone (de Marinis *et al.* 2005). Here again, the *terramare* seem to be an exception, with arboreal plant pollen records weaker than 30%, attesting more intensive deforestation in the central-eastern Po Plain (Cremaschi *et al.* 2006; Vanzetti 2013). The presence of possible shifts in settlement development at a multi-decadal scale appears more related to aspects such as ecological susceptibility and territorial sustainability than to large-scale climatic influences. Nevertheless, the convergence of both types of factors should not be excluded, and these factors could have contributed to the two major gaps in wetland-settlement history in northern Italy (*i.e.* between the second half of the 19th and the first decades of the 18th century BC, and at the end of the *terramare* culture around 1200 BC).

What about the Late Bronze Age and the end of the lake-dwellings?

Unfortunately, the rather poor representation of dendrochronological data in northern Italy does not allow a common extension of the dendro-typological application to this phase. Therefore, this sub-section summarises only the major developments known in the north domain, with particular focus on the beginning of the last disappearance of the lake-dwelling tradition in the mid-/late 9th century BC. Some consideration will, however, be given to the state of research in the southern domain with respect to the few dendrochronological records obtained there.

Bearing in mind the regional study of Köninger and Schöbel (2010) that embraced the hinterland context of wetland settlements in the south Federsee bog and on Lake Constance during the LBA, the settlement developments of these areas can be highlighted by dendro-typological means, as follows. In both areas, these developments are characterised by first settlement foundations being built in the middle of the 11th century BC, flourishing expansion around 1000 BC, and a recession phase around 850 BC. As shown by the frequency of negative tree-growth pointer years, attesting increasing wet conditions in the intermediate phases (Billamboz, 2009), one may assume that such 'triptych development' was principally triggered by climatic factors. Under the same reference, the replication of a similar settlement development on the lake shores of the Swiss Plateau underpins this conclusion.

Consequently, and with the exception of two short interims of climate depletion around 1020 and 900 BC, the LBA period is considered to have been a rather warm period favouring long-lasting settlement conditions in wetlands. However, as stated by

Pétrequin and Pétrequin (2013), it is worth underlining the defensive character of the LBA wetland settlements, as they were constructed at exposed places, in bogs, on river beds, and (particularly on Lake Constance) on dried delta, bank, and island positions.

A greater difference between the two sub-regions can be found within the scope of ecology. The example of Wasserburg-Buchau, attesting the systematic use of bog pine (*Pinus rotundata*) for building purposes, shows that substantial oak timber resources were probably no longer present in the surroundings of the southern Federsee bog. In regard to the model developed for Siedlung-Forschner at the end of the EBA (see above), this can be explained by woodland overuse and a subsequent lack of forest regeneration, as well as due to the effect of drought on oak dieback, as known from actual observations in the beech-dominated forest stands of the Swabian Alpine foreland. According to the more continental conditions of the climate, the most common oak species growing in the region is the pedunculate oak (*Quercus robur* L.), a species that is rather sensitive to water stress. Contrary to the Federsee, oak wood is well represented in the building structures of the lake-dwellings on Lake Constance.

Dendro-typological assemblages at Unteruhldingen-Stollenwiesen (Uu) (Billamboz and Schöbel, 1994) show settlement development and woodland management; this follows the LBA model sequence A-B-C described above. The foundation phase A is missing in the dendrochronological records, but its dating position around 1050 BC can easily be derived from the growth starting point of the oak trees felled for the construction of the villages Uu1 (975–966, 954 BC) and Uu2 (930–927, 917 BC). These trees, which were ~80 years old and ~120 years old at the time of felling, respectively, reflect the two-step management of the corresponding old coppice formations (sequence B). During the last settlement Uu3 (863–850, 843 BC), the increasing crisis character of type C in the model sequence is illustrated by the strong distribution of oak timber in two classes of age: old trees as markers of the woodland thinning and very young coppice trees as a result of premature cutting operations. These considerations are of particular interest in addressing the question of the abandonment of the lake-dwelling tradition. The impact of the major deterioration in the climate between 850 and 750 BC is hard to dispute, and the peak in radiocarbon production (with the highest value for the whole Holocene Period) merely acts to illustrate the argument (Van Geel *et al.* 1998).

However, cultural adaptations are rarely explained by single-factor events such as climatic change – a combination of factors occurring parallel to the change (*e.g.* woodland overuse, which may lead to the loss of major resources) is considered more influential to processes of re-adaptation and drastic transformations of the subsistence strategy. Such ecological conditions have already been concluded for settlement in other periods, namely the Neolithic lake-shore occupation around 2400 BC (Billamboz 2014). Recalling the hypothesis of a retreating attitude (see model C above), one may assume that the defence strategy was probably also a consequence of a far-reaching ecological crisis (*i.e.* not only within wetland environments but also within a wider hinterland background). It is therefore possible that the lake-dwellings were not the only ones involved in that process. However, they were also affected by the repercussions of natural events and cultural developments at the regional scale or even wider.

In northern Italy, dendrochronological research (and its dendro-typological application) is unfortunately much more limited than in the domain north of the Alps for the LBA period. However, the very last phase of wetland settlement has also been examined from an archaeological point of view. In fact, although *Bronzo Recente* was a phase of major demographic expansion, only a few pile-dwellings were developed during the period. Regarding the beginning of the subsequent period (*Bronzo Finale)*, a gap with the previous settlement pattern is generally acknowledged; the number of sites became rather low – especially in the southern Po Plain – and pile-dwellings became extremely rare. Nevertheless, two of the most relevant settlements of the period were wet sites: Peschiera and San Gaetano in the old lagoon of Caorle (Fozzati *et al.* in preparation).[7] A spot of 'wetland occupation' occurred towards the transition to the Iron Age, when the wetland settlement of Stagno (located in the former lagoon of Livorno and dating to the early 11th century cal BC) was constructed (Zanini and Martinelli 2005).

The first results are sometimes confirmed by other disciplines. For example, the strong evidence of settlement reduction towards the end of *Bronzo Recente* is supported by geohydrological studies linking the end of the *terramare* phenomenon in the Po Plain to the reduced water availability at the beginning of the warmer LBA period (Cremaschi *et al.* 2006). On the other hand, further dendrochronological developments at Lake Ledro could lead to a better assessment of the results obtained there with multi-disciplinary research, assuming the resilience of the lake settlers to remain in the lacustrine areas despite worsening climatic conditions (Magny *et al.* 2009; see also Chapter 4, this volume).

Conclusions

During the last few decades, advances in dendrochronology applied to archaeology have been made, particularly in terms of going beyond simple dating. Within this scope, dendro-typology has been presented as a method to evaluate in different ways the information of large timber series, acting in this manner as a reliable interface between archaeology and natural sciences. From the perspective of chronological achievements concerning the annual time-resolution, an attempt has been made to compare the dendro-typological assemblages from pile-dwellings dated EBA–MBA in northern Italy with those performed in south-western Germany. This analysis, based on patterns of forest dynamics, could lead to a better understanding of and responses to the questions relating to the interactions between people and forests. Through this strong degree of contextuality, dendro-typology underlines the regional character of settlement development, acting as an interpretative tool to enhance our comprehension of the relationship between woodland development, timber properties, and architectural adaptations, as illustrated at Siedlung-Forschner (Billamboz 2009). Here, for instance, the house units of the first building phases (SF1a–b) were constructed on small-section piles converted from thin, elongated trunks grown under high competition (*i.e.* trees growing in dense forest stands). In the subsequent building phases (SF1c, SF2–3), more developed constructions with tightened piles at ground level are found in conjunction with the use of bigger trunks extracted from less-dense forest. From the pile-dwelling *sensu stricto* to the *Bonifica* building structures,[8] the EBA and MBA wetland settlements in northern

Italy show high variability in architectural adaptations, which offers possibilities to establish such relationships. Furthermore, ecological parameters can be involved in this approach; for example, one may refer to the cockchafer signal particularly registered in young oak series (Billamboz 2014a), where the question of a relationship between clearing activities and the mass development of cockchafer populations is stressed in terms of facultative synanthropy, as defined by Kenward (1997).

Finally, as has clearly emerged, the potential of dendro-typology could be extended to other areas of Circum-Alpine pile-dwelling research, offering the possibility of including a large variety of ecosystems and wood species, as well as a number of related ecofacts. Consequently, the strong relationship between settlement development and forest dynamics should lead to a greater consideration of more science-oriented forestry studies within environmental archaeology. From both chronological and ecological perspectives, further challenges require stronger cooperation between archaeology and dendrochronology. On the one hand, dendrochronology and dendro-typology can lead to a better understanding of settlement developments, not only in terms of simple continuity and gaps but also more in terms of intensity and fluctuations. On the other hand, though, as detailed in past publications, it is down to archaeological excavations to provide more wood suitable to fill the gaps in regional chronologies. Let us not forget the famous beam HH-39 (from the pueblo ruins of Show Low, pointedly sampled by A. E. Douglass and archaeologists L. L. Hardgrave and E. W. Haury), which finally allowed the bridging of both yellow pine chronologies of the American South West, linking the absolute dated one – relating to living trees – and the floating one based on archaeological woods (Webb 1983). Looking closer at dendro-typological patterns and models of woodland/settlement developments should help us to find the various 'missing links', at least within the span of specific cultural periods such as the Bronze Age.

Notes

1. In the southern slopes of the Alps, standard chronologies for dating purposes at an annual resolution begin in the last centuries of the 1st millennium AD, reaching the present day (Martinelli 2005; Čufar *et al.* 2008).
2. Nineteen sites from northern Italy are component parts of the UNESCO's World Heritage Sites – *Prehistoric pile dwellings around the Alps.*
3. Martinelli, N. and Valzolgher, E. 2013. *Revisione della curva dendrocronologica regionale GARDA 3.* Poster displayed at XLVIII Riunione Scientifica dell'Istituto Italiano di Preistoria e Protostoria 'Preistoria e Protostoria del Veneto', held in Padoa, 5th–9th November 2013.
4. The investigation is part of the project 'The end of the lake-dwelling phenomenon: cultural versus environmental change', which is being funded by the Swiss National Science Foundation and is based at the Institute of Prehistory and Archaeological Science, Basel University.
5. DG-series are averaged series of DC-series integrated into a dendro-group. DC-series are single tree-ring series.
6. In Fig. 3.2, among the bars indicating the dendro-dates of the main phases of building activities, the data coming from the chronology from Lavagnone sites has been inserted: the data elaborated by the Dendrodata Laboratory (part of the GARDA 1 chronology) and that developed in the Cornell Tree-Ring Laboratory. In this case, for the latter, the cross-dating position against the regional chronology GARDA 1 (Martinelli 2007) has been preferred to the one calculated from the

independent wiggle-matching carried out at the Cornell Tree-Ring Laboratory (Griggs *et al.* 2002), in order to allow comparison at the one-year scale with other sites that have been inserted into the chronology. Cross-dating test values between Lavagnone site chronology from Cornell and GARDA 1 are: TVBP = 7.00, TVH = 7.9, CDI = 55, GL% = 74, 99.9.

7. Fozzati, L., Leonardi, G., Martinelli, N., Aspes, A., Balista, C., Gonzato, F., and Salzani, L. 2013. *Wetlands. Palafitte e siti umidi nell'Età del bronzo del Veneto: cronologia assoluta, territorio e funzione.* Paper presented at XLVIII Riunione Scientifica dell'Istituto Italiano di Preistoria e Protostoria 'Preistoria e Protostoria del Veneto', held in Padua, 5th–9th November 2013.

8. Constructions on wet soils built on different kinds of wooden foundations at ground level (Balista and Leonardi 1996).

References

Arnold, B. and Langenegger, F. (2012) *Bevaix-Sud: plongée dans le passé, fouille subaquatique d'un village du Bronze final.* Plateau de Bevaix 8. Neuchâtel: Archéologie neuchâteloise.

Aspes, A., Baroni, C. and Fasani, L. (1998) Umweltveränderungen und ihre Folgen für die bevölkerung der Bronzezeit in Norditalien. In B. Hänsel (ed.) *Mensch und Umwelt in der Bronzezeit Europas. Abschußtagung der Kampagne des Europarates: Die Bronzezeit das erste goldene Zeitalter Europas an der Freien Universität Berlin, 17–19 März 1997*: 419–426. Kiel: Oetker-Voges Verlag.

Badino, F., Baioni, M., Castellano, L., Martinelli, N. Perego, R. and Ravazzi, C. (2011) Fundation, development and abandoning of a Bronze Age pile-dwelling ('Lucone D', Garda Lake) recorded in the palinostratigraphic sequence of the pond offshore the settlement. *Il Quaternario. Italian Journal of Quaternary sciences* 24 (Special number: AIQUA, Roma 02/2011): 177–179.

Baioni, M., Bocchio, G. and Mangani, C. (2007) Il Lucone di Polpenazze: storia delle ricerche e nuove prospettive. In F. Morandini and M. Volontè (eds) *Contributi di archeologia in memoria di Mario Mirabella Roberti. Atti del XVI Convegno Archeologico Benacense, Cavriana (Mantova) 15–16 Ottobre 2005*: 83–102. Gussago (Brescia): Annali Benacensi XIII–XIV.

Balista, C. and Leonardi, G. (1996) Gli abitati di ambiente umido nel Bronzo Antico dell'Italia settentrionale. In D. Cocchi Genick (ed.) *L'antica età del Bronzo in Italia. Atti del Congresso di Viareggio (9–12 gennaio 1995)*: 199–228. Firenze: Octavo.

Becker, B., Billamboz, A., Egger, H., Gassmann, P., Orcel, A., Orcel, Chr. and Ruoff, U. (1985) *Dendrochronologie in der Ur- und Frühgeschichte. Die absolute Datierung von Pfahlbausiedlungen nördlich der Alpen im Jahrringkalender Mitteleuropas.* Basel: Antiqua 11.

Billamboz, A. (2009) Jahrringuntersuchungen in der Siedlung Forschner und weiteren bronze- und metallzeitlichen Feuchtbodensiedlungen Südwestdeutschlands. Aussagen der angewandten Dendrochronologie in der Feuchtbodenarchäologie. In A. Billamboz, J. Köninger, H. Schlichtherle and W. Torke (Regierungspräsidium Stuttgart, Landesamt für Denkmalpflege, Esslingen, ed.) *Die früh- und mittelbronzezeitliche 'Siedlung Forschner' im Federseemoor. Befunde und Dendrochronologie*: 399–355. Stuttgart: Siedlungsarchäologie im Alpenvorland XI, Forsch. u. Ber. Vor. Frühgesch. Baden-Württemberg 113.

Billamboz, A. (2011) Applying dendrotypology to large timber series. In P. Fraiture (ed.) Tree Rings, Art, Archaeology. Proceedings of the Conference in *Brussels, Royal Institute for Cultural Heritage, 10–12 February 2010*: 177–188. Brussels: Scientia Artis 7.

Billamboz, A. (2013) Der Standpunkt der Dendroarchäologie zu Auswirkungen der Thera-Eruption nördlich der Alpen. In H. Meller, F. Bertemes, H.-R. Bork and R. Risch (eds) *1600 – Kultureller Umbruch im Schatten des Thera-Ausbruchs? 4. Mitteldeutscher Archäologentag vom 14. bis 16. Oktober 2011 in Halle (Saale)*: 89–99. Halle (Saale): Tagungen des Landesmuseums für Vorgeschichte Halle 9.

Billamboz, A. (2014a) Dendroarchaeology and cockchafers north of the Alps: regional patterns of a middle frequency signal in oak tree-ring series. *Environmental Archaeology* 19/2: 114–123.

Billamboz, A. (2014b) Regional patterns of settlement and woodland developments. Dendroarchaeology in the Neolithic pile-dwellings on Lake Constance (Germany). *The Holocene* 24/10: 1278–1287.

Billamboz, A. and Martinelli, N. (1996) La recherche dendrochronologique en Europe pour l'Age du Bronze ancien. In C. Mordant and O. Gaiffe (eds) *Cultures et sociétés du bronze ancien en Europe. Actes du 117e Congrès national des Sociétés historiques et scientifiques. Fondements culturels, techniques, économiques et sociaux des débuts de l'Âge du Bronze, 27–29 oct. 1992, Clermont-Ferrand:* 85–95. Paris: CTHS.

Billamboz, A. and Schöbel G. (1996) Dendrochronologische Untersuchungen in den spätbronzezeitlichen Pfahlbausiedlungen am nördlichen Ufer des Bodensees. In G: Schöbel (Regierungspräsidium Stuttgart, Landesdenkmalamt Baden-Württemberg, Stuttgart, ed.) *Die Spätbronzezeit am nordwestlichenBodensee. Taucharchäologische Untersuchungen in Hagnau und Unteruhldingen 1982–1989:* 203–220. Stuttgart: Siedlungsarchäologie im Alpenvorland VI, Forsch. u. Ber. Vor. Frühgesch. Baden-Württemberg 47.

Bronk Ramsey, C. (2009) Bayesian analysis of radiocarbon dates, *Radiocarbon* 51(1): 337–360.

Corboud, P. and Pugin, C. (2008) L'organisation spatiale d'un village littoral du Bronze ancien lémanique : Préverenges I (VD). *Annuaire de l'Archéologie Suisse* 91: 39–58.

Cremaschi, M., Pizzi, C. and Valsecchi, V. (2006) Water management and land use in the terramare and a possible climatic co-factor in their abandonment: The case study of the terramara of Poviglio Santa Rosa (northern Italy). *Quaternary International* 151: 87–98.

Čufar, K., De Luis, M., Zupančič, M., Eckstein, D. (2008) A 548-year tree-ring chronology of oak (*Quercus* spp.) for southeast Slovenia and its significance as a dating tool and climate archive. *Tree-ring Research* 64(1): 3–15.

David-Elbiali, M. and David, W. (2009) Le Bronze ancien et le début du Bronze moyen: cadre chronologique et liens culturels entre l'Europe nordalpine occidentale, le monde danubien et l'Italie du Nord. In A. Richard, P. Barral, A. Daubigney, G. Kaenel, C. Mordant and J.-F. Piningre (eds) *L'isthme européen Rhin-Saône-Rhône dans la Protohistoire. Approches nouvelles en hommage à Jacques-Pierre Millotte. Actes du Colloque.* Besançon, 16–18.10.2006: 311–340. Besançon:

De Marinis, R. C. (2002) Towards a Relative and Absolute Chronology of the Bronze Age in Northern Italy. *Notizie Archeologiche Bergomensi* 7: 23–100.

De Marinis, R. C., Rapi, M., Ravazzi, C., Arpenti, E., Deaddis, M. and Perego., R. (2005) Lavagnone (Desenzano del Garda): new excavations and palaeoecology of a Bronze Age pile dwelling site in northern Italy. In Ph. Delle Casa and M. Trachsel (eds) *WES'04. Wetland economies and societies. Proceedings of the international conference Zurich, 10–13 March 2004:* 221–232. Zürich: Collectio Archeologica 3 (Schweizerisches Landesmuseum).

Fasani L., Martinelli, N. (1996) Cronologia assoluta e relativa dell'antica età del Bronzo nell'Italia settentrionale (dati dendrocronologici e radiometrici). In D. Cocchi Genick (ed.) *L'antica età del Bronzo in Italia. Atti del Congresso di Viareggio (9–12 gennaio 1995):* 19–32. Firenze: Octavo.

Fozzati, L., Bressan, F., Martinelli, N. and Valzolgher, E. (2006) Underwater archaeology and prehistoric settlement dynamic in a great alpine lake: the case study of Lake Garda. In A. Hafner, U. Niffeler and U. Ruoff (eds) *Die neue Sicht. Unterwasserarchaeologie und Geschichtsbild. Proceedings of the IKUWA2 Congress (Zurigo 2004):*78–91. Basel: Antiqua 40.

Griggs, C. B., Kuniholm, P. I., and Newton, M. W. (2002) Lavagnone di Brescia in the early Bronze Age: Dendrochronological Report. *Notizie Archeologiche Bergomensi* 10: 19–33.

Kenward, H. K. (1997) Synanthropic insects and the size, remoteness and longevity of archaeological occupation sites: applying concepts from biogeography to past 'islands' of human occupation. *Quaternary Proceedings* 5: 135–152.

Köninger, J. (2006) *Bodman-Schachen I, Die frühbronzezeitlichen Ufersiedlungen von Bodman-Schachen I – Befunde und Funde aus den Tauchsondagen 1982–84 und 1986.* Stuttgart: Siedlungsarchäologie im Alpenvorland. VIII. Forsch. u. Ber. Vor- u. Frühgesch. Baden-Württemberg 85.

Köninger, J. and Schöbel, G. (2010) Bronzezeitliche Fundstellen zwischen Bodensee und Oberschwaben. In I. Matuschik, Chr. Strahm, *et al.* (eds) *Vernetzungen. Festschrift für H. Schlichtherle*: 385–438. Freiburg im Breisgau: Lavori Verlag.

Magny, M. (2013) Orbital, ice-sheet, and possible solar forcing of Holocene lake-level fluctuations in west-central Europe: A comment on Bleicher. *The Holocene* published online 30 April 2013: DOI: 10.1177/0959683613483627.

Magny, M., Galop, D., Bellintani, P., Desmet, M., Didier, J., Haas, J. N., Martinelli, N., Pedrotti, A., Scandolari, R., Stock, A. and Vannière, B. (2009) Late-Holocene climatic variability south of the Alps as recorded by lake-level fluctuations at Lake Ledro, Trentino, Italy. *The Holocene* 19: 575–589.

Martinelli, N. (1996) Datazioni dendrocronologiche per l'età del Bronzo dell'area alpina. In K. Randsborg (ed.) *Absolute Chronology. Archaeological Europe 2500–500 BC, Proceedings of the Conference, Verona, Italy, 20–23 April 1995*: 315–326. Copenhagen: Acta Archaeologica 67, Acta Archaeologica Supplementa, Munsksgaart, vol. I.

Martinelli, N. (2003) Le indagini dendrocronologiche nella palafitta del Sabbione: datazione assoluta ed evoluzione della struttura abitativa. In M. A. Binaghi Leva (ed.) *Le palafitte del lago di Monate. Ricerche archeologiche e ambientali nell'insediamento preistorico del Sabbione*: 121–131, 151–152. Gavirate: Nicolini Editore.

Martinelli, N. (2005) Dendrocronologia e Archeologia: situazione e prospettive della ricerca in Italia. In P. Attema, A. Nijboer and A. Zifferero (eds) *Communities and settlements from the Neolithic to the Early Medieval period, Proceedings of the 6th Conference of Italian Archaeology, Groningen, The Netherlands, 15–17 April 2003*: 437–448. Oxford: Papers in Italian Archaeology, VI, BAR International Series, 1452 (I).

Martinelli, N. (2007) Dendrocronologia delle palafitte dell'area gardesana: situazione delle ricerche e prospettive. In F. Morandini and M. Volonté (eds) *Contributi di archeologia in memoria di Mario Mirabella Roberti, Atti del XVI Convegno Archeologico Benacense, Cavriana, Italy, 15–16 October 2005*: 103–120. Cavriana: Annali Benacensi, XIII–XIV.

Martinelli, N. (2013) Dendro-typology in Italy: The case studies of the pile-dwelling villages Lucone D (Brescia) and Sabbione (Varese). In N. Bleicher, P. Gassmann, N. Martinelli and H. Schlichtherle (eds) *DENDRO ... -Chronologie, -Typologie, -Ökologie. Festschrift für André Billamboz zum 65. Geburtstag*: 117–124. Freiburg im Breisgau: Janus Verlag.

Martinelli, M., Čufar, K. and Billamboz, A. (in press) Dendroarchaeology between teleconnection and regional patterns. In *Le Palafitte: Ricerca, valorizzazione, Conservazione*, Convegno a Desenzano del Garda (Brescia) 2011.

Martinelli, N. and Kromer, B. (1999) High precision ^{14}C dating of a new tree-ring Bronze Age chronology from the pile-dwelling of Frassino I (Northern Italy). In *Actes du 3ème congres international, Archeologie et ^{14}C, Lione 6–10 Aprile 1998*: 119–122. Paris: Revue d'Archéométrie Suppl. 1999 et Soc. Préhist. Fr. Mémoire 26.

Martinelli, N., Pappafava, M. and Tinazzi, O. (1998) Datazione dendrocronologica dei resti strutturali. In C. Balista and P. Bellintani (eds) *Canàr di San Pietro Polesine. Ricerche archeo-ambientali sul sito palafitticolo*: 105–113. Rovigo: Padusa Quaderni 2.

Marzatico, F. (2004) 150 years of lake-dwelling research in northern Italy. In F. Menotti (ed.) *Living on the lake in prehistoric Europe. 150 years of lake-dwelling research*: 83–97. London: Routledge.

Menotti, F. (2001) *'The missing period': Middle Bronze Age lake-dwellings in the Alps.* Oxford: Archaeopress.

Menotti, F., Rubat Borel, F., Köninger, J. and Martinelli, N. (2012) Viverone (Bi) – Azeglio (To), sito palafitticolo Vil-Emissario: indagini subacquee e campionamento dendrocronologico. *Quaderni della Soprintendenza Archeologica del Piemonte* 27: 196–201.

Pétrequin, M., Magny, M. and Bailly, M. (2004) Habitat lacustres du Néolithique et de l'âge du Bronze dans les lacs alpins francais: bilan des connaissances et perspectives. In Ph. Della Casa and M. Trachsel (eds) *WES'04 – Wetland Economies and Societies, Proceedings of the International Conference, Zurich, Switzerland, 10–13 March 2004*: 143–168. Zurich: Chronos Verlag.

Pétrequin, P. and Pétrequin, A. M. (2013) Pourquoi des palafittes? Des villages dans un milieu répulsif. *Dossiers d'Archéologie* 355: 24–27.

Poggiani Keller, R., Binaghi Leva, M. A., Menotti, E. M., Roffia, E., Pacchieni, T., Baioni, M., Martinelli, N., Ruggiero, M. G. and Bocchio, G. (2005) Siti di ambiente umido della Lombardia: rilettura di vecchi dati e nuove ricerche. In Ph. Della Casa and M. Trachsel (eds) *WES'04 – Wetland Economies and Societies, Proceedings of the International Conference, Zurich, Switzerland, 10–13 March 2004*: 233–250, Zürich: Chronos ed., Collectio Archeologica, X.

Reimer, P. J. Bard, E., Bayliss, A., Warren Beck, J., Blackwell, P. G., Bronk Ramsey, C., Buck, C. E., Cheng, H., Lawrence Edwards, R., Friedrich, M., Grootes, P. M., Guilderson, T. P., Haflidason, H., Hajdas, I., Hatté, C., Heaton, T. J., Hoffmann, D. L., Hogg, A. G., Hughen, K. A., Kaiser, K. F., Kromer, B., Manning, S. W., Niu, M., Reimer, R. W., Richards, D. A., Scott, E. M., Southon, J. R., Staff, R. A., Turney, C. S. M., van der Plicht, J. (2013) IntCal13 and Marine13 radiocarbon age calibration curves 0–50.000 years cal BP. *Radiocarbon* 55(4): 1869–1887.

Ruckdeschel, W. (1978) *Die frühbronzezeitlichen Gräber Südbayerns*. Bonn: Antiquitas 11.

Ruoff, U. (1987) Die frühbronzezeitlichen Ufersiedlungen in Meilen-Schellen, Kanton Zürich. Tauchgrabung 1985. *Jahrbuch der Schweizerischen Gesellschaft für Urgeschichte* 70: 51–64.

Schmidheiny, M. (2011) *Zürich 'Mozartstrasse'. Neolithische und bronzezeitliche Ufersiedlungen. Band 4: Die Bronzezeitliche Besiedlung*. Zürich und Egg: Monogr. Kantonsarchäologie Zürich 42.

Usoskin, I. G. (2008) A History of solar activity over millennia. *Living Review in Solar Physics*. 5, [online article]: http://www.livingreviews.org/lrsp-2008–3.

Van Geel, B., Van der Pflicht, J., Killian, M.R., Klaver, E. R., Kouwenberg, J. H. M., Renssen, H., Renaud-Farrera, J. and H. T. Waterbolk (1998) *The sharp rise of Δ^{14}C c. 800 cal BC: possible causes, related climatic teleconnections and the impact on human environments*. Radiocarbon 40/1: 535–550.

Vanzetti, A. (2013) 1600? The rise of the Terramara system (Nothern Italy). In H. Meller, F. Bertemes, H.-R. Bork and R. Risch (eds) *1600 – Kultureller Umbruch im Schatten des Thera-Ausbruchs? 4. Mitteldeutscher Archäologentag vom 14. bis 16. Oktober 2011 in Halle (Saale)*: 267–282. Halle (Saale):Tagungen des Landesmuseums für Vorgeschichte Halle 9.

Webb, G. E. (1983) *Tree rings and Telescopes. The scientific career of A. E. Douglass*. Tucson: The University of Arizona Press.

Winiger, A. (2008) *La station lacustre de Concise, 1. Stratigraphie, datations et contexte environnemental*. Lausanne: Cahiers d'archéologie romande 111

Zanini, A. and Martinelli, N. (2005) *The absolute chronology of the Late Bronze Age in central Italy*. BAR International Series 1337 Section 11–19, 147–155.

Chapter 4

Climatic variations in the Circum-Alpine area during the period 4500–2500 cal BP, as reflected by palaeohydrological changes

Michel Magny

Introduction

In the Circum-Alpine region, the period around 4500–2500 cal BP (which coarsely spans the Bronze Age) was punctuated by major climatic changes, such as that of the transition from the Middle to the Late Holocene at *c.* 4200 cal BP (Walker *et al.* 2012), or the 2700 cal BP cold event, which marks the transition from the regional Subboreal to Subatlantic pollen zones (van Geel *et al.* 1996). A lot of data based on various proxies, including glacier history, pollen, tree-rings, speleothems, lake and alluvial sediments, and chironomids (Holzhauser *et al.* 2005; Giraudi 2005; Nicolussi *et al.* 2005, 2009; Mangini *et al.* 2005; Haas *et al.* 1998; Tinner *et al.* 2003; Heiri *et al.* 2003; Zolitschka *et al.* 2003; Arnaud *et al.* 2012; Wessels 1998), has been collected in recent decades to document the Holocene climatic variability in and around the Alpine area. However, as the topic of the present volume centres on questions concerning the Bronze Age lake-dwellings in the Circum-Alpine region, this chapter mainly focuses on climatic variations that were reflected by palaeohydrological changes. More specifically, it looks at lake-level fluctuations, which could have been crucial to the general environmental conditions of the Bronze Age lake-shore villages.

The chapter first presents a general overview of the palaeohydrological records available for the Circum-Alpine region (Fig. 4.1) to document the major climatic oscillations that occurred during the Bronze Age time window. It successively considers two distinct regions: (1) north of the Alps, including the Jura and the Swiss Plateau, and (2) the southern Alpine foreland, including the northern half of the Italian peninsula, where a peculiar chronological pattern of Bronze Age wetland site developments has been observed (Guidi and Bellintani 1996; Cremaschi *et al.* 2006). After debating the possible significance of the palaeohydrological data in terms of palaeoclimatic changes and their various parameters, the final discussion considers the possible impacts of these climatic variations on the Circum-Alpine Bronze Age societies.

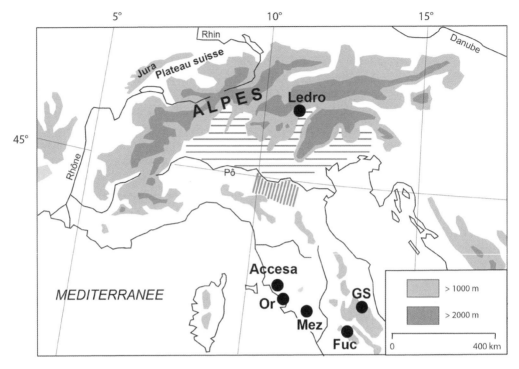

Figure 4.1. Geographical map of the Circum-Alpine area, with the location of regions and reference sites cited in the text. Horizontal and vertical hatching corresponds to zones occupied by lake-dwellings and terramare respectively. Fuc: Lake Fucino; GS: Gran Sasso Massif; Mez: Lake Mezzano; Or: Ombrone River.

Palaeohydrological and palaeoclimatic oscillations north and south of the Alps during the Bronze Age

North of the Alps

Over the last three decades, using a specific technique (Magny 1998, 2004, 2006), systematic sedimentological investigations have been developed in western-central Europe, in order to reconstruct Holocene lake-level fluctuations. Supported by a series of radiocarbon and tree-ring dates, lake-level data from 26 lake basins has allowed a robust regional pattern of palaeohydrological changes to be established (Fig. 4.2). Thus, the period 4500–2500 cal BP appears to have been characterised by an alternation of lake-level lowstands and highstands. Major phases of higher lake-level conditions developed around 4300–3750, 3350–3100, and 2750–2300 cal BP (Magny 2004, 2006, 2013). As illustrated by records presented in Fig. 4.2, the chronologies of these successive events may show slight differences that are related to uncertainties linked to the radiocarbon dating, which depends upon the sensitivity of the studied catchment areas, as well as the proxies used for the reconstruction. The sediment sequence of Lake Clairvaux (France), for instance, suggests that the lake-level highstand centred at *c.* 3300–3200 cal BP may have been initiated as early as 1650–1600 BC (*i.e.*

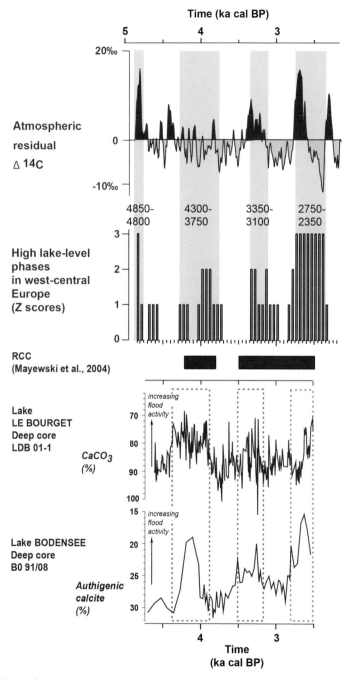

Figure 4.2. Palaeohydrological records reconstructed north of the Alps. Upper panel: comparison between the phases of high lake level reconstructed in west-central Europe (Magny 2004, 2006, 2013) with the atmospheric residual radiocarbon record (Stuiver et al. 1998). Mid panel: phases of rapid climate change (RCC) defined by Mayewski et al. (2004). Lower panel: Palaeohydrological records established from deep cores from Lakes Bourget (Arnaud et al. 2012) and Bodensee (Wessels 1998).

3600–3550 cal BP) (Magny 2013). Precise tree-ring dates and the wiggle-matching approach place the abrupt climate change at the Subboreal/Subatlantic transition; more precisely, it is placed before *c.* 2764 cal BP (Magny *et al.* 2012a ; Magny 2013) and between *c.* 2800–2750 cal BP (Speranza *et al.* 2000).

In discussing the possible impacts of these palaeohydrological/palaeoclimatic changes on the Bronze Age societies of the Circum-Alpine region, it is important to rule out any naïve interpretations of the pluri-secular high versus low lake-level phases that have been reconstructed from sedimentological studies. High-resolution lake-level records, as well as significant sediment accumulations in lake-shore archaeological sites (Winiger 2008), have shown that phases of high/low lake levels should not be considered as homogenous periods of permanent high/low water tables but rather as intervals marked by higher frequencies of high/low water-table spells, reflecting the decadal- to centennial-scale climatic variability behind these lake-level fluctuations. Considered as a whole, the three multi-century phases of general lake-level highstands dated to *c.* 4300–3750, 3350–3100, and 2750–2300 cal BP appear to have been broadly synchronous with phases of wetter and cooler climatic conditions marked in the French, Swiss, and Austrian Alps by glacier advances and timberline declines (Patzelt 1977; Zoller 1977; Haas *et al.* 1998; Nicolussi *et al.* 2005, 2009; Schmidt *et al.* 2002; Holzhauser 2007; Lieman and Niessen 1994; Deline and Orombelli 2005; Le Roy 2012).

A well-dated high-resolution lake-level record from Lake Bourget in the northern French Pre-Alps has recently shown the possible complexity of the lake-level highstand that occurred between *c.* 4300 and 3750 cal BP, which was interrupted by a lowering episode around 4100 cal BP (Magny *et al.* 2012a). As pointed out by Mayewski *et al.* (2004), this phase coincided with the period of rapid climate change (RCC) that developed around 4000 cal BP on a global scale. Concerning the possible causes of this climatic reversal, which developed during a phase of above-average solar activity, as shown by rather high values in [10]Be and ^{14}C records (Bond *et al.* 2001), Zhao *et al.* (2010) have hypothesised that it may reflect a nonlinear response of the climate system to an orbitally driven gradual decrease in insolation – the key seasonal and inter-hemispherical changes in the insolation distribution that developed around this time interval are also part of the equation (Fig. 4.2). This orbital 'forcing' resulted in a general re-organisation of the atmospheric circulation, with a southward shift of the ITCZ (Intertropical Convergence Zone) (Haug *et al.* 2001) and more frequent westerlies (prevailing winds from the west) responsible for more humidity over the mid-European latitudes (Magny, 2004, 2006, 2013). It also marks the transition from the Middle to the Late Holocene, as characterised by prevailing positive to negative NAO (North Atlantic Oscillation) modes of atmospheric circulation in the North Atlantic area (Magny *et al.* 2013; Wirth *et al.* 2013).

The higher lake-level phases around 3350–3100 and 2750–2300 cal BP also corresponded to major global-scale climatic changes, with contrasting palaeohydrological patterns from the Tropics to the mid-European latitudes, as shown by Magny *et al.* (2009a) for the climatic event around 3300 cal BP (Fig. 4.3) and by van Geel *et al.* (1996) for the climatic event around 2750 cal BP. They may be considered as two successive parts of the RCC event dated to 3500–2500 cal BP by Mayewski *et al.* (2004) (Fig. 4.2). Both successive events

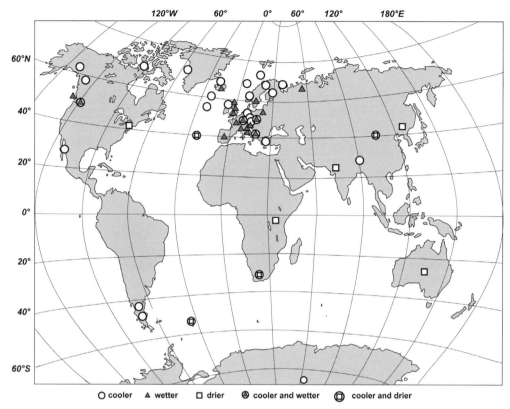

Figure 4.3. Sites documenting a widespread climate change around 3600–3300 cal BP (from: Magny et al. 2009c).

may be clearly related to a solar 'forcing' well marked by decreasing values in the ¹⁰Be and ¹⁴C records (Stuiver *et al.* 1998; Bond *et al.* 2001), a hypothesis supported by recent high-resolution studies of floods in the Alpine area (Martin-Puertas *et al.* 2012; Czymzik *et al.* 2013; Swierczynski *et al.* 2013; Wirth *et al.* 2013).

Regarding the significance of these palaeohydrological oscillations in terms of climatic parameters, Figure 4.4 presents pollen-based and lake-level-based quantitative estimates, which were reconstructed from data collected at the site of Tresserve, Lake Bourget (eastern French Pre-Alps) for the period *c.* 3800–2600 cal BP (Magny *et al.* 2009b), using the best analogue method (Guiot *et al.* 1993). Seven climatic variables have been reconstructed: total annual precipitation (PANN), summer precipitation (PSUM), winter precipitation (PWIN), mean annual temperature (TANN), mean temperatures of the coldest month (MTCO) and the warmest month (MTWA), and the growing degree days (GDD5) (*i.e.* the total number of days with temperatures above 5°C, which characterises the growing season). Considered as a whole, phases of higher lake-level conditions coincided with decreases in MTCO and TANN and with increases in PANN and PSUM, while lowstand phases corresponded to the opposite processes. The magnitude of the changes reached

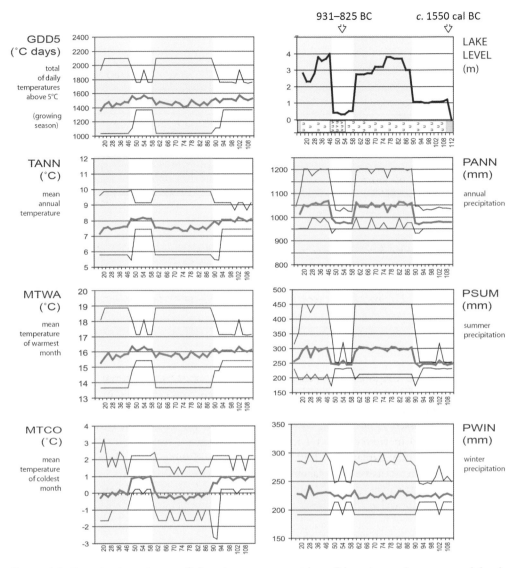

Figure 4.4. Quantitative estimates of climatic parameters with confidence interval reconstructed for the period c. 3500–2500 cal BP from pollen and lake-level data at the site of Tresserve, Lake Bourget (eastern France; Magny et al. 2009b).

c. 70–100 mm for PANN, 50–70 mm for PSUM, 1–1.2°C for MTCO, and 0.8°C for TANN. Unclear oscillation may be observed from the PWIN curve. Despite the fact that they are not statistically significant, the oscillations shown by the MTWA and GDD5 curves are consistent with indications evidenced by the MTCO and TANN curves and suggest that the lake-level highstands corresponded to a decrease in MTWA by c. 1°C and in GDD5 by c. 200 days (*i.e.* there was a substantial reduction in the growing season).

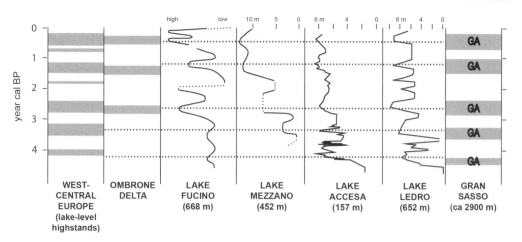

Figure 4.5. Comparison between (1) palaeohydrological records reconstructed south of the Alps at Fucino (Giraudi 1998), Mezzano (Giraudi 2004; Sadori et al. 2004), Accesa (Magny et al. 2007), Ledro (Magny et al. 2012b), Ombrone river delta (Bellotti et al. 2004), Gran Sasso on the higher Apennine massifs (Giraudi 2005); and (2) lake-level fluctuations in west-central Europe north of the Alps (Magny 2013).

Regarding the magnitude of changes in temperature, the estimates reconstructed at Tresserve are consistent with values inferred from other proxies in the Alpine area (Bortenschlager 1977; Patzelt 1985; von Grafenstein *et al.* 1994; Haas *et al.* 1998; Heiri *et al.* 2003; Renssen *et al.* 2009). In general, they are also consistent with environmental changes observed in western-central Europe: the decrease in temperature and the increase in precipitation may explain the higher lake-level conditions in the Jura Mountains and on the Swiss Plateau, as well as glacier advances and tree-limit declines in the Alps. Taken together, this data suggests that relatively limited changes in climatic parameters may have resulted in substantial environmental changes and possible major difficulties for Bronze Age societies.

South of the Alps

As illustrated by Fig. 4.5, several palaeohydrological records document the late Holocene south of the Alps, including variations in river discharge (Bellotti *et al.* 2004), lake-level fluctuations (Giraudi 1998; Sadori *et al.* 2004; Magny *et al.* 2007, 2012b), and glacier advances and retreats (Giraudi 2005). Of particular interest are the well-dated high-resolution lake-level records recently established at Lake Ledro in northern Italy (southern slope of the Alps), and Lake Accesa (Tuscany) in central Italy. The records of both sites have been reconstructed using the same method as that used for the lake-level records north of the Alps (Magny 2004, 2006, 2013), allowing a direct comparison to be developed between data obtained north and south of the Alps.

Keeping in mind the inherent uncertainties in radiocarbon dating and taking into account the fact that records may have been established using different methods (and also may differ in the precision of their temporal resolution and chronology), Fig. 4.5 suggests that the lake-level records from Ledro, Fucino, Mezzano, and Accesa present similarities, with highstands around 4000, 3400, 2700, 1200, and 400 cal BP. This palaeohydrological pattern established from lake data is also supported by data collected in the delta of the Ombrone River in Tuscany (Bellotti *et al.* 2004) and around the Calderone glacier in the Gran Sasso Massif (Central Apennines) (Giraudi 2005). In addition, Fig. 4.5 suggests that the regional pattern of palaeohydrological changes reconstructed south of the Alps in northern and central Italy have strong similarities with those established north of the Alps (Magny 2004, 2006, 2013).

A unique feature of the region south of the Alps may be the fact that the climatic oscillation around 4000 cal BP (*i.e.* during the Early Bronze Age) appears to have been more marked than north of the Alps. This event corresponds to an abrupt rise in the lake levels at Lakes Ledro and Accesa (Magny *et al.* 2007, 2012b) and at Lake Maliq in Albania (Magny *et al.* 2009c). This climatic oscillation also marks a significant increase in the sedimentation rate at Lake Iseo (Lauterbach *et al.* 2012) and even coincides with major environmental changes in the high mountains of the Central Apennines, resulting in a growth of the Calderone glacier and marking the onset of the Apennine 'Neoglacial' (Zanchetta *et al.* 2012). By contrast, north of the Alps, the Neoglacial was probably initiated earlier at *c.* 5500 cal BP (Magny *et al.* 2004). However, as suggested by lake-level records from the Lakes Bourget, Ledro, and Accesa, the climate change around 4000 cal BP seems to present a similar possible complexity north and south of the Alps (Magny *et al.* 2009c, 2012b). This marked climatic event has also been supported by records of palaeo-floods on the southern slope of the Alps (Vannière *et al.* 2013; Wirth *et al.* 2013).

To summarise, the data presented above clearly indicates that, on the centennial to pluri-centennial scale, the regions located immediately north and south of the Alps appear to have been characterised by similar climatic changes both in terms of timing and general characteristics, with an alternation of (1) warmer and drier phases responsible for lake-level lowstands and decreasing river discharge, as well as glacier retreats in more elevated areas; and (2) cooler and wetter phases leading to opposite environmental changes around 4300–3800, 3400–3200, and 2800–2200 cal BP (Magny and Peyron 2008; Magny *et al.* 2013).

From the history of the climate to that of Bronze Age societies

This final section does not aim to provide an exhaustive discussion of the possible impacts of climate variations on the Bronze Age societies in the Circum-Alpine region. More modestly, it attempts to outline tracks for thought and to illustrate the possible complexities of the processes, the diversity of situations, and the variety of responses given by societies to environmental and climatic changes.

Climate and lake dwellings

Fig. 4.6 presents a comparison between (1) the climatic conditions as reflected by lake-level records; and (2) the frequency of Late Neolithic – Bronze Age lake-dwellings north and

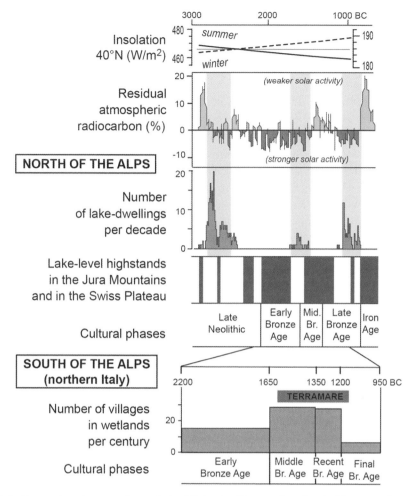

Figure 4.6. Comparison between the periods of lake-dwellings and wetland villages north and south of the Alps; and palaeohydrological (palaeoclimatic) records. GA: glacier advance.

south of the Alps. Two distinct patterns may be observed. North of the Alps, there is general agreement on the variations in the climate conditions and the frequency of lake-dwellings, which were clearly encouraged by warmer and drier conditions associated with stronger solar activity. In contrast, cooler and wetter phases coincided with a strong decrease in the number of lake-shore villages. Recent studies have given evidence of the relatively late abandonment of Bronze Age lake-dwellings at Lake Bourget at *c.* 814 BC (*i.e.* 2764 cal BP, corresponding to one of the youngest tree-ring-dated wooden piles) in comparison with tree-ring dates obtained from other subalpine lakes that indicate that the general abandonment of lake shores happened north of the Alps between 860 and 830 BC (*i.e.* 2810–2780 cal BP) (with the exception of Ürschhausen-Horn, Lake Nussbaum, Switzerland – see Chapter 3), in line with the development of wetter conditions well dated by wiggle-matching to *c.* 2800–2750 cal BP (Speranza *et al.* 2000). In fact, the sedimentological data collected at Chatillon, Lake Bourget, clearly indicates that the lake level began to rise before the abandonment of the Late Bronze Age village. It also shows that the village was developed during the final part of the highstand corresponding to the climate reversal centred on *c.* 3300–3200 cal BP. Altogether, this suggests that, even if the development of prehistoric lake-dwellings displays an apparent coincidence with phases of warmer and drier climatic conditions, the Bronze Age inhabitants were able to adapt the techniques for the construction of their houses to a certain magnitude of changes in the water table (Menotti *et al.* 2014).

South of the Alps, particularly in northern Italy, the Bronze Age chronology significantly contrasts with that reconstructed in the northern Circum-Alpine region, as illustrated by Fig. 4.6. South of the Alpine Mountains, archaeologists have observed that not only was a relative continuity of lake dwellings maintained throughout almost the entire Early Bronze Age but also that the Middle Bronze Age (3600–3300 cal BP) seems to mark a maximal development in lake-shore and wetland pile-dwelling villages (Perini 1994; Guidi and Bellintani 1996; Martinelli 2005; Magny and Peyron 2008). The regional peculiarity of the area is even confirmed by the so-called *terramare*, which were fortified villages developed in the wetlands of the Po Plain during the Middle and early Late Bronze Age (*Bronzo Finale*), between 3550 and 3100 cal BP (Cremaschi *et al.* 2006). This contrasts with the general abandonment of the lake shores observed north of the Alps at the same time.

The lake-level data presented in the preceding section clearly indicates that the singularity of the Italian humid settlements during the Middle and early Late Bronze Age did not result from a peculiar climatic history. Thus, the sedimentological data collected at Lake Ledro gives evidence that a rise in the lake level at around 3400 cal BP was responsible for the overlaying of a peat layer by lacustrine carbonate deposits, while pollen data suggests that the maximum human impact on the vegetation cover occurred during the start of the climate reversal (Magny *et al.* 2009a).

As a working hypothesis, this flourishing of Bronze Age settlements in Italian humid areas during a period marked by wetter climatic conditions points to a peculiar socio-economic organisation of Bronze Age societies in northern Italy, as discussed by Magny *et al.* (2009a). In addition, archaeological investigations at Fiavè-Carera (Trentino, northern Italy) have highlighted the ability of Bronze Age people to build true *palafitte* (Perini 1994). In the specific case of *terramare*, Cremaschi *et al.* (2006) have shown how their development was linked with an original management of water supply to fields through a network of irrigation ditches and how an increasing dryness after 3100 cal BP could have threatened such an organisation (see Chapter 3).

Climate and Bronze Age societies

Following our previous line of argument, climate oscillations may have affected not just the locations of the villages but also their socio-economic equilibrium. Phases of cooler and wetter climatic conditions may have provoked harvest failures, particularly due to wetter summer conditions, at least north of the Alps. Thus, in agreement with the quantitative estimates of climatic parameters obtained at Tresserve, Lake Bourget (Fig. 4.4; Magny *et al.*

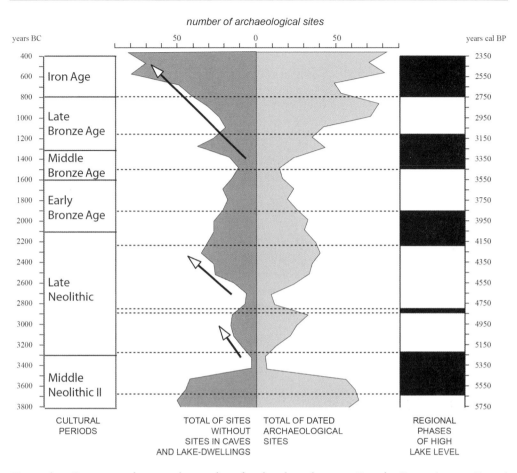

Figure 4.7. Comparison between the number of archaeological sites in Franche-Comté (eastern France) from the Neolithic to the early Iron Age; and (right) palaeoclimatic oscillations as reflected by regional changes in lake-level (from: Pétrequin et al. 2005; Magny et al. 2009b).

2009b), Tinner *et al.* (2003) have also suggested (on the basis of pollen records) that, during climate reversals, an increase in precipitation probably had a more decisive impact than a temperature decrease on former settlements in moderately elevated areas like the Alpine foreland. In Germany, Zolitschka *et al.* (2003) have also come to similar conclusions, noting that phases of cooler and wetter climatic conditions coincided with a decrease in human activities, from the Bronze Age to the beginning of the Migration Period (also known as the Barbarian Invasions).

However, other data invites us to rule out an excessive environmentally deterministic view of human history. Thus, the data presented in Fig. 4.7 shows how the chronological distribution of archaeological sites recognised in the region of Franche-Comté in eastern France from the mid-Neolithic to the early Iron Age (Pétrequin *et al.* 2005) does not directly and continuously match the climate history as reflected by lake-level records.

During the Neolithic, the two marked decreases in regional settlement at *c.* 5400 and 4800 cal BP may have been correlated with successive climatic reversals; by contrast, the period 4200–3500 cal BP appears to have been characterised by a general decrease in the population density, which cannot be simply attributed to a climatic reversal limited to *c.* 4200–3850 cal BP. In addition, the number of archaeological sites (especially inland settlements) suggests a general trend towards increasing population density from the Middle Bronze Age until the early Iron Age (inclusive). This contrasts with a more variable climatic history but is in agreement with the increase in anthropogenic disturbances shown by the regional pollen records for the same period (Richard and Gauthier 2007). In comparison with the Neolithic societies, such observations suggest, at least for the region of Franche-Comté, progress in the relative emancipation of the protohistoric societies from climatic conditions. Recent research also shows that a similar situation was present in other regions of the northern Circum-Alpine foreland, starting from the Late Bronze Age and perpetuating throughout the Iron Age (Jennings 2014; see also Chapter 8, this volume).

Conclusions

Considered as a whole, the period 4500–2500 cal BP was punctuated by three major phases of higher lake-level conditions north and south of the Alps at around 4300–3750, 3350–3100, and 2750–2300 cal BP, as reflected by the available palaeohydrological data. These lake-level highstand phases appear to have been broadly synchronous with phases of wetter and cooler climatic conditions marked in the French, Swiss, and Austrian Alps by glacier advances and timberline declines in response to the possible influences of variations in solar activity and/or orbitally driven changes in insolation. Quantitative estimates suggest that phases of higher (and inversely, lower) lake levels may have corresponded to decreasing (increasing) mean annual and winter temperatures, increasing (decreasing) annual and summer precipitation, and a shortening (lengthening) of the growing season.

While phases marked by wetter conditions coincided north of the Alps with a general abandonment of Bronze Age lake-dwellings, northern Italy shows a contrasting pattern, with relative continuity of lake-dwellings being maintained throughout almost the entire Bronze Age, with maximal development of lake-shore and wetland pile-dwelling villages during the Middle Bronze Age. The regional peculiarity of the region south of the Alps could reflect (i) the specific socio-economic organisations of Bronze Age societies in northern Italy; (ii) original architectural techniques; and/or (iii) original water management.

Finally, it is important to keep in mind that climate oscillations may have affected not just the locations of villages but also the socio-economic structures of societies, with harvest failures triggered by phases of cooler and wetter climatic conditions. However, archaeological data invites us to rule out excessive environmentally deterministic views of human history and suggests, at least for certain areas, a relative emancipation of protohistoric societies from climatic conditions.

References

Arnaud, F., Révillon, S., Debret, M., Revel, M., Chapron, E., Jacob, J., Giguet-Covex, C., Poulenard, J. and Magny, M. (2012) Lake Bourget regional erosion patterns reconstruction reveals Holocene NW European Alps soil evolution and paleohydrology. *Quaternary Science Reviews* 51: 81–92.

Bellotti, P., Caputo, C., Davoli, L., Evangelista, S., Garzanti, E., Pugliese, F. and Valeri, P. (2004) Morpho-sedimentary characteristics and Holocene evolution of the emergent part of the Ombrone River delta (southern Tuscany). *Geomorphology* 61: 71–90.

Bond, G., Kromer, B., Beer, J., Muscheler, R., Evans, M. N., Showers, W., Hoffmann, S., Lotti-Bond, R., Hajdas, I. and Bonani, G. (2001) Persistent solar influence on North Atlantic climate during the Holocene. *Science* 294: 2130–2136.

Bortenschlager, S. (1977) Ursachen and Ausmass postglazialer Waldgrenzschwankungen in den Ostalpen. In B. Frenzel (ed.) *Dendrochronologie und postglaziale Klimaschwankungen in Europa*: 260–26. Steiner Verlag, Wiesbaden.

Cremaschi, M., Pizzi, C. and Valsecchi, V. (2006) Water management and land use in the terramare and a possible climatic co-factor in their abandonment: the case study of the terramara of Poviglio Santa Rosa (northern Italy). *Quaternary International* 151: 87–98.

Czymzik, M., Brauer, A., Dulski, P., Plessen, B., Naumann, R., von Grafenstein, U. and Scheffler, R. (2013) Orbital and solar forcing of shifts in Mid- to Late Holocene flood intensity from varved sediments of pre-Alpine Lake Ammersee (southern Germany). *Quaternary Science Reviews* 61: 96–110.

Deline, P. and Orombelli, G. (2005) Glacier fluctuations in the western Alps during the Neoglacial, as indicated by the MIage morainic amphitheater. *Boreas* 34: 456–467.

Giraudi, C. (1998) Late Pleistocene and Holocene lake-level variations in Fucino Lake (Abruzzo, central Italy) inferred from geological, archaeological and historical data. In S. P. Harrison, B. Frenzel, U. Huckried and M. Weiss (eds) *Palaeohydrology as reflected in lake-level changes as climatic evidence for Holocene times*, 1–17. Paläoklimaforschung 25.

Giraudi, C. (2005) Late Holocene alluvial events in the central Apennines (Italy). *The Holocene* 15: 768–773.

Grafenstein (von), U., Erlenkeuser, H., Kleinmann, A., Müller, J. and Trimborn, P. (1994) High-frequency climatic oscillations during the last deglaciation as revealed by oxygen-isotope records of benthic organisms (Ammersee, southern Germany). *Journal of Paleolimnology* 11: 349–357.

Guidi, C. and Bellintani, P. (1996) Gli abitati 'palafitticoli' dell'Italia settentrionale. *Origini, Preistoria e protostoria delle civilta antiche* 20: 165–231.

Guiot, J., Harrison, S. P. and Prentice, I. C. (1993) Reconstruction of Holocene pattern of moisture in Europe using pollen and lake-level data. *Quaternary Research* 40: 139–149.

Haas, J. N., Richoz I., Tinner, W. and Wick, L. (1998) Synchronous Holocene climatic oscillations recorded on the Swiss Plateau and at timberline in the Alps. *The Holocene* 8: 301–304.

Haug, G. H., Hughen, K. A., Sigman, D. M., Peterson, L. C. and Röhl, U. (2001) Southward migration of the Intertropical Convergence Zone through the Holocene. *Science* 293: 1304–1308.

Heiri, O., Lotter, A. F., Hausmann, S. and Kienast F. (2003) A chironomid-based Holocene summer air temperature reconstruction from the Swiss Alps. *The Holocene* 13: 477–484.

Holzhauser, H. (2007) Holocene glacier fluctuations in the SWISS ALPS. In H. Richard, M. Magny, and C. Mordant (eds) *Environnements et cultures à l'âge du Bronze en Europe occidentale*: 29–43. Paris: Editions du CTHS.

Holzhauser, H., Magny, M. and Zumbühl, H. J. (2005) Glacier and lake-level variations in west-central Europe over the last 3500 years. *The Holocene* 15: 789–801.

Jennings, B. (2014) Travelling Objects: Changing Values. Incorporation of the northern Alpine lake-dwelling communities in exchange and communication networks during the Late Bronze Age. Oxford: Archaeopress.

Leeman, A. and Niessen, F. (1994) Holocene glacial activity and climatic variations in the Swiss Alps: reconstructing a continuous record from proglacial lake sediments. *The Holocene* 4: 259–268.

Le Roy, M. (2012) Reconstitution des fluctuations glaciaires holocènes dans les Alpes occidentales. PhD Université de Grenoble.

Lauterbach, S., Chapron, E., Brauer, A., Hüls, M., Gilli, A., Arnaud, F., Piccin, A., Nomade, J. and Desmet, M. (2012) A sedimentary record of Holocene surface runoff events and earthquake activity from Lake Iseo (Southern Alps, Italy). *The Holocene* 22: 749–760.

Magny, M. (2004) Holocene climatic variability as reflected by mid-European lake-level fluctuations, and its probable impact on prehistoric human settlements. *Quaternary International* 113: 65–79.

Magny, M. (2006) Holocene fluctuations of lake levels in west-central Europe: methods of reconstruction, regional pattern, palaeoclimatic significance and forcing factors. *Encyclopedia of Quaternary Geology*, Elsevier, 1389–1399.

Magny, M. (2013) Orbital, ice-sheet and possible solar forcing of Holocene lake-level fluctuations in west-central Europe. A comment on Bleicher (2013). *The Holocene* 23: 1202–1212.

Magny, M., Arnaud, F., Billaud Y. and Marguet, A. (2012a) Lake-level fluctuations at Lake Bourget (eastern France) around 4500–3500 cal. BP and their palaeoclimatic and archaeological implications. *Journal of Quaternary Sciences* 26: 171–177.

Magny, M., de Beaulieu, J. L., Drescher-Schneider, R., Vannière, B., Walter-Simonnet, A. V., Miras, Y., Millet, L., Bossuet, G., Peyron, O., Brugiapaglia, E. and Leroux, A. (2007) Holocene climate changes in the central Mediterranean as recorded by lake-level fluctuations at Lake Accesa (Tuscany, Italy). *Quaternary Science Reviews* 26: 1736–1758.

Magny, M. Combourieu-Nebout, N., de Beaulieu, J. L., Bout-Roumazeilles, V., Colombaroli, D., Desprat, S., Francke, A., Joannin, S., Ortu, E., Peyron, O., Revel, M., Sadori, L., Siani, L., Sicre, M. A., Samartin, S., Simonneau, A., Tinner, W., Vannière, B., Wagner, B., Zanchetta, G., Anselmetti, F., Brugiapaglia, E., Chapron, E., Debret, M., Desmet, M., Didier, J., Essallami, L., Galop, D., Gilli, A., Haas, J. N., Kallel, N., Millet, L., Stock, A., Turon, J. L. and Wirth, S. (2013) North–south palaeohydrological contrasts in the central Mediterranean during the Holocene: tentative synthesis and working hypotheses. *Climate of the Past* 9: 2043–2071.

Magny, M., Galop, D., Bellintani, P., Desmet, M., Didier, J., Haas, J. N., Martinelli, N., Pedrotti, A., Scandolari, R., Stock, A. and Vannière B. (2009a) Late-Holocene climatic variability south of the Alps as recorded by lake-level fluctuations at Lake Ledro, Trentino, Italy. *The Holocene* 19: 575–589.

Magny, M., Joannin, S., Galop, D., Vannière, B., Haas, J. N., Bassetti, M., Bellintani, P., Scandolari, R. and Desmet, M. (2012b) Holocene palaeohydrological changes in the northern Mediterranean borderlands as reflected by the lake-level record of Lake Ledro, northeastern Italy. *Quaternary Research* 77: 382–396.

Magny, M., Leuzinger, U., Bortenschlager, S. and Haas J. N. (2006) Tripartite climate reversal in Central Europe 5600–5300 years ago. *Quaternary Research* 65: 3–19.

Magny, M. and Peyron, O. (2008) Variations climatiques et histoire des sociétés à l'Age du Bronze au nord et au sud des Alpes. In J. Guilaine (ed.) *Villes, villages, campagnes de l'Age du Bronze*: 159–176. Paris: Editions Errance.

Magny, M., Peyron, O., Gauthier, E., Rouèche, H., Bordon, A., Billaud, Y., Chapron, E., Marguet, A., Pétrequin, P. and Vannière, B. (2009b) Quantitative reconstruction of climatic variations during the Bronze and early Iron ages based on pollen and lake-level data in the NW Alps, France. *Quaternary International* 200: 102–110.

Magny, M., Vannière, B., Zanchetta, G., Fouache, E., Touchais, G., Petrika, L., Coussot, C., Walter-

Simonnet, A. V., Arnaud, F. (2009c) Possible complexity of the climatic event around 4300–3800 cal BP in the central and western Mediterranean. *The Holocene* 19: 823–833.

Mangini, A., Spötl, C. and Verdes, P. (2005) Reconstruction of temperature in the Central Alps during the past 2000 years from a $\delta^{18}O$ stalagmite record. *Earth and Planetary Science Letters* 235: 741–751.

Martinelli, N. (2005) Dendrocronologia e Archeologia: situazione e prospettive della ricerca in Italia. *British Archaeological Reports International Serie* 1452 (1): 437–448.

Martin-Puertas, C., Matthes, K., Brauer, A., Muscheler, R., Hansen, F., Petrick, C., Aldahan, A., Possnert, G. and van Geel, B. (2012) Regional atmospheric circulation shifts induced by a grand solar minimum. *Nature Geoscience* 5: 397–401.

Mayewski, P. A., Rohling, E. E., Stager, J. C., Karlén, W., Maasch, K. A., Meeker, L. D., Meyerson, E. A., Gasse, F., van Kreveld, S., Holmgren, K., Lee-Thorp, J., Rosqvist, G., Rack, F., Staubwasser, M., Schneider, R. R. and Steig, E. J. (2004) Holocene climate variability. *Quaternary Research* 62: 243–255.

Menotti, F., Jennings, B. and Gollnisch-Moos, H. (2014) 'Gifts for the Gods': lake-dwellers' macabre remedies against floods in central Europe Bronze Age. *Antiquity* 88(340): 456–469

Nicolussi, K., Kaufmann, M., Melvin, T. M., van der Plicht, J., Schiessling, P. and Thurner, A. (2009) A 9111 year long conifer tree-ring chronology for the European Alps: a base for environmental and climatic investigations. *The Holocene* 19: 909–920.

Nicolussi, K., Kaufmann, M., Patzelt, G., van der Plicht, J. and Thurner, A. (2005) Holocene tree-line variability in the Kauner valley, central eastern Alps, indicated by dendrochronological analysis of living trees and subfossil logs. *Vegetation History and Archaeobotany* 14: 221–234.

Patzelt, G. (1977) Der zeitliche Ablauf und das Ausmass postglazialer Klimaschwankungen in den Alpen. In B. Frenzel (ed.) *Dendrochronologie und postglaziale Klimaschwankungen in Europa*, 248–259. Steiner Verlag, Wiesbaden.

Patzelt, G. (1985) The period of glacier advances in the Alps, 1965 to 1980. *Zeitschrift für Gletscherkunde and Glazialgeologie* 21: 403–407.

Perini, R. (1994) *Scavi archeologici nella zona palafitticola di Fiave-Carera, Parte III*. Patrimonio storico e artistico del trentino 10. Trento: Servizio Beni Culturali della Provincia Autonoma di Trento.

Pétrequin, P., Magny M. and Bailly M. (2005) Habitat lacustre, densité de population et climat. L'exemple du Jura français. In P. Della Casa and M. Trachsel (eds) *WES'O4, Wetland Economies and Societies*: 140–168. Zurich: Collectio Archaeologica 3.

Renssen, H., Seppä, H., Heiri, O., Roche, D. M., Goosse, H. and Fichefet, T. (2009) The spatial and temporal complexity of the Holocene thermal maximum. *Nature Geoscience* 2: 411–414.

Richard, H. and Gauthier, E. (2007). Bilan des données polliniques concernant l'âge du Bronze dans le Jura et le nord des Alpes. Actes du Colloque CTHS, Besançon, 19–24 avril 2004.

Sadori, L., Giraudi, C., Petitti, P. and Ramrath, A. (2004) Human impact at Lago di Mezzano (central Italy) during the Bronze Age: a multidisciplinary approach. *Quaternary International* 113: 5–17.

Schmidt, R., Koinig, K. A., Thompson, R. and Kamekik, C. (2002) A multi proxy core study of the last 7000 years of climate and alpine land-use impacts on an Austrian mountain lake (Unterer Landschitzsee, Niedere Tauern). *Palaeogeography, Palaeoclimatology, Palaeoecology* 187: 101–120.

Speranza, A., van der Plicht, J. and van Geel, B. (2000) Improving the time control of the Subboreal/Subatlantic transition in a Czech peat sequence by ^{14}C wiggle-matching. *Quaternary Science Reviews* 19: 1589–1604.

Stuiver, M., Reimer, P. J., Bard, E., Beck, J. W., Burr, G. S., Hughen, K. A., Kromer, B., McCormac, G., van der Plicht, J. and Spurk, M. (1998) Intcal98 radiocarbon age calibration, 24,000–0 cal BP. *Radiocarbon* 40: 1041–1083.

Swierczynski, T., Lauterbach, S., Dulski, P., Delgado, J., Merz, B. and Brauer, A. (2013) Mid- to late-Holocene flood frequency changes in the northeastern Alps as recorded in varved sediments of Lake Mondsee (Upper Austria). *Quaternary Science Reviews* 80: 78–90.

Tinner, W., Lotter, A. F., Ammann, B., Conedera, M., Hubschmid, P., van Leeuwen, J. F. N. and Wehrli, M. (2003) Climatic change and contemporaneous land-use phases north and south of the Alps 2300 BC to 800 AD. *Quaternary Science Reviews* 22: 1447–1460.

van Geel, B., Buurman, J. and Waterbolk, H. T. (1996) Archaeological and palaeoecological indications of an abrupt climate change in the Netherlands and evidence for climatological teleconnections around 2650 BP. *Journal of Quaternary Science* 11: 451–460.

Vannière, B., Magny, M., Joannin, S., Simonneau, A., Wirth, S., Hamann, Y., Chapron, E., Gilli, A., Desmet, M. and Anselmetti, F. (2013) Orbital changes, variations in solar activity and increased anthropogenic activities: controls on the Holocene flood frequency in the Lake Ledro area, Northern Italy. *Climate of the Past* 9: 1193–1209.

Walker, M. J. C., Berkelhammer, M., Bjorck, S., Cwynar, L. C., Fisher, D. A., Long, A., Lowe, J. J., Newnham, R. M., Rasmussen, S. O. and Weiss, H. (2012) Formal subdivision of the Holocene Series/Epoch: a Discussion Paper by a Working Group of INTIMATE (Integration of ice-core, marine and terrestrial records) and the Subcommission on Quaternary Stratigraphy (International Commission on Stratigraphy). *Journal of Quaternary Science* 27: 649–659.

Wessels, M. (1998) Natural environmental changes indicated by Late Glacial and Holocene sediments from Lake Constance, Germany. *Palaeogeography, Palaeoclimatology, Palaeoecology* 140: 421–432.

Winiger, A. (2008) *La station lacustre de Concise 1. Stratigraphie, datations et contexte environnemental.* Lausanne: Cahiers d'Archéologie Romande 111.

Wirth, S., Glur, L., Gilli, A. and Anselmetti, F. (2013) Holocene flood frequency across the Central Alps – solar forcing and evidence for variations in North Atlantic atmospheric circulation. *Quaternary Science Reviews* 80: 112–128.

Zanchetta, G., Giraudi, C., Sulpizio, R., Magny, M., Drysdale, R. N. and Sadori, L. (2012) Constraining the onset of the Holocene 'Neoglacial' over the central Italy using tephra layers. *Quaternary Research* 78: 236–247.

Zhao, C., Yu, Z. and Zhao, Y. (2010) Holocene climate trend, variability, and shift documented by lacustrine stable-isotope record in the northeastern United States. *Quaternary Science Reviews* 29: 1831–1843.

Zolitschka, B., Behre, K. E. and Schneider, J. (2003) Human and climatic impact on the environment as derived from coluvial, fluvial and lacustrine archives – examples from the Bronze Age to the Migration period, Germany. *Quaternary Science Reviews* 22: 81–100.

Zoller, H. (1977) Alter und Ausmass postglazialer Klimaschwankungen in den Schweizer Alpen. In B. Frenzel (ed.) *Dendrochronologie und postglaziale Klimaschwankungen in Europa*: 271–281. Wiesbaden: Steiner Verlag.

Chapter 5

Micromorphological studies of wetland site formation processes: additional help for a better understanding of the lake-dwellings' final disappearance

Philipp Wiemann and Philippe Rentzel

Introduction

Lakes are generally considered to be useful palaeoenvironmental archives; for instance, they form the basis of research areas such as palaeolimnology (Cohen 2003). This is because lake sediments are seen as highly detailed archives of environmental and climatic changes (Gaillard *et al.* 1994) on the one hand and of anthropogenic impacts (Wirth *et al.* 2011) on the other. Prehistoric lake-dwellings, however, also provide exceptionally good preservation conditions and are invaluable archaeological archives that are studied by archaeologists as well as archaeobotanists, zooarchaeologists, and researchers from a host of disciplines within the area of natural scientific archaeology. It is generally accepted that the profundal zones of large lakes contain undisturbed sediments that, deposited as varves, allow us to reconstruct the palaeoenvironment, ideally in a continuous sequence with only minor gaps or none at all. It is also accepted that organic remains in lake-dwellings generally exhibit excellent preservation conditions due to their waterlogged state, making them preferred objects of research for the disciplines mentioned and many more besides. This is shown by the example of the site Arbon-Bleiche 3 (Jacomet *et al.* 2004). However, we can state that the locations of lake-dwellings on lake shores can also have many drawbacks in terms of certain research objectives. The morphodynamic processes in the littoral zones (above all, wave action), for instance, can cause severe erosion and reworking (see Table 5.1). This is, in fact, the greatest danger that lake-dwelling sites face nowadays. As a consequence, a variety of conservation measures have been put in place in order to bring this problem under control (Ramseyer *et al.* 1996; Ramseyer and Roulière-Lambert 2006).

These often underestimated negative effects also have an impact on the study of the features at lake-dwelling sites. The fact that the preservation conditions for finds – be they artefacts or ecofacts – are particularly good, can, indeed, pose something of a paradox. In fact, very few other structural remains of dwellings are preserved besides piles, organic

Profundal	Littoral
Calm depositional milieu	Dynamic depositional milieu
Slow and more or less continuous sedimentation	Comparatively rapid, and usually discontinuous sedimentation and severe erosion
Seasonal events	Fragmentary preservation
Severely 'diluted' anthropogenic signals (*e.g.* micro-charcoal, changes in pollen spectra)	Partially high resolution in terms of individual events
Partially terrigeneous inwash (*e.g.* as a result of onshore run-off processes)	Usually very strong anthropogenic signals (particularly near the settlement) and patchwork-like layers/features (if preserved)
Low rate of sedimentation	High rate of sedimentation
Laminated deposits	Usually no laminated sediments (horizontal layering)
Hardly any lateral changes in facies	Lentoid layers, often cannot be traced over long stretches, frequent lateral changes in facies

Table 5.1. Summary table listing the characteristics of the depositional milieu in the profundal and littoral zones.

layers, and clay features, unless the site silted and sealed up quickly, as was, for instance, the case at Arbon-Bleiche 3. A look at the settlements in the Federsee bog, with its excellently preserved features that included entire house floors (Schlichtherle 2004), clearly shows how much information has been lost on the architecture of the houses and the lifestyles of their inhabitants around the hydrologically more active lakes in the Swiss Pre-Alps (such as Lake Constance and Lake Zurich). Preliminary studies have shown that it is around these lakes in particular that geoarchaeological – and specifically micromorphological – analyses can help make the most of the available information (Wallace 1999, 2003a) that cannot be detected macroscopically.

This is mainly based on the fact that deposits at archaeological sites not only bear information in the shape of finds, macro-remains, and animal bones but that the sites themselves can be bearers of information. It is possible by micromorphological means to recognise seemingly unremarkable stratigraphical changes caused by pedogenic, geological, and anthropogenic processes/events and to attribute the changes to these processes. Therefore, one can view the anthropogenically impacted sediments, and the finds and features within them, as part of the 'archaeological memory' (Altekamp 2004), which needs to be deciphered. However, it must be borne in mind that this process of decipherment is by no means simple, as past behaviour cannot directly be deduced from archaeological material. It is often overlooked that this material was, as a rule, gradually 'discarded' or abandoned and is thus today found outside of its normal context of utilisation (Bernbeck 1997: 66–67). The patchy nature of the 'archaeological memory' inevitably results in a gap between the theoretical concepts and the actual archaeological data. Researchers in the English-speaking tradition have attempted to bridge this gap in two different ways (Bernbeck 1997: 65): both the middle-range theory applied by Binford (1977: 6–8) and the treatises on formation processes developed by Schiffer (1983) deal with the nature of the archaeological data. They both consider it crucially important to study the processes that led to the formation of archaeological features (Eggert 2001: 350). Other researchers have attempted to bridge the problematic gaps in the theoretical concepts by following systems-theoretical lines of approach (Bernbeck 1997: 109–129).

The New Archaeology of the early 1960s (*e.g.* Binford 1962) adopted many of its theoretical ideas from the natural sciences (Bernbeck 1997: 65). This is also reflected in Clarke's 'Analytical Archaeology' (1978), first published in England in the late 1960s. The most important objective of the middle-range theory, however, was to link the static archaeological context with the dynamics of the past cultural system within which it was formed (Bernbeck 1997: 66). Before studying the past cultural system, one must first study the processes that produced the archaeological context. Schiffer presented the most comprehensive overview on his theories, which he first introduced and further developed in many articles, in two textbook treatises, although these theories are still being developed and adapted (LaMotta and Schiffer 2001). One of the two works was entitled 'Behavioral Archaeology' (Schiffer 1976), and was closely intertwined with Schiffer's second broad topic: the formation processes (Schiffer 1987). The latter comprises a theoretical approach that is intended to facilitate the link between the 'reality' of the archaeological data and Schiffer's behavioural archaeology. Although formation processes cannot be considered an invention of behavioural archaeology (Schiffer *et al.* 2010: 31), the theory has largely been established in archaeological research. While Schiffer's approach was adopted by geoarchaeologists and ultimately provided the theoretical framework for the natural and cultural formation processes discussed in this chapter, his theories were not met with a positive response by theoretical archaeologists. Schiffer is mainly lauded for the fact that he recognised the impact of natural processes on archaeological features. However, as it was not his main objective to study natural transforms, Schiffer's behavioural archaeology must not be neglected. On the contrary, the natural transforms actually disguise the cultural transforms that are really important to his approach (see below), as they ultimately speak to the behaviour exhibited by human beings. While this 'behaviouristic' approach was and continues to be advocated by Schiffer and his pupils/colleagues (LaMotta and Schiffer 2001), it has not become established to the same extent as formation processes have. By the time Schiffer's book was published (Schiffer 1987), theoretical archaeologists had already begun to move towards post-processual archaeology, replacing the systemic approach with a perspective orientated more towards symbols and the individual. Although Schiffer's work can assist in providing a theoretical framework for micromorphological results, the following fact must not be forgotten among all the theoretical reflections:

> 'geoarchaeology, like geology and archaeology, is a field-based endeavour that relies on empirical data. No matter how much we might like to theorise in either discipline, the bottom line is that we are constrained by the observations we make first in the field and later in the laboratory' (Goldberg and Macphail 2006: 28).

What can micromorphology contribute? Macphail *et al.* (1990: 168) specifically state with regard to microscopic studies of sediments that the reconstruction of layer-formation processes is one of the crucial areas where micromorphological research can make a contribution towards understanding a site. This comprises not only questions of preservation, but can also provide essential clues concerning the biography (or taphonomy) of a site. According to Schiffer, the aim must be to decipher the natural and cultural transforms of a deposit at the microscopic level. Incidentally, one must bear in mind the definitions of formation processes and taphonomy, as the latter in particular is not always applied very concisely in archaeological research (Lyman 2010).

Micromorphological studies are still not as common as they perhaps should be in lake-dwelling research. Nevertheless, more and more scholars are contributing to the development of the discipline; for instance, Krier (1997) has undertaken off-site studies, and Wallace (1999, 2003a, 2003b), Ismail-Meyer (2010; Ismail-Meyer *et al.* 2013 and Ismail-Meyer and Rentzel 2004, 2007) have done pioneering micromorphological work at lake-dwelling sites in the Alpine forelands. In recent years, Lewis (2007) and Karkanas (2010) have also made contributions (from Lithuania and Greece, respectively) to this field of study.

Approach

In order to study the different syn-sedimentary, post-sedimentary, and abandonment processes, samples were taken from six lake-dwelling sites located north (five sites) and south (one site) of the Alps (Fig. 5.1). The choice of sites spanned the Neolithic to the Bronze Age, because using a long time span allowed us to carry out a diachronic study of the phenomena observed. The geographical emphasis was on the lower basin of Lake Zurich (three sites: Zurich-Kanalisationssanierung Seefeld, Zurich-Opéra, and Zurich-Alpenquai – see Table 5.2), where there was an actual settlement cluster consisting of a multitude of lake-dwellings, which encompassed the aforementioned period. Samples from Greifensee-Böschen (Lake Greifen, Switzerland), Zug-Riedmatt (Lake Zug, Switzerland), and Viverone-Emissario I (Lake Viverone, Italy) were added to this body of evidence.

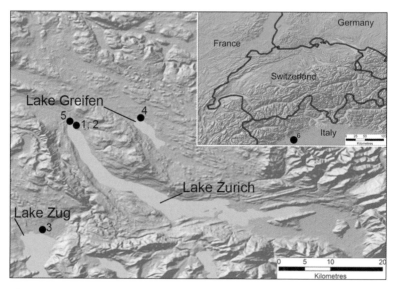

Figure 5.1. The sites studied. 1. Zurich-Kanalisationssanierung Seefeld; 2. Zurich-Opéra; 3. Zug-Riedmatt; 4. Greifensee-Böschen; 5. Zurich-Alpenquai; 6. Viverone – Emissario I.

Site	Country	Canton	Lake	Period	Columns
Zurich-Kananalisations-sanierung Seefeld	Switzerland	Zurich	Lake Zurich	Neolithic	1
Zurich-Opéra	Switzerland	Zurich	Lake Zurich	Neolithic	13
Zug-Riedmatt	Switzerland	Zug	Lake Zug	Neolithic	2
Viverone I – Emissario	Italy	Piedmont	Lake Viverone	Middle Bronze Age	2
Greifensee-Böschen	Switzerland	Zurich	Lake Greifen	Late Bronze Age	2
Zurich-Alpenquai	Switzerland	Zurich	Lake Zurich	Late Bronze Age	2

Table 5.2. Basic information on the sites examined as part of the study.

Samples in the shape of undisturbed columns were available from all the sites. They were taken by means of large window flower boxes (up to 80 cm in length), small plastic boxes (up to 25 cm in length), or tubes (10 cm in diameter). The samples were described in detail and a photographic record was compiled in the laboratory. In the case of the flower boxes, sub-samples were taken by means of smaller sample containers (20–25 cm in height). The samples were air-dried at room temperature over the course of 2–3 months and were subsequently cast in epoxy resin under vacuum conditions. The resin blocks were then sawn into 1-cm thick slices, on which the positions for the thin sections were marked. The thin sections themselves were 48×48 mm in size and were prepared by Thomas Beckmann (Gifhorn, Germany) and Willy Tschudin (Basel, Switzerland). The analysis was carried out using a polarisation microscope with a magnification of up to 630×. The thin sections were described using generally established standards (Stoops, 2003). The comprehensive reference collection on archaeological micromorphology in Basel was also available.

Based on the rather broadly defined aims and objectives, two hypotheses were put forward for testing:

1. The lake-dwelling deposits were exposed to processes of alteration, both during and after their deposition
2. By deciphering and precisely identifying these processes and their causes, it is possible to gather potential clues as to the reasons that led to the abandonment of a given settlement

Site occupation: different formation processes

Geoarchaeological methods such as micromorphology use the deposits at a given lake-dwelling site as an archive from which to reconstruct the various layer-formation processes (Ismail-Meyer *et al.* 2013). The aim is to identify both natural and anthropogenic formation processes, to explain them, and to distinguish one from the other. As the lake-dwellings examined were located around Perialpine lakes, the bodies of water and their immediate hinterlands are of particular significance as sedimentary environments. Limnic and littoral processes can be identified in the littoral zone, with the limnic sediments of the sublittoral zone comprising the construction ground for the lake-dwelling in a broader sense and the littoral processes representing the building ground in a stricter sense. There is usually a marked and abrupt change – sometimes mediated by a so-called installation horizon – to

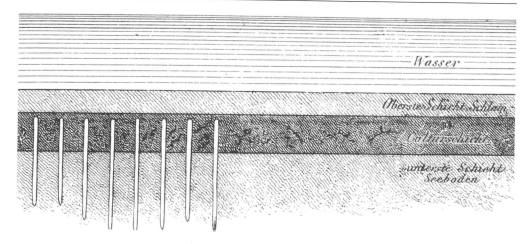

Figure 5.2. Depiction of the stratigraphical sequence of a lake-dwelling site (after: Keller 1854: plate 1, fig. 2).

a deposit that is usually completely organic; this is the actual cultural layer. Moreover, at certain sites, terrigenous-detrital sediments (*e.g.* run-off sediments) point to (periodical) influences from the surrounding elevated areas.

Before dealing with the different processes that contributed to the formation of the sediments mentioned, it makes sense to explain briefly why only the processes (or sedimentary facies and microfacies) are named instead of using the established terminology employed in lake-dwelling research. The term 'cultural layer' (*Culturschicht*), for instance, was introduced by Keller's first report on pile dwellings in 1854 (Keller 1854; Fig. 5.2) and was not only disseminated throughout German-speaking areas but was also introduced into other languages by translations of pile-dwelling studies (Trachsel 2008: 116). In the context of lake-dwellings, the term 'cultural layer' is used for organic deposits that contain finds and were deposited on top of or (more often) between lake sediments. Micromorphological research, however, shows that one cannot speak about *a* cultural layer but that the deposits termed 'cultural layers' by field archaeologists actually consist of complex anthropogenic deposits (Fig. 5.3.A) that reflect the entire sequence of events in the history of a house (Ismail-Meyer and Rentzel 2004) or even of a whole village. Therefore, a process-orientated approach is adopted here, which takes into account the variety of layers that are present at lake-dwelling sites.

Natural formation processes

Because the samples never reached down as far as the glacial lacustrine clays, the formation of lake marl was not only the oldest process identified in the stratigraphical sequences studied but it was also – though not only – found at the very bottom of these sequences. The beginning of the process of lake marl formation in lakes throughout the temperate regions, which continued throughout the entire Holocene, can be traced back to a phase of climate warming during the last glacial interstadial (Magny 1995; for Zurich-Opéra, also Flavio Anselmetti, pers. comm. 2013). It is a very fine micrite with components of mollusc shells and ostracods, stems and fruiting bodies (oogonia) of *characeae*, and sand and sparite chains (Fig. 5.3.B–C). According to Schindler (1976), 'true lake marls' have a CaCO$_3$ content exceeding 75%. They are formed in calm limnic conditions due to the metabolism of aquatic algae and bacteria. This requires water cover of 0.5 to 12 m (Brochier 1983; Schindler 1976); according to Schindler, the 12 m boundary is explained by the 12°C isotherm, which is located roughly at that water depth during the summer months and disappears in the winter. Lake marl can contain a certain amount of sand, particularly near the lake shore, which points to fluvial inwash or terrigenous input.

Another phenomenon that can occur near the lake shore is that the precipitation of the lake marl and the erosion due to wave action balance each other out, leading to the formation of horizontal lake-shore platforms (Ismail-Meyer *et al.* 2013). The areas that are thus created are ideal building grounds for lake-dwellings, not least because piles could fairly easily be driven into the sediment (Menotti and Pranckėnaitė 2008). Climatic oscillations and changeable weather conditions during the Holocene period are generally credited with having a direct impact on the levels of the lakes in the foothills of the Alps (Magny 2004). It is a model that is largely accepted but has met with criticism in respect of smaller oscillations and its universal validity for all lakes in the foothills of the Alps (Bleicher 2013). In any case, there were periods during which the lake-shore platforms dried out or at least ended up in the littoral zone. This can be reflected micromorphologically in a less homogenous lake marl with higher porosity; in mollusc and ostracod shells being affected by microborers (Cutler 1995) and wave action; and in a localised increase in the sandy components. Ismail-Meyer *et al.* (2013, table III) published criteria that allow us to make a rough estimate of the water depth and the conditions that prevailed at the time of the deposition of whichever lake marl is being studied, based on the aforementioned factors and some additional characteristics.

Anthropogenic formation processes

The most important anthropogenic process in the area of the lake shores was clearly the accumulation of organic and minerogenous material, which led to the formation of organic deposits or the so-called cultural layers (see above). The crucial factor is to identify the anthropogenic causes behind the accumulation. This is based first and foremost on the massive input of wood, bark, charcoal, clay, seeds of useful plants, subfossil dung of domestic animals, and artefacts such as pottery or flint.

Deposits that exhibit initial (discrete) indications of such a process of accumulation combined with trampling indicators are termed 'installation horizons' (Ismail-Meyer *et al.* 2013). The term was also used by Pétrequin (1997), for instance, and has been incorporated into the micromorphological analysis of lake-dwelling sites (Ismail-Meyer and Rentzel 2004). Archaeologists often encounter a layer at the base of the cultural layer, whose matrix still consists mainly of micrite but also contains isolated organic remains (*e.g.* wood waste and bark) and tiny loam aggregates. Here is the beginning of the anthropogenic accumulation,

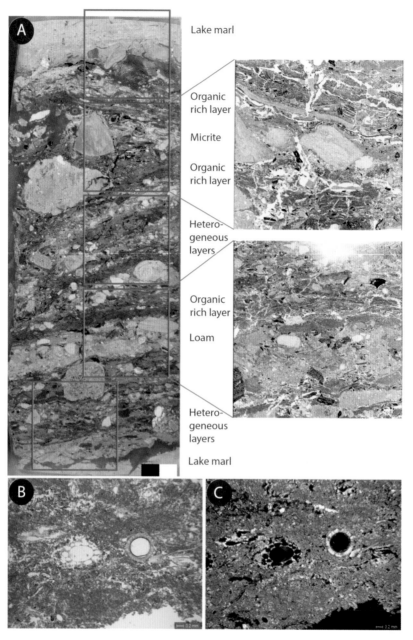

Figure 5.3. A) Sample 2240 from Zurich-Opéra. The impregnated sample shows a fine stratification with many sublayers representing changes in the depositional milieu. The whole sequence covers only one of the various settlement phases of the site. Scans of the thin sections with many details add to the before mentioned assessment of the sample and hint on the potential for microscopic studies. The postion of the thin sections are indicated by red rectangles and the scale bar measures 2 cm. Microphotographs from Zurich-Opéra with examples of the processes and facies described: B) Lake marl with mollusc shells, stems and fruiting bodies (oogonia) of characeae; C) Same picture as before: the micrite exhibits a crystallitic b-fabric in cross-polarized light.

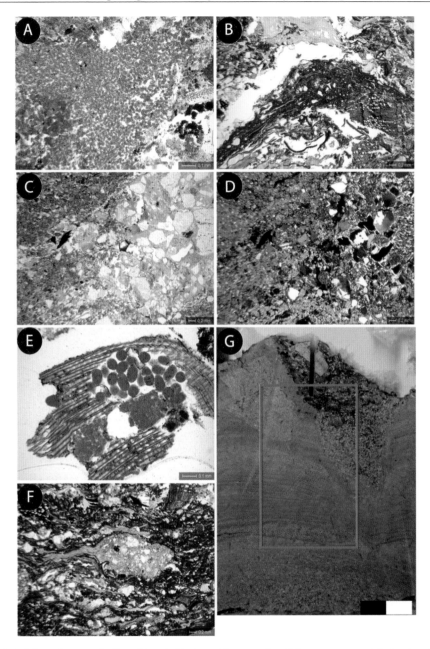

Figure 5.4. Microphotographs from Zurich-Opéra with examples of the processes and facies described A) Organic rich cultural layer with ash; B) Possible coprolite of a ruminant; C) Clayey loam ped (right) in micrite; D) Same picture as before: in cross-polarized light the clay content appears bright yellow; E) Organic fabric with mite droppings; F) Example of a heterogeneous layer, in which loam (centre) is only found in fragments and mixed with organic material; G) Intrusion into the layer fabric from diagonally above, possibly due to the recovery of finds. The red rectangle indicates the position of the thin section and the scale bar measures 2 cm.

which probably attests to the first building activities. This therefore explains the presence of timber remnants and loam aggregates, with the wood chips probably deriving from the trimming of the piles and the loam deriving from the rendering of the walls and the construction of hearths. At the Neolithic lake-dwelling site of Arbon-Bleiche 3, compaction of the surface of the lake marl mixed with sand, loam, charcoal, and bark and indicators of lake regression have been observed and interpreted as evidence of the dried-out lake-shore platform having been trampled on (Ismail-Meyer and Rentzel 2004).

The highly organic deposit (*i.e.* the cultural layer in the stricter sense), which is clearly recognisable as a dark brown band in the profiles of lake-dwelling sites, has one distinctive feature: it is mostly non-calcareous (with the exception of wood ash). In other words, neither field tests using dilute hydrochloric acid nor thin-section analyses show any hint of the presence of lake marl. This situation was encountered, for instance, at the Zurich-Opéra site, albeit not in all samples. Apparently, the organic remains accumulated without any recognisable lake sediment content. This means that the change from a natural sedimentary environment with a limnic influence to an almost purely anthropogenic sedimentary environment was abrupt. The deposits are composed largely of organic material, quartz sand, and loam aggregates. They are quite heterogeneous, and deposits identified in the field as cultural layers can often be divided into a multitude of microfacies by carrying out micromorphological analyses.

One possibility is that there are layers which contain large amounts of wood remains (bark, twigs, leaves, conifer needles, *etc.*), some of which can be identified as construction waste. Other possible interpretations include firewood, litter, insulation layers, or leaf fodder (Ismail-Meyer 2010). Various seeds (strawberry, raspberry, blackberry, poppy, *etc.*), cereal remains, bones, and fish remains can be seen as the remnants of food preparation or as layers of waste. They are sometimes charred and associated with charcoal and wood ash (Fig. 5.4.A), pointing to midden deposits (Wiemann *et al.* 2012). It appears as though the contents of hearths were disposed of here. Units of organic layers also regularly contain coprolites, particularly of herbivores (sheep/goat, cattle, Fig. 5.4.B) and more rarely of carnivores (dog) and omnivores (pig) (Ismail-Meyer *et al.* 2013). Herbivore coprolites can also be present in a highly fragmented state, in the form of shreds from horizontally dispersed organic material, and are thus hardly recognisable macroscopically – as opposed to subfossil cowpats recorded elsewhere (Akeret and Rentzel 2001). Units of organic layers often also contain loam aggregates in various sizes and quantities, as well as entire surfaces or layers. Loam was used as wall plaster and in the construction of hearths and floors. Loam layers once again provide direct evidence, proving that this was an accumulation of anthropogenic material, as the petrographic analysis of the loam shows that it was extracted from the Al and Bt horizons of a Luvisol (Fig. 5.4.C–D). These types of soil form on moraines, which are present in the surroundings of many sites on the Swiss Plateau. Other sites, however, have also provided evidence to suggest that lake marl was used as a construction material (Ismail-Meyer and Rentzel 2004). For this purpose, it was mixed with sand and fine gravel, which resulted in an easy-to-use building material – the authors assume that it was used as daub.

In summary, a succession from limnic to littoral sediments can be observed within the analysed stratigraphical sequences. In other words, the lake levels fell during phases of regression, thus allowing settlers to build their houses on the flat lake-shore platforms. Both the limnic sediments and the indications of falling lake levels can be attested by micromorphology, albeit the exact amount of water coverage remains hard to determine. Moreover, the thin sections show a first anthropogenic input associated with the process of founding the settlement and with its usually gradual expansion. This is subsequently followed by a particularly distinctive transition from sediments, consisting predominantly of lake marl, to a highly organic layer with only rare lake marl precipitation. The predominant process is now the anthropogenic accumulation of food remnants, waste from construction and crafts, the keeping and feeding of animals, and much more. Fragments of bark and wood chippings may also have been deposited intentionally in order to drain and insulate the permanently-moist ground or to enhance the insulation of house floors. In fact, the sedimentary regime changed considerably from limnic conditions to a peat-like environment, combined with an increase in the anthropogenically influenced sedimentation rate.

Environmental and cultural influence on sediments

By using micromorphological methods, three categories of the characteristics of a layer can essentially be distinguished (Renfrew and Bahn 2008: 242): 1) those related to the source of the sediment; 2) those linked to soil-formation processes; and 3) those caused or modified by human impact. Most importantly, though, we attempt to recognise those characteristics in a sediment, which provide information about its source or origin. In the case of the layer-formation processes, one can further divide them into cultural (C-transforms) and natural (N-transforms) layer-formation processes (see above). Erecting buildings or settlements, or abandoning them, falls into the category of the cultural formation processes, while natural processes subsequently determine how artefacts and settlement remains are buried and preserved (Renfrew and Bahn 2008: 54). Using occupation surfaces, in particular of tell settlements, Gé *et al.* (1993) defined four fundamental processes of human action: accumulation, depletion, redistribution, and transformation. This chapter uses these processes not only to analyse human actions but also to describe natural influences.

Studies on lake-dwelling sites have so far mainly dealt with questions regarding the positions of the houses in relation to the lake water level (Wallace 1999; Ismail-Meyer and Rentzel 2004). While syn- and post-sedimentary processes have been taken into consideration, they have never been at the centre of the investigations. It is, however, of crucial importance to understand the formation processes and to identify as many of the processes as possible that were involved in controlling what exactly happened during and after the deposition. The first question that needs to be answered is what exactly we mean when we speak about syn-sedimentary and post-sedimentary processes. Both terms are taken from geology and characterise processes that occur during the deposition of a layer (= syn-sedimentary) on the one hand and after the formation of a layer (= post-sedimentary) on the other. The main focus of this study is on the syn- and post-sedimentary processes and on examining their impacts on layer formation at lake-dwelling sites.

To begin, we will deal with the N-transforms identified. First and foremost, there is the influence of weathering and the depletion or humification of the organic material. The generally excellent state of preservation of the artefacts made from organic materials and of the macrobotanical remains is only possible because the area was quickly covered (by water) or because the components were embedded in a water-saturated environment and the preserved sediments never dried out after the material was deposited, in some cases over a period of 5,000 years or more. Nevertheless, micromorphological studies on organic layers from lake-dwelling sites regularly encounter short-term flooding, be it by streams flowing from the hinterland or by the lake itself, which can lead to erosion, re-deposition, and/or modification by another sediment (*e.g.* fluviatile sand or limnic carbonate). In conjunction with C-transforms such as local waste disposal, keeping animals in pens, and houses or entire settlements being consumed by fire, a palimpsest is created, upon which syn- and post-sedimentary processes lead to the alteration of the layer that was deposited originally. This can either occur in a very subtle manner and within a unit of deposits that can almost be perceived in the field as one and the same layer (*e.g.* Ismail-Meyer and Rentzel 2004) or it can result in a very clear sequence of alternating layers of loam, organic matter, and lake marl (Wiemann *et al.* 2012).

Subaerial weathering, or the depletion of organic material, was identified more often than one would expect in view of the generally excellent preservation conditions at lake-dwelling sites. Nevertheless, Zurich-Alpenquai and Zurich-Opéra in particular exhibited depletion of the organic material to the point where a jelly-like transformation substance which resembles dopplerite (Stolt and Lindbo 2010) had been formed. Fungal spores and mite droppings in organic tissue and wood remnants (Fig. 5.4.E) are further indications of weathering processes. In order for such processes to take effect, one may assume that the water level periodically decreased. This is probably a reflection of seasonal lake-level fluctuations.

Many of the layers contain plant material in extremely fine particles (less than 1 mm). This matter is called organic detritus and consists of extremely fine organic tissue, individual cells, and amorphous organic fine material – such layers were also identified at Zurich-Opéra. The formation process of such detritus has been compared to that of the upper acrotelm of a bog (Ismail-Meyer *et al.* 2013; Lindsay 2010). During phases of low water levels in the summer, the upper part of the organic layer can dry out, leading to the formation of fine detritus. It is also conceivable that a reworking of the organic sediments due to wave action or a combination of both processes took place. The thin sections of such layers show mainly amorphous organic fine material and individual cells.

Moreover, both Zurich-Opéra and Zug-Riedmatt yielded layers whose matrix was composed of micrite and fine detritus. In the case of Zug-Riedmatt, these layers helped us to separate the four settlement phases identified. A preliminary micromorphological analysis of these layers revealed that they were deposited under the influence of low-energy flooding (Wiemann in press). The botanical results, which identified high values of *Naja minor*, point in the same direction (Jacomet and Antolin, pers. comm. 2011), hinting at shallow water conditions and a calm depositional milieu.

C-transforms are often more difficult to identify than natural processes. Nevertheless, the study recorded various clues in regard to C-transforms. Traces of occupation or trampling are phenomena that are well known from studies carried out on terrestrial settlements

(Courty *et al.* 1989) and have also been recreated in experiments (Rentzel and Narten 2000). Their identification in organic sediments in waterlogged conditions, however, is considered difficult (Ismail-Meyer *et al.* 2013).

The formation of the loam aggregates mentioned can be associated with clumps of daub falling off walls due to natural weathering phenomena or with renovation work, which means that loam aggregates can constitute N-transforms or C-transforms. Furthermore, loam can be present as a homogenous and compact loam layer or as a heterogeneous layer composed of large quantities of loam aggregates, charcoal, and organic remains (Fig. 5.4.F). Layers of the first-mentioned type can be associated with loam floors, stores of building materials, or the construction of hearths, whereas layers of the latter type can derive from the disposal of hearths or (in special cases) from house fires (Ismail-Meyer *et al.* 2013).

Post-sedimentary processes mainly include the influence of water (*i.e.* fluctuating lake levels) on the sediments deposited on the lake shores, and this water often had a destructive effect on the sediments. In many cases, compaction of the organic layers (due to overload) is detectable macroscopically. At Zurich-Opéra, for example, the settlement area in the 19th century was covered by deposits linked with the construction of an embankment, which meant that the organic layers had to bear a heavy load. Similar phenomena are also known from Zug-Riedmatt, where overloading by delta deposits of several metres in thickness led to a change in the organic layers (Gross *et al.* 2013). In most cases, we can presume that the organic layers were fairly quickly covered by water and then by lake marl after the settlement had been abandoned and the lake level had risen. Nevertheless, an erosion of the uppermost layers is usually discernable. Finally, the circumstances would subsequently have stabilised (Kenward and Hall 2000), resulting in favourable preservation conditions and consequently an absence of major post-sedimentary processes of weathering. Still, Greifensee-Böschen, for instance, would later be exposed to perhaps several phases of sinking lake levels, associated with the erosion of the organic layer by wave action (Eberschweiler *et al.* 2007). This was linked to penetration by extant reed roots, which was particularly severe in the samples from this site. Once again, the identification of C-transforms presents greater difficulties than that of the N-transforms mentioned earlier. The records for Viverone-Emissario I show intense phases of artefact recovery by scuba divers (Palafittes 2009), which, unfortunately, probably left traces of intrusion / modern perturbation in the samples analysed (Fig. 5.4.G). Ultimately, all modern intrusions, such as the artificial sinking of the level of Lake Zug at Risch-Oberrisch (Hochuli *et al.* 2010) or the covering of the site at Zurich-Opéra by fill material for the embankment, can be considered to be post-sedimentary C-transforms.

In conclusion, one must ask the question as to whether a lake-dwelling site is limited in its value as a source by the numerous transformations that have already occurred even at a syn-sedimentary level. This problem was touched upon by Bleicher (2006) in a debate on whether a stratigraphical sequence can be considered a closed find after Montelius (1903). Because the decisive criterion for a closed find according to Montelius is simultaneous deposition, Bleicher (2006) concludes that, in this case, a layer cannot be viewed as a closed find in the strict sense. Regarding an entire stratigraphical sequence, however, the situation is different – Bleicher defines a stratigraphical sequence as a deposition over a certain period of time. This is why, in a settlement context, the term 'simultaneous' must be viewed as the period of occupation of the settlement. In respect of the individual layers, 'simultaneous' would mean the period during which the deposit lay exposed. While both recent and prehistoric abrasion must be considered sources of disturbance that, however, possibly only had an effect on the peripheral areas of the stratigraphical unit, it is worth nothing that drift lines, bands of sand, horizontal displacement, and peripheral erosion by the lake on the one hand and vertical displacement by new piles being driven into the ground on the other are no reason not to talk about a 'closed stratigraphical sequence'. After all, both effects occurred while the settlement was still occupied, which is why they can be seen equally as part of the stratigraphical sequence or as disturbances. The identification of these and other effects (see above; Gé *et al.* 1993) provides evidence of a variety of phenomena, including lake-level fluctuations.

We may therefore conclude that while a stratigraphical sequence at a lake-dwelling site is always a palimpsest that was created by a variety of syn-sedimentary N- and C-transforms, this actually confirms the first hypothesis formulated (see above). If, however, post-sedimentary processes with a negative impact have largely failed to occur, they still constitute an important source of cultural and natural history. The aim must be to decipher the different transforms and to associate them with human actions or natural phenomena. In this respect, micromorphology – in combination and close collaboration with other natural scientific analyses – is one method (among others) that holds a lot of promise.

Investigating settlement abandonment and the different theoretical approaches

The one aspect that all archaeological sites have in common is that they were abandoned (Cameron and Tomka 1996, front matter), and this can be seen almost as a prerequisite to becoming the subject of an archaeological study. There are a multitude of ways in which, and reasons why, a settlement was abandoned. An attempt was made in the past to identify these various processes on the basis of archaeological and ethnographical data and to publish them in an edited volume (Cameron and Tomka 1996), although the examples highlighted – many of them settlements in the dry southwest of the United States – cannot be readily transposed to the lake-dwelling sites. This present chapter seeks to examine whether micromorphological analyses at lake-dwelling sites can provide evidence pointing to the reasons and modalities behind the abandonment of settlements and regions. Why were the settlements on the lake shores abandoned at certain periods of time? Can the human actions associated with this abandonment be reconstructed using the analytical methods highlighted here? These questions are based on the ideas of Schiffer (1987), outlined earlier, that it is ultimately necessary to study the formation processes in order to examine human behaviour. Basically, the processes of abandonment can be divided according to the concept of the 'level of analysis' generally used in social sciences (Babbie 2004). The macro-level is the level at which the abandonment of the lake-dwellings is examined as a general phenomenon. This incorporates a certain array ranging from the concept of a lake-dwelling to conglomerations of settlements as well as settlement areas. The meso-level is the level at which settlements and their inherent dynamics can be analysed. The micro-

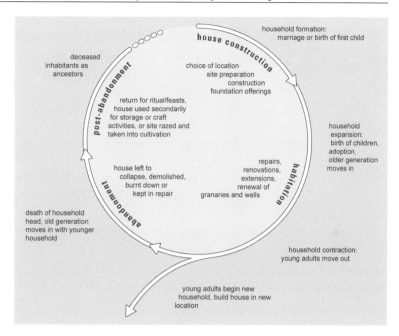

Figure 5.5. Diagram showing a possible cultural biography of a single-phase house (after: Gerritsen 2003: 40, fig. 3.1).

level can refer to houses or house locations (Ebersbach 2010) and also to sample columns. As the term implies, micromorphological studies take place at the micro-level. By calling on other disciplines and drawing on theoretical concepts, but mainly by analysing several sample columns from a settlement and therefore potentially distinguishing between localised micro-phenomena and meso-phenomena, micromorphologists also attempt to make general statements concerning the entire settlement.

In order to bridge the gap between the artefact within a behavioural system and its present position in or on the ground, the concepts of systemic and archaeological contexts were introduced into behavioural archaeology (Schiffer 1972). The term 'systemic context' refers to artefacts and locations at a time when they were still active components in a behavioural system (Schiffer *et al.* 2010: 20). Artefacts that no longer interact with anything outside of their natural environment, products of decay, and other artefacts are situated in an archaeological context. It must be noted, however, that objects can in fact change several times from one type of context to the other and back. Influenced by a paper written by Ascher (1968), Schiffer (1972) developed a flowchart by which the 'lifecycles' of an artefact and its transition from the systemic to the archaeological context can be described. The essential processes it undergoes are procurement, manufacture, and use, as well as potential reuse, maintenance, and ultimately disposal. In principle, these cycles can also be translated to dwellings. Though not directly based on this concept, but bearing certain similarities, Gerritsen's (2003) biographical model for a house was developed on the basis of a study on houses dating from the Late Bronze Age to the Roman period in the Meuse-Demer-Scheldt region (Fig. 5.5). It outlines an example of a possible house biography including the associated actions within the inner circle, as well as the events in the lives of its occupants outside of it. The latter are obviously hardly ever identifiable by micromorphological means.

The actions or processes inside Gerritsen's cycle diagram, on the other hand, can be associated with N- and C-transforms without any major difficulty. An interesting example of a house biography is the study carried out by Ismail-Meyer and Rentzel (2004) at the Neolithic lake-dwelling site Arbon-Bleiche 3. A micromorphological analysis combined with other natural scientific disciplines and, most importantly, with good-quality dendrochronological dates traced a detailed biography of a house that had fallen victim to a fire at one stage, had been subsequently repaired, and, after its abandonment, had continued to be used as an open pen for livestock (see also Menotti 2012: 272–273).

The issues concerning the abandonment and the eventual definitive absence of lake-dwellings in the Circum-Alpine region were traced on the basis of two Late Bronze Age settlements: Greifensee-Böschen (Lake Greifen) and Zurich-Alpenquai (Lake Zurich). While an organic layer was preserved in the Hallstatt B1-period settlement at Greifensee-Böschen, it consisted of little more than coarse components. Bast fibre strings from the lake marl just above the organic layer yielded radiocarbon dates from the Early Middle Ages. Other finds dating from more recent periods were also found in the same context. It must be noted that post-sedimentary processes resulted in severely limited micromorphological diagnostic potential, particularly in regard to the abandonment of the settlement. We must assume that the organic layer was exposed to wave action (several times) after the settlement was abandoned and thus experienced phases of reduction. This was largely confirmed by the macroscopic observations made during the excavation (Eberschweiler *et al.* 2007).

Two main organic layers separated by a layer of lake marl were excavated at the settlement Zurich-Alpenquai (Fig. 5.6). The sequence was divided into four phases, A–D (Künzler Wagner 2005: 14–18). Phase A was dendrochronologically dated to between 1041 and 976 BC. Phase B only yielded a *terminus post quem* of 978 BC, but certain evidence suggested that the phase can be dated to around the mid-10th century BC. Only a small number of piles could be associated with phase C and dated it to between 900 and 860 BC. The most recent date at Zurich-Alpenquai was 844 BC. It is not certain, however, whether it

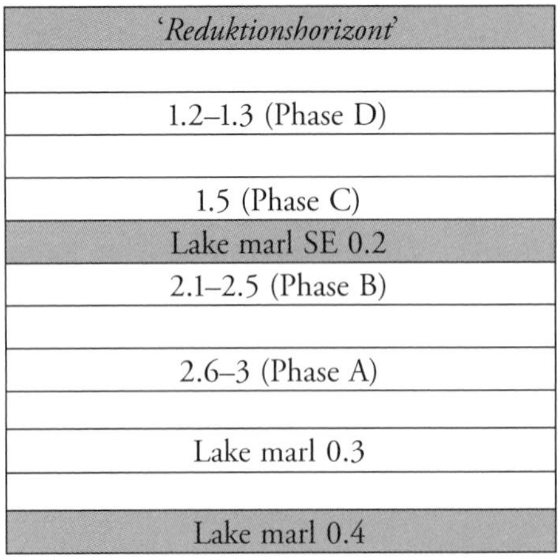

'Reduktionshorizont'
1.2–1.3 (Phase D)
1.5 (Phase C)
Lake marl SE 0.2
2.1–2.5 (Phase B)
2.6–3 (Phase A)
Lake marl 0.3
Lake marl 0.4

Figure 5.6. Zurich-Alpenquai. Diagram of the stratigraphical sequence showing the four settlement phases and lake marl layers (after: Künzler Wagner 2005: fig. 6).

belonged to the upper settlement layer (which yielded another date of 863 BC) or to the uppermost '*Reduktionshorizont*' (condensed layer). The latter reflects the most recent event: the formation of a lag deposit.

The settlement was excavated by means of a mechanical digger in the early 20th century; this was followed by several minor inspections and test excavations, which were carried out by divers in the second half of the 20th century. An area of 60 m² was excavated around the turn of the 21st century, and the findings were subsequently published as a monograph by Künzler Wagner (2005). A multi-disciplinary study (micromorphology, archaeobotany, archaeozoology, and material culture studies) was carried out recently on samples taken during the latest excavations (Wiemann *et al.* 2012), and a brief summary of the results is given below.

The results of the micromorphological and archaeobotanical (macro-remains and pollen) analyses corresponded rather well and allowed us to make statements regarding layer-formation processes and both syn- and post-sedimentary transformations. The results were enhanced by the archaeozoological study and a material culture analysis, although they could not avail the same sample columns and had to fall back on lower-resolution surface samples. Because special emphasis was put on clues pointing to the abandonment of the settlement, the study focused on phases B to D.

The layers of phase B were characterised by high loam content and only a small amount of organic material. Some of the loam bore traces of burning, which, in conjunction with the archaeological features (Künzler Wagner 2005: 14), pointed to a fire. Diatoms were discovered in the upper areas, indicating a stronger influence of water. Erosion indicators increased and eventually the layer merged into a layer of lake marl, which separated settlement phases B and C. While the influence of the lake is still clearly detectable in phase C, it is in fact once again an accumulation evidently caused by human actions (organic material, loam, and charcoal). During phase D, which presents itself as a highly organic layer without any detectable limnic influence, lake levels must have decreased significantly. Organic material including loam, charcoal, and dung accumulated. The pollen spectrum and macrobotanical remains also suggested that the area silted up to some degree. The uppermost layer of phase D showed a slight increase of aquatic plant diaspores, and this continued into the '*Reduktionshorizont*'. This increase and a spread of alluvial forests containing *alnus* and *betula* were also identified in a nearby core that had previously been analysed (Heitz-Weniger 1977). Furthermore, it is assumed that the uppermost layer (*i.e.* the '*Reduktionshorizont*') reflects a settlement hiatus.

Unfortunately, no precise dendrochronological dates were available for Zurich-Alpenquai to create a house biography as was possible in the case of Arbon-Bleiche 3 mentioned above. Therefore, identifying the potential house locations and phases with precision, and linking them with the results from the analysis, was almost impossible. Nevertheless, even the association with the rather vague dating of the phases paints an interesting picture: the four settlement phases and the events of flooding had to be 'fitted into' a period of just 200 years. During this period, the settlement was completely inundated at least once (between phases B and C) for a period long enough for the sedimentation of lake marl to occur. Another event of at least partial flooding could be recognised during phase A.

Short periods of settlement are, in fact, not unusual at lake-dwelling sites (see, for instance, Greifensee-Böschen (Eberschweiler *et al.* 2007) or Arbon-Bleiche 3 (Leuzinger 2000)), and individual houses, in particular, are presumed to have lasted no longer than 10–20 years in the Late Neolithic (Ebersbach 2013). We may therefore conclude that the inhabitants of a lake-dwelling did, in fact, build several houses throughout their lives (Ebersbach 2013). Assuming by way of a hypothesis that the same community settled at Alpenquai over the 200 years (this notion is at least supported by the fact that the exact same settlement location was sought out repeatedly), it must have been a fairly mobile community with 'dry quarters' to fall back on. Similarly mobile communities have also been postulated for the Neolithic (Ebersbach 2013).

Therefore, Gerritsen's (2003) house biographies were played out at short intervals on the lake shores. The resolution of Zurich-Alpenquai as an archive, however, was not high enough to reconstruct the individual processes – particularly those linked with the abandonment of the site and those that occurred after the abandonment – in any greater detail. Nevertheless, the dynamics inherent in human behaviour can clearly be recognised. Dealing with longer periods of flooding must have been part of the oral history of these communities, making such events more manageable. Contrary to perhaps our modern views, having to abandon a house or even a settlement location would have been no disaster but was probably part of the cultural biography of these populations. In terms of the second hypothesis, it was shown that the analysis of a closed stratigraphical sequence (including all the processes involved and their causes) can provide information about the topic of the abandonment of a settlement; however, the resolution of this information is strongly mitigated by the prevailing preservation conditions.

Synthesis

The diachronic analysis of the syn- and post-sedimentary changes and abandonment processes that occurred at six lake-dwelling sites dating from the Neolithic to the Late Bronze Age revealed both similarities and differences. Overall, the organic layers from the Neolithic appear to have been better preserved than those from the Late Bronze Age. This observation is supported by examples from outside the study, though exceptions can also be cited, particularly from smaller lakes (Ürschhausen, Lake Nussbaum, Switzerland: Gollnisch-Moos 1999; Roseninsel, Lake Starnberg, Germany: Schlitzer 2009). This could be explained by distinctive lake-level fluctuations during or after the Neolithic, which resulted in substantial lake marl coverage, while similar overlying strata at Late Bronze Age settlements were exposed to more frequent or more severe wave action (Magny 2004). Another hypothesis predicts that Late Bronze Age lake-dwellings were built in areas of lake-shore platforms that were located closer to the lakes than the Neolithic lake-dwellings and were thus more exposed to erosion (Primas 2008: 33).

In terms of the settlement history, various formation processes due to natural and anthropogenic factors were identified. They suggest that the lake levels sank before the settlements were built and reflect the settlers' actions. The most distinctive changes were those from lake marl to anthropogenic accumulations of organic layers, which very often contained only sporadic patches of limnic carbonates or none at all. These layers represent various human activities. The study encountered evidence of construction activity, food preparation, animal husbandry, waste disposal, and, possibly, disasters (house fires). In general, these events led to an anthropogenically driven high sedimentation rate within a special amphibious environment.

We were also able to show that the lake-dwelling sites were exposed to a multitude of syn- and post-sedimentary transformations (both natural and cultural). However, once the layers of a lake-dwelling site are viewed as a closed stratigraphical sequence, the syn-sedimentary transformations become an integral component of that stratigraphy. The aim must therefore be to study and decipher the syn-sedimentary transformations besides the general layer-formation processes in order to make the most of the potential information of a closed stratigraphical sequence. Various post-sedimentary processes were also identified. On the one hand, they provide an opportunity to verify the sources; on the other hand, they constitute an archive in their own right, from which it is possible to discern specific environmental influences and types of human actions.

Two micromorphologically recognisable processes can be associated with the abandonment of a settlement. These are events of fire and lake-level increases after the abandonment of the settlement, as well as the associated erosion and subsequent lake marl coverage. Erosion, however, makes it very difficult to study in detail the phase of abandonment, which tends to be fairly short. Because of erosion, the final phase might not even survive in the archaeological record – as seen in the most recent phase at Zurich-Alpenquai and also at Greifensee-Böschen. Nevertheless, the analysis of Zurich-Alpenquai showed that the inhabitants of this settlement were increasingly and repeatedly forced to deal with high lake levels between settlement phases, which were long enough for considerable amounts of lake marl to be deposited. This supports the generally held views on the discontinuation of lake-dwellings at the end of the Late Bronze Age (Schöbel 2010) but also clearly shows that this would not have been due to a single catastrophic event. It was, rather, a long-term process, probably linked with other external and internal factors (Jennings 2012), which ultimately resulted in the end of the history of settlement on the lake shores in the Circum-Alpine region. After that period, only limited settlement traces (Gollnisch-Moos 1999: 155–157) or special installations (*e.g.* fishing stations) (Köninger 2001), are found on lake shores.

Conclusion and outlook

The chapter has clearly shown that micromorphology should be viewed as more than just a specialised technique to solve certain detail problems – it should be employed as an indispensable component in the analysis of archaeological stratigraphical sequences. Furthermore, it is germane that other disciplines such as botanical macro-remains analysis, archaeozoology, pollen analysis, and material culture studies are included in the general archaeological reasoning. One has to notice, though, that the highly dynamic interaction between people and their environment (identified, for instance, at Zurich-Alpenquai and other settlements) has shown that while the different natural scientific methods can clearly identify and highlight the phenomena, they sometimes run into difficulties when it comes to explaining and interpreting how past populations reacted to them. This is undoubtedly one of the most difficult undertakings, but an integrative research design that combines archaeological and natural scientific analyses with experimental and actualistic studies, ethnographical analogies, and cognitive approaches can result in a more in-depth understanding of abandonment processes.

Monument conservation is another aspect of the micromorphological analysis of syn-sedimentary and, actually more importantly, post-sedimentary processes, which must be borne in mind. The evaluation of the preservation conditions and site monitoring (*i.e.* keeping destruction/erosion under control) (Hafner *et al.* 2009) was a topic of serious concern even before the lake-dwelling sites were accorded UNESCO World Heritage status. We are of the opinion that, due to its ability to identify these processes in minute detail and to assess the state of the organic layers, micromorphology is highly suitable for the assessment and monitoring of lake-dwelling sites and their significance to our cultural heritage.

References

Akeret, Ö. and Rentzel, P. (2001) Micromorphology and Plant Macrofossil Analysis of Cattle Dung from the Neolithic Lake Shore Settlement of Arbon Bleiche 3. *Geoarchaeology* 16: 687–700.

Altekamp, S. (2004) Das archäologische Gedächtnis. In M. K. Ebeling and S. Altekamp (eds) *Die Aktualität des Archäologischen in Wissenschaft, Medien und Künsten*: 211–232. Frankfurt am Main: Fischer.

Ascher, R. (1968) Time's Arrow and the Archaeology of a Contemporary Community. In K. C. Chang (ed.) *Settlement Archaeology*: 43–52. Palo Alto: National Press Books.

Babbie, E. (2004). *The Practice of Social Research* (10th edn). Belmont, CA: Wadsworth, Thomson Learning Inc.

Bernbeck, R. (1997) *Theorien in der Archäologie*. Tübingen, Basel: Francke.

Binford, L. R. (1962) Archaeology as Anthropology. *American Antiquity* 28: 217–225.

Binford, L. R. (ed.) (1977) *For theory building in archaeology*. New York: Academic Press.

Bleicher, N. (2006) Die Kleinhölzer von Hornstaad-Hörnle I A. Archäologische und dendrochronologische Untersuchungen zur Bedeutung einer Fundgattung und zur Schichtgenese. In B. Dieckmann, A. Harwath, and J. Hoffstadt (eds) *Hornstaad-Hörnle IA. Die Befunde einer jungneolithischen Pfahlbausiedlung am westlichen Bodensee*: 419–454. Stuttgart: Theiss.

Bleicher, N. (2013) Summed radiocarbon probability density functions cannot prove solar forcing of Central European lake-level changes. *The Holocene* 23: 755–765.

Brochier, J. L. (1983) L'habitat lacustre préhistorique: Problèmes géologiques. *Archiv des Sciences de Genève* 36: 247–260.

Cameron, C. M. and Tomka, S. A. (eds) (1996) *Abandonment of settlements and regions. Ethnoarchaeological and archaeological approaches*. Cambridge: Cambridge University Press.

Clarke, D. L. (1978) *Analytical archaeology*. New York: Columbia University Press (2nd edn).

Cohen, A. S. (2003) *Paleolimnology. The history and evolution of lake systems*. New York: Oxford University Press.

Courty, M. A., Goldberg, P. and Macphail, R. I. (1989) *Soils and Micromorphology in Archaeology*. Cambridge: Cambridge University Press.

Cutler, A. H. (1995) Taphonomic implications of shell surface textures in Bahia la Choya, northern Gulf of California, *Palaeogeography, Palaeoclimatology, Palaeoecology* 114: 219–240.

Ebersbach, R. (2010) Vom Entstehen und Vergehen. Überlegungen zur Dynamik von Feuchtbodenhäusern und -siedlungen. In I. M. Matuschik, C. Strahm, B. Eberschweiler, G. Fingerlin, A. Hafner, M. Kinsky, M. Mainberger and G. Schöbel (eds) *Vernetzungen. Aspekte siedlungsarchäologischer Forschung; Festschrift für Helmut Schlichtherle zum 60. Geburtstag*: 41–50. Freiburg im Breisgau: Lavori.

Ebersbach, R. (2013) Houses, households and settlements: architecture and living spaces. In F. Menotti and A. O'Sullivan (eds) *The Oxford Handbook of Wetland Archaeology*: 283–301. Oxford. Oxford University Press.

Eberschweiler, B., Riethmann, P. and Ruoff, U. (2007) *Das spätbronzezeitliche Dorf von Greifensee-Böschen*. Zürich and Egg: Fotorotar.

Eggert, M. K. H. (2001) *Prähistorische Archäologie. Konzepte und Methoden*. Tübingen: Francke.

Gaillard, M., Birks, H., Emanuelsson, U., Karlsson, S., Lageras, P. and Olausson, D. (1994) Application of modern pollen/land-use relationships to the interpretation of pollen diagrams – reconstructions of land-use history in south Sweden, 3000–0 BP. *Review of Palaeobotany and Palynology* 82: 47–73.

Gé, T., Courty, M., Matthews, W. and Wattez, J. (1993) Sedimentary Formation Processes of Occupation Surfaces. In P. Goldberg, D. T. Nash and M. D. Petraglia (eds) *Formation processes in Archaeological context*: 149–163. Madison, Wisconsin: Prehistory Press.

Gerritsen, F. A. (2003) *Local identities. Landscape and community in the late prehistoric Meuse-Demer-Scheldt region*. Amsterdam: Amsterdam University Press.

Goldberg, P. and Macphail, R. I. (2006) *Practical and Theoretical Geoarchaeology*. Malden: Blackwell.

Gollnisch-Moos, H. (1999) *Ürschhausen-Horn. Haus- und Siedlungsstrukturen der spätestbronzezeitlichen Siedlung*. Frauenfeld: Departement für Erziehung und Kultur des Kantons Thurgau.

Gross, E., Huber, R., Schaeren, G, de Capitani, A. and Reinhard, J. (2013) Wohnen mit Seesicht – damals wie heute bevorzugt. *Archäologie Schweiz* 36/2: 29–37.

Hafner, A., Achermann, M., Haab, R., Krebs, R., Matile, L., Marti, A. and Rentzel, P. (2009) Seedorf, Lobsigensee. Erste Arbeiten zum Monitoring der neolithischen Fundstelle im Jahr 2008. *Archäologie Bern. Jahrbuch des Archäologischen Dienstes des Kanton Bern*: 102–105.

Heitz-Weniger, A. (1977) Zur Waldgeschichte im unteren Zürichseegebiet während des Neolithikums und der Bronzezeit. Ergebnisse pollenanalystischer Untersuchungen. *Bauhinia* 6: 61–81.

Hochuli, S., Huber, R. and Schaeren, G. (2010) Seeufersiedlungen am Zugersee: Geschichte und Stand der Forschung. In I. Matuschik *et al.* (eds) *Vernetzungen. Aspekte siedlungsarchäologischer Forschung. Festschrift für Helmut Schlichtherle zum 60. Geburtstag*: 377–383. Freiburg im Breisgau: Lavori Verlag.

Ismail-Meyer, K. (2010) Mikromorphologische Analyse zweier Profilkolonnen aus den Tauchsondagen von 1999 und 2007. In K. Altorfer *Die prähistorischen Feuchtbodensiedlungen am Südrand des Pfäffikersees. Eine archäologische Bestandesaufnahme der Stationen Wetzikon-Robenhausen und Wetzikon-Himmerich*. 86–96. Zürich and Egg: Fotorotar.

Ismail-Meyer, K. and Rentzel, P. (2004) Mikromorphologische Untersuchung der Schichtabfolge. In S. Jacomet, U. Leuzinger and J. Schibler (eds) *Die jungsteinzeitliche Seeufersiedlung Arbon Bleiche 3. Umwelt und Wirtschaft:* 66–80. Frauenfeld: Huber.

Ismail-Meyer, K. and Rentzel, P. (2007) Chollerpark 1999/2000: geologische Untersuchungen. In B. Röder and R. Huber (eds) *Archäologie in Steinhausen 'Sennweid' (Kanton Zug). Ergebnisse der Untersuchungen von 1942 bis 2000*: 80–98. Basel: Archäologie Schweiz.

Ismail-Meyer, K., Rentzel, P. and Wiemann, P. (2013) Neolithic Lakeshore Settlements in Switzerland: New Insights on Site Formation Processes from Micromorphology. *Geoarchaeology* 28: 317–339.

Jacomet, S., Leuzinger, U. and Schibler, J. (eds) (2004) *Die jungsteinzeitliche Seeufersiedlung Arbon Bleiche 3. Umwelt und Wirtschaft.* Frauenfeld: Huber.

Jennings, B. (2012) When the Going Gets Tough…? Climatic or Cultural Influences for the LBA Abandonment of Circum-Alpine Lake-Dwellings. In J. Kneisel, W. Kirles, M. Dal Corsa, N. Taylor and V. Tiedtke (eds) *Collapse of continuity? Environment and development of bronze age human landscapes*: 85–99. Bonn: Habelt.

Karkanas, P., Pavlopoulos, K., Kouli, K., Ntinou, M., Tsartsidou, G., Facorellis, Y. and Tsourou, T. (2010) Palaeoenvironments and site formation processes at the Neolithic lakeside settlement of Dispilio, Kastoria, Northern Greece. *Geoarchaeology* 26: 83–117.

Keller, F. (1854) *Pfahlbauten, erster Bericht.* Zürich: Zürcherische Gesellschaft für vaterländische Alterthümer.

Kenward, H. and Hall, A. (2000) Decay of delicate organic remains in shallow urban deposits: are we at a watershed? *Antiquity* 74: 519–525.

Köninger, J. (2001) Zum vorläufigen Abschluss der Sondagen in der eisenzeitlichen Fischfanganlage bei Oggelshausen-Bruckgraben, Kreis Biberach. *Archäologische Ausgrabungen Baden-Württemberg 2000*: 59–62.

Krier, V. (1997) Premières observation micromorphologiques sur la coupe de Chalain 3. In P. Pétrequin (ed.) *Chalain station 3. 3200–2900 av. J.-C.*: 95–99. Paris: Edition de la Maison des sciences de l'homme.

Künzler Wagner, N. (2005) *Seeufersiedlungen. Zürich-Alpenquai V. Tauchgrabungen 1999–2001. Funde und Befunde.* Zürich: Baudirektion Kanton Zürich Hochbauamt Kantonsarchäologie.

LaMotta, V. M. and Schiffer, M. B. (2001) Behavioral Archaeology. Toward a New Synthesis. In I. Hodder (ed.) *Archaeological Theory Today*: 14–64. Cambridge: Polity.

Leuzinger, U. (2000) *Die jungsteinzeitliche Seeufersiedlung Arbon, Bleiche 3. Befunde.* Frauenfeld: Departement für Erziehung und Kultur des Kantons Thurgau.

Lewis, H. (2007) Pile dwellings, drainage and deposition: preliminary soil micromorphology study of cultural deposits from underwater sites at Lake Luokesas, Moletai Region, Lithuania. *Journal of Wetland Archaeology* 7: 33–50.

Lindsay, R. (2010) *Peatbogs and carbon: a critical synthesis to inform policy development in oceanic peat bog conservation and restoration in the context of climate change.* Available from: www.rspb.org. uk/images/peatbogs_and_carbon_tcm9-255200.pdf.

Lyman, R. L. (2010) What taphonomy is, what it isn't and why taphonomists should care about the difference. *Journal of Taphonomy* 8: 1–16.

Macphail, R. I., Courty, M. and Goldberg, P. (1990) Soil micromorphology in archaeology. *Endeavour* 14: 163–171.

Magny, M. (1995) *Une histoire du climat, des derniers mammouths au siècle de l'automobile.* Paris: Editions Errance.

Magny, M. (2004) Holocene climate variability as reflected by mid-European lake-level fluctuations and its probable impact on prehistoric human settlements. *Quaternary International* 113: 65–79.

Menotti, F. (2012) *Wetland Archaeology and Beyond: Theory and Practice.* Oxford: Oxford University Press.

Menotti, F. and Pranckėnaitė, E. (2008) Lake-dwelling building techniques in prehistory: driving wooden piles into lacustrine sediments. *EuroRAE* 5: 3–7.

Montelius, O. (1903) *Die typologische Methode.* Stockholm: Beckmans.

Palafittes (2009) *IT-PM-01.Viverone (BI)/Azeglio (TO)- Vi1-Emissario.* Prehistoric Pile Dwellings around the Alps. Site Database for the UNESCO World Heritage Application Version 3.

Pétrequin, P. (1997) Stratigraphie et stratégie de fouille. In P. Pétrequin (ed.) *Les sites littoraux néolithiques de Clairvaux-les-Lacs et de Chalain (Jura) III. Chalain station 3, 3200–2900 av. J.-C.*: 37–64. Paris: Éditions de la Maison des Sciences de l'Homme.

Primas, M. (2008) *Bronzezeit zwischen Elbe und Po. Strukturwandel in Zentraleuropa, 2200–800 v. Chr.* Bonn: Habelt.

Ramseyer, D., Lourdaux, S. and Pétrequin, P. (eds) (1996) *Archéologie et érosion. Mesures de protection pour la sauvegarde des sites lacustres et palustres / actes de la Rencontre internationale de Marigny – Lac de Chalain – 29–30 septembre 1994*, Centre Jurassien du Patrimoine, Lons-le-Saunier.

Ramseyer, D. and Roulière-Lambert, M. (eds) (2006) *Archéologie et érosion 2. Zones humides en péril: actes de la deuxième Rencontre Internationale Neuchâtel, 23–25 septembre 2004*, Centre Jurassien du Patrimoine, Lons-Le-Saunier.

Renfrew, C. and Bahn, P. (2008) *Archaeology. Theories, methods and practice.* London: Thames & Hudson.

Rentzel, P. and Narten, G. (2000) Zur Entstehung von Gehniveaus in sandig-lehmigen Ablagerungen. Experimente und archäologische Befunde. *Jahresbericht Archäologische Bodenforschung des Kantons Basel-Stadt 1999*: 107–127.

Schiffer, M. B. (1972) Archaeological Context and Systemic Context. *American Antiquity* 37: 156–165.

Schiffer, M. B. (1976) *Behavioral archeology,* New York, London: Academic Press.

Schiffer, M. B. (1983) Toward the Identification of Formation Processes. *American Antiquity* 48: 675–706.

Schiffer, M. B. (1987) *Formation processes of the archaeological record.* Albuquerque: University of New Mexico Press.

Schiffer, M. B., Hollenback, K. L., Skibo, J. M. and Walker, W. H. (2010) *Behavioral archaeology. Principles and practice.* London: Equinox.

Schindler, C. (1976) Eine geologische Karte des Zürichsees und ihre Deutung *Eclogae geologicae Helvetiae* 69: 125–138.

Schlichtherle, H. (2004) Große Häuser – kleine Häuser. Archäologische Befunde zum Siedlungswandel am neolithischen Federsee. In H. Schlichtherle (ed.) *Ökonomischer und ökologischer Wandel am vorgeschichtlichen Federsee. Archäologische und naturwissenschaftliche Untersuchungen*: 13–56. Gaienhofen-Hemmenhofen: Landesdenkmalamt Baden-Württemberg.

Schlitzer, U. (2009) Seeufersiedlungen in Bayern. Die Roseninsel im Starnberger See und das Problem der bayerischen Lücke. In J. M. Bagley, C. Eggl, D. Neumann and M. Schefzik (eds) *Alpen, Kult und Eisenzeit. Festschrift für Amei Lang zum 65. Geburtstag*: 493–504. Rahden/Westf.: Verlag Marie Leidorf.

Schöbel, G. (2010) The end of the lake-dwelling settlements of the north-western alps. *Scienze dell'antichità, Storia Archeologia Antropologia* 15: 596–619.

Stolt, M. H. and Lindbo, D. L. (2010) Soil Organic Matter. In G. Stoops, V. Marcelino and F. Mees *Interpretation of micromorphological features of soils and regoliths*: 369–396. Amsterdam: Elsevier.

Stoops, G. (2003) *Guidelines for Analysis and Description of Soil and Regolith Thin Sections.* Madison: Soil Science Society of America Inc.

Trachsel, M. (2008) *Ur- und Frühgeschichte. Quellen, Methoden, Ziele.* Zürich: Orell Füssli.

Wallace, G. E. (1999) *A Microscopic View of Neolithic Lakeside Settlements on the Northern Rim of the European Alps.* PhD Thesis, Cambridge.

Wallace, G. E. (2003a) Die Erde als Artefakt. Mikromorphologie in der Archäologie mit Beispielen aus Feuchtbodensiedlungen. *Germania* 81: 25–45.

Wallace, G. E. (2003b) Using narrative to contextualise micromorphological data from Neolithic Houses. *Journal of Wetland Archaeology* 3: 73–90.

Wiemann, P., Kühn, M., Heitz-Weniger, A. Stopp, B., Jennings, B., Rentzel, P. and Menotti, F.

(2012) Zurich-Alpenquai: a multidisciplinary approach to the chronological development of a Late Bronze Age lakeside settlement in the northern Circum-Alpine region. *Journal of Wetland Archaeology* 12: 58–85.

Wiemann, P. (in press) Mind the gap(s): Micromorphological investigations on site manipulation and destruction in lake-dwellings. In *Proceedings of the International Conference Palafitte 2011 – Pile dwellings: investigation, preservation, and enhancement.*

Wirth, S. B., Girardclos, S., Rellstab, C and Anselmetti, F. S. (2011) The sedimentary response to a pioneer geo-engineering project: Tracking the Kander River deviation in the sediments of Lake Thun (Switzerland). *Sedimentology* 58: 1737–1761.

Chapter 6

Vegetation history and plant economy in the Circum-Alpine region Bronze Age and early Iron Age environments: stability or major changes?

Marlu Kühn and Annekäthi Heitz-Weniger

Introduction

The Bronze Age and Early Iron Age (the Hallstatt period) were characterized by highly fluctuating climatic conditions, changes in the vegetation and types of land use, an expansion of long-distance contacts, varying settlement types, and technological innovations. From an archaeobotanical point of view, one might raise the question as to why the people, and in particular lake-dwellers, decided to cultivate new plants, change their farming methods, intensify their approach to their natural environment, and finally abandon the lake-shore and bog settlement areas at the transition from the Late Bronze Age to the Hallstatt period.

By means of analysing microbotanical and macrobotanical remains, the field of archaeobotany provides an important input on the journey towards finding answers to these questions. Palynology (the examination of microbotanical remains) is a way of researching the natural environment; it helps identify long-term changes in the composition of the vegetation caused by climatic changes and/or anthropogenic influences. While macrobotanical analysis mainly deals with examining seeds and fruits, other plant components (*e.g.* buds, leaf epidermises, mosses, *etc.*) can also be identified. In this way, the economic factors (*i.e.* cultural/useful plant spectra, agricultural methods, subsistence strategies, and the exploitation of natural resources) can be recorded and changes that may have occurred over time can be identified (*e.g.* Jacomet 2013; Jacomet and Kreuz 1999).

Vegetation and climate history

Palynology has a long-standing tradition in vegetation history research, particularly in relation to lake-dwelling sites. This suggests that we have a good understanding today of the history of vegetation. There are, in fact, an impressive number of pollen diagrams from the second half of the 20th century, which outline the basic course of vegetation history

(Burga and Perret 1998). These diagrams, however, have one disadvantage: the methods available at the time did not allow the diagrams to be dated with sufficient precision, leaving their chronological correlation uncertain. As a result, they are difficult to include in today's research.

Over the past 15 years, pollen diagrams have been dated more precisely by means of AMS dating (supplemented by examining further botanical and zoological remains and palaeoclimatic data), and have been incorporated into multi-proxy studies, allowing us to draw detailed conclusions in regard to vegetation and climate history. Unfortunately, the Early Iron Age radiocarbon dates fall into an age plateau when they are calibrated, and are therefore not reliable.

This brief overview on the vegetation and land-use history is based on the palaeoecological multi-proxy data gleaned from four bogs at Soppensee, Lobsigensee, Lago di Origlio, and Lago di Muzzano, whose pollen diagrams all cover the period from 2300 BC to AD 800 and have been closely analysed and AMS dated (Tinner *et al.* 2003). The first two lakes mentioned are located on the Swiss Plateau north of the Alps and are typical of central European sites, while the latter two are situated south of the Alps in the border region between Switzerland and Italy and are characteristic of the sub-Mediterranean region of southern Europe.

After the decline of elm (*Ulmus*) and lime (*Tilia*) on the Swiss Plateau, fir (*Abies*) and beech (*Fagus*) became predominant from 5000 BC onwards and, apart from human influence, the forest history subsequently remained relatively stable until the Roman period. A possible further decline of elm around the Nussbaumersee, Lobsigensee, and Soppensee has been explained by human impact (Ammann 1988, 1989; Lotter 1999; Rösch 1985), and the frequent forest fires caused by humans changed the forest-scape around Seedorfsee (Canton Fribourg) from the Neolithic onwards (Richoz 1998). From the Late Bronze Age onwards, beech began to extend its foothold in some places (Hadorn 1994; Heitz-Weniger 1978; Liese-Kleiber 1985). Around 800 BC, hornbeam (*Carpinus betulus*) became established in the colline zone on the Swiss Plateau; researchers generally agree that this was the transition from the Subboreal to the Subatlantic phase.

South of the Alps, however, people had much more of an impact on the forest vegetation from the Neolithic onwards because they tended to use fire to clear pastures and arable land, which led to a distinct increase in forest fires. Fire-sensitive species such as beech, fir, lime, and elm gradually disappeared from the forests and left behind depleted oak-alder (*Quercus-Alnus*) forests. It was not until the Roman period that these species were replaced by sweet chestnut (*Castanea sativa*).

Sporadic pollen of cereals and anthropogenic indicators found at all four sites suggest that human impact during the Neolithic was not very high. On-site studies, however, have yielded very varied pollen spectra, suggesting that the cultivation of land played quite a significant role (Brombacher and Hadorn 2004; Haas and Magny 2004a). Continuous pollen curves of the anthropogenic indicators begin in 2300 BC at Lobsigensee, in 1950 BC at Soppensee, and in 2250 BC at Lake Origlio and Lake Muzzano (*i.e.* in the final Neolithic or the Early Bronze Age). It is only from then on that one can argue that human impact seems to have increased. Around 2000 BC, the diagrams from the Lobsigensee and Lago di Origlio yield higher NAP (non-arboreal pollen) values, thus pointing to large-scale forest clearances. Around 1350 BC, all four sites simultaneously show a marked decrease in tree pollen and an increase in cereals and ribwort plantain (*Plantago lanceolata*), which reflects an expansion of pastureland, meadows, and arable land during the Late Bronze Age. Palynological analyses carried out elsewhere have also yielded evidence of a distinct opening up of the landscape from the Bronze Age or at least from the Late Bronze Age onwards (Hadorn 1994; Ollive *et al.* 2009). The diagrams from the Soppensee and Lago di Origlio show a cereal minimum around 800–700 BC, and a decrease in human impact can be detected.

Cultural indicators once again increased while tree pollen decreased considerably at all four lakes on both sides of the Alps around 650–400 BC (*i.e.* during the Iron Age) (HaD). Meadow and ruderal plants spread north and south of the Alps; at Lake Origlio, these included plants of the pink family (Caryophyllaceae), germander (*Teucrium*), and heather (*Calluna*), while plants of the carrot (Apiaceae), pea (Fabaceae), and cabbage families (Brassicaceae) were present at Lobsigensee.

Oxygen isotope analyses carried out in Greenland by GRIP (Greenland Ice Core Project) resulted in the identification of warm and cold phases and a reconstruction of the climatic variations. The warm phases dated to between 1450 and 1250 BC and to between 650 and 450 BC coincide with the tree pollen minima, and with increased pollen-based anthropogenic indicators at all four lakes (Tinner *et al.* 2003). It is important to note, however, that the warm phases mentioned above do not coincide with the findings of some more recent palaeoclimatological studies. Haas *et al.* (1998) have, for instance, reached different conclusions: based on their examinations of the bogs at the Seedorfsee (Canton Fribourg), Gouillé Rion (Valais), and Lago Basso (Italy, Splügen Pass area) and combined with palaeoclimatic data, one of the cold phases dated from between 3500 and 3200 BP in the Middle Bronze Age and corresponded with the '*Tiefengletscher/Löbben*' cold phase, while the other dated from between 2600 and 2350 BP in the Iron Age and corresponded with the '*Göschenen I*' cold phase (see also Magny, Chapter 4 this volume; and Fig. 2.1).

Changes in the vegetation caused by human impact

Both the climate and human impact brought about changes in the vegetation during the late Holocene. In order to identify these changes and balance them against one another, some recent pollen diagrams from a few lakeside settlements typical of the Late Bronze and Early Iron Age north and south of the Alps have been chosen as examples, and a comparative analysis has been carried out. To this end, the results gleaned from the actual settlement layers, so-called on-site diagrams, were used on the one hand, and pollen diagrams from deposits with very little or no human impact (such as lake sediments and bog sites away from settlements), so-called off-site diagrams, were studied on the other.

The following diagrams were used in the study. On-site pollen diagrams are available from two sites, Chindrieux and Tresserve, on Lac du Bourget in Savoy (France) (Gauthier and Richard 2009; Magny *et al.* 2009b, 2012). An off-site pollen diagram from the bog of Fénay near Dijon in Bourgogne (France) reflects the impact (attested to by burial finds) that the settlers had on the local vegetation (Laine *et al.* 2010). Another off-site diagram from

Lac d'Antre in the southern area of the French Jura Mountains (Franche-Comté) traces the development since the first signs of human activity around 5850–4300 cal BP (Doyen *et al.* 2012). Zurich-Alpenquai (Heitz-Weniger 1978; Künzler Wagner 2005; Wiemann *et al.* 2012) on Lake Zurich (Switzerland) was one of the last lake-dwelling sites, and it has yielded on-site diagrams. Both on-site and off-site diagrams are available from some of the latest lakeside settlements on the Nussbaumersee (Canton Thurgau, Switzerland), which is a small lake in the area of the end moraine of the Thur Glacier (Haas and Hadorn 1998; Rösch 1983; Rösch 1995). The Federsee (Lake Feder) in Upper Swabia (Germany), which is today almost completely silted up except for a remaining area of 1.5 km², is one of the best-examined bog settlement areas palynologically, and it has also yielded off-site diagrams (Liese-Kleiber 1993, 1990). South of the Alps, pollen diagrams were examined from very near a Bronze Age settlement on Lago di Ledro (Trentino, Italy) and from Lago Lucone (Magny *et al.* 2009a; Valsecchi *et al.* 2006).

Listed chronologically, the following statements can be made on the basis of the diagrams mentioned above:

Neolithic

The off-site pollen diagrams attest to only small-scale forest clearances for the Neolithic. Despite warm climate conditions, human impact on Lac du Bourget was still quite limited during the period of transition from the Neolithic to the Bronze Age. The Chindrieux diagram shows no forest clearance indicators, and strikingly few plants of the grass family (Poaceae) were present, while beech forests appear to have been widespread.

Early and Middle Bronze Ages

Variable NAP curves on Lac d'Antre from the Early Bronze Age onwards (from 3900 cal BP) reflect the change in human impact on the vegetation. A slightly higher human impact can also be seen around Lac du Bourget, while a colder and more humid climate is attested during the Middle Bronze Age (1550–1150 cal BC), alongside a decline in anthropogenic indicators.

The Federsee diagrams also show a thinning out of the forests as a result of human activity. The off-site diagram 'Wildes Ried', however, also shows that human impact on the vegetation did not cease between the Siedlung-Forschner settlement, which dated from the Early and Middle Bronze Age (starting in 1767 BC) (Billamboz 2009a), and the settlement at Wasserburg-Buchau, which dated from the Urnfield culture (starting in 1058 BC) (Billamboz, 2009b). Consequently, this attests the continuous human impact and unbroken human activity in the area.

South of the Alps, pollen diagrams from the immediate vicinity of the Bronze Age settlement on Lago di Ledro reflect a considerable increase in human impact, with high values for cereals and anthropogenic indicators. By contrast, fir (*Abies*), spruce (*Picea*), yew (*Taxus*), and elm (*Ulmus*) decreased (Magny *et al.* 2009a).

Late Bronze Age, 1300–800 BC

Increased human impact can be detected during the Late Bronze Age. High cereal values in both diagrams from Lac du Bourget suggest that threshing took place within the settlement. However, the fields were probably not very large yet, and moist grassland is attested for the surroundings. It is not until the Late Bronze Age that the Tresserve diagram shows a decrease in tree pollen, indicating that the landscape had been opened up. Cereals, ruderals, and pasture plants in the bog of Fénay also point to modest human impact in the form of forest clearances and the development of pastureland. A gradual decrease of beech (*Fagus*) around Lac d'Antre allows us to conclude that the forests were thinning out, and rather small-scale and intermittent pastures and fields are attested.

An off-site diagram from the middle of the Nussbaumersee shows only slight traces of the Late Bronze Age. The pollen spectra suggest that pastures and arable land were not located near the lake shore – it is also conceivable that cereal cultivation became more difficult during the climate deterioration and thus decreased. The pollen spectrum of the on-site diagram, however, does suggest that cereals were processed at the settlement (850–800 BC).

Two on-site pollen diagrams from the lakeside settlement Zurich-Alpenquai attest to a changeable history for the period before the lake-dwellings were abandoned. Towards the end of the Late Bronze Age (HaB2 late), the upper part of the bottom stratigraphic unit shows pioneer vegetation on uncultivated fallow land. The settlement was subsequently flooded, and the diagram reflects a regeneration of the forest. High values for segetals and meadow plants in the subsequent settlement phase (layer C, HaB3, between 900 and 860 BC) suggest that the forest was cleared and meadows existed near the lake shore. Varied pollen spectra of pasture plants attest to further thinning out of the forests at the very end of the Late Bronze Age (HaB3, 900–860 BC), which is confirmed by pollen diagrams from the Zurich-Grosser Hafner site. This final phase of the Late Bronze Age, which was characterised by an open landscape, was also a turbulent period around Lac du Bourget – two anthropogenic peaks were separated by a decrease in cultural indicators, allowing us to conclude that the settlement was flooded and its occupation interrupted for a short while. This hiatus can also be detected at Lac Clairvaux (Gauthier 2004; Richard and Gauthier 2007).

South of the Alps, around Lago di Ledro, a clear decrease in crop cultivation and pasture farming and a considerable increase in pine (*Pinus*) can be detected from 3185 BP onwards, and human impact once again increased after that time. A period of climate deterioration is reflected in an increase of alder around Lago Lucone at the beginning of the Late Bronze Age around 1300–1100 BC. These results correspond with other palynological data from northern Italy.

Hallstatt period, 800–450 BC

Changes towards a more humid climate and floods have been recorded at numerous settlement sites and correspond with a climate deterioration that occurred throughout Europe between 800 and 400 BC (see Chapter 4 this volume; Fig. 2.1). From *c.* 800 BC onwards, lake-shore forests with alder (*Alnus*) and ash (*Fraxinus*) became more widespread around Lac du

Bourget. The forest around the lake became denser once again and there is little evidence of agriculture; the settlements on the lake shores were abandoned. People eventually settled in the hinterland, and other lake-shore activities such as fishing became more important. The diagram from the bog of Fénay (900–580 BC) attests to a more humid environment and high lake-level fluctuations, with alder (*Alnus*) declining as a result of the alluvial forest being flooded and water plants increasing – the occupation of the area, however, continued. Lake Zurich also experienced a phase of flooding and widespread alluvial alder forest growth. The off-site diagrams from Buchau-Torfwerk and Oedenahlen on the Federsee show a phase of transgression during the Hallstatt period between 800 and 570 cal BC.

Many of the diagrams show a massive increase in alder (*Alnus*) during the later Hallstatt period, for instance at the Greifensee (Wick 1988), Egelsee (Rüti), Spitzenmoos and Hüttnersee (Hufschmid 1983), and Egelsee (Diemtigen) (Welten 1982), which attests to more humid conditions. A phase of reforestation occurred as a result of this climate change. A distinct decrease in herb pollen and a lack of anthropogenic indicators with a simultaneous increase in tree pollen can be seen in the diagrams from the Nussbaumersee. The area around Lac du Bourget also became more wooded, and there is little evidence of agriculture; the settlements on the lake shore were abandoned. Conversely, significant forest clearances, in areas of varying size, took place around Lac d'Antre *c.* 2700 cal BP, before the forests once again experienced a phase of regeneration around 2500 cal BP.

La Tène period, 450–100 BC

Human impact was once again more obvious and the landscape around the Nussbaumersee more open during the La Tène period. From 2350 cal BP onwards, pastureland was being reclaimed by clearing beech (*Fagus*) forest around Lac d'Antre. These clearances, however, were not on a larger scale than those of the Bronze Age, and the archaeological record suggests that the number of settlements was quite limited, as elsewhere in elevated areas of the Jura Mountains (Gauthier 2004; Gauthier and Richard 2009; Richard and Gauthier 2007).

The water plants in the bog of Fénay declined and alder (*Alnus*) greatly increased locally due to succession in the eutrophic bog; water levels were low and conditions became drier. Human impact is constantly detectable, and the pollen curves attest to continuous occupation in the area.

Climate and people

In general, changes in lake-shore vegetation around settlements and the wider surroundings are repeatedly detectable north and south of the Alps from the Bronze Age onwards, pointing to a series of climate fluctuations.

The Late Bronze Age and Hallstatt period were particularly variable phases from a climatic point of view, with alternating cold and warm phases. Several minor cold and warm phases have been identified for the end of the Late Bronze Age and the Early Iron Age (Jacomet *et al.* 1999b, Tinner *et al.* 2003), which had a different impact locally and cannot be seen in all pollen diagrams. Both these minor climate changes and their major supra-regional counterparts did not necessarily have an impact on the vegetation in all the settlements simultaneously. The local vegetation can have different reaction times, depending on edaphic conditions, the local climate, and successional factors. General statements about any particular region can only be made to a limited extent.

Apart from these minor climate changes, however, significant climate deterioration is attested for the wider region at the transition from the Late Bronze Age to the Hallstatt period. The reaction of alder is visible in the pollen diagrams because alder is directly dependent on lake levels. Depending on the topography and vegetation succession in the immediate vicinity of a settlement, a lake-level rise can cause alluvial alder forests to spread or decline. Many pollen diagrams show a major increase in alder during that period of time. The forests further away from the lake shores show an increase in the shade-tolerant beech (*Fagus*), while oak (*Quercus*), elm (*Ulmus*), and lime (*Tilia*) decreased. A general, large-scale regeneration of forests occurred at the beginning of the Iron Age.

Besides changes in the vegetation caused by climate and successional conditions, human impact was also a factor. The gradual opening up of the landscape became more obvious from the Late Bronze Age onwards. Forest clearances increased, which is attested by higher herb pollen values and a more varied herb pollen spectrum. During phases of climate deterioration, however, pollen of anthropogenic-indicator species often decreased; these included plants of the grass family (Poaceae), cereals, plantain (*Plantago*), and other herb species. While cultural indicators decreased in cold and humid phases on the one hand, the pollen spectra, on the other, point to continuous settlement even throughout phases of climate deterioration. While it was no problem to grow cereals in colder temperatures (Zoller and Erny-Rodman 1994), the increased humidity may have caused difficulties in cereal cultivation. People were able to cope with the colder phases, probably due to their technological advances, though it sometimes involved abandoning the peripheral areas of their settlements for a while; a temporary decrease in forest clearances can also be detected.

Subsistence, economy and land use during the Bronze Age and Hallstatt period

The first overviews on Bronze Age and Iron Age archaeobotanical research in central Europe were published in the 1990s (Jacomet *et al.* 1999b; Jacomet and Karg 1996; Jacomet *et al.* 1998), and they were based on 20 Bronze Age and ten Iron Age sites from Switzerland. Since then, the macrobotanical remains of 90 further sites have been examined. The following observations are based on data gleaned from 118 sites from the entire Bronze and Iron Ages; 14 of the sites had wetland preservation conditions. Despite the considerably improved data sets available, it is difficult to compare the plant spectra. Sites dating from the Early and Middle Bronze Age and from the Hallstatt period, for instance, are clearly underrepresented. The sites are also unevenly spread throughout the different regions in Switzerland, mainly due to urban construction activities and the expansion of the road network over the past 20 years, so the eastern Swiss Plateau and the Jura Mountains are marginally better represented.

This diachronic overview on the subsistence economy and land use from the Bronze Age to the Hallstatt period is based on data from sites throughout present-day Switzerland, divided into the greater geographical regions of the Jura Mountains, the Swiss Plateau, and the Alps (see Table 6.1, at the end of the chapter). In order to ensure that the comparisons are appropriate, data from the final Neolithic and from the La Tène period is used as a reference. The comparison with neighbouring regions throughout the Circum-Alpine region is based on 306 selected sites (see Table 6.2, at the end of the chapter). For an overview on the plant economy in Bronze Age Europe, see Stika and Heiss (2013).

Tables 6.3 to 6.6 (at the end of the chapter) show the distribution of the sites across chronological periods and greater geographical regions (see also Chapter 7 for the geographical locations of some of the sites).

The data gathered from the individual sites was influenced by a variety of factors; the preservation conditions, taphonomic processes, the type and number of sampled features, and the methods of processing and recording the plant remains all played an important role. For a detailed description and discussion of the methods, see Jacomet (2006b, 2007, 2008) and also Jacomet and Brombacher (2009).

All the cultivated plants and the most important gathered plants were recorded for each site, and, for the purpose of the study, the different remain types of the firmly identified species were added together, irrespective of their preservation. The data were evaluated by means of a spreadsheet (Excel) and a statistical package called PAST (Hammer 1999–2012; Hammer *et al.* 2001). Cereals are the most important group of cultivated plants; they are regularly found at the sites and often in large numbers. It is therefore particularly easy to ascertain any potential climatic and/or cultural differences between the chronological periods and/or the different regions when comparing the cereal ranges and the degree to which they were used. The nomenclature of the plant species (scientific names) follows that of the National Centre for the Data and Information Network of Swiss Flora (www.crsf.ch). The English names follow Stace (1999).

Cereal use in Switzerland – changes over time and space

The time factor

During the final Neolithic (2800–2200 BC) and up to the transition to the Bronze Age, barley (*Hordeum vulgare*) and emmer (*Triticum dicoccon*) were the most important cereals cultivated (see Figs 6.1 and 6.2). Einkorn (*Triticum monococcum*) and hexaploid naked wheat (also known as bread wheat, *Triticum aestivum*) were rarely grown. The decline of tetraploid naked wheat, which had begun in the Late Neolithic, continued during the final Neolithic. This wheat was either macaroni wheat (*Triticum durum*) or rivet wheat (*Triticum turgidum*) (for the differentiation between the types of naked wheat, see Jacomet (2006a), Jacomet *et al.* (1989), and Maier (1998)). Spelt (*Triticum spelta*) appeared for the first time at a few of the sites with the beginning of the Bell Beaker culture around 2400 BC (Akeret 2005; Jacomet 2008; on genetics, see Blatter *et al.* 2004; Giles and Brown 2006).

Barley does not require soils of particularly good quality and, if cultivated during the summer, has an extremely short growing season. Moreover, it is resistant to the cold and immune to heat and drought. These features make it particularly suitable for cultivation in marginal areas and elevations, for instance on high ground or in summer-dry regions

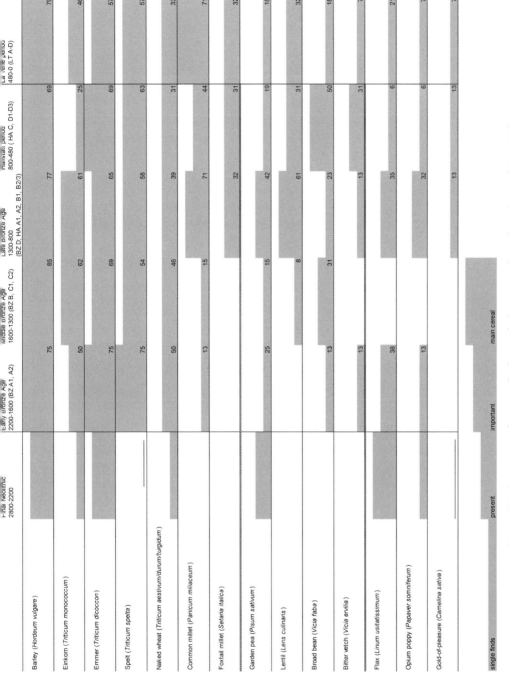

Figure 6.1. Swiss sites: ubiquity of cultivated plants, per chronological period (n = 96).

(Jacomet *et al.* 1989; Schilperoord 2012). Emmer can be grown in winter and summer – in temperate humid climates, however, summer cultivation is better because of its sensitivity to frost. Emmer prefers a rather dry climate with short, hot summers and does not require very good-quality soils. Einkorn can also be grown in both winter and summer; it is quite resistant to the cold and can be grown in poor-quality soils. Hexaploid bread wheat thrives in colder temperate zones, and it requires more nutrient-rich soils than glume wheats (spelt, emmer, and einkorn). Tetraploid naked wheat is better grown in the summer because of its low resistance to the cold. Finally, spelt is a typical winter grain as it is not very sensitive to frost and does not require high-quality soils.

During the Bronze Age and Hallstatt period, barley was the most important grain besides emmer and spelt (see Figs 6.1 and 6.2). Not only does barley exhibit high ubiquity but it is also usually found in large quantities. Besides barley and emmer, the 'newcomer' spelt became widespread during the Early Bronze Age and quickly became one of the most important cereals cultivated. Einkorn and naked wheat are regularly found, although naked wheat in rather limited quantities.

The earliest Swiss find of common millet was made at the Early Bronze Age site of Spiez-Einigen (Bern – Switzerland) (Cooper *et al.* 2010). Common millet (*Panicum miliaceum*) and foxtail millet (*Setaria italica*) were important Bronze Age introductions – they originated in China and gradually moved west over the course of the Neolithic (see various authors in Colledge and Conolly 2007). Millet is not resistant to the cold and therefore cannot be cultivated at high altitudes. However, it only needs a little soil moisture, which makes it particularly suitable to summer-dry regions, and, because it has a very short growing season, it can be combined with a preceding or following crop (broad beans and garden peas are for instance particularly well suited as preceding crops, because they are unsusceptible to the cold and can thus be sown early in the year and harvested at the beginning of summer). Furthermore, as its seeds are very small, millet requires a carefully prepared seed bed with even, fluffy soil. It must also be hoed and weeded several times; as a result, it would have been cultivated in garden-like cultivated areas – as opposed to the other cereals.

The so-called 'new glume wheat', which was first cultivated in other regions (*e.g.* Lavagnone and Lucone, Italy – Perego, in preparation; Clermont-Ferrand Le Petit Beaulieu/ Puy Long, France – Durand and Thirault, pers. comm. 2013) from the Early Bronze Age onwards, has not, as yet, been found in Switzerland.

A slight decrease in the ubiquity of emmer and spelt can be observed during the Middle Bronze Age. Emmer continued to be found in large quantities, while the amounts of spelt decreased compared to the Early Bronze Age sites. Einkorn, on the other hand, became more important. A small number of grains of common millet were found at Rekingen AG Bierkeller (Jacomet and Brombacher 1995), while a considerable number came to light at Payerne (Vaud) En Planeise (Jacquat 2012). Barley and millet were the main cereals cultivated in the Late Bronze Age: both show high ubiquity values and are found in large quantities (see Figs 6.1 and 6.2). All glume wheats were also important; they have high ubiquity values and are sometimes found in quite large quantities. Foxtail millet was a new species (in the Late Bronze Age) that occurred at several sites. During the Hallstatt period, the cereals of barley, emmer, and spelt remained the main cereals cultivated, while emmer was in decline.

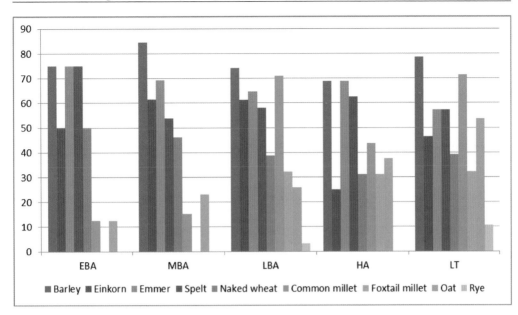

Figure 6.2. Swiss sites: ubiquity of main cereal species, per chronological period (n = 96). Key: EBA = Early Bronze Age; MBA = Middle Bronze Age; LBA = Late Bronze Age; HA = Hallstatt period; LT = La Tène period.

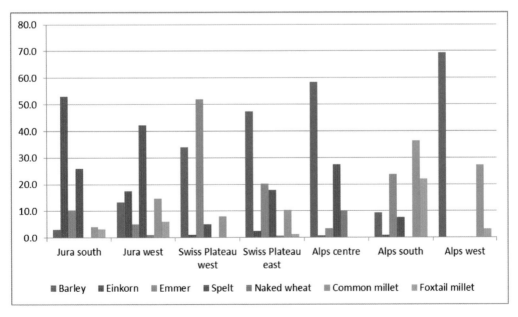

Figure 6.3. Swiss sites: proportion of cereal species cultivated regionally (sites with ≥50 cereal remains; data from La Tène period sites excluded; n = 43).

Einkorn was also decreasing everywhere, except at the southern foot of the Jura Mountains (see below). Common millet also experienced a slight decline. The diversity of cultivated plants considerably increased during the La Tène period. Barley – together with common millet – was one of the main crops, but glume wheats also played a fairly important role. A newly cultivated cereal from the La Tène period onwards was oat (*Avena sativa*). Individual finds of rye (*Secale cereale*) also occurred, although its cultivation in Switzerland before the Roman period has yet to be proven.

Apart from the new species (common millet and foxtail millet), the chronological differences in the cereal spectra remained small until the beginning of the La Tène period – cultivation of the established species of barley, emmer, spelt, and einkorn continued, and the percentages of large-fruited cereals hardly changed in relation to the dating of the sites.

The space factor

As pointed out above, barley was generally cultivated throughout Switzerland and was usually the main cereal grown (see Fig. 6.3). On the western Swiss Plateau, barley was paired with emmer and/or spelt and millet – einkorn and naked wheat were more rarely grown. The western Swiss Plateau is characterised by fertile soils and favourable climate conditions, which allowed farmers to concentrate on one or two main cereals without running the risk of losing significant amounts of the harvest due to extreme short-term weather fluctuations.

On the eastern Swiss Plateau, barley was also the most important cereal cultivated. It was associated with emmer and/or spelt, as well as one or (often) two other cereals (einkorn, millet, or naked wheat). The cultivation of frost-sensitive emmer played a less important role on the eastern Swiss Plateau, where the climate was not as favourable as on the western Swiss Plateau. Crop diversity served to minimise risks (see Kreuz and Schäfer 2008) and to guarantee a decent harvest, even with short spells of extreme weather conditions.

The cereal spectrum in the Jura region was slightly different (see Fig. 6.3). While barley was also cultivated there, the main cereals were einkorn and spelt. Emmer also played a much less significant role than on the Swiss Plateau, possibly due to its higher susceptibility to the cold. The climate along the southern foot of the Jura Mountains was milder, allowing farmers to concentrate on the cultivation of two cereal species, with einkorn being the main one before spelt. The latter was predominant in the north-western parts of the Jura region, where the risks were minimised by crop diversity (including einkorn, emmer, and both species of millet). Sites located south of the Alps (*e.g.* Fiavè, Lake Carera, Italy – Jones and Rowley-Conwy 1984, 1985; Lavagnone and Lucone, Italy – Perego, in preparation) yielded higher percentages of einkorn. This unusual emphasis on einkorn – at the southern foot of the Jura Mountains in particular – possibly points to an intensive cultural exchange with southern populations.

Very few sites in the Alps have been archaeobotanically examined (see Jacomet *et al.* 1999a). Three regions can currently be distinguished based on the range of species. The first is the central Alpine sites in the Grisons (GR), which exhibit a dominance of barley followed by spelt – both species are characterised by low requirements in regard to their location and can be grown on higher ground. Other types of cereal (such as einkorn and emmer) do not perform very well in extreme conditions, particularly on higher ground, and this is probably the reason why they played a minor role in the central Alpine sites. Naked wheat was only found at Scuol-Munt Baselgia (GR), and it was possibly cultivated only in fields located on lower ground (Hopf 1983; Jacomet *et al.* 1999a). Regarding the second region, in Ticino (TI) (especially at Roveredo, located at an altitude of 298m a.s.l. – see Brombacher 2008), millet species constituted almost 60% of the cereal grown, followed by emmer – barley only played a minor role. Finally, the third region is Valais, where the site of Brig-Glis/Waldmatte (Switzerland) (Curdy *et al.* 1993, 1998), is situated in an inner Alpine dry valley with warm and dry summers; this site yielded barley and millet, while other species were absent. Cultivated as summer crops, both taxa have a short growing season and are resistant to drought.

Other cultivated plants

Pulses and oil/fibre plants are generally not very likely to be identified in the records (see, for instance, Jacomet 2007, 2013); this results in the frequent underestimation of their importance for the human diet and as a raw material resource (see Fig. 6.1).

The garden pea (*Pisum sativum*) was regularly cultivated as early as the Neolithic. The earliest evidence of broad bean (*Vicia faba*) and lentil (*Lens culinaris*) in the Alpine settlements, on the other hand, starts from the Early and Middle Bronze Age (*e.g.* Savognin-Padnal (Grison) – Jacomet *et al.* 1999a; Bartholomäberg Friaga, Vorarlberg (Austria) – Schmidl and Oeggl 2005). From the Late Bronze Age onwards, all three pulses were well established north of the Alps. Broad bean and garden pea are extremely weather resistant and are well suited to being cultivated on higher ground.

The oldest known finds of bitter vetch (*Vicia ervilia*) come from the Early Bronze Age site of Bevaix/Treytel-À Sugiez (Neuchâtel) (Akeret and Geith-Chauvière 2011a; Akeret and Geith-Chauvière 2011b). Individual finds within the Late Bronze Age contexts are found throughout Switzerland, but their limited numbers suggest that bitter vetch grew as a weed among other pulses or in fields of grain. Only in the Hallstatt period did its cultivation become more regular, and two sites actually yielded quite large amounts (Brig-Glis/Waldmatte (Valais) – Curdy *et al.* 1993; Cortaillod-Champ Basset (Neuchâtel) – Akeret and Geith-Chauvière 2011b; and pers. comm. 2013); this suggests a localized cultivation. In the La Tène period, bitter vetch almost completely disappeared from the records. The plant originated from the Mediterranean region and is regularly found in Neolithic and Bronze Age settlements in the Balkans and in Turkey.

Flax (*Linum usitatissimum*) and opium poppy (*Papaver somniferum*) appear to have played a less important role during the Metal Ages than they did at the end of the Neolithic. Their absence from Middle Bronze Age settlements is probably due to the limited number of sites during that period and poor preservation conditions in mineral soils. Gold-of-pleasure (*Camelina sativa*) began to occur from the Late Bronze Age onwards but in very limited quantities, and it is difficult to conclude whether it was grown and used on a regular basis.

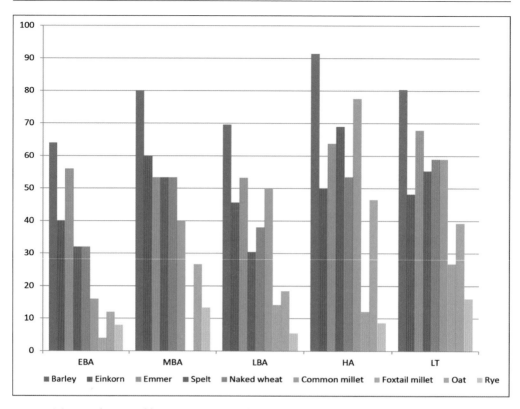

Figure 6.4. Sites from neighbouring countries: ubiquity of main cereal species, per chronological period (n = 243). Key: EBA = Early Bronze Age; MBA = Middle Bronze Age; LBA = Late Bronze Age; HA = Hallstatt period; LT = La Tène period.

While they were regularly found in Neolithic sites (particularly lake-dwellings) north of the Alps, celery (*Apium graveolens*) and dill (*Anethum graveolens*) had disappeared by the Bronze Age (see Jacomet 2006b, 2007; Jacomet and Karg 1996; Jacomet *et al.* 1998), with the only exception at the Late Bronze Age site Zurich-Alpenquai. Perhaps they were too complicated to grow or did not appeal to the (cultural) taste preferences of the Bronze Age populations.

The seeds and fruits of woad (*Isatis tinctoria*) found at the Late Bronze Age settlement of Zurich-Alpenquai can be viewed as evidence of contact with the Mediterranean region (see Hall 1995; Hegi 1958; Wiemann *et al.* 2012; Zech-Matterne and Leconte 2010). Woad originates from the Mediterranean region and western Asia, and it is a ruderal plant that grows in dry and sunny places such as on wasteland and fallows, as well as on poor grassland. Archaeological evidence in the form of seeds, fruits, dyed textiles, and mills is quite rare. Evidence for woad in central Europe includes blue-dyed fibres from the Late Neolithic cave l'Adaouste (Bouches-du-Rhône, Provence-Alpes-Côte d'Azur, France) and woad-dyed woollen textile fragments from the Bronze Age and Iron Age (1400–400 BC) salt mines in Hallstatt, Austria. Dyed textiles and plant parts (seeds, fruits, fruit stems, and

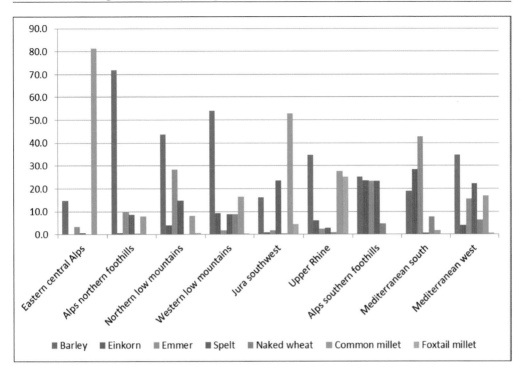

Figure 6.5. Sites from neighbouring countries: proportion of cereal species cultivated regionally (sites with ≥ 50 cereal remains; data from La Tène period sites excluded; n = 56).

impressions on pottery) are more often found in archaeological contexts dating from the Iron Age onwards. Over the course of the La Tène period and under increasing Roman influence, the diversity of garden plants (vegetables, herbs, and spices) and cultivated fruit increased considerably (see Jacomet and Brombacher 2009).

In regard to cultivated plants, one may state that the established species (including barley, emmer, spelt, einkorn, and garden pea) continued to be grown. The choice of which cultivated cereal species were chosen and combined with one another in any particular area would largely have depended on the environmental and topographical conditions. The sites were clearly more discriminated by the 'space' variable than the 'time' variable. However, from the Late Bronze Age onwards, diversity among the range of cultivated plants became more pronounced, even though the whole process had already begun in the Early Bronze Age. It is interesting to notice that plants such as common millet, foxtail millet, broad bean, lentil, bitter vetch, and woad all point to exchange/trade/contact with southern and south-eastern cultural groups.

The position of Swiss cultivated plant spectra in the Circum-Alpine context

The neighbouring countries exhibit a similar trend in regard to their cereal spectra as can be seen at the Swiss sites: regional differences (*e.g.* environment and topography) have a greater impact on the range of uses for the large-fruited cereals than chronological differences (see Figs 6.4 and 6.5).

In all the regions studied, barley was the most important or at least one of the most important cereals; it was grown together with emmer, einkorn, spelt, naked wheat, and millets in various quantities. In the northern foothills of the Alps (Germany: southern Baden-Württemberg and southern Bavaria) and in the northern low mountain regions (Germany: northern Baden-Württemberg, Saarland, and Rhineland-Palatinate; France: Lorraine), barley was grown in combination with emmer and the 'uncomplicated spelt'. The spectra in both regions can be compared with that of the eastern Swiss Plateau (see above), which also had great cereal diversity that included barley and spelt. In the western low mountain regions (France: mainly Bourgogne), all wheat species (einkorn, spelt, naked wheat, and emmer) were cultivated alongside barley, although emmer was not grown as often as in the northern low mountain regions. It remains unclear how the unusual spectra in the south-western Jura (France: Franche-Comté and Rhône-Alpes) and Upper Rhine regions (France: Alsace; Germany: western Baden-Württemberg) should be interpreted.

Similarly to the central and western Alpine sites in Switzerland, the eastern central Alps (Austria: Vorarlberg; Italy: Trentino-Alto Adige), only represented by two sites, also exhibited little diversity in regard to the range of cereals cultivated there. Undemanding and suitable for cultivation on higher ground, barley was yet again important. Common millet was also identified (by a cereal store in Schluderns, Ganglegg, Italy – Schmidl 2005). Unlike at the Swiss sites, spelt appears to have been quite insignificant in the eastern central Alps.

Contrary to the inner Alpine sites and those located north of the Alps, the more demanding naked wheat was quite well represented south of the Alps. Further studies are required to ascertain whether this referred to both hexaploid and tetraploid naked wheat, as was seen in Lavagnone and Lucone (both in northern Italy – Perego in preparation). In the southern foothills of the Alps (Italy: Lombardia, Trentino-Alto Adige, and in the Cévennes), all glume wheats were grown alongside barley and naked wheat, while spelt and millet are quite rarely found, especially at more Mediterranean sites (Italy: Liguria, Toscana).

In summary, the cereal spectra in all the regions studied can be characterised as follows: the diversity in the regions with a less favourable climate can be explained as a measure to minimise the risks. In regions with a favourable climate (*i.e.* the Mediterranean region and the western Swiss Plateau), more demanding species (naked wheat and emmer) were cultivated alongside barley. Farmers on higher ground concentrated on one or two robust types of cereal (barley and spelt).

Pulses not only came into use earlier at the sites south of the Alps (see above) but there was also greater diversity, with lupin (*Lupinus*) at the Middle Bronze Age site of Belvedere, S. Maria, Italy (Carra *et al.* 2003); chick pea (*Cicer arietinum*) at the Middle Bronze Age site of Greve, San Lorenzo, Italy (Bellini *et al.* 2007, 2008; Mariotti Lippi *et al.* 2009) and at the Late Bronze Age site of Leghorn, Stagno, Italy (*e.g.* Bellini *et al.* 2008; Giachi *et al.* 2010); and finally vetchling (*Lathyrus*) at various sites in the south of France and also at Leghorn, Stagno, Italy from the Late Bronze Age onwards (Bellini *et al.* 2008; Bouby *et al.* 1999; Bouby and Ruas 2005; Giachi *et al.* 2010). Because these species prefer a milder climate, they are not very well suited to cultivation in central Europe.

Crop cultivation

The introduction of new crops brought profound changes to the types of land use. The cultivation of the winter crop spelt and the summer crop barley would have resulted in a clearer distinction between the typical winter crop weeds and the typical summer crop weeds. Many new weeds, which appeared from the Late Bronze Age onwards, of winter crops and root crops are now also regularly found, some in large quantities. While a detailed study of the weeds found at Swiss sites has yet to be completed, basic tendencies have already been observed and are supported by studies from central Europe (*e.g.* Kreuz and Schäfer 2008; Rösch 2005, 2008).

Species that were new to the region included bur chervil (*Caucalis platycarpos*), cornflower (*Centaurea cyanus*), fluellen (*Kickxia*), prickly poppy (*Papaver argemone*), small-flowered catchfly (*Silene gallica*), and field madder (*Sherardia arvensis*) (see Fig. 6.6; Wiemann *et al.* 2012). They originated from the eastern and southern steppes and dry grasslands. This fits in perfectly with the origins of the new cultivated plants in the Bronze Age. Like the cultivated plants, the weeds mentioned also occurred much earlier in the arable fields south of the Alps.

The occurrence of these new weeds also suggests that the cereals (particularly the winter crop spelt) were grown in larger and extensively farmed fields from the Late Bronze Age at the latest. This stands in contrast to the findings from studies of the Neolithic, which so far have pointed to a garden-like and intensive type of farming (Bogaard 2004, 2011). Palynological analyses also show a distinct increase in forest clearances and areas of arable land compared to during the Neolithic.

Finds of perennial weeds such as chicory (*Cichorium intybus*), which also originated in the Mediterranean region, suggest that the fields lay fallow for a short while after harvesting and during that time were probably used as pastureland (Brombacher and Jacomet 1997; Jacomet and Brombacher 2009; Kreuz and Schäfer 2008; Rösch 2005; Wiemann *et al.* 2012; see also Fig. 6.6). Palynological analyses carried out at the Late Bronze Age settlement Zurich-Alpenquai also yielded evidence of fallow land.

In terms of the cultivation of summer crops and also the garden-like cultivation of pulses and millets, an increase in the number of root crop weeds can be seen from the Bronze Age (mainly from the Late Bronze Age) onwards. These weeds include species such as sun spurge (*Euphorbia helioscopia*), petty spurge (*Euphorbia peplus*), and fumitory (*Fumaria*).

The (Late) Bronze Age range of cultivated plants and weeds reflects a division of arable land into two areas: on the one hand, large and extensively farmed grain fields that were probably not located in the immediate vicinity of the settlements and, on the other hand, intensively used nutrient-rich areas in, or very near, the settlements where root crops were cultivated. As already argued in detail by Jacomet and Brombacher (2009: 62, 69), this was the first time that cultivated fields were divided in the same way as they would be later on in time; it was, therefore, the beginning of the traditional cultural landscape.

Such new production structures were facilitated by technological innovations. It was from the Bronze Age onwards that hook-ploughs pulled by cows or oxen started to be used. This not only made it quicker to prepare the existing fields but also facilitated the use of,

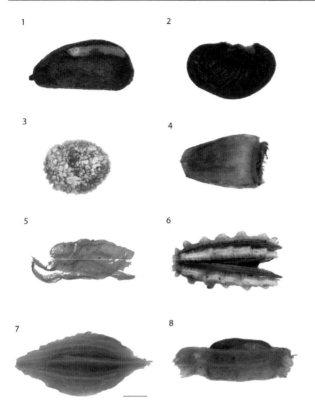

Figure 6.6. Plant finds from the Late Bronze Age site Zurich-Alpenquai, waterlogged preservation (compare Künzler Wagner 2005; Wiemann et al. 2012). 1. Common juniper (Juniperus communis), seed; 2. Prickly poppy (Papaver argemone), seed; 3. Fluellen (Kickxia), seed; 4. Chicory (Cichorium intybus), fruit; 5. Clover (Trifolium), petal; 6. Bur chervil (Caucalis platycarpos), fruit; 7. Woad (Isatis tinctoria), fruit; 8. Woad (Isatis tinctoria), fruit fragment with seed.

for instance, very loamy marginal soils. For the first time, sickles with metal blades were available for harvesting and for cutting fodder/litter for domestic animals.

Animal husbandry and land use

The higher settlement and population density during the Bronze Age not only resulted in an expansion of the cultivated areas but also inevitably led to stronger utilisation of the forests (extraction of construction timber, firewood, wild fruits, *etc.*; see, for instance, Machatschek 1999). Bigger domestic animal herds also meant that enough fodder had to be procured all year round without overexploiting the resources available or causing conflicts with neighbouring settlements due to unrestricted pasture. It is highly likely that our present-day grasslands were formed due to the increased opening up of the landscape. South of the Alps (Lavagnone, Lucone), grassland would have existed as far back as the Early Bronze Age, and this is attested by palynological analyses on Lago di Ledro (Magny *et al.* 2009a).

North of the Alps, there is evidence of widespread grassland areas that were used as pastures and meadowland from the Late Bronze Age onwards. The domestic animals grazed the grassland areas in the spring – after harvesting the grain, the fallow land was again available for pasture; some of the animals may have even been brought to higher ground for the summer months. The grassland plants that had grown in the meantime were cut in the autumn to make hay. This scenario is based on the examination of pollen and macro-remains from the dung of small ruminants on the one hand and from the cultural layers at the site Zurich-Alpenquai on the other (see also Jacomet and Brombacher 2009; Jacomet and Karg 1996).

Cow parsley (*Anthriscus sylvestris*), hogweed (*Heracleum sphondylium*), common mouse-ear (*Cerastium fontanum*), red clover (*Trifolium pratense*), and oxeye daisy (*Leucanthemum vulgare*) are indicators of the use of grassland as meadowland (*i.e.* for the making of hay). Grazing is attested by the presence of species such as crested dog's-tail (*Cynosurus cristatus*), white clover (*Trifolium repens*), selfheal (*Prunella vulgaris*), creeping cinquefoil (*Potentilla reptans*), greater plantain (*Plantago major*), cat's-tails (*Phleum*), creeping buttercup (*Ranunculus repens*), and common juniper (*Juniperus communis*) (see Fig. 6.6; Wiemann *et al.* 2012).

The stricter division between arable fields, grassland, and woodland also resulted in changes to the management of domestic animals. Stabling/fencing in of the animals during the winter and feeding them with grass/herbaceous hay, as is presumed to have taken place at various settlements from the final Neolithic onwards, led to a more regulated and possibly more sustainable use of the individual areas; pastureland, hedges, and forests were thus protected from being overexploited and were given an opportunity to regenerate. A further aspect to housing animals is the targeted accumulation of dung, which could be spread on the fields and meadows in spring.

It has been postulated that animals were kept indoors at the final Neolithic settlement of Alleshausen-Täschenwiesen on the Federsee, Baden-Württemberg, Germany (Kühn *et al.* 2013); at the final Neolithic settlement of Hombrechtikon-Feldbach West (Canton Zürich, ZH) on Lake Zurich, Switzerland; at the Early Bronze Age settlements of Wädenswil-Vorder Au (ZH) and Horgen-Scheller (ZH), Switzerland; and at the Late Bronze Age site of Zurich-Alpenquai, Switzerland (Kühn *et al.* in press). It is presumed that the animals were fed grass or herbaceous hay at all the settlements mentioned, except at Alleshausen-Täschenwiesen. Transhumance during the summer months would also have protected the surroundings of the settlements from overgrazing. It is conceivable that those animals that were not needed in the settlements as working animals and/or a source of milk were summered in this way. Although it is difficult to provide evidence of transhumance by macrobotanical means, we may however assume that, along with the exploitation of higher elevations in the Alps in order to extract raw materials, the utilization of Alpine grasslands for grazing was also intensified (see Stopp, Chapter 7 this volume).

Gathering

As in the Neolithic, the gathering of wild plants remained an important cornerstone of human nutrition in the Bronze and Early Iron Ages. Fruit such as crab apple (*Malus sylvestris*), blackberry (*Rubus fruticosus*), raspberry (*Rubus idaeus*), strawberry (*Fragaria vesca*), and rose hip (*Rosa*) played a considerable role. When dried, they could be stored easily and were thus also available over the winter months. Hazelnuts (*Corylus avellana*) were very popular and have a high calorie count due to their high oil content. Starchy acorns (*Quercus*) and beechnuts (*Fagus sylvatica*) were also regularly gathered (Karg and Haas 1996). South of the Alps, the range of gathered plants was more varied and included species that do not grow in the northern region for climate reasons, for example mastic (*Pistacia lentiscus*) (Sète, La Fangade – Bouby *et al.* 1999). From the Bronze Age onwards at the latest, grape (*Vitis*) and fig (*Ficus carica*) were also gathered (or perhaps cultivated). They have been found at the Early Bronze Age sites of Lavagnone and Lucone, Italy (Perego in preparation) and at the Middle Bronze Age Italian sites of Greve (Bellini *et al.* 2007, 2008; Mariotti Lippi *et al.* 2009), Montale (Mercuri *et al.* 2006), and Lavagnone (Perego in preparation).

Innovation and continuity – concluding remarks

The Late Bronze and Early Iron Ages were characterised by changeable climate conditions (see above) – warm and dry phases alternating with cool and humid phases led to lake-level fluctuations and highly changeable environmental conditions, particularly on lake shores. Regarding the cooler phases, off-site pollen diagrams often show a decline in anthropogenic-indicator pollen such as cereals and plantain (*Plantago*), while their values rise during the warmer periods (Tinner *et al.* 2003; also see above). We may therefore conclude that the climate had a decisive impact on the economy of the population. A fairly prolonged phase of marked and widespread climate deterioration is attested for the end of the Late Bronze Age around 800 BC. Because the abandonment of the lake shores as an area of settlement falls into this period, the climate might have contributed to this abandonment. High lake levels and a climate that did not favour the cultivation of cereals may have resulted in the population resorting to different types of settlements and economic systems. However, even though it is possible that cooler climatic conditions influenced a reduction in the extent of land cultivated, the spectrum of cereal species remained unchanged. Barley, which is highly adaptable, shows consistent predominance during both favourable and less favourable phases. Moreover, less favourable (colder, more humid) phases did not lead to a noticeable decline of millet species, which were more demanding, or of emmer.

Trade and exchange with both neighbouring and far-away populations were extremely important during the Bronze Age. The cultivated plant spectrum and the subsequent range of weeds point to intensive contact with the Mediterranean and eastern regions. This was how common millet, foxtail millet, pulses, woad, and spices came from the south and southeast into the region north of the Alps. Discoveries of these 'new' cultivated plants in the regions south of the Alps and in the Alps themselves often date from earlier periods than those from sites north of the Alps. This indicates potential exchange routes for commodities and knowledge, suggesting that the Alps were possibly 'opened up' from the south (but see Jennings, Chapter 8 this volume).

The aim of a subsistence economy (not only in the Bronze Age and Hallstatt period) was to secure enough resources to ensure that a growing number of people could be fed. Long-established cultivated plants (such as the undemanding species of barley and garden pea) continued to play a significant role throughout the entire Circum-Alpine region well into the Iron Age. Regional spectra, however, were highly variable; which species were grown alongside barley and garden pea in any given region ultimately depended on the localised conditions in each natural environment. The range of cultivated plants that had been known since the Neolithic was expanded by new species and became more varied from the Bronze Age onwards. As the examples of spelt, millet, lentil, and broad bean show, innovations in the range of cultivated plants were quickly incorporated throughout the entire region. The cultivation of spelt, millet, and pulses fitted ideally into the range of agricultural activities over the course of the year. Moreover, greater diversity in the spectrum of cultivated plants kept harvest losses due to short-term climate oscillations to a minimum. All this would have facilitated the acceptance and integration of new species into the subsistence strategies of Bronze Age populations. New cultivated plants, new technologies, and population growth required changes to production techniques, land use, and animal husbandry (see, for instance, Ebersbach *et al.* 2012; Jacomet 2007; Jennings 2012a, 2012b; Schibler *et al.* 1997). The division of economic spaces as we know it today appears to have originated in the Bronze Age.

Our archaeobotanical analyses of pollen and plant macro-remains show that a combination of various factors led to changes in the range of cultivated plants, the types of land use, and the exploitation of new living spaces, which included supra-regional contacts and cultural preferences, changes in the landscape due to local climate conditions, climate oscillations throughout larger and/or smaller areas. Both settlement and population density would have also played a crucial role. It is obvious, however, that one of the main goals of the Circum-Alpine region Bronze Age lacustrine groups was the optimisation of subsistence, regardless of internal/external factors.

Tables

Bronze Age and Iron Age sites in Switzerland

Site (comune)	Site (field/street)	Canton	Dating	Number of remains	Recording of data	References
Airolo-Madrano	In Grop	Tessin	BA	?	q	Della Casa *et al.*, 2009, Jacquat *et al.*, 2011
Airolo-Madrano	In Grop	Tessin	LT	>3000	q	Della Casa *et al.*, 2009, Jacquat *et al.*, 2011
Alle	Pré au Prince	Jura	LT	2859	q	Klee, 2010
Alle	Sur Noir Bois	Jura	LT	9304	q	Jacquat and Mermod, 1998, Klee, 2010
Allschwil	Neuweilerstrasse	Basel-Land	LT ?	6891	q	Kühn, unpubl.
Benken	Hämmenried	Zürich	LBA	377	q	Vandorpe, unpubl.
Benken	Hämmenried	Zürich	LT	24	q	Vandorpe, unpubl.
Basel	Gasfabrik	Basel-Stadt	LT	25097	q	Iseli, unpubl., Iseli and Jacomet 1994, Kühn, unpub., Kühn and Iseli, 2008, Moosbrugger and Kühn, unpubl., Steiner and Kühn, unpubl., Stopp *et al.*, 1999
Basel	Martinsgasse 6+8	Basel-Stadt	LT	3479	q	Martinoli, unpubl.
Basel	Rittergasse 4	Basel-Stadt	LT	55	q	Iseli, unpubl.
Bern-Enge	Reichenbachstrasse 87	Bern	LT	0	q	Klee and Brombacher, unpubl.
Bevaix	Le Bataillard	Neuenburg	EBA	5	q	Akeret and Geith-Chauvière, 2011b, Leducq *et al.*, 2008
Bevaix	Le Bataillard	Neuenburg	MBA	311	q	Akeret and Geith-Chauvière, 2011b, Leducq *et al.*, 2008
Bevaix	Le Bataillard	Neuenburg	HA	1	q	Akeret and Geith-Chauvière, 2011b, Leducq *et al.*, 2008
Bevaix	Le Bataillard	Neuenburg	LT	162	q	Akeret and Geith-Chauvière, 2011b, Leducq *et al.*, 2008
Bevaix	Les Chenevières	Neuenburg	IA	19	q	Akeret and Geith-Chauvière, 2011b & unpubl.
Bevaix	Les Chenevières	Neuenburg	LT	200	q	Akeret and Geith-Chauvière, 2011b & unpubl.
Bevaix	Les Pâquiers	Neuenburg	MBA	561	q	Akeret and Geith-Chauvière, 2006a/b, 2011b
Bevaix	Les Pâquiers	Neuenburg	LBA	2804	q	Akeret and Geith-Chauvière, 2006a/b, 2011b
Bevaix	Les Pâquiers	Neuenburg	HA	17	q	Akeret and Geith-Chauvière, 2006a/b, 2011b
Bevaix	Les Pâquiers	Neuenburg	LT	54	q	Akeret and Geith-Chauvière, 2006a/b, 2011b
Bevaix	Treytel-À Sugiez	Neuchâtel	EBA	2045	q	Akeret and Geith-Chauvière, 2011a/b
Bevaix	Treytel-À Sugiez	Neuchâtel	LBA	1	q	Akeret and Geith-Chauvière, 2011a/b
Bevaix	Treytel-À Sugiez	Neuchâtel	IA	29	q	Akeret and Geith-Chauvière, 2011a/b
Birmensdorf	Stoffel	Zürich	MBA	347	q	Brombacher and Klee, 2001

Table 6.1. Sites in Switzerland. Continued pp. 147–149.

Bronze Age and Iron Age sites in Switzerland

Site (comune)	Site (field/street)	Canton	Dating	Number of remains	Recording of data	References
Boudry	Chézard-Littorail	Neuenburg	LBA	42	q	Akeret and Geith-Chauvière, unpubl.
Brig-Glis	Waldmatte	Wallis	HA	9612	q	Curdy *et al.*, 1993, 1998, Jacomet *et al.*, 1999a
Bussy	Pré de Fond	Fribourg	HA	238	q	Vandorpe, unpubl.
Cham Oberwil	Hof	Zug	MBZ	6683	q	Zibulski, 2001
Chevenez	Combe en Vaillard	Jura	LT	416	q	Brombacher *et al.*, 2010
Chevenez	Combe Ronde	Jura	LT	216	q	Klee and Brombacher, 2010, Schlumbaum, 2010
Cheyres	Roche Burnin	Fribourg	LT	22274	q	Martinoli and Brombacher, unpubl.
Chur	Areal Ackermann	Graubünden	IA	<100KP	q	Jacomet *et al.*, 1999a
Chur	Karlihof	Graubünden	LBA	>500	q	Jacomet *et al.*, 1999a
Cortaillod	Champ Basset	Neuenburg	HA	2835	q	Akeret and Geith-Chauvière, 2011b & unpubl.
Cortaillod	Petit Ruz	Neuenburg	MBA	36	q	Akeret and Geith-Chauvière, 2010, 2011b, Geith-Chauvière *et al.*, 2010
Cortaillod	Petit Ruz	Neuenburg	LBA	336	q	Akeret and Geith-Chauvière, 2010, 2011b, Geith-Chauvière *et al.*, 2010
Cortaillod	Petit Ruz	Neuenburg	HA	11956	q	Akeret and Geith-Chauvière, 2010, 2011b, Geith-Chauvière *et al.*, 2010
Cortaillod	Petit Ruz	Neuenburg	LT	926	q	Akeret and Geith-Chauvière, 2010, 2011b, Geith-Chauvière *et al.*, 2010
Cortaillod	Petit Ruz	Neuenburg	LT	40467	q	Akeret and Geith-Chauvière, 2010, 2011b, Geith-Chauvière *et al.*, 2010
Cortaillod	Sur les Rochettes	Neuenburg	HA	23	q	Akeret and Geith-Chauvière, 2011b & unpubl.
Courtételle	Tivila	Jura	LT	39115	q	Brombacher, 2012
Cugy	Les Combes	Fribourg	LT	2049	q	Martinoli and Brombacher, unpubl.
Dachsen	Langroggenacker	Zürich	LBA	1	q	Vandorpe and Schlumbaum, unpubl.
Delémont	En la Pran	Jura	LBA	5497	q	Brombacher, unpubl.
Delémont	En la Pran	Jura	BA	1215	q	Brombacher, unpubl.
Delémont	En la Pran	Jura	HA	2235	q	Brombacher *et al.*, 2012
Delémont	En la Pran	Jura	LT	698	q	Brombacher *et al.*, 2012
Delémont	La Beuchille	Jura	LBA	662	q	Klee, 2011
Fällanden	Maurstrasse	Zürich	LBA	27	q	Martinoli and Brombacher, unpubl.
Frasses	Praz au Doux	Fribourg	HA	6615	q	Jacomet *et al.*, 1999b, Mauvilly *et al.*, 1997
Greifensee	Böschen	Zürich	LBA	>10000	sq	Küster, unpubl.
Haldenstein	Auf dem Stein	Graubünden	LBA	?	sq	Jacomet, unpubl.
Hauterive	Champréveyres	Neuchâtel	LBA	>10000	q	Jacquat, 1988, 1989
Ipsach	Räberain	Bern	BA	5	q	Klee and Brombacher, 2005

Bronze Age and Iron Age sites in Switzerland

Site (comune)	Site (field/street)	Canton	Dating	Number of remains	Recording of data	References
Langenthal	Geissbergweg	Bern	LT	178	q	Brombacher, unpubl.
Jegenstorf	Kirchgasse	Bern	LBA	47	q	Ramstein et al., 2012
Kernenried	Oberholz	Bern	IA	9	q	Klee and Brombacher, unpubl.
Kleinandelfingen	Boden-Buck	Zürich	HA	20	q	Vandorpe and Schlumbaum, unpubl.
Koppigen	Usserfeld	Bern	LBA	4	q	Klee and Brombacher, 2005
La Sarraz	Le Mormont	Waadt	LT	>1000	sq/q	Akeret, unpubl.
Langenthal	Unterhard	Bern	HA	32	q	Klee, 2008
Lantsch	Bot da Loz	Graubünden	HA	>10000	q	Jacomet et al., 1999a
Leuk	Pfyngut	Wallis	IA	14	q	Brombacher and Mermod, unpubl.
Lumbrein-Surin	Crestaulta	Graubünden	MBA	>1000	sq	var. authors in Burkart 1946, Jacomet et al., 1999a
Maladers	Tummihügel	Graubünden	EBA	>1000	q	Jacomet et al., 1999a
Marthalen	Obere Schillingstrasse	Zürich	LBA	131	q	Akeret, unpubl.
Meinisberg	Hintere Gasse	Bern	LBA	114	q	Vandorpe, unpubl.
Meinisberg	Hintere Gasse	Bern	HA	591	q	Vandorpe, unpubl.
Möhlin	Hinter der Mühle	Aargau	HA_LT	?	sq	Brogli and Schibler, 1999
Mörigen		Bern	LBA	?	sq	Uhlmann, 1874
Münchenwiler	Im Loch 1	Bern	LBA	3893	q	Brombacher et al., 2005a
Müstair	Kloster St. Johann	Graubünden	BA	492	q	Brombacher et al., 2007
Neunkirch	Tobeläcker	Schaffhausen	HA	1389	q	Dick, 1989
Oberriet	Montlingen	St. Gallen	BA	0	q	Akeret, unpubl.
Orbe	Boscéaz	Waadt	LT	12344	q	Jacquat, unpubl.
Otelfingen	Bonenberg	Zürich	HA	260	q	Brombacher, 1996
Ostermundigen	Dennikofe	Bern	BA	88	q	Klee, unpubl.
Ostermundigen	Dennikofe	Bern	MBA	14656	q	Klee, unpubl.
Ostermundigen	Dennikofe	Bern	LBA	0	q	Klee, unpubl.
Payerne	En Planeise	Waadt	MBA	645	q	Jacquat, unpubl.
Pieterlen	Under Siedebrunnen	Bern	BA	281	q	Brombacher and Schlumbaum, unpubl.
Pieterlen	Vorem Holz 3	Bern	BA_IA	3	q	Brombacher, 2005
Posieux	La Pila	Fribourg	LBA	89	q	Vandorpe, unpubl.
Posieux	La Pila	Fribourg	EBA	5443	q	Vandorpe, unpubl.
Reinach	Mausacker	Basel Land	BA	16	q	Akeret, unpubl.
Reinach	Mausacker	Basel Land	LT	26750	q	Akeret, unpubl.
Rekingen	Bierkeller	Aargau	MBA	686	q	Jacomet and Brombacher, unpubl.
Roveredo	San Fedele Valasc	Graubünden	BA	?	q	Brombacher, unpubl.
Roveredo	San Fedele Valasc	Graubünden	IA	?	q	Brombacher, unpubl.
Saint-Aubin	Derrière la Croix	Neuchâtel	LBA	39	q	Akeret and Geith-Chauvière, 2003, 2011b
Savognin	Padnal	Graubünden	EBA	>20000	q	Jacomet et al., 1999 a,b
Savognin	Padnal	Graubünden	MBA	>10000	q	Jacomet et al., 1999 a,b

Table 6.1. Sites in Switzerland continued.

Bronze Age and Iron Age sites in Switzerland

Site (comune)	Site (field/street)	Canton	Dating	Number of remains	Recording of data	References
Savognin	Padnal	Graubünden	LBA	>10000	q	Jacomet *et al.*, 1999 a,b
Schleitheim	Auf der Egg	Schaffhausen	LBA	9442	q	Martinoli and Brombacher, unpubl.
Schleitheim	Auf der Egg	Schaffhausen	LT	4714	q	Martinoli and Brombacher, unpubl.
Scuol	Avant Muglins	Graubünden	BA	2348	q	Akeret, unpubl.
Scuol	Munt Baselgia	Graubünden	HA	>10000	q	Hopf, 1983, Jacomet *et al.*, 1999a
Spiez	Einigen Holleeweg 3	Bern	EBA	34	q	Cooper *et al.*, 2010
Spiez	Thunstrasse	Bern	HA_LT	365	q	Kühn, unpubl.
Sursee	Hofstetterstrasse	Luzern	IA	keine	q	Akeret, unpubl.
Therwil	Baslerstr./Fichtenrain	Basel-Land	LT	8942	q	Jacomet *et al.*, 1999b, Jacomet *et al.*, unpubl.
Thunstetten	Längmatt	Bern	IA	5473	q	Klee and Brombacher, unpubl.
Toos-Waldi	Waldi	Thurgau	MBA	>20000	q	Behre, 1988, Jacomet and Behre, 2008
Trimmis	Kirchgemeindehaus	Graubünden	LT	510	q	Brombacher and Schlumbaum, unpubl.
Uerschhausen	Horn	Thurgau	LBA	>15000	q	Feigenwinter, 1992
Volketswil	In der Höh	Zürich	LBA	1066	q	Vandorpe, unpubl.
Wädenswil	Vorder Au	Zürich	EBA	13683	q	Brombacher *et al.*, 2005b
Wartau	Ochsenberg	St. Gallen	LT	109	q	Heiss, 2008
Wittnau	Hüttenweg	Aargau	MBA	115	q	Brombacher, unpubl.
Zug	Chollerpark	Zug	BA	3176	q	Jacomet and Martinoli, 2004a/b
Zug	Rathauswiese	Zug	MBA	2242	q	Zibulski, unpubl.
Zug	Sumpf	Zug	LBA	?	q	Jacomet and Karg, 1996
Zürich	Alpenquai	Zürich	LBA	?	sq	Neuweiler, 1919, 1925, 1931, Zibulski, 2005
Zürich	Alpenquai	Zürich	LBA	65470	q	Wiemann *et al.*, 2012
Zürich	Mozartstrasse	Zürich	EBA	>10000	q	Brombacher, 1986, Brombacher and Dick, 1987, Jacomet *et al.*, 1989
Zürich	Mozartstrasse	Zürich	LBA	>5000	q	Brombacher, 1986, Brombacher and Dick, 1987, Jacomet *et al.*, 1989
Zürich	Wollishofen	Zürich	LBA	?	sq	Neuweiler, 1919, 1925

q = quantitative
sq = semi-quantitative
BA = Bronze Age
EBA = Early Bronze Age
MBA = Middle Bronze Age
LBA = Late Bronze Age
IA = Iron Age
HA = Hallstatt period
LT = La Tène period

Bronze Age and Iron Age sites from neighbouring countries

Site (comune)	Site (field, street)	Country	State/Province/ Region/District	References	Number of remains
BRONZE AGE					
Kelchalpe bei Kitzbühel		A	Tirol	Oeggl, 1992	?
Neuburg Horst?		A	Vorarlberg	Oeggl, 1992	?
Diebeshöhle Sangerhausen		D	Sachsen-Anhalt	Hopf, 1982	?
Döttingen		D	Baden-Württemberg	Hopf and Blankenhorn, 1983/84	?
Ehrenburg		D	Bayern	Hopf and Blankenhorn, 1983/84	?
Fellbach		D	Baden-Württemberg	Hopf and Blankenhorn, 1983/84	?
Haltnau		D	Baden-Württemberg	Hopf and Blankenhorn, 1983/84	?
Heuneburg (Hundersingen)		D	Baden-Württemberg	Fuchs, 1975, Hopf and Blankenhorn, 1983/84, Körber-Grohne, 1981	?
Kallmünz		D	Bayern	Hopf and Blankenhorn, 1983/84; Küster 1991	?
Kochertürn		D	Baden-Württemberg	Hopf and Blankenhorn, 1983/84	?
Lauf (Pegnitz)		D	Bayern	Hopf and Blankenhorn, 1983/84	?
Mainz Bretzenheim		D	Rheinland-Pfalz	Hopf, 1982, Hopf and Blankenhorn, 1983/84	?
Mistelbach		D	Bayern	Hopf and Blankenhorn, 1983/84	?
Neckarwestheim		D	Baden-Württemberg	Hopf and Blankenhorn, 1983/84	?
Ödenbühl, Federsee		D	Baden-Württemberg	Hopf and Blankenhorn, 1983/84	?
Rauenegg, Konstanz		D	Baden-Württemberg	Hopf and Blankenhorn, 1983/84	?
Siegenshöhle		D	Baden-Württemberg	Hopf and Blankenhorn, 1983/84	?
Weinzierlein		D	Bayern	Hopf and Blankenhorn, 1983/84	?
Charavines	Lac du Paladru	F	Rhône-Alpes	Lundström-Baudais, 1993	?
Couternon	Larrey	F	Bourgogne	Wiethold, 2011	70
Crévéchamps	Tronc du Chêne	F	Lorraine	de Hingh, 2000	>2484
Lac du Chalin		F	Franches-Comté	Bertsch and Bertsch, 1947	?
Castelgandolfo	Villaggio delle Macine	I	Lazio	Carra, 2007	?
Castellaro Lagusello		I	Lombardia	Carra, 2007	?
Molina di Ledro, Trient		I	Trentino-Alto Adige	Oeggl, 1992	?
Pienza	Cava Barbieri	I	Toscana	Bellini *et al.*, 2008	25
Riparo-Gaban, Trient		I	Trentino-Alto Adige	Oeggl, 1992	?
Seeberg-Sarntal, Bozen		I	Trentino-Alto Adige	Oeggl, 1992	?
St. Lögg, Kurburg, Bozen		I	Trentino-Alto Adige	Oeggl, 1992	?

Table 6.2. Sites in the Circum-Alpine region neighbouring countries. Continued pp. 151–158.

Bronze Age and Iron Age sites from neighbouring countries

Site (comune)	Site (field, street)	Country	State/Province/ Region/District	References	Number of remains
EARLY BRONZE AGE					
Aiterhofen		D	Bayern	Bakels, 1986, Küster, 1991	?
Bodman	Schachen	D	Baden-Württemberg	Bertsch and Bertsch, 1947, Frank, 1989	>1300
Burgdorf		D	Niedersachsen	Hopf, 1982	?
Butzbach		D	Hessen	Hopf, 1982	?
Freising		D	Bayern	Küster, 1992a	?
Mühlhausen-Ehingen	Kai	D	Baden-Württemberg	Rösch, 2003	51
Niederbayern, div. Fundorte		D	Bayern	Küster, 1991	?
Riekofen		D	Bayern	Hopf and Blankenhorn, 1983/84	?
Straubing	Grabfeld Ortler	D	Bayern	Hopf and Blankenhorn, 1983/84	?
Straubing, Dendl.?		D	Bayern	Hopf and Blankenhorn, 1983/84	?
Thüringen, unbek. Fundorte		D	Thüringen	Hopf, 1982	?
Crévéchamps	Sous Velle	F	Lorraine	de Hingh, 2000	10
Frouard	Haut de Penotte	F	Lorraine	de Hingh, 2000	>123
Frouard	ZAC du Saule Gaillard I	F	Lorraine	de Hingh, 2000	187
Goin	Aéroport régional de Lorraine, zone D	F	Lorraine	de Hingh, 2000	99
Lyon-Vaise	Boulevard périphérique nord	F	Rhône-Alpes	Jacquet *et al.*, 1998	?
Yutz	Contournement sud-est, site 17	F	Lorraine	de Hingh, 2000	?
Belvedere (sul Monte Cetona)	S. Maria	I	Toscana	Carra *et al.*, 2003	519
Monte Covolo		I	Lombardia	Pals and Vorrips, 1979	?
Monte Covolo, Brescia		I	Lombardia	Pals and Vorrips, 1979	?
San Pietro Polesine	Canàr	I	Veneto	Castelletti *et al.*, 2001, Castiglioni *et al.*, 1998	?
Valeggio am Mincio, Prov. Verona		I	Veneto	Villaret-von Rochow, 1958	?
Lavagnone		I	Lombardia	De Marinis, 2002, De Marinis *et al.*, 2005, Perego, unpubl.	65136
Lucone		I	Lombardia	Perego, unpubl.	357158
EARLY BRONZE AGE / MIDDLE BRONZE AGE					
Altdorf		D	Bayern	Bakels, 1986, Küster, 1991	
MIDDLE BRONZE AGE					
Bartholomäberg	Friaga	A	Vorarlberg	Schmidl and Oeggl, 2005	3086
Bretten-Gölshausen	Steinäcker	D	Baden-Württemberg	Rösch, unpubl.	?
Büschdorf	Weichenförstchen	D	Saarland	Wiethold, 2000a	6763
Langenisarhofen		D	Bayern	Bakels, 1986, Küster, 1991	?
Uhingen		D	Baden-Württemberg	Karg, 1988	?

Bronze Age and Iron Age sites from neighbouring countries

Site (comune)	Site (field, street)	Country	State/Province/ Region/District	References	Number remains
Erstein	Grasweg	F	Alsace	Martinoli, unpubl.	?
Erstein	Grasweg	F	Alsace	Martinoli, unpubl.	?
Belvedere (sul Monte Cetona)	S. Maria	I	Toscana	Carra *et al.*, 2003	930
Fiavé Carera		I	Trentino-Alto Adige	Jones and Rowley-Conwy, 1984	>10,000
Greve	San Lorenzo	I	Toscana	Bellini *et al.*, 2007, 2008, Mariotti Lippi *et al.*, 2009	238
Millesimo	Bric Tana	I	Liguria	Nisbet and Scaife, 1998	62
Montale Rangone		I	Emilia-Romagna	Mercuri *et al.*, 2006, Forlani, 1988	78359
Lavagnone		I	Lombardia	De Marinis, 2002, De Marinis *et al.*, 2005, Perego, unpubl.	16250
Künzing-Bruck			Bayern	Küster, 1992a	?
Candalla	Riparo del Lauro	I	Toscana	Nisbet, 1987	386
MIDDLE BRONZE AGE / LATE BRONZE AGE					
Schluderns	Ganglegg/ Hahnehütterbödele	I	Trentino-Alto Adige	Heiss, 2008	425
Fort Harrouard (Eure-et-Loir)		F	Centre	Bakels, 1982	?
LATE BRONZE AGE					
Feldkirch-Altenstadt	Grütze	A	Vorarlberg	Heiss, 2008	1005
St. Nikolai	Sölkpass	A	Steiermark	Heiss, 2008	3
Stillfried		A	Niederösterreich	Kohler-Schneider, 2001	10097
Altheim		D	Bayern	Bakels, 1986	?
Atting		D	Bayern	Hopf and Blankenhorn, 1983/84	?
Berghülen-Treffensbuch		D	Baden-Württemberg	Karg, 1989	?
Buchau	Wasserburg	D	Baden-Württemberg	Bertsch, 1931, Hopf and Blankenhorn, 1983/84	?
Butzbach		D	Hessen	Hopf, 1982	?
Dobeneck, Gem. Talnitz		D	Sachsen	Hopf, 1982	?
Dullenried (bei Bad Buchau)		D	Baden-Württemberg	Hopf and Blankenhorn, 1983/84	?
Erfurt		D	Thüringen	Hopf, 1982	?
Federsee (bei Bad Buchau)		D	Baden-Württemberg	Hopf and Blankenhorn, 1983/84	?
Fritzlar		D	Hessen	Hopf, 1982	?
Greding		D	Bayern	Kroll, 1997	49376
Hagnau-Burg		D	Baden-Württemberg	Rösch, 1991, 1996	12220
Hamm		D	Nordrhein-Westfalen	Hopf, 1982	?
Herringen, Hamm	Nordherringen	D	Nordrhein-Westfalen	Hopf, 1982	?
Ichtershausen		D	Thüringen	Hopf, 1982	?
Kersheim, Forchheim		D	Bayern	Hopf and Blankenhorn, 1983/84	?
Knittlingen-Mittelfeld		D	Baden-Württemberg	Rösch, 1995	?

Table 6.2. Sites in the Circum-Alpine region neighbouring countries continued.

Bronze Age and Iron Age sites from neighbouring countries

Site (comune)	Site (field, street)	Country	State/Province/Region/District	References	Number of remains
Konstanz Langenrain		D	Baden-Württemberg	Hopf and Blankenhorn, 1983/84, Bertsch, 1932	?
Konstanz-Staad	Hörlepark	D	Baden-Württemberg	Günther, 2005	?
Langenisarhofen		D	Bayern	Bakels, 1986	?
Mannheim Vogelstang		D	Baden-Württemberg	Hopf and Blankenhorn, 1983/84	?
Mannheim, div. FO		D	Baden-Württemberg	Hopf and Blankenhorn, 1983/84	?
Neckargartach, Heilbronn		D	Baden-Württemberg	Hopf and Blankenhorn, 1983/84	?
Niederbayern, div. Fundorte		D	Bayern	Küster, 1991	?
Oberolm		D	Rheinland-Pfalz	Hopf and Blankenhorn, 1983/84	?
Oettersdorf		D	Thüringen	Hopf, 1982	?
Pöhl		D	Sachsen	Hopf, 1982	?
Radldorf		D	Bayern	Hopf and Blankenhorn, 1983/84	?
Säckingen		D	Baden-Württemberg	Hopf, 1969, Hopf and Blankenhorn, 1983/84	?
Stuttgart-Mühlhausen		D	Baden-Württemberg	Piening, 1988a	36
Unterechingen		D		Hopf and Blankenhorn, 1983/84	?
Unteruhldingen	Stollenwiese	D	Baden-Württemberg	Rösch, 1993a	1625
Vogtsburg-Burkheim	Burgberg	D	Baden-Württemberg	Küster, 1988a	?
Wiesloch	Weinäcker	D	Baden-Württemberg	Rösch, 1993b	?
Ay-sur-Moselle	Les Velers Jacques	F	Lorraine	Wiethold, 2011	40
Ay-sur-Moselle		F	Lorraine	de Hingh, 2000	1814
Carcassonne	Carsac	F	Languedoc-Roussillon	Erroux, 1986	?
Chaley	Balme Gontran	F	Rhône-Alpes	Bouby *et al.*, 2005, Coquillat, 1955	22537
Champagnole	La Planchette	F	Franches-Comté	Wiethold, 2012	103
Chens-sur-Léman	Touges	F	Rhône-Alpes	Baudais-Lundström, unpubl.	?
Conques-sur-Orbiel	Font Juvénal	F	Languedoc-Roussillon	Marinval, 1988	?
Crévéchamps	Sous Velle	F	Lorraine	de Hingh, 2000	?
Curtil	Brenot	F	Bourgogne	Coquillat, 1964	?
Ennery	Solotra	F	Lorraine	de Hingh, 2000	12
Etigny	Le Brassot	F	Bourgogne	Wiethold, 1998	52
Ettendorf	Gaentzbruch	F	Alsace	Wiethold, 2011	28
Fort Harrouard (Eure-et-Loir)		F	Centre	Bakels, 1982	?
Grésine	Lac du Bourget	F	Rhône-Alpes	Bouby and Billaud, 2001	?
Grotte des Planches, Jura		F	Franches-Comté	Petrequin *et al.*, 1985	?
Guénange	Gravières G.S.M.	F	Lorraine	Wiethold, 2011	300

Bronze Age and Iron Age sites from neighbouring countries

Site (comune)	Site (field, street)	Country	State/Province/ Region/District	References	Number remains
Liéhon	Aéroport régional de Lorraine, zone G	F	Lorraine	de Hingh, 2000	11
Lyon-Vaise	Boulevard périphérique nord	F	Rhône-Alpes	Jacquet *et al.*, 1998	?
Marly	La Grange aux Ormes	F	Lorraine	Wiethold, 2011	2398
Marly	Le Clos des Sorbiers	F	Lorraine	de Hingh, 2000	93
Meistratzheim	Foegel	F	Alsace	Wiethold, 2011	968
Montclus	Grotte du Prével Supérieur	F	Languedoc-Roussillon	Roudil, 1972	?
Ouroux	Curtil-Brenot	F	Bourgogne	Coquillat, 1964	?
Ouroux	Marnay	F	Bourgogne	Hopf, 1985	?
Passy- Véron	La Truie pendue	F	Bourgogne	Wiethold, 2011	167
Rettel	Chemin die Sierck	F	Lorraine	de Hingh, 2000	210
Saint-Apollinaire	Sur le petit Pré I	F	Bourgogne	Wiethold and Dálnoki, 2000, Labeaune and Wiethold, 2007	285
Saint-Apollinaire	Sur le Pré de Crot I	F	Bourgogne	Wiethold and Dálnoki, 2000	130
Saint-Bonnet-du-Gard	Oppidum du Marduel	F	Languedoc-Roussillon	Marinval, 1988	?
Saxon-Sion	Butte de Sion/ Vaudémont	F	Lorraine	Wiethold, 2011	785
Sète	La Fangade	F	Languedoc-Roussillon	Bouby *et al.*, 1999	25346
Tharaux	Grotte du Hasard	F	Languedoc-Roussillon	Roudil, 1972	?
Trèves	Baume Layrou	F	Languedoc-Roussillon	Bouby *et al.*, 2005, Erroux and Fages, 2001	20794
Varois-et-Chaignot	Le Pré du Plancher	F	Bourgogne	Wiethold, 2011	204
Vendres	Portal Vielh	F	Languedoc-Roussillon	Bouby *et al.*, 1999	929
Vergigny	La Grande Folie	F	Bourgogne	Wiethold, 1998	49
Villeneuve-la-Guyard	Les champs Boissier	F	Bourgogne	Wiethold, unpubl.	16
Yutz	Contournement sud-est, site 13	F	Lorraine	de Hingh, 2000	>21
Belvedere (sul Monte Cetona)	S. Maria	I	Toscana	Carra *et al.*, 2003	
Bibbiani		I	Toscana	Bellini *et al.*, 2008, Balducci and Fenu, 2005	?
Chiusi	I Forti	I	Toscana	Bellini *et al.*, 2008	?
Custoza	Sommacampagna	I	Veneto	Nisbet, 1996/1997	?
Fiavé Carera		I	Trentino-Alto Adige	Jones and Rowley-Conwy, 1984	>50
Manciano	Scarceta	I	Toscana	Rottoli, 1999	67
Schlern	Burgstall	I	Trentino-Alto Adige	Heiss, 2008	24
Schluderns	Ganglegg	I	Trentino-Alto Adige	Schmidl and Oeggl, 2005	23913
Seeberg	Schwarzsee/Lago Nero	I	Trentino-Alto Adige	Castiglioni and Cottini, 2000, Niederwanger and Tecchiati, 2000	?
Uscio	Castellaro	I	Liguria	Nisbet, 1990	1243

Table 6.2. Sites in the Circum-Alpine region neighbouring countries continued.

Bronze Age and Iron Age sites from neighbouring countries

Site (comune)	Site (field, street)	Country	State/Province/Region/District	References	Number of remains
Uscio	Castellaro	I	Liguria	Nisbet, 1990	214
Zignago	Castellaro	I	Liguria	Castelletti, 1974	>300
Budersberg-Dudelange	Ponk	L	Luxemburg	de Hingh, 2000	790
Peppange	Keitzenberg	L	Luxemburg	de Hingh, 2000	193
Konstanz	Rauenegg	D	Baden-Württemberg	Bertsch and Bertsch, 1947	?
Saint-Etienne-de-Gourgas		F	Languedoc-Roussillon	Erroux, 1981	?
BRONZE AGE / IRON AGE					
Ay-sur-Moselle	Les Velers Jacques	F	Lorraine	Wiethold, 2011	?
Les Trois Domaines	La Hachie	F	Lorraine	Wiethold, 2011	110
LATE BRONZE AGE / HALLSTATT PERIOD					
Saint-Apollinaire	Sur le petit Pré I	F	Bourgogne	Labeaune and Wiethold, 2007	574
Fliess	Pillerhöhe	A	Tirol	Oeggl, unpubl.	>429
Maneidtal	Grubensee	I	Trentino-Alto Adige	Heiss, 2008	435
Bussy-Lettré	Vatry, Mont Lardon, site 16	F	Champagne-Ardenne	Matterne, 2005	?
Changis-sur-Marne	Les Pétraux	F	Île-de-France	Matterne, 2001	349
Plancy-l'Abbaye	St. Martin	F	Champagne-Ardenne	Toulemonde, 2009a	89
Vigny	Aéroport régional de Lorraine, zone C	F	Lorraine	de Hingh, 2000	133
Ville-Saint-Jacques	Les bois d'échalas	F	Île-de-France	Toulemonde, 2009b	252
Leghorn	Stagno	I	Toscana	Bellini *et al.*, 2008, Gambogi *et al.*, 1995, Giachi *et al.*, 2010, Zanini, 1997, Zanini and Martinelli, 2005	6867
IRON AGE					
Bretten	Bauerbach	D	Baden-Württemberg	Rösch, unpubl.	?
Freiberg-Beihingen		D	Baden-Württemberg	Stika, 1996, 1999	?
Gerlingen		D	Baden-Württemberg	Stika, unpubl.	?
Heilbronn-Klingenberg		D	Baden-Württemberg	Stika, 1996, 1999	369
Niedererlbach		D	Bayern	Küster, 1988b, 1992b, 1995	?
Schwalheim		D	Hessen	Kreuz and Boenke, 2001, 2003	?
Crévéchamps	Tronc du Chêne	F	Lorraine	de Hingh, unpubl.	198
Ettendorf	Gaentzbruch II	F	Alsace	van der Plaetsen, 2004	624
Gondreville	site 4	F	Lorraine	de Hingh, 2000	?
Les Trois Domaines	La Hachie	F	Lorraine	Wiethold, 2011	72
Passy-Véron	La Truie pendu	F	Bourgogne	Wiethold, 2011	341415
Pierry	Les Forges	F	Champagne-Ardenne	Wiethold, 2011	16
Pluvet	Larrivoux	F	Bourgogne	Wiethold and Labeaune, 2005, Wiethold, 1998	1385
Pluvet	Larrivoux	F	Bourgogne	Wiethold and Labeaune, 2005	2121
Pont-sur-Seine	La Gravière	F	Champagne-Ardenne	Toulemonde, 2009c	5933
Pont-sur-Yonne	Les Basses Veuves	F	Bourgogne	Wiethold, 2011	207
Quetigny	Les Grebillons	F	Bourgogne	Wiethold, 2011	519
Schaeffersheim		F	Alsace	Märkle, 2011	?

Bronze Age and Iron Age sites from neighbouring countries

Site (comune)	Site (field, street)	Country	State/Province/ Region/District	References	Number remain.
Sorcy-St-Martin	La Louvière	F	Lorraine	Wiethold, 2011	5
Como	Via Tito Livio	I	Lombardia	Castiglioni and Cottini, 1998	?
Rémerschen	Schwengerwis	L	Grevenmacher	de Hingh, 2000	99
HALLSTATT PERIOD					
Borg	Seelengewann	D	Saarland	Wiethold, 2000b, c	1552
Echzell-Mühlbach		D	Hessen	Wiethold *et al.*, 2008	?
Freiberg-Geisingen		D	Baden-Württemberg	Piening, 1988b	<500
Heilbronn-Neckargartach		D	Baden-Württemberg	Piening, 1982	42
Mühlhausen-Ehingen	Kai	D	Baden-Württemberg	Rösch, 2004a	?
Niederachdorf		D	Bayern	Küster, 1988b, 1995	?
Sehndorf	Hinter'm Dellchen	D	Saarland	Henz, 2000	14
Steinheim		D	Bayern	Bloos and Gregor, 1984, Küster, 1988b, 1995, Poschlod, 1984	?
Tamm-Hohenstange		D	Baden-Württemberg	Piening, 1982	574
Wierschem	Auf Buhrmorgen	D	Rheinland-Pfalz	Kroll, 1998, 2001	198
Ars-sur-Moselle	rue Foch	F	Lorraine	de Hingh, 2000	1
Ay-sur-Moselle	Les Velers Jacques	F	Lorraine	Wiethold, 2011	11
Bezannes	La Bergerie	F	Champagne-Ardenne	Toulemonde, 2009d	77
Champagnole	La Planchette	F	Franches-Comté	Wiethold, 2012	
Chamvres	Les Grands Malades	F	Bourgogne	Wiethold, 1998	4
Chargey-les-Gray		F	Franche-Comté	Wiethold, 1998	3
Charney-les-Chalon		F	Bourgogne	Alary, 1994	?
Chassenard	La Générie	F	Auvergne	Wiethold, 1999	?
Clermont-Ferrand		F	Auvergne	Hajnalova, 1998	?
Couternon	Larrey	F	Bourgogne	Wiethold, 2011	54
Crévéchamps	Tronc du Chêne	F	Lorraine	de Hingh, unpubl.	>133
Frébécourt	La Fourche	F	Lorraine	Wiethold, 2011	5
Frouard	Haut de Penotte	F	Lorraine	de Hingh, 2000	?
Guénange	Gravières G.S.M.	F	Lorraine	Wiethold, 2011	30
Hattstatt	Ziegelscheuer	F	Alsace	Achard-Corompt *et al.*, 2004, Wiethold, 2011	997
Illfurth	Britzgyberg	F	Alsace	Fischer, unpubl.	?
Jouy-aux-Arches	La Machotte	F	Lorraine	de Hingh, 2000	41
Marlenheim	Contournement routier, site 1	F	Alsace	Cayrol, 2004	4
Marlenheim	La Couronne d'Or	F	Alsace	Wiethold, 2011	27
Marlenheim	Maison Apprederis	F	Alsace	Wiethold, 2011	12
Marly	La Grange aux Ormes	F	Lorraine	Wiethold, 2011	47579
Meaux	ZAC Luxembourg	F	Île-de-France	Matterne, 2001	?
Meistratzheim	Foegel	F	Alsace	Wiethold, 2011	600
Merxheim	Trummelmatten	F	Alsace	Wiethold, unpubl.	20
Molinet	Taillis des Gouttes	F	Auvergne	Wiethold and Dálnoki, 2000	67
Passy-Véron	La Truie pendu	F	Bourgogne	Wiethold, 2011	121
Reims	ZAC Croix Blandin	F	Champagne-Ardenne	Toulemonde, 2009e	179

Table 6.2. Sites in the Circum-Alpine region neighbouring countries continued.

Bronze Age and Iron Age sites from neighbouring countries

Site (comune)	Site (field, street)	Country	State/Province/Region/District	References	Number of remains
Reims	ZAC Dauphinot	F	Champagne-Ardenne	Wiethold, 2011	418
Rosoy	La Plaine de Nange	F	Bourgogne	Wiethold, 2011	2065
Saint-André-les-Vergers	Echenilly	F	Champagne-Ardenne	Toulemonde, 2010	163
Saint-Apollinaire	La pièce derrière La Grange I	F	Bourgogne	Wiethold, 2011	14
Saint-Apollinaire	La Tirbaude 2	F	Bourgogne	Wiethold and Dálnoki, 2000, Labeaune and Wiethold, 2007	283
Saint-Apollinaire	Les Petits Gorguenots	F	Bourgogne	Wiethold and Dálnoki, 2000	336
Saint-Apollinaire	Les Petits Gorguenots 2	F	Bourgogne	Wiethold, 2011	338
Saint-Apollinaire	Sur le Pré Crot 3	F	Bourgogne	Wiethold, 2011	36
Tomblaine	Hasbergen	F	Lorraine	Wiethold, 2011	56
Varois-et-Chaignot	Les Épenottes	F	Bourgogne	Labeaune and Wiethold, 2007	498
Varois-et-Chaignot	Les Marchemailles	F	Bourgogne	Labeaune and Wiethold, 2007	3469
Vigny	Aéroport régional de Lorraine, zone B	F	Lorraine	de Hingh, 2000	26
Ville-Saint-Jacques	Les Bois d'échalas	F	Île-de-France	Toulemonde, 2009b	14797
Vrigny	Les Côtes chéries	F	Champagne-Ardenne	Matterne, 2003, 2009	12
Vrigny	Les Cumines Basses	F	Champagne-Ardenne	Matterne, 2003, 2009	106
Yutz	Contournement sud-est, site 15	F	Lorraine	de Hingh, 2000	>612
Yutz	ZAC Olypmpe II	F	Lorraine	Wiethold, 2011	1629
Pietra Ligure	Monte Trabocchetto (saggio O)	I	Liguria	Arobba *et al.*, 2003	2656
Montagnieu	La Roche-Noire		Rhône-Alpes	Wiethold and Treffort, 2002	13376
Montagnieu	Pré de la Cour		Rhône-Alpes	Marinval, 1993	?
LA TÈNE PERIOD					
Dürrnberg		A	Salzburg	Wiethold, 2000b	?
Kundl		A	Tirol	Henz, 2000	?
Pfaffenhofen	Trappeleacker	A	Tirol	Heiss, 2008	9
Roseldorf	Sandberg	A	Niederösterrreich	Caneppele and Kohler-Schneider, 2008, 2009	?
Wattens	Himmelreich	A	Tirol	Wiethold, 2000a; Oeggl, 1999	?
Bad Nauheim		D	Hessen	Kreuz and Boenke, 2001, 2003	?
Bondorf		D	Baden-Württemberg	Körber-Grohne and Piening, 1979	?
Büdesheim		D	Hessen	Wiethold *et al.*, 2008	?
Büschdorf	Weichenförstchen	D	Saarland	Wiethold, 2000a	352
Dünsberg		D	Hessen	Kreuz and Hopf, 2001	?
Feldkirchen		D	Bayern	Wiethold *et al.*, 2008	?
Gauting		D	Bayern	Wiethold *et al.*, 2008	?
Goddelau		D	Hessen	Kreuz, 1993	269
Hochdorf		D	Baden-Württemberg	Stika, 1995, 1999	?
Ilsfeld		D	Baden-Württemberg	Piening, 1982	1711

Bronze Age and Iron Age sites from neighbouring countries

Site (comune)	Site (field, street)	Country	State/Province/Region/District	References	Number remains
Kalbach		D	Hessen	Kreuz, 2005	?
Kehlheim	'Mitterfeld'	D	Bayern	Wiethold et al., 2008	?
Kirchheim am Ries - Benzenzimmern	Ohrenberg	D	Baden-Württemberg	Rösch, 2004b	14:
Lauffen		D	Baden-Württemberg	Piening, 1983	294:
Manching		D	Bayern	Küster, 1992b, 1998	?
Mardorf 23		D	Hessen	Kreuz and Wiethold, 2002, Wiethold et al., 2008	?
Münchhausen	Christenberg	D	Hessen	Kreuz, 1993	1690
Niederpöring		D	Bayern	Küster, 1992b	?
Pankofen		D	Bayern	Wiethold et al., 2008	?
Riedlingen	'Klinge'	D	Baden-Württemberg	Bouchette and Rösch, 1996	?
Steinbach		D	Hessen	Kreuz, 2005	?
Stephansposching		D	Bayern	Wiethold et al., 2008	?
Stuttgart-Mühlhausen		D	Baden-Württemberg	Piening, 1988a	>30(
Wallendorf		D	Saarland	Kroll, 2000	?
Wierschem	Auf Buhrmorgen	D	Rheinland-Pfalz	Kroll, 1998, 2001	1306(
Alésia	En Curiot	F	Bourgogne	Wiethold et al., 2008	?
Aulnat	Puy-de-Dòme	F		Collis et al., 1979	?
Bailly	Le Crapaud, Le Mérisier	F	Île-de-France	Matterne, 2001	388(
Bussy-Lettré	Le Petit Vau Bourdin	F	Champagne-Ardenne	Wiethold, 2011	575:
Bussy-Saint-Georges	Le Champ Fleuri nord	F	Île-de-France	Matterne, 2001	208(
Damary	Aisne-Tal, N-Frankreich	F	Picardy	Bakels, 1999	?
Entzheim-Geispolsheim	Aéroparc (LIDL-CUS)	F	Alsace	Schaal, 2007	46:
Fossé de Pandours		F	Alsace	Wiethold, 2002	?
Gevrey-Chambertin	Au Dessus de Bergis	F	Bourgogne	Wiethold, 2009	33:
Larchant	Les Groues	F	Île-de-France	Wiethold, 2008	15:
Marly	Le Clos des Sorbiers	F	Lorraine	de Hingh, 2000	2(
Matzenheim	Les Berges du Panama	F	Alsace	Martinoli, unpubl.	?
Mont Beuvray	Fontaine Saint-Pierre	F	Bourgogne	Wiethold, 1994	26:
Mont Beuvray	La Croix du Rebout	F	Bourgogne	Wiethold, 1995	?
Mont Beuvray	La Terasse 'Le coffre'	F	Bourgogne	Wiethold, 1996	599!
Mont Beuvray	Pâture du Couvent	F	Bourgogne	Wiethold, 1998	14:
St.-Julien-du-Sault	W-Burgund	F	Bourgogne	Wiethold et al., 2008	?
Verdun-sur-le-Doubs	Le Petit Chauvort	F	Bourgogne	Wiethold, 1998	?
Villemanoche	Verpilliers	F	Bourgogne	Wiethold, 2011	834(
Bergeggi	Castellaro	I	Liguria	Nisbet, 1994	1:
Campi	Monte S. Martino	I	Veneto	Castiglioni, 2007	?
Este	Fondo Baratella	I	Veneto	Pasternak, 2005	?
Este	Meggiaro	I	Veneto	Motella de Carlo, 2002	?
Ulten	St. Walburg	I	Trentino-Alto Adige	Heiss, 2008	437!
Dudelange	Angeldall	L	Luxemburg	Kroll, 1997	303
St Martin	Prati del Putia	I	Trentino-Alto Adige	Cottini et al., 2007	?

acc. to = according to

Table 6.2. Sites in the Circum-Alpine region neighbouring countries continued.

Chronological period	Sites total, n = 118	Sites with ≥ 50 cereal remains, n = 58
Bronze Age	11	1
Early Bronze Age	8	6
Middle Bronze Age	13	10
Late Bronze Age	31	15
Bronze Age / Iron Age	1	0
Iron Age	10	2
Hallstatt period	16	9
La Tène period	28	15

Table 6.3. Number of Swiss sites considered, per chronological period.

Jura south	8
Jura west	3
Swiss Plateau west	7
Swiss Plateau east	16
Alps centre	7
Alps south	1
Alps west	1

Table 6.4. Number of Swiss sites considered, per geographical region (sites with ≥50 cereal remains; data from La Tène period sites excluded; n = 43).

Chronological period	Sites total, n = 306	Sites with ≥ 50 cereal remains, n = 68
Bronze Age	29	0
Early Bronze Age	24	4
Early / Middle Bronze Age	1	1
Middle Bronze Age	15	9
Middle / Lage Bronze Age	2	0
Lage Bronze Age	92	20
Bronze Age / Iron Age	11	2
Iron Age	21	4
Hallstatt period	57	16
La Tène period	56	12

Table 6.5. Number of sites (per chronological period) from the Circum-Alpine region neighbouring countries considered.

Geographical region	Sites with ≥ 50 cereal remains
Eastern central Alps	2
Alps northern foothills	5
Northern low mountains	14
Western low mountains	14
Jura southwest	2
Upper Rhine	7
Alps southern foothills	5
Mediterranean south	4
Mediterranean west	3

Table 6.6. Number of sites (per geographical region) from the Circum-Alpine region neighbouring countries (sites with ≥50 cereal remains; data from La Tène period sites excluded; n = 56).

Table References

Achard-Corompt, N., Dumont, A., Tegel, W., Treffort, J.-M. and Wiethold, J. (2004) Archéologie préventive et sites de milieux humides: les exemples protohistoriques de Hattstatt et de Vrigne-aux-Bois. In J. Burnouf and P. Leveau (eds) *Fleuves et marais, une histoire au croisement de la nature et de la culture. Sociétés préindustrielles et milieux fluviaux, lacustres et palustres: pratiques sociales et hydrosystèmes*: 45–56. Paris: Ministère de l'Education nationale, de l'Enseignement supérieur et de la Recherche.

Akeret, Ö. and Geith-Chauvière, I. (2003) Les macrorestes végétaux. In S. Wüthrich (ed.) *Saint-Aubin/Derrière la Croix – Un complexe mégalithique durant le Néolithique moyen et final*: 281–293, 341–355. Hauterive: Service et musée cantonal d'archéologie de Neuchâtel.

Akeret, Ö. and Geith-Chauvière, I. (2006a) Données carpologiques. In M. Bednarz, J. Kraese, P. Reynier and J. Becze-Deák (eds) *Plateau de Bevaix 2. Histoire et préhistoire d'un paysage rural: le site des Pâquiers*: 110–111. Neuchâtel: Service et musée cantonal d'archéologie.

Akeret, Ö. and Geith-Chauvière, I. (2006b) Occupations néolithiques et protohistoriques: cadre et environnement. Données carpologiques. In M. Bednarz, J. Kraese, P. Reynier and J. Becze-Deak (eds) *Plateau de Bevaix, 2. Histoire et préhistoire d'un paysage rural: le site des Paquiers*: 110–111. Neuchâtel.

Akeret, Ö. and Geith-Chauvière, I. (2010) Analyses carpologiques des structures archéologiques. In R. Anastasiu and F. Langenegger (eds) *Plateau de Bevaix 5: Cortaillod/Petit Ruz: impacts humains et évolution d'un terroir, du Néolithique à l'époque gallo-romaine, sur un kilomètre d'autoroute*: 1, sowie 43 Tabellen. Hautrive: Office et musée cantonal d'archéologie de Neuchâtel.

Akeret, Ö. and Geith-Chauvière, I. (2011a) Les macrorestes végétaux. In M.-H. Grau Bitterli and E. Fierz-Dayer (eds) *Plateau de Bevaix 6. Bevaix/Treytel – À Sugiez: histoire d'un complexe mégalithique néolithique, témoins d'habitats du Campaniforme et du Bronze ancien*: 311–321. Neuchâtel.

Akeret, Ö. and Geith-Chauvière, I. (2011b) Plateau de Bevaix 7. L'histoire de la relation entre hommes et plantes utiles: synthèse des données carpologiques. Hautrive: Office et musée d'archéologie de Neuchâtel.

Alary, J.-C. (1994) L'archéologie dans le Verdunois. Trois rivières. *Bulletin du Groupe d'Études Historiques de Verdun-sur-le-Doubs* 44: 15–38.

Arobba, D., Caramiello, R. and Del Lucchese, A. (2003) Archaeobotanical investigations in Liguria: preliminary data on the early Iron Age at Monte Trabocchetto (Pietra Ligure, Italy). *Vegetation History and Archaeobotany* 12: 253–262.

Bakels, C. (1982) Les graines carbonisées de Fort-Harrouard (Eure-et-Loir). *Antiquités Nationales* 14/15: 59–63.

Bakels, C. (1986) Pflanzenreste aus Niederbayern – Beobachtungen in rezenten Ausgrabungen. *Berichte der Bayrischen Bodendenkmalpflege* 24/25: 157–166.

Bakels, C. (1999) Archaeobotanical investigations in the Aisne valley, northern France, from the Neolithic up to the early Middle Ages. In Proceedings of the 11th IWGP Symposium Toulouse 1998. *Vegetation History and Archaeobotany* 8: 71–77.

Balducci, C. and Fenu, P. (2005) Bibbiani (Capraia e Limite, Firenze). In P. Fenu (ed.) *Echi dalla Preistoria*: 142–145. Firenze: Edizioni Polistampa.

Behre, K.-E. (1988) Getreidefunde aus der bronzezeitlichen Höhensiedlung Toos-Waldi, Kanton Thurgau (Schweiz). In H. Küster (ed.) *Der prähistorische Mensch und seine Umwelt. Festschrift für Udelgard Körber-Grohne*: 239–243. Stuttgart: Konrad Theiss Verlag.

Bellini, C., Capretti, C., Giachi, G., Gonnelli, T., Macchioni, N., Mariotti Lippi, M. and Mori Secci, M. (2007) Indagini arceobotaniche nella struttura ipogeica della Media Età del Bronzo di San Lorenzo a Greve a Firenze. *Riv. Sc. Preist.* 57: 255–262.

Bellini, C., Mariotti-Lippi, M., Mori Secci, M., Aranguren, B. and Perazzi, P. (2008) Plant gathering and cultivation in prehistoric Tuscany (Italy) *Vegetation History and Archaeoabotany* 17: 103–112.

Bertsch, K. (1931) Wasserburg Buchau. In Paläobotanische Monographie des Federseeriedes. *Bibliotheca botanica* 103: 41–43.

Bertsch, K. (1932) Die Pflanzenreste der Pfahlbauten von Sipplingen und Langenrain im Bodensee. *Badische Fundberichte* 2: 305–320.

Bertsch, K. and Bertsch, F. (1947) *Geschichte unserer Kulturpflanzen*. Stuttgart: Wissenschaftliche Verlagsgesellschaft GmbH.

Bloos, G. and Gregor, H.-J. (1984) Geologie und fossile Makroflora der Älteren Fluviatilen Schichten (Riss-Glazial) von Steinheim a.d. Murr. *Documenta naturae* 18: 1–9.

Bouby, L. and Billaud, Y. (2001) Économie agraire à la fin de l'âge du Bronze sur les bords du lac du Bourget (Savoie, France). *Sciences de la Terre et des Planètes/Earth and Planetary Sciences* 333: 749–756.

Bouby, L., Fages, G. and Treffort, J. M. (2005) Food storage in two Late Bronze Age caves of Southern France: palaeoethnobotanical and social implications. *Vegetation History and Archaeobotany* 14: 313–328.

Bouby, L., Leroy, F. and Carozza, L. (1999). Food plants from lage Bronze Age lagoon sites in Languedoc, southern France: reconstruction of farming economy and environment. *Vegetation History and Archaeoabotany* 8: 53–69.

Bouchette, A. and Rösch, M. (1996) Keltische Pflanzenfunde aus Riedlingen, Kreis Biberach. *Archäologische Ausgrabungen in Baden-Württemberg* 1995: 132–137.

Brogli, W. and Schibler, J. (1999) Zwölf Gruben aus der Späthallstatt-/Frühlatènezeit in Möhlin (mit Beiträgen von Heiner Albrecht, Stefanie Jacomet und Marcel Joos). *Jahrbuch der Schweizerischen Gesellschaft für Ur- und Frühgeschichte* 82: 79–116.

Brombacher, C. (1986) *Untersuchungen der botanischen Makroreste des prähistorischen Siedlungsplatzes Zürich-Mozartstrasse I (Endneolithikum bis Spätbronzezeit)*. (unpubl.) Inaugural- Dissertation, Universität Basel.

Brombacher, C. (1996) Pflanzliche Makroreste aus der späthallstattzeitlichen Siedlung Otelfingen-Bonenberg, Kt. Zürich, Schweiz. In D. Fort-Linksfeiler Ein späthallstattzeitlicher Siedlungsbefund aus Otelfingen, Kt. Zürich, Schweiz. *Archaeologia Austriaca* 80: 211–215.

Brombacher, C. (2005) Archäobotanik. In M. Ramstein and A. Cueni Koppigen – Usserfeld. Spätbronzezeitliche Gräber. *Archäologie im Kanton Bern* 556. Bern.

Brombacher, C. (2012) Etude carpologique des plantes carbonisées et imbibées. In L. Frei Paroz and I. Gaume (eds) *Delémont – En La Pran 4 (Jura, Suisse). Occupations des Premier et Second âges du Fer dans le bassin de Delémont*: 128–132; 152–153. Porrentruy: Office de la culture. Sociéte jurassienne d'Emulation.

Brombacher, C. and Dick, M. (1987) Die Untersuchungen der botanischen Makroreste. In E. Gross, C. Brombacher, M. Dick and K. Diggelman (eds) *Zürich 'Mozartstrasse', Neolithische und bronzezeitliche Ufersiedlungen*: 198–212. Zürich.

Brombacher, C. and Klee, M. (2001) Untersuchungen der botanischen Makroreste. In C. Achour-Uster and J. Kunz (eds) *Die mittelbronzezeitliche Siedlungsstelle von Birmensdorf-Stoffel (Grabungen 1995–1996)*: 60–67. Zürich: Fotorotar AG.

Brombacher, C., Ernst, M. and Martinoli, D. (2010) Etude archéobotanique. In C. Deslex, E. Evéquoz, C. Bélet-Gonda and S. Saltel (eds) *Occupations protohistoriques à Chevenez: de l'âge du Bronze à la fin de l'âge du Fer*: 83–85. Delémont.

Brombacher, C., Ghiggi, D. and Jacomet, S. (2005a) Untersuchung der pflanzlichen Makroreste. In A.-C. Conscience (ed.) *Wädenswil – Vorder Au. Eine Seeufersiedlung am Übergang vom 17. zum 16. Jh. v. Chr. im Rahmen der Frühbronzezeit am Zürichsee. Unter besonderer Berücksichtigung der frühbronzezeitlichen Funde und Befunde von Meilen-Schellen*: 25–32. Zürich, Egg: Baudirektion Kanton Zürich. Hochbauamt. Kantonsarchäologie.

Brombacher, C., Klee, M. and Jacomet, S. (2005b) Münchenwiler – Im Loch 1. Botanische Makroreste aus einer spätbronzezeitlichen Grube. In P. J. Suter and M. Ramstein (eds) *Fundberichte und Aufsätze. Chroniques archéologique et textes*: 559–568. Bern: Archäologischer Dienst des Kantons Bern.

Brombacher, C., Klee, M. and Martinoli, D. (2007) Bronzezeitliche und mittelalterliche Pflanzenfunde aus dem Kloster St. Johann in Müstair. In H. R. Sennhauser (ed.) *Müstair Kloster St. Johann, Band 4. Naturwissenschaftliche und technische Beiträge*: 75–98. Zürich:

Brombacher, C., Martinoli, D. and Klee, M. (2012) Etude carpologique. In L. Frei Paroz and I. Gaume (eds) *Delémont – En La Pran 4 (Jura, Suisse). Occupations des Premier et Second âges du Fer dans le bassin de Delémont*: 72–77, 150–151, 87, 96. Porrentruy: Office de la culture. Sociéte jurassienne d'Emulation.

Burkart, W. (1946) Crestaulta. Eine bronzezeitliche Hügelsiedlung bei Surin im Lugnez. *Monographien zur Ur- und Frühgeschichte der Schweiz V.*

Caneppele, A. and Kohler-Schneider, M. (2008) Ein Nachweis von Kulturwein aus dem Heiligtum der keltischen Siedlung bei Roseldorf. In E. Lauermann and P. Trebsche (eds) *Heiligtümer der Druiden. Opfer und Rituale der Kelten*: 85–89. Asparn an der Zaya.

Caneppele, A. and Kohler-Schneider, M. (2009) Archäobotanische Untersuchung eines latènezeitlichen Getreidespeichers aus der 'Keltensiedlung Sandberg' bei Roseldorf (Weinviertel, Niederösterreich). In V. Holzer (ed.) *Roseldorf. Interdisziplinäre Forschungen zur grössten keltischen Zentralsiedlung Österreichs.*: 103–143. Wien.

Carra, M. (2007) Ambiente ed economia di sussistenza nell'età del bronzo. Analisi paleocarpologica dei siti perilacustri di 'Villaggio delle Macine' (Castelgandolfo, Roma) e Castellaro Lagusello (Mantova): due realtà a confronto. *Annali dell'Università degli Studi di Ferrara. Museologia Scientifica e Naturalistica* 79–82.

Carra, M. L., Cattani, L. and Zanni, C. (2003) Aspetti palethnobotanici dell'area insediativa protostorica di S. Maria in Belvedere sul Monte Cetona (Siena). *Riv Sc Preist* 53: 505–518.

Castelletti, L. (1974) Castellaro di Zignago. In I. I. P. Protost (ed.) *Atti XVI Riunione Scientifica in Liguria, 3–5 November 1973*: 175. Firenze.

Castelletti, L., Castiglioni, E. and Rottoli, M. (2001) L'agricoltura dell'Italia settentrionale dal Neolitico al Medioevo. In O. Failla and G. Forni (eds) *Le piante coltivate e la loro storia. Dalle origini al transgenico in Lombardia nel Centenario della riscoperta della genetica di Mendel*: 33–84.

Castiglioni, E. (2007) Resti botanici dai contesti dell'età del Ferro. In G. Cuirletti (ed.) *Monte S. Martino: Fra il Garda e le Alpi di Ledro; il luogo di culto (ricerche e scavi 1969–1979)*: 195–207. Provincia Autonoma di Trento, Soprintendenza per i Beni Archeologici.

Castiglioni, E. and Cottini, M. (1998) I resti botanici dalla necropoli di via Tito Livio a Como. *Revista Archeologica dell'Antica Provincia e Diocesi di Como* 180: 127–140.

Castiglioni, E. and Cottini, M. (2000) Die pflanzlichen Makroreste am Schwarzsee, Seeberg. In G. Niederwanger and U. Tecchiati (eds) *Wasser – Feuer – Himmel. Ein Brandopferplatz spätbronzezeitlicher Bergknappen*: 36–37. Bozen: Folio.

Castiglioni, E., Motella de Carlo, S. and Nisbet, R. (1998) Indagini sui resti vegetali macroscopici. In C. Balista and P. Bellintani (eds) *Canàr di San Pietro Polesine. Ricerche archeo-ambientali sul sito palafitticolo*: 115–123.

Cayrol, J. (2004) Données paléoenvironnementales. In S. Tristan, E. Boës and S. Rotillon (eds) *Marlenheim (Bas-Rhin), Contournement routier: Deux habitats rubanés et une occupation hallstattienne. DFS de saufetage urgent (6 octobre–19 décembre 2003)*: 59–62. Dijon, Strasbourg: Inrap GES, SRA d'Alsace.

Collis, J. R., Périchon, R. and Chopelin, C. (1979) Étude de céréales sur le site protohistorique d'Aulnat. *Revue Archéologique du Centre* 35–38.

Cooper, C., Harbeck, M., Kühn, M., Rast-Eicher, A., Schweissing, M., Ulrich-Bochsler, S. and Vandorpe, P. (2010) Spiez-Einigen, Holleeweg 3. Naturwissenschaftliche Untersuchungen zu den bronzezeitlichen Bestattungen. In A. f. K. Erziehungsdirektion des Kantons Bern, Archäologischer Dienst des Kantons Bern (ed.) *ArchBE. Archäologie Bern/Archéologie bernoise. Jahrbuch des Archäologischen Dienstes des Kantons Bern 2010. Fund- und Kurzberichte 2009 sowie die Aufsätze. Spiez-Einigen, Holleeweg 3. Attiswil, Wybrunne. Burgdorf, Kirchbühl 20–22. Ein 'Repräsentatives Inventar' für den Kanton Bern.*: 175–198. Bern: Rub Media.

Coquillat, M. (1955) Sur les graines des foyers protohistoriques de La Balme Gontran, Commune de Chaley (Ain). *Bulletin de la Société des Naturalistes d'Oyonnax* 9: 47–58.

Coquillat, M. (1964) Etude paléobotanique et détermination des graines. In L. Bonnamour (ed.) *Un habitat protohistorique à Ouroux-sur-Saône (Saône-et-Loire)*: 143–153.

Cottini, M., Mascino Murphy, C., Pilli, A. and Tecchiati, U. (2007) Un luogo di culto dell'età del Ferro in Val Badia, località Prati del Putia (Comune di San Martino – BZ). *Ladinia* 31: 7–44.

Curdy, P., Mottet, M., Nicoud, C., Baudais, D., Lundström-Baudais, K. and Moulin, B. (1993) Brig-Glis/Waldmatte, un habitat alpin de l'âge du Fer. Fouilles archéologiques N9 en Valais. *Archäologie der Schweiz* 16: 138–151.

Curdy, P., Nicoud, C. and Schindler, M. P. (1998) Dynamique villageoise et datation. L'exemple de l'habitat du 1er âge du Fer de Brigue-Glis/Waldmatte (Valais). *Bulletin d'études préhistoriques et archéologiques alpines* 9: 117–120.

de Hingh, A. E. (2000) *Food production and food procurement in the Bronze Age and Early Iron Age (2000–500 BC).* Leiden: Faculty of Archaeology, Leiden University.

De Marinis, R. C. (ed.) (2002) *Studi sull'abitato dell'età del Bronzo del Lavagnone, Desenzano del Garda,* Bergamo: Comune di Bergamo. Assossorato alla Cultura. Civico Museo Archeologico.

De Marinis, R. C., Rapi, M., Ravazzi, C., Arpenti, E., Deaddis, R. and Perego, R. (2005) Lavagnone (Desenzano del Garda): new excavations and palaeoecology of a Bronze Age pile dwelling site in northern Italy. In P. Della Casa and M. Trachsel (eds) *WES'04 – Wetland Economies and Societies. Proceedings of the International Conference in Zürich, 10–13 March 2004*: 221–232. Zürich: Chronos.

Della Casa, P., Jochum Zimmermann, E. and Jacquat, C. (2009) Eine Alpine Siedlung der Bronze- und Eisenzeit in Airolo-Madrano (Kt. Tessin, Schweiz) – archäologische und paläoökologische Grundlagen. *Archäologisches Korrespondenzblatt* 39: 193–212.

Dick, M. (1989) Untersuchungen pflanzlicher Grossreste. In B. Ruckstuhl Hallstattzeitliche Seidlungsgruben aus Neunkirch-Tobeläcker (SH). *Jahrbuch der Schweizerischen Gesellschft für Ur- und Frühgeschichte* 72: 91–95.

Erroux, F. (1981) Etude des graines de sites préhistoriques des causses: La Poujade, St. Etienne-de-Gourgas, Pompignan. *Paléobiologie continentale* 12: 273–278.

Erroux, J. (1986) Les céréales cultivées du site de Carsac. In J. Guilaine and *et al.* (eds) *Carsac: une agglomération protohistorique en Languedoc*: 215–217. Toulouse: Centre d'Anthropologie des Sociétés Rurales.

Erroux, J. and Fages, G. (2001) Analyse des graines carbonisées de l'Age du Bronze final de la Baume Layroux, Trèves (Gard). In P. Marinval (ed.) *Histoire d'hommes, histoire de plantes. Hommage au professeur Jean Erroux*: 25–36. Toulouse: Editions Monique Mergoil.

Feigenwinter, F. 1992. Bestandsaufnahme der botanischen Makroreste und Vergleich zweier Hausstandorte der spätbronzezeitlichen Siedlung Ürschhausen-Horn am Nussbaumersee / Kt. Thurgau. Diplomarbeit, Bot. Institut, Universtität Basel.

Forlani, L. (1988) I Legni delle Terramare di S. Ambrogio e di Montale. In A. Cardarelli (ed.) *Modena dalle origini all'anno Mille. Studi de Archeologia e Storia 1*: 208–209. Modena.

Frank, K.-S. (1989) Untersuchung von botanischen Makroresten aus der archäologischen Tauchgrabung der Seeufersiedlungen Bodman-Schachen am nordwestlichen Bodensee unter besonderer Berücksichtigung der Morphologie und Anatomie der Wildpflanzenfunde (Frühe bis Mittlere Bronzezeit). Teil I. *Diplomarbeit, Universität Hohenheim.*

Fuchs, C. (1975) Bestimmung und Auswertung von Abdrücken prähistorischer Nutzpflanzen aus der bronze- und hallstattzeitlichen Siedlungsschichten der Heuneburg (SW-Rand der Schwäbischen Alb). Universität Stuttgart-Hohenheim.

Gambogi, P., Nanni, M. and Zanini, A. (1995) L'abitato protostorico di Livorno-Stagno. Nota preliminare. In N. Negrino Batacchio (ed.) *Preistoria e Protosotria in Etruria. Atti del Secondo Incontro di Studi*: 93–101.

Geith-Chauvière, I., Tegel, W. and Akeret, Ö. (2010) Analyses archéobotaniques des tombes à incinérations du site de Cortaillod/Petit Ruz. In R. Anastasiu and F. Langenegger (eds) *Plateau de Bevaix 5: Cortaillod/Petit Ruz: impacts humains et évolution d'un terroir, du Néolithique à l'époque gallo-romaine, sur un kilomètre d'autoroute*: 10, sowie 1 Tabellen. Hautrive: Office et musée cantonal d'archéologie de Neuchâtel.

Giachi, G., Mori Secchi, M., Pignatelli, O., Gambogi, P. and Mariotti Lippi, M. (2010) The prehistoric pile-dwelling settlement of Stagno (Leghorn, Italy): wood and food resource exploitation. *Journal of Archaeological Science* 37/6: 1260–1268.

Günther, D. (2005) *Archäobotanik der Pfahlbausiedlung Konstanz-Staad Hörlepark (Baden-Württemberg). Subsistenz und Vegetation in der Urnenfelderzeit.* Norderstedt: GRIN Verlag.

Hajnalová, M. 1998. *Plant remains from two sites in the Auvergne (France). Rapport d'étude.* Multigraphié.

Heiss, A. G. (2008) *Weizen, Linsen, Opferbrote. Archäobotanische Analysen bronze- und eisenzeitlicher Brandopferplätze im mittleren Alpenraum. Doktorarbeit, Universität Innsbruck.* SVH (Süddeutscher Verlag für Hochschulschriften).

Henz, K.-P. (2000) Eisenzeitliche Gebäudegrundrisse von Sehndorf Hinter'm Dellchen, mit einem Beitrag von Julian Wiethold. In A. Miron (ed.) *Archäologische Untersuchungen im Trassenverlauf der Bundesautobahn A8 im Landkreis Merzig-Wadern*: 421–428.

Hopf, M. (1969) Säckingen. In E. Gersbach (ed.) *Urgeschichte des Hochrheins. Funde und Fundstellen in den Landkreisen Säckingen und Waldshut*: 70.

Hopf, M. (1982) Vor- und frühgeschichtliche Kulturpflanzen aus dem nördlichen Deutschland. *Kataloge vor- und frühgeschichtlicher Altertümer* 22: 108, 188.

Hopf, M. (1983) Getreide und Hülsenfrüchte von Scuol-Munt Baselgia. In L. Stauffer-Isenring (ed.) *Die Siedlungsreste von Scuol-Munt Baselgia (Unterengadin GR)*: Basel: Schweizerische Gesellschaft für Ur- und Frühgeschichte.

Hopf, M. (1985) Bronzezeitliche Sämereien aus Ouroux-Marnay, dép. Saône-et-Loire. *Jahrbuch des römisch-germanischen Zentralmuseums* 32: 255–264.

Hopf, M. and Blankenhorn, B. (1983/84) Kultur- und Nutzpflanzen aus vor- und frühgeschichtlichen Grabungen Süddeutschlands. *Bericht der Bayerischen Bodendenkmalpflege* 24/25: 76–111.

Iseli, M. and Jacomet, S. (1994) Erste Ergebnisse der Untersuchungen der botanischen Makroreste aus dem keltischen Basel. In P. Jud (ed.) *Die spätkeltische Zeit am südlichen Oberrhein*: 78–81. Basel: Archäologische Bodenforschung des Kantons Basel-Stadt.

Jacomet, S. and Behre, K.-E. (2008) Der Mittelbronzezeitliche Getreidefund. In A. N. Lanzrein (ed.) *Die befestigte Höhensiedlung Toos-Waldi von der Frühbronzezeit bis in die Spätantike (mit Beiträgen von Stefanie Jacomet, Karl-Ernst Behre und Hansjörg Brem)*: 71–79. Frauenfeld.

Jacomet, S. and Karg, S. (1996) Ackerbau und Umwelt der Seeufersiedlungen von Zug-Sumpf im Rahmen der mitteleuropäischen Spätbronzezeit. Ergebnisse archäobotanischer Untersuchungen. In Regierungsrat des Kantons Zug (ed.) *Die spätbronzezeitlichen Ufersiedlungen von Zug-Sumpf, Band 1: Die Dorfgeschichte*: 198–303 und 365–368. Zug: Kantonales Museum für Urgeschichte.

Jacomet, S. and Martinoli, D. (2004a) Archäobotanik: das obere Schichtpaket – spätbronzezeitlicher Siedlungsbrandschutt. In B. Eberschweiler (ed.) *Bronzezeitliches Schwemmgut vom 'Chollerpark' in Steinhausen (Kanton Zug). Bemerkenswerte Holzfunde vom nördlichen Zugersee sowie weitere bronzezeitliche Hölzer von Fundplätzen an Gewässern der Zentral- und Ostschweiz*: 107–108. Basel: Schweizerische Gesellschaft für Ur- und Frühgeschichte.

Jacomet, S. and Martinoli, D. (2004b) Archäobotanik: das untere Schichtpaket – eine mittelbronzezeitliche 'Off-site'-Situation. In B. Eberschweiler (ed.) *Bronzezeitliches Schwemmgut vom 'Chollerpark' in Steinhausen (Kanton Zug). Bemerkenswerte Holzfunde vom nördlichen Zugersee sowie weitere bronzezeitliche Hölzer von Fundplätzen an Gewässern der Zentral- und Ostschweiz*: 50–51. Basel: Schweizerische Gesellschaft für Ur- und Frühgeschichte.

Jacomet, S., Brombacher, C. and Dick, M. (1989) *Archäobotanik am Zürichsee*. Zürich: Orell Füssli Verlag.

Jacomet, S., Brombacher, C. and Schraner, E. (1999a) Ackerbau und Sammelwirtschaft während der Bronze- und Eisenzeit in den östlichen Schweizer Alpen – vorläufige Ergebnisse. In P. Della Casa (ed.) *Prehistoric alpine environment, society, and economy. Papers of the International Colloquium PAESE '97 in Zürich*: 231–244. Zürich.

Jacomet, S., Jacquat, C., Winter, M. and Wick, L. (1999b) Umwelt, Ackerbau und Sammelwirtschaft. In F. Müller, G. Kaenel and G. Lüscher (eds) *Eisenzeit*: 98–115. Basel: Verlag Schweizerische Gesellschaft für Ur- und Frühgeschichte.

Jacquat, C. (1988) Hauterive-Champréveyres 1. Les plantes de l'âge du Bronze. Catalogue des fruits et graines. *Archéologie Neuchâteloise* 7: 162.

Jacquat, C. (1989) Hauterive-Champréveyres 2. Les plantes de l'âge de Bronze. Contribution à l'histoire de l'environnement et de l'alimentation. In Musée Cantonal d'Archéologie (ed.) *Archéologie Neuchâteloise*. Neuchâtel et St. Blaise: Editions Ruau.

Jacquat, C. and Mermod, O. C. (1998) Alle, Noir Bois (JU). Archéobotanique. Rapport préliminaire. In Masserey, Catherine: Le site d'Alle, Noir Bois (JU, Suisse). Protohistoire, activités 1997. *Archéologie et Transjurane* 62A: 31–49.

Jacquat, C., Della Casa, P. and Studer, J. (2011) Airolo-Madrano 'In Grop', Haute Léventine (Tessin, Suisse): première esquisse de l'espace archéologique et du paléoenvironnement d'un site montagnard aux àge du Bronze et du Fer. In J. Studer, M. David-Elbiali and M. Besse (eds) *Paysage ... Landschaft ... Paesaggio.... L'impact des activités humaines sur l'environnement du Paléolithique à la période romaine (actes du colloque du Groupe de travail pour les recherches préhistoriques en Suisse (GPS/AGUS), qui s'est tenu les 15–16 mars 2007 à Genève au Muséum d'histoire naturelle)*: 83–92.

Jacquet, P., Bouby, L., Franc, O., Bertran, P., Fabre, L. and Argant, J. (1998) Paléoenvironnement, économie et peuplement. In P. Jacquet (ed.) *Habitats de l'âge du Bronze à Lyon-Vaise (Rhône)*: 214–238. Paris: Maison des Sciences de l'Homme.

Jones, G. E. M. and Rowley-Conwy, P. (1984) Plant remains from the North Italian lake dwellings of Fiavé (1400–1200 BC). In R. Perini (ed.) *Scavi archeologici nella zona palafitticole di Fiavé-Carera. Parte 1*: 323–355. Trento.

Karg, S. (1988) Pflanzenreste aus zwei Bodenproben der frühmittelbronzezeitlichen Siedlung Uhingen – Römerstrasse 91 (Kreis Göppingen). In H. Küster (ed.) *Der prähistorische Mensch und seine Umwelt. Festschrift Körber-Grohne*: 231–237. Stuttgart: Konrad Theiss Verlag.

Karg, S. (1989) Verkohlte Pflanzenreste aus der urnenfelderzeitlichen Siedlung. In J. Rehmet Bronze- und eisenzeitliche Fundstelle in Treffensbach. *Fundberichte aus Baden-Württemberg* 14: 246–249.

Klee, M. (2008) Botanik. In M. Ramstein and C. Hartmann (eds) *Langenthal, Unterhard. Gräberfeld und Siedlungsreste der Hallstatt- und Latènezeit, der römischen Epoche und des Frühmittelalters*: 202–211. Bern: Verlag Rub Media.

Klee, M. (2010) Alle, Pré au Prince 2 et sur Noir Bois: les restes végétaux carbonisés (La Tène). In J.-

D. Demarez and B. Othenin-Girard (eds) *Etablissements ruraux de la Tène et de l'Epoque romaine à Alle et à Porrentruy (Jura, Suisse)*: 289–295. Porrentruy.

Klee, M. (2011) Graines et fruits carbonisés provenant des fosses 13 et 17. In O. Wey (ed.) *Occupations protohistoriques au sud de Delémont: de l'âge du Bronze final au Second âge du Fer*: 51–54. Porrentruy: Office de la culture et Société jurassienne d'Emulation.

Klee, M. and Brombacher, C. (2005) Archäobotanik. In M. Ramstein (mit Beiträgen von Ch. Brombacher, E. Büttiker-Schumacher, S. Frey-Kupper, M. Klee, M. Maggetti, D. Rüttimann und S. Ulrich-Bochsler), Ipsach – Räberain. Spätbronzezeitliche Siedlungen und römischer Gutshof. In P. J. Suter and M. Ramstein (eds) *Archäologie im Kanton Bern*: 569–614. Bern: Archäologischer Dienst des Kantons Bern.

Klee, M. and Brombacher, C. (2010) Analyse carpologique. In C. Deslex, E. Evéquoz, C. Bélet-Gonda and S. Saltel (eds) *Occupations protohistoriques à Chevenez: de l'âge du Bronze à la fin de l'âge du Fer*: 154–158. Delémont:

Kohler-Schneider, M. (2001) *Verkohlte Kultur- und Wildpflanzenreste aus Stillfried an der March als Spiegel spätbronzezeitlicher Landwirtschaft im Weinviertel, Niederösterreich (Habilitationsschrift)*. Wien: Verlag der Österreichischen Akademie der Wissenschaften.

Körber-Grohne, U. (1981) Pflanzliche Abdrücke eisenzeitlicher Keramik – Spiegelbild damaliger Nutzpflanzen. *Fundberichte in Baden-Würtemberg*. 6: 165–211.

Körber-Grohne, U. and Piening, U. (1979) Verkohlte Nutz- und Wildpflanzenreste aus Bondorf, Kreis Böblingen. *Fundberichte aus Baden Württemberg* 4: 152–169.

Kreuz, A. (1993) Frühlatènezeitliche Pflanzenfunde aus Hessen als Spiegel landwirtschaftlicher Gegebenheiten des 5.-4. Jh. v. Chr. *Berichte der Kommission für Archäologische Landesforschung in Hessen* 2: 147–170.

Kreuz, A. (2005) *Forschungen der hessischen Landesarchäologie zu Umwelt, Landwirtschaft und Ernährung der Vorzeit*. Landesamt für Denkmalpflege Hessen Abteilung Archäologische und Paläontologische Denkmalpflege.

Kreuz, A. and Boenke, N. (2001) Archäobotanische Ergebnisse der eisenzeitlich-keltischen Fundstellen Bad Nauheim 'Im Deut' und Schwalheim, Bad Nauheim 'Wilhelm-Leuchner-Strasse' (Wetteraukreis). *Berichte der Kommission für Archäologische Landesforschung in Hessen* 6: 233–256.

Kreuz, A. and Boenke, N. (2003) Hirsebrei, Feigen und... Landwirtschaft, Umwelt und Ernährung im Bad Nauheimer Raum. In B. Kull, Landesamt für Denkmalpflege Hessen and Archäologische und Paläontologische Denkmalpflege (eds) *Sole & Salz schreiben Geschichte. 50 Jahre Landesarchäologie – 150 Jahre Archäologische Forschung Bad Nauheim*: 249–255. Mainz am Rhein: Verlag Philipp von Zabern.

Kreuz, A. and Hopf, M. (2001) Ein Gerstenfund vom keltischen Oppidum Dünsberg bei Giessen. In S. Hansen and V. Pingel (eds) *Archäologie in Hessen. Neue Funde und Befunde. Festschrift für Fritz-Rudolf Herrmann zum 65. Geburtstag*: 165–169.

Kreuz, A. and Wiethold, J. (2002) Kontinuität und Wandel? Archäobotanische Untersuchungen zur eisenzeitlichen und kaiserzeitlichen Landwirtschaft der Siedlung Mardorf 23. *Denkmalpflege und Kulturgeschichte* 1: 40–43.

Kroll, H. (1997) Zur eisenzeitlichen Wintergetreide-Unkrautflora von Mitteleuropa. Mit Analysenbeispielen archäologischer Grossreste aus Feudvar in der Vojvodina, aus Greding in Bayern und aus Dudelange in Luxemburg. *Praehistorische Zeitschrift* 72/1: 106–114.

Kroll, H. (1998) Die latènezeitlichen Mohn-Äcker von Wierschem, Kreis Mayen-Koblenz. In A. Müller-Karpe and et al. (eds) *Studien zur Archäologie der Kelten, Römer und Germanen in Mittel- und Westeuropa. Alfred Hafner zum 60. Geburtstag gewidmet*: 353–359.

Kroll, H. (2000) Zum Ackerbau in Wallendorf in vorrömischer und römischer Zeit. *Kelten, Germanen, Römer im Mittelgebirgsraum zwischen Luxemburg und Thüringen. Akten des Internationelen Kolloquiums zum DFG-Schwerpunktprogramm Romanisierung in Trier vom 28. bis 30. September*

1998: Bonn: Dr. Rudolf Habelt GmbH.

Kroll, H. (2001) Die Pflanzenfunde von Wierschem. In C. A. Jost Die späthallstatt- und frühlatènezeitliche Siedlung von Wierschem, Kreis Mayen-Koblenz. Ein Beitrag zur eisenzeitlichen Besiedlung an Mittelrhein und Untermosel. *Berichte zur Archäologie an Mittelrhein und Mosel. Trierer Zeitschrift 7, Beiheft* 25: 531–546.

Kühn, M. and Iseli, M. (2008) Botanische Makroreste aus der spätlatènezeitlichen Siedlung Basel-Gasfabrik, Grabung 1989/5. In P. Jud (ed.) *Die Töpferin und der Schmied. Basel-Gasfabrik, Grabung 1989/5*: 293–324. Basel: Archäologische Bodenforschung des Kantons Basel-Stadt.

Küster, H. (1988a) Urnenfeldzeitliche Pflanzenreste aus Burkheim, Gemeinde Vogtsburg, Kreis Breisgau-Hochschwarzwald (Baden-Württemberg). In H. Küster (ed.) *Der prähistorische Mensch und seine Umwelt, Festschrift für Udelgard Körber-Grohne*: 261–268. Stuttgart: Konrad Theiss Verlag.

Küster, H. (1988b) Pflanzenreste der Späthallstatt-/Frühlatèneeit aus Niedererlbach (Niederbayern). *Bayrisches Vorgeschichtsblatt* 53: 77–82.

Küster, H. (1991) Ackerbau in Niederbayern von der Jungsteinzeit bis zum Mittelalter. *Vorträge 9. Niederbayrischer Archäologentag* 191–198.

Küster, H. (1992a) Early Bronze Age plant remains from Freising, southern Bavaria. *Review of Palaeobotany and Palynology* 73: 205–211.

Küster, H. (1992b) Vegetationsgeschichtliche Untersuchungen. In F. Maier, U. Geilenbrügge, E. Hahn, H.-J. Köhler and S. Sievers (eds) *Ergebnisse der Ausgrabungen 1984–1987 in Manching*: 433–476. Stuttgart: Franz Steiner Verlag.

Küster, H. (1995) *Postglaziale Vegetationsgeschichte Südbayerns. Geobotanische Studien zur prähistorischen Landschaftskunde.* Berlin.

Küster, H. (1998) Neue Analysen an Pflanzenresten aus Manching [New analysis of plant remains from Manching]. Vorbericht über die Ausgrabungen 1996–1997 in Manching. *Germania* 76: 659–661.

Labeaune, R. and Wiethold, J. (2007) L'habitat du Premier âge du Fer dans le Dijonnais (Cote-d'Or) d'après les fouilles récentes: résultats archéologiques et carpologiques. In P. Barral, A. Daubigney, C. Dunning, G. Kaennel and M.-J. Roulière-Lambert (eds) *L'age du Fer dans l'arc jurassien et ses marges. Depots, lieux sacrés et territorialité à l'age du Fer. Actes du XXIXe colloque international de l'AFEAF.*: 73–100. Bienne, 5–8 mai 2005: Besançon: Presses universitaires de Franches-Comté (Annales littéraires; série 'environnement, sociétés et archéologie').

Leducq, A., Rordorf Duvaux, M., Tréhoux, A. and Adatte, T. (2008) *Bevaix/Le Bataillard : occupations terrestres en bordure de marais.* Hauterive: Office et musée cantonal d'archéologie de Neuchâtel.

Lundstrom-Baudais, K. and Mignot, C. (1993) Le milieu végétal au XIe siècle: macrorestes et paléosemences. In M. Colardelle and E. Verdel (eds) *Les habitats du lac de Paladru (Isère) dans leur environnement. La formation d'un terroir au XIe siècle*: 77–97. Paris: Editions de la maison des sciences de l'homme.

Marinval, P. (1988) *Cueillette, agriculture et alimentation végétale de l'épipaléolithique jusqu'au 2è age du fer en France méridionale. Apports paléthnographiques de carpologie.* Thèse pour le Doctorat, Ecole des hautes études en sciences sociales.

Marinval, P. (1993) Analyse des paéosemences. In J. Vital (ed.) *Habitats et sociétés du Bronze final au Premier âge du Fer dans le Jura. Les occupations protohistoriques et néolithiques du Pré de la Cour à Montagnieu (Ain)*: 50–52. Paris: CNRS Éditions.

Mariotti Lippi, M., Bellini, C., Mori Secci, M. and Gonnelli, T. (2009) Comparing seeds/fruits and pollen from a Middle Bronze Age pit in Florence (Italy). *Journal of Archaeological Science* 36: 1135–1141.

Märkle, T. (2011) Plant macro-remains from a late Iron Age well at Schaeffersheim (Bas-Rhin, Alsace). Avec la collaboration de Eric Boes. In J. Wiethold (ed.) *Carpologia. Articles réunis à la mémoire de Karen Lundström-Baudais. Actes de la table ronde organisée par Bibracte, Centre archéologique européen, et le Centre de Recherches Archéologiques de la Vallée de l'Oise, 9–12 juin 2005, Glux-en-Glenne*: 51–61. Bibracte, Glux en Glenne.

Matterne, V. (2001) *Agriculture et alimentation végétale durant l'âge du Fer et l'époque gallo-romaine en France septentrionale.* Montagnac: Editions Monique Mergoil.

Matterne, V. (2003) Rapport d'étude carpologique d'évaluations et de fouilles réalisées sur le tracé du futur TGV est (section Champagne-Ardenne). Compiègne: CRAVO/Inrap.

Matterne, V. (2005) Etude carpologique des sites protohistoriques de l'Europort Vatry. In C. Lagatie and J. Vanmoerkerke (eds) *Les pistes de l'archéologie. Quand la plaine n'était pas déserté*: 79–83. Langrés, Châlons-en-Champagne, Paris: Editions Dominique Guéniot.

Matterne, V. (2009) Premier aperçu des activités agricoles en plaine champenoise à partir d'études carpologiques. In J. Vanmoerkerke (ed.) *Le basin de la Vesle du Bronze final au Moyen Âge à travers les fouilles du TGV est*: 45–56.

Mauvilly, M., Antenen, I., Brombacher, C., Gassmann, P., Guélat, M., Morina-Curty, L., Olive, C., Pillonel, D., Richoz, I. and Studer, J. (1997) Frasses 'Praz au Doux' (FR), un site du Hallstatt ancien en bordure de rivière. *Archäologie der Schweiz* 20: 112–125.

Mercuri, A. M., Accorsi, C. A., Bandini Mazzanti, M., Bosi, G., Cardarelli, A., Labate, D., Marchesini, M. and Grandi, G. T. (2006) Economy and environment of Bronze Age settlements – Terramaras – on the Po Plain (Northern Italy): first results from the archaeobotanical research at the Terramara di Montale. *Vegetation History and Archaeobotany* 16: 43–60.

Motella de Carlo, S. (2002) I resti botanici nel pozzo. In A. R. Serafini (ed.) *Este preromana: una città e i suoi santuari*: 198–229. Treviso: Canova.

Neuweiler, E. (1919) Die Pflanzenreste aus den Pfahlbauten am Alpenquai in Zürich und von Wollishofen sowie einer interglazialen Torfprobe von Niederwenigen (Zürich). *Vierteljahrsschrift der Naturforschenden Gesellschaft in Zürich* 64: 617–648.

Neuweiler, E. (1925) Pflanzenreste aus den Pfahlbauten vom Hausersee, Greifensee und Zürichsee. *Vierteljahrsschrift der Naturforschenden Gesellschaft in Zürich* 70: 225–233.

Neuweiler, E. (1931) Die Pflanzenreste aus dem spätbronzezeitlichen Pfahlbau Sumpf bei Zug. *Vierteljahrsschrift der Naturforschenden Gesellschaft in Zürich* 76: 116–132.

Niederwanger, G. and Tecchiati, U. (eds) (2000) *Wasser – Feuer – Himmel. Ein Brandopferplatz spätbronzezeitlicher Bergknappen.*, Bozen: Folio.

Nisbet, R. (1987) L'utilizzazione delle piante al Riparo del Lauro durante l'età del Bronzo. In D. Cocchi Genik (ed.) *Il riparo del Lauro di Candalla nel Quadro del Bronzo medio iniziale dell'Italia centrooccidentale*: 175–183.

Nisbet, R. (1990) Uso del legno ed economia agricola al Castellaro di Uscio. In R. Maggi (ed.) Archeologia dell'Appennino Ligure. Gli scavi del Castellaro di Uscio: un insediamento di Crinale occupato dal Neolitico alla Conquista Romana. *Istitito Internazionale di Studi Liguri, Collezione di Monografie Preistoriche ed Archeologiche* 8: 197–208.

Nisbet, R. (1994) I vegetali carbonnizzati del Castellaro di Bergeggi. *Rivista Ingauna Intermelia* 46/47(1/4): 102–103.

Nisbet, R. (1996/1997) Offerte votive e analisi botaniche. In L. Salzani (ed.) *Il sito protostorico di Custoza (Sommacampagna – Verona)*: 15–16.

Nisbet, R. and Scaife, R. G. (1998) Analisi archeobotaniche: storia forestale ed uso delle piante. In A. Del Lucchese and et al. (eds) *L'insediamento dell'età del Bronzo di Bric Tana (Millesimo, Savona). Primi risultati delle ricerche*: 273–280.

Oeggl, K. (1992) *Zur Besiedlung des mittleren Alpenraumes während der Bronze- und Eisenzeit: Die Vegetationsverhältnisse.* In J. Kovar-Eder (ed.) *Palaeovegetational development in Europe and regions relevant to its palaeofloristic evolution. Proceedings of the Pan-European palaeobotanical conference, Vienna, 19.–23. September 1991.*

Oeggl, K. (1999) Die Pflanzenreste der jungsteinzeitlichen Siedlung auf dem Himmelreich bei Wattens. Gedenkschrift für Franz Aufschnaiter. *Heimatkundliche Blätter* 8: 33–42.

Pals, J. P. and Voorips, A. (1979) Seed, fruits and charcoals from two prehistoric sites in northern Italy. *Archaeo-Physika* 8: 217–235.

Pasternak, R. (2005) Archäobotanische Untersuchungen der Aschenaltäre aus dem Reitia-Heiligtum von Este, Venetien (Este IV, 4./3. Jh. v. Chr.). In H. Riemer (ed.) *Die Aschenaltäre aus dem Reitia-Heiligtum von Este im mitteleuropäischen und mediterranen Vergleich / Gli altari di ceneri de santuario di Reitia a Este nel contesto-Europeo e mediterraneo*: 425–427. Mainz: Verlag Philipp von Zabern.

Pétrequin, P., Chaix, L., Pétrequin, A.-M. and Piningre, J.-F. (1985) *La grotte de Planches-près-Arbois (Jura), Proto-Cortaillod et Age du Bronze final*. Paris: Editions de la maison des sciences de l'homme.

Piening, U. (1982) Botanische Untersuchungen an verkohlten Pflanzenresten aus Nordwürttemberg (Neolithikum bis römische Zeit). *Fundberichte aus Baden-Württemberg* 7: 239–271.

Piening, U. (1983) Verkohlte Pflanzenreste der Frühlatènezeit von Lauffen am Neckar, Kreis Heilbronn. *Fundberichte aus Baden-Württemberg* 8: 47–54.

Piening, U. (1988a) Kultur- und Wildpflanzenreste aus Gruben der Urnenfelder- und Frühlatènezeit von Stuttgart-Mühlhausen. In H. Küster (ed.) *Der prähistorische Mensch und seine Umwelt. Festschrift für Udelgard Körber-Grohne*: 269–280. Stuttgart: Konrad Theiss Verlag.

Piening, U. (1988b) Neolithische und hallstattzeitliche Pflanzenreste aus Freiberg-Geisingen (Kreis Ludwigsburg). In H. Küster (ed.) *Der prähistorische Mensch und seine Umwelt. Festschrift für Udelgard Körber-Grohne zum 65. Geburtstag.*: 213–228. Stuttgart: Konrad Theiss Verlag.

Poschlod, P. (1984) Ein rezent- ökologisches Modell für die fossile Makroflora von Steinheim a.d. Murr. *Documenta naturae* 18: 12–17.

Ramstein, M., Cueni, A., Vandorpe, P. and Schlumbaum, A. (2012) Das bronzezeitliche Brandgrab von Jegenstort BE-Kirchgasse. In A. Boschetti-Maradi, A. de Capitani and S. Hochuli (eds) *Form, Zeit und Raum. Grundlagen für eine Geschichte aus dem Boden. Festschrift für Werner E. Stöckli zu seinem 65. Geburtstag.*: 169–177. Basel: Reinhardt AG.

Rösch, M. (1991) Archäobotanik und Pflanzensoziologie – Auswertungsmöglichkeiten subfossiler Floren (Beispiel Hagnau-Burg, Urnenfelderkultur, Hornstaad-Hörnle IA, Jungneolithikum). Palaeoethnobotany and Archaeology. International Work-Group for Palaeoethnobotany 8th Symposium Nitra-Nové Vozokany 1989. *ACTA* 7: 273–284.

Rösch, M. (1993a) Pflanzenreste der Spätbronzezeit aus der Ufersiedlung Unteruhldingen-Stollenwiesen (Bodenseekreis). *Plattform. Zeitschrift des Vereins für Pfahlbau und Heimatkunde* 2: 38–55.

Rösch, M. (1993b) Zum Ackerbau der Urnenfelderkultur am nördlichen Oberrhein. Botanische Untersuchungen am Fundplatz Wiesloch-Weinäcker, Rhein-Neckar-Kreis. *Archäologische Ausgrabungen in Baden-Württemberg* 1992: 95–99.

Rösch, M. (1995) Die Pflanzenreste. Aussergewöhnliche Funde der Urnenfelderzeit aus Knittlingen, Enzkreis. Bemerkungen zu Kult und Kultgerät der Spätbronze. *Fundberichte aus Baden-Württemberg* 20: 423–448.

Rösch, M. (1996) Archäobotanische Untersuchungen in der spätbronzezeitlichen Ufersiedlung Hagnau-Burg (Bodenseekreis). In G. S. Schöbel (ed.) *Siedlungsgeschichte im Alpenvorland IV. Die Spätbronzezeit am nordwestlichen Bodensee. Taucharchäologische Untersuchungen in Hagnau und Unteruhldingen 1982–1989*: 239–312. Stuttgart: Konrad Theiss Verlag.

Rösch, M. (2003) Pflanzenreste der frühen Bronzezeit von Mühlhausen-Ehingen, Kreis Konstanz. *Archäologische Ausgrabungen in Baden-Württemberg* 2002: 65–66.

Rösch, M. (2004a). Eisenzeitliche und frühmittelalterliche Pflanzenreste aus Mühlhausen-Ehingen, Kreis Konstanz. *Archäologische Ausgrabungen in Baden-Württemberg* 2003: 46–48.

Rösch, M. (2004b) Pflanzenreste aus Gruben der keltischen Siedlung am Ohrenberg bei

Benzenzimmern, Gde. Kirchheim am Ries, Ostalbkreis. In R. Krause and K.-H. Pfeffer (eds) *Studien zum Ökosystem einer keltisch-römischen Siedlungskammer am Nördlinger Ries*: 287–301. Tübingen: Geographisches Institut der Universität.

Rottoli, M. (1999) Le analisi archeobotaniche. *Scarceta di Manciano (GR) – Un centro abitativo e artigianale dell'Età del Bronzo sulle rive del Fiora. Comune di Manciano, Comunità Montana delle Colline del Fiora 'Zona S' – Pitigliano, Ministero per i Beni e le Attività Culturali*: 151–157.

Roudil, J. L. (1972) L'Age du Bronze en Languedoc oriental. *Mém Soc Préhist Fr* 10: 1–303.

Schaal, C. (2007) Les plantes. In M. Landolt, M. van Es, O. Putelat, D. Bouquin, C. Schaal, E. Boës, a. l. c. de, E. Baccharetti, D. Bevilaqua and I. Dechanez-Clerc (eds) *Entzheim-Geispolsheim (Alsace, Bas-Rhin), Aéroparc (LIDL-CUS), Rapport de fouille préventive. Les occupations protohistoriques*: 326–329. Séléstat: Pôle d'Archéologie Interdépartemental Rhénan.

Schlumbaum, A. (2010) Analyse anthracologique. In C. Deslex, E. Evéquoz, C. Bélet-Gonda and S. Saltel (eds) *Occupations protohistoriques à Chevenez: de l'âge du Bronze à la fin de l'âge du Fer*: 159–161. Delémont.

Schmidl, A. and Oeggl, K. (2005) Subsistence strategies of two Bronze Age hill-top settlements in the eastern Alps – Friaga/Bartholomäberg (Vorarlberg, Austria) and Ganglegg/Schluderns (South Tyrol, Italy). *Vegetation History and Archaeobotany* 14: 303–312.

Stika, H.-P. (1995) Ackerbau und pflanzliche Nahrungsmittel zur Keltenzeit in Südwestdeutschland. *Archäologische Informationen aus Baden-Württemberg* 28: 81–87.

Stika, H.-P. (1996) *Vorgeschichtliche Pflanzenreste aus Heilbronn-Klingenberg*. Stuttgart: Kommissionsverlag, Konrad Theiss Verlag.

Stika, H.-P. (1999) Approaches to reconstruction of early Celtic land-use in the central Neckar region in southwestern Germany. *Vegetation History and Archaeobotany* 8: 95–103.

Stopp, B., Iseli, M. and Jacomet, S. (1999) Die Landwirtschaft der späten Eisenzeit. *Archäologie der Schweiz* 22/1: 27–30.

Toulemonde, F. (2009a) Rapport d'étude carpologique du site protohistorique de Plancy-l'Abbaye 'St Martin' (Aube). In L. a. INRAP Grand-est Nord (ed.) *Rapport d'étude carpologique*. Chalôns-en-Champagne.

Toulemonde, F. (2009b) Étude carpologique des occupations protohistoriques des sites de Ville-St-Jacques 'Les Cailloux noirs', 'Le fond des vallées' et 'Le bois d'échalas'. In R. Issenmann, N. Ameye, G. Auxiette, D. Bardel, L. Bedault, P. Bertin, I. Bertrand, F. Bostyn, V. Delattre, K. Meunier, R. Peake, F. Pilon, I. Praud, J.-M. Seguier, I. Sidera, F. Toulemonde and J. Wiethold (eds) *Ville-Saint-Jacques 'Le fond des vallées'/'Le Bois d'échalas' (Seine-et-Marne, Ile-de-France). Occupations du Néolithique ancien, du Bronze final, du Hallstatt moyen, du Hallstatt final, de La Tène ancienne et de l'époque gallo-romaine*: 168–183. Pantin.

Toulemonde, F. (2009c) Rapport d'étude carpologique du site protohistorique de Pont-sur-Seine 'La Barvière' (Aube). Châlons-en Champagne: Inrap GEN.

Toulemonde, F. (2009d) Etude carpologique de l'occupation protohistorique de Bezannes 'La Bergerie'. Rapport d'étude carpologique. In V. Riquier, G. Achard-Corompt, C. Ampe, G. Auxiette, F. Avival, Y. Devos, B. Duchene, D. Duda, K. Fechner, I. Fortaillier, F. Gauvain, L. Huart, R. Irribarria, S. Loiseau, V. Peltier, M. Poifier, M. Saurel, F. Toulemonde and I. Ture (eds) *Bezannes 'La Bergerie' (Marne). Rapport final d'opération.* Saint-Martin-sur le Pré, Châlons-en-Champagne: Inrap Grand-Est nord, SRA Champagne-Ardenne.

Toulemonde, F. (2009e) Rapport d'étude carpologique du site protohistorique de Reims 'ZAC Croix Blandin' (Marne). Châlons-en Champagne: Inrap GEN.

Toulemonde, F. (2010) Etude carpologique de l'occupation protohistorique de Saint-André-les-Vergers 'Echenilly' (Aube). In V. Riquier, C. Ampe, G. Auxiette, E. Boitard-Bidaut, S. Culot, S. Desbrosse-Degobertiere, A. Demecquenem, D. Duda, D. Durost, K. Fechner, R. Irribarria, S. Loicq, S.

Loiseau, V. Marchaisseau, S. Oudry, E. Segain, M. Saurel, F. Toulemonde, I. Ture and K. Zipper (eds) *Saint-André-les-Vergers (10) 'Echenilly'. Rapport final d'opération, vol. 2*. Saint-Martin-sur le Pré, Châlons-en-Champagne: Inrap Grand-Est nord, SRA Champagne-Ardenne.

Uhlmann, J. (1874) Einiges über Pflanzenreste aus der Pfahlbaustation Mörigen am Bielersee (Bronzezeit). *Anzeiger für Schweizerische Alterthumskunde* 3: 532–535.

Van der Plaetsen, L. (2004) Botanique. Détermination d'essance de charbon de bois et de macrorestes carbonisés provenant des fosses et silos, site de Baentzbruch II à Ettendorf (67350). *Rapport d'étude, Archéolabs*. Saine Bonnet de Chavagne.

Villaret – von Rochow, M. (1958) Die Pflanzenreste der bronzezeitlichen Pfahlbauten von Valeggio am Mincio. *Bericht des geobotanischen Forschungsinstitutes Rübel in Zürich* 96–114.

Wiemann, P., Kühn, M., Heitz-Weniger, A., Stopp, B., Jennings, B., Rentzel, P. and Menotti, F. (2012) Zurich-Alpenquai: a multidisciplinary approach to the chronological development of a Late Bronze Age lakeside settlement in the northern Circum-Alpine Region. *Journal of Wetland Archaeology* 12: 58–85.

Wiethold, J. (1994) Analyse de macrorestes végétaux du Mont Beuvray. In J.-L. Flouest (ed.) *Centre européen d'archéologie du Mont Beuvray. Activités 1993. Prévision 1994. Rapport scientifique de la campagne de recherche 1993 Bibracte sur le Mont Beuvray*: 247–254. Glux-en-Glenne.

Wiethold, J. (1995) Analyse de macrorestes végétaux du Mont Beuvray. In J.-L. Flouest (ed.) *Bibracte, Centre archéologique européen du Mont Beuvray. Rapport scientifique intermédiaire. Activités 1994*: 255–265. Glux-en-Glenne.

Wiethold, J. (1996) Fonctionnement socio-economique de l'oppidum du 2° s. av. J.-C. au 1° s. ap. J.-C. Analyse de macrorestes végétaux du Mont Beuvray. *Bibracte. Centre archéologique européen du Mont Beuvray. Document final de synthèse, rapport triennal 1993–1995*: 3–13.

Wiethold, J. (1998) Recherches archéobotaniques en France du centre-est. In C. M. Beuvray (ed.) *Rapport annuel d'activité scientifique* 1998: 217–240.

Wiethold, J. (1999) Annexe 3. Macrorestes végétaux carbonisés des périodes Bronze final/début Hallstatt et La Tène finale provenant de chantier archéologique de 'La Générie' à Chassenard (Allier). In C. Vermeulen (ed.) *R.C.E.A. Allier. Route Centre Europe Atlantique, zones d'emprunt. Chassenard, La Générie, site n° 03.063.013 AH. Rapport de l'opération préventive de fouille, 30 novembre 1998–16 avril 1999*: Clermont-Ferrand: Multigraphié.

Wiethold, J. (2000a) Verkohlte Pflanzenreste der Bronze- und Eisenzeit aus Büschdorf Weichenförstchen I. In A. Miron (ed.) *Archäologische Untersuchungen im Trassenverlauf der Bundesautobahn A8 im Landkreis Merzig-Wadern*: 73–96.

Wiethold, J. (2000b) Kontinuität und Wandel in der landwirtschaftlichen Produktion und Nahrungsmittelversorgung zwischen Spätlatènezeit und gallorömischer Epoche. Archäobotanische Analysen in der römischen Grossvillenanlage von Borg, Kr. Merzig-Wadern. In A. Haffner and S. von Schnurbein (eds) *Kelten, Germanen, Römer im Mittelgebirgsraum zwischen Luxemburg und Thüringen. Akten des Internationalen Kolloquiums zum DFG-Schwerpunktprogramm 'Romanisierung' in Trier vom 28. bis 30. September 1998*: 147–159. Bonn: Dr. Rudolf Habelt GmbH.

Wiethold, J. (2000c) Verkohlte Pflanzenreste aus der späthallstattzeitlichen Siedlung von Borg Seelengewann. In A. Miron (ed.) *Archäologische Untersuchungen im Trassenverlauf der Bundesautobahn A8 im Landkreis Merzig-Wadern*: 403–420.

Wiethold, J. (2002) Pflanzenreste aus einem spätlatènezeitlichen Brunnen vom *oppidum* Fossé de Pandours, Col de Saverne (Bas-Rhin) – Vorbericht zu den archäobotanischen Analysen. In S. Fichtl and A.-M. Adam (eds) *L'oppidium médiomatrique du Fossé des Pandours au Col de Saverne (Bas-Rhin). Rapport triennal 2000–2002*: 177–186. Strassbourg.

Wiethold, J. (2008) Annexe 4. Larchant (Seine-et-Marne) 'Les Groues'. Macro-restes végétaux provenant des silos et des fosses du Bronze final et de La Tène ancienne sur le site de 'Les Groues' à Larchant (Seine-et-Marne, Île-de-France) (Rapport d'etude carpologique 2008/14). In R. Issenmann (ed.) *Larchant, 'Les Groues' (Seine-et-Marne, Île-de-France). Structure du bronze final et occupations rurales de La Tène ancienne*: 107–127. Pantin: Inrap CIF.

Wiethold, J. (2009) Etude des macro-restes végétaux. Gevrey-Chambertin (Côte d'Or) 'Au Dessus de Bergis'. Agriculture *et ali*mentation végétale du Néolithique moyen (II) jusqu'à La Tène ancien déduite d'analyse carpologique: Les macro-restes végétaux provenant des fosses, silos et trous de poteaux (Rapport d'étude carpologique 2009/2). In S. Chevrier, N. Cantin, F. Ducreux, J.-P. Garcia, L. Jacottey, J.-B. Lajoux, D. Lalai, J. Wiethold, C. Moreau, C. Tristan and R. Symonds (eds) *Gevrey-Chambertin 'Au-Dessus-de-Bergis': une occupation diachronique au pied de la Côte de Nuits. Rapport final d'opération*: 169–186. Dijon: Inrap Grand-Est sud.

Wiethold, J. (2011) Ay-sur-Moselle, Moselle (57), 'Les Velers Jacques'. Les macro-restes végétaux d'occupations de l'âge du Bronze et du premier âge du Fer. In L. a. INRAP Grand-est Nord (ed.) *Rapport archéobotanique 2011/8.* Metz.

Wiethold, J. (2012) Étude anthracologique et paléobotanique des restes végétaux. In F. Ducreux (ed.) Champagnole, Jura, La Planchette. Structures à pierres chauffantes de la fin de l'âge du Bronze et occupation d premier äge du Fer au pied du Mont-Rivel. Campagnole.

Wiethold, J. and Dálnoki, O. (2000) Recherches archéobotaniques en France du Centre-Est. Campagne 2000. *Rapport annuel d'activité 2000 du Centre archéologiques européen du Mont Beuvray*: 309–325.

Wiethold, J. and Labeaune, R. (2005) Pluvet 'Larrivoux'. Un habitat de plaine du premier âge du Fer: premiers résultats sur les macro-restes. In C. Petit (ed.) *Occupation et gestion des plaines alluviales dans le Nord de la France de l'âge du Fer à l'époque gallo-romaine. Actes de la table-ronde de Molesme 17–18 septembre 1999*: 197–211. Besancon: Presses Universitaires de Franche-Comté.

Wiethold, J. and Treffort, J.-M. (2002) Archäobotanische Funde als Hinweis auf Handels- und Kulturkontakte zum Mittelmeergebiet in der Hallstattzeit? Das Beispiel des Fundplatzes von 'Roche Noire', Montagnieu (Ain), Frankreich. In A. Lang and V. Salac (eds) *Fernkontakte in der Eisenzeit. Konferenz Liblice 2000*: 379–394. Praha: Archäologisches Institut der Akademie der Wissenschaften der Tschechischen Republik.

Wiethold, J., Schäfer, E. and Kreuz, A. (2008) Archäobotanische Untersuchungen der eisenzeitlichen und kaiserzeitlichen Siedlung von Mardorf 23. In M. Meyer (ed.) *Mardorf 23, Lkr. Marburg-Biedenkopf. Archäologische Studien zur Besiedlung des deutschen Mittelgebirgsraumes in den jahrhunderten um Christi Geburt*: 353–427. Rahden: VML.

Zanini, A. (1997) A.21 Stagno (Collesalvetti). In A. Zanini (ed.) *Dal Bronzo al Ferro. Il II Millenio A.C. nella Toscana centro occidentale*: 103–115. Livorno.

Zanini, A. and Martinelli, N. (2005) New data on the absolute chronology of Late Bronze Age in Central Italy. BAR International Series. *The Bronze Age in Europe and the Mediterranean* 1337: 147–155.

Zibulski, P. (2001) Archäobotanische Untersuchungen der Makroreste (Samen, Früchte und Dreschreste). In U. Gnepf Horisberger and S. Hämmerle (eds) *Cham-Oberwil, Hof (Kanton Zug). Befunde und Funde aus der Glockenbecherkultur und der Bronzeit*: 150–166, 285–295, 333–339. Basel: Verlag Schweizerische Gesellschaft für Ur- und Frühgeschichte.

Zibulski, P. (2005) Botanische Makroreste. In N. Künzler Wagner (ed.) *Zürich-Alpenquai V: Tauchgrabungen 1999–2001. Funde und Befunde*: 53–55. Zürich und Egg: Baudirektion Kanton Zürich, Hochbauamt, Kantonsarchäologie.

References

Akeret, Ö. (2005) Plant remains from a Bell Beaker site in Switzerland, and the beginnings of *Triticum spelta* (spelt) cultivation in Europe. *Vegetation History and Archaeobotany* 14: 279–286.

Akeret, Ö. and Geith-Chauvière, I. (2011a) Les macrorestes végétaux. In M.-H. Grau Bitterli and E. Fierz-Dayer (eds) *Plateau de Bevaix 6. Bevaix/Treytel – À Sugiez: histoire d'un complexe mégalithique néolithique, témoins d'habitats du Campaniforme et du Bronze ancien*: 311–321. Hautrive: Office et musée d'archéologie de Neuchâtel.

Akeret, Ö. and Geith-Chauvière, I. (2011b) Plateau de Bevaix 7. L'histoire de la relation entre hommes et plantes utiles: synthèse des données carpologiques. Hautrive: Office et musée d'archéologie de Neuchâtel.

Ammann, B. (1988) Palynological Evidence of Prehistoric Anthropogenic Forest Changes on the Swiss Plateau. In H. Birks, H. H. Birks, P. E. Kaland and D. Moe (eds) *The cultural Landscape – Past, Present and Future*. Cambridge Univ. Press.

Ammann, B. (1989) Late-Quaternary palynology at Lobsigensee. Regional vegetation history and local lake development. *Dissertationes Botanicae* 137: 157.

Bellini, C., Capretti, C., Giachi, G., Gonnelli, T., Macchioni, N., Mariotti Lippi, M. and Mori Secci, M. (2007) Indagini arceobotaniche nella struttura ipogeica della Media Età del Bronzo di San Lorenzo a Greve a Firenze. *Riv. Sc. Preist.* 57: 255–262.

Bellini, C., Mariotti-Lippi, M., Mori Secci, M., Aranguren, B. and Perazzi, P. (2008) Plant gathering and cultivation in prehistoric Tuscany (Italy) *Vegetation History and Archaeoabotany* 17: 103–112.

Billamboz, A. (2009a) Jahrringuntersuchungen in der Siedlung Forschner und weiteren bronze- und eisenzeitlichen Feuchtbodensiedlungen Südwestdeutschlands. Aussagen der angewandten Dendrochronologie in der Feuchtbodenarchäologie. In Landesamt für Denkmalpflege (ed.) *Siedlungsarchäologie im Alpenvorland XI.* 399–556. Stuttgart: Konrad Theiss Verlag.

Billamboz, A. (2009b) The Absolute Dating of Wasserburg Buchau: A Long Story of Tree-ring Research. In S. W. Manning and M. J. Bruce (eds) *Tree-Rings, Kings and Old World Archaeology and Environment: Papers Presented in Honor of Peter Ian Kuniholm.* 33–40. Oxford: Oxbow Books.

Blatter, R., Jacomet, S. and Schlumbaum, A. (2004) About the origin of European spelt (*Triticum spelta* L.): allelic differentiation of the HMW Glutenin B1–1 and A1–2 subunit genes. *Theoretical and Applied Genetics* 108: 360–367.

Bogaard, A. (2004) *Neolithic farming in Central Europe. An archaeobotanical study of crop husbandry practices*. London: Routledge.

Bogaard, A. (2011) Farming practice and society in the central European Neolithic and Bronze Age: an archaeobotanical response to the secondary products revolution model. In A. Hadjikoumis, E. Robinson and S. Viner (eds) *The Dynamics of Neolithisation in Europe. Studies in honour of Andrew Sherratt*: 266–283. Oxbow Books.

Bouby, L., Leroy, F. and Carozza, L. (1999) Food plants from Late Bronze Age lagoon sites in Languedoc, southern France: reconstruction of farming economy and environment. *Vegetation History and Archaeoabotany* 8: 53–69.

Bouby, L. and Ruas, M.-P. (2005) Prairies et fourrages: réflexions autour de deux exemples carpologiques de l'Âge de Fer et des Temps Modernes en Languedoc. *Anthropozoologica* 40: 109–145.

Brombacher, C. (2008) Unpublished data from Bronze Age and Iron Age Roveredo GR San Fedele Valasc. Basel University.

Brombacher, C. and Hadorn, P. (2004) Untersuchungen der Pollen und Makroreste aus den Profilsäulen. In S. Jacomet, U. Leuzinger and J. Schibler (eds) *Die jungsteinzeitliche Seeufersiedlung Arbon Bleiche 3. Umwelt und Wirtschaft*: 50–65. Frauenfeld: Amt für Archäologie des Kantons Thurgau.

Brombacher, C. and Jacomet, S. (1997) Ackerbau, Sammelwirtschaft und Umwelt: Ergebnisse archäobotanischer Untersuchungen. In J. Schibler, H. Hüster-Plogmann, S. Jacomet, C. Brombacher, E. Gross-Klee and A. Rast-Eicher (eds) *Ökonomie und Ökologie neolithischer und bronzezeitlicher Ufersiedlungen am Zürichsee*: 220–299. Zürich, Egg: Fotorotar AG.

Burga, C. A. and Perret, R. (1998) *Vegetation und Klima der Schweiz seit dem jüngeren Eiszeitalter*. Thun: Ott Verlag.

Carra, M. L., Cattani, L. and Zanni, C. (2003) Aspetti palethnobotanici dell'area insediativa protostorica di S. Maria in Belvedere sul Monte Cetona (Siena). *Rivista Scientifca Preistorica* 53: 505–518.

Colledge, S. and Conolly, J. (2007) *The Origins and Spread of Domestic Plants in Southwest Asia and Europe*. Walnut Creek: Left Coast.

Cooper, C., Harbeck, M., Kühn, M., Rast-Eicher, A., Schweissing, M., Ulrich-Bochsler, S. and Vandorpe, P. (2010) Spiez-Einigen, Holleeweg 3. Naturwissenschaftliche Untersuchungen zu den bronzezeitlichen Bestattungen. In Erziehungsdirektion des Kantons Bern, Amt für Kultur, Archäologischer Dienst des Kantons Bern (ed.) *ArchBE. Archäologie Bern/Archéologie bernoise. Jahrbuch des Archäologischen Dienstes des Kantons Bern 2010*: 175–198. Bern: Rub Media.

Curdy, P., Mottet, M., Nicoud, C., Baudais, D., Lundström-Baudais, K. and Moulin, B. (1993) Brig-Glis/Waldmatte, un habitat alpin de l'âge du Fer. Fouilles archéologiques N9 en Valais. *Archäologie der Schweiz* 16: 138–151.

Curdy, P., Nicoud, C. and Schindler, M. P. (1998) Dynamique villageoise et datation. L'exemple de l'habitat du 1er âge du Fer de Brigue-Glis/Waldmatte (Valais). *Bulletin d'études préhistoriques et archéologiques alpines* 9: 117–120.

Doyen, E., Vannière, B., Bichet, V., Gauthier, E., Richard, H. and Petit, C. (2012) Vegetation history and landscape management from 6500 to 1500 cal. BP at Lac d'Antre, Gallo-Roman sanctuary of Villards d'Héria, Jura, France. *Vegetation History and Archaeoabotany*. Online first.

Ebersbach, R., Kühn, M., Stopp, B. and Schibler, J. (2012) Die Nutzung neuer Lebensräume in der Schweiz und angrenzenden Gebieten im 5. Jtsd. v. Chr. – Siedlungs- und wirtschaftsarchäologische Aspekte. *Jahrbuch Archäologie Schweiz* 95: 7–34.

Gauthier, E. (2004) *Forêts et Agriculteurs du Jura. Les quatre derniers millénaires*. Besançon.

Gauthier E. and Richard, H. (2009) Bronze Age at Lake Bourget (NW Alps, France): vegetation, human impact and climatic change. *Quat Int* 200: 11–119.

Giachi, G., Mori Secchi, M., Pignatelli, O., Gambogi, P. and Mariotti Lippi, M. (2010) The prehistoric pile-dwelling settlement of Stagno (Leghorn, Italy): wood and food resource exploitation. *Journal of Archaeological Science* 37/6: 1260–1268.

Giles, R. J. and Brown, T. A. (2006) GluDy allele variations in Aegilops tauschii and Triticum aestivum: implications for the origins of hexaploid wheats. *Theorertical and Applied Genetics* 112: 1563–1572.

Haas, J. N. and Hadorn, P. (1998) Die Vegetations- und Kulturlandschaftsgeschichte des Seebachtals von der Mittelsteinzeit bis zum Frühmittelalter anhand von Pollenanalysen. In A. Hasenfratz and M. Schnyder (eds) *Das Seebachtal. Eine archäologische und paläoökologische Bestandesaufnahme*: 221–255. Frauenfeld: Huber & Co AG.

Haas, J. N. and Magny, M. (2004a) Schichtgenese und Vegetationsgeschichte. In S. Jacomet, U. Leuzinger and J. Schibler (eds) *Die neolithische Seeufersiedlung Arbon Bleiche 3. Umwelt und Wirtschaft*: 43–49. Frauenfeld: Amt für Archäologie des Kantons Thurgau.

Haas, J. N., Richoz, I., Tinner, W. and Wick, L. (1998) Synchronous Holocene climatic oscillations recorded on the Swiss Plateau and at timberline in the Alps. *The Holocene* 8/3: 301–309.

Hadorn, P. (1994) *Saint-Blaise/Bains des Dames 1 – Palynologie d'un site néolithique et histoire de la végétation des derniers 16'000 ans*. Neuchâtel: Musée cantonal d'archéologie.

Hall, A. R. (1995) Archaeological evidence for woad *Isatis tinctoria* L. from Medieval England and Ireland. In H. Kroll and R. Pasternak (eds) *Res archaeobotanicae – 9th Symposium IWGP*: 33–38. Kiel: Oetker-Voges-Verlag.

Hammer, Ø. (1999–2012) *PAST: Paleontological statistics, Version 2.14. Reference manual.* Oslo: Natural History Museum, University of Oslo.

Hammer, Ø., Harper, D. A. T. and Ryan, P. D. (2001) PAST: Paleontological statistics software package for education and data analysis. *Paleontologia Electonica 4 (1)* 9pp.

Hegi, G. (1958) Isatis tinctoria. In G. Hegi (ed.) *Illustrierte Flora von Mittel-Europa*: 126–131. München.

Heitz-Weniger, A. (1978) Pollenanalytische Untersuchungen an den neolithischen und bronzezeitlichen Seerandsiedlungen 'Kleiner Hafner', 'Grosser Hafner' und 'Alpenquai' im untersten Zürichsee (Schweiz). *Botanische Jahrbücher für Systematik, Pflanzengeschichte und Pflanzengeographie* 99, 1: 48–107.

Hopf, M. (1983) Getreide und Hülsenfrüchte von Scuol-Munt Baselgia. In L. Stauffer-Isenring (ed.) *Die Siedlungsreste von Scuol-Munt Baselgia (Unterengadin GR)*: Basel: Schweizerische Gesellschaft für Ur- und Frühgeschichte.

Hufschmid, N. (1983) *Pollenanalytische Untersuchungen zur postglazialen Vegetationsgeschichte rund um den Zürichsee anhand von anthropogen unbeeinflussten Moor- und Seesedimenten.* Inaugural-Dissertation, Universität Basel.

Jacomet, S. (2006a) *Identification of cereal remains from archaeological sites.* Basel: IPAS, Basel University.

Jacomet, S. (2006b) Plant economy of the northern Alpine lake dwellings – 3500–2400 cal. BC. *Environmental Archaeology* 11: 65–85.

Jacomet, S. (2007) Neolithic plant economies in the northern alpine foreland from 5500–3500 BC cal. In S. Colledge and J. Conolly (eds) *The origins and Spread of Domestic Plants in Southwest Asia and Europe*: 221–258. Walnut Creek CA: Left Coast Press.

Jacomet, S. (2008) Subsistenz und Landnutzung während des 3. Jahrtausends v. Chr. aufgrund von archäobotanischen Daten aus dem südwestlichen Mitteleuropa. In W. Dörfler and J. Müller (eds) *Umwelt – Wirtschaft – Siedlungen im dritten vorchristlichen Jahrtausend Mitteleuropas und Südskandinaviens*: 355–377. Neumünster: Wachholtz Verlag.

Jacomet, S. (2013) Archaeobotany. Analyses of plant remains from waterlogged archaeological sites. In F. Menotti and A. O'Sullivan (eds) *The Oxford Handbook of Wetland Archaeology*: 497–514. Oxford: Oxford University Press.

Jacomet, S. and Brombacher, C. (2009) Geschichte der Flora in der Regio Basiliensis seit 7500 Jahren: Ergebnisse von Untersuchungen pflanzlicher Makroreste aus archäologischen Ausgrabungen. *Mitteilungen der Naturforschenden Gesellschaften beider Basel* 11: 27–106.

Jacomet, S., Brombacher, C. and Dick, M. (1989) *Archäobotanik am Zürichsee.* Zürich: Orell Füssli Verlag.

Jacomet, S. and Brombacher,C. (1995) Unpublished data from Bronze Age Rekingen AG Bierkeller. Basel University.

Jacomet, S., Brombacher, C. and Schraner, E. (1999a) Ackerbau und Sammelwirtschaft während der Bronze- und Eisenzeit in den östlichen Schweizer Alpen – vorläufige Ergebnisse. In P. Della Casa (ed.) *Prehistoric alpine environment, society, and economy. Papers of the International Colloquium PAESE '97 in Zürich*: 231–244. Bonn: Rudolf Habelt

Jacomet, S., Jacquat, C., Winter, M. and Wick, L. (1999b) Umwelt, Ackerbau und Sammelwirtschaft. In F. Müller, G. Kaenel and G. Lüscher (eds) *Eisenzeit*: 98–115. Basel: Verlag Schweizerische Gesellschaft für Ur- und Frühgeschichte.

Jacomet, S. and Karg, S. (1996) Ackerbau und Umwelt der Seeufersiedlungen von Zug-Sumpf im

Rahmen der mitteleuropäischen Spätbronzezeit. Ergebnisse archäobotanischer Untersuchungen. In Regierungsrat des Kantons Zug (ed.) *Die spätbronzezeitlichen Ufersiedlungen von Zug-Sumpf, Band 1: Die Dorfgeschichte*: 198–303 und 365–368. Zug: Kantonales Museum für Urgeschichte.

Jacomet, S. and Kreuz, A. (1999) *Archäobotanik*. Stuttgart: Verlag Eugen Ulmer.

Jacomet, S., Rachoud-Schneider, A.-M., Zoller, H. and Burga, C. A. (1998) Vegetationsentwicklung, Vegetationsveränderung durch menschlichen Einfluss, Ackerbau und Sammelwirtschaft. In S. Hochuli, U. Niffeler and V. Rychner (eds) *Bronzezeit*: 141–170. Basel: Verlag Schweizerische Gesellschaft für Ur- und Frühgeschichte.

Jacquat, C. (2012) Analyse carpologique du contenu de trous de poteau, de fosses et de jarres. In D. Castelle, J.-F. Buard, M. David-Elbiali, C. Jacquat, P. J. Northover and C. Olive (eds) *L'habitat de l'âge du Bronze moyen de Payerne 'En Planeise' (canton de Vaud, Suisse). Fouilles 1991–1994*: 237–245. Lausanne: IRL+ Lausanne SA.

Jennings, B. (2012a) Settling and Moving: a biographical approach to interpreting patterns of occupation in LBA Circum-Alpine lake-dwellings. *Journal of Wetland Archaeology* 12: 1–21.

Jennings, B. (2012b) When the going gets tough...? Climatic or cultural influences for the LBA abandonment of Circum-Alpine lake-dwellings. In J. Kneisel, W. Kirleis, M. Dal Corso, N. Taylor and V. Tiedtke (eds) *Collapse or continuity? Environment and development of Bronze Age human landscapes. – Proceedings of the international workshop 'Socio-environmental dynamics over the last 12,000 years: the creation of landscapes II (24th–18th March 2011)' in Kiel*: 85–99. Bonn: Rudolf Habelt GmbH.

Jones, G. E. M. and Rowley-Conwy, P. (1984) Plant remains from the North Italian lake Dwellings of Fiavé (1400–1200 BC). In R. Perini (ed.) *Scavi archeologici nella zona palafitticole di Fiavé-Carera. Parte 1*: 323–355. Trento.

Jones, G. E. M. and Rowley-Conwy, P. (1985) Agricultural diversity and sub-alpine colonization: spatial analysis of plant remains from Fiavé. *Papers in Italian Archaeology* 4, BAR 244: 282–295.

Karg, S. and Haas, J. N. (1996) Indizien für den Gebrauch von mitteleuropäischen Eicheln als prähistorische Nahrungsressource. *Tübinger Monographien für Urgeschichte* 11: 429–435.

Kreuz, A. and Schäfer, E. (2008) Archaeobotanical considerations of the development of Pre-Roman Iron Age crop growing in the region of Hesse, Germany, and the question of agricultural production and consumption at hillfort sites and open settlements. *Vegetation History and Archaeobotany* 17, Suppl 1: 159–179.

Kühn, M., Maier, U., Herbig, C., Ismail-Meyer, K., Le Bailly, M. and Wick, L. (2013) Methods for the examination of cattle, sheep and goat dung in prehistoric wetland settlements with examples of the sites Alleshausen-Täschenwiesen and Alleshausen-Grundwiesen (around cal 2900 BC) at Lake Federsee, south-west Germany. *Environmental Archaeology* 18(1): 5–19.

Kühn, M., Wick, L., Perego, R., Heitz, A. and Jacomet, S. (in press) Animal husbandry regimes in Late Neolithic and Bronze Age lake dwellings in the Alpine foreland. *Vegetation History and Archaeobotany*.

Künzler Wagner, N. (ed.) 2005 *Seeufersiedlungen – Zürich-Alpenquai V: Tauchgrabungen 1999–2001, Funde und Befunde*, Zürich, Egg.

Laine, A., Gauthier, E., Gracia, J.-P., Petit, C., Cruz, F. and Richard, H. (2010) A three-thousand-year history of vegetation and human impact in Burgundy (France) reconstructed from pollen a non-pollen palynomorphs analysis. *Comptes Rendus Biologies* 333: 850–857.

Liese-Kleiber, H. (1985) *Pollenanalysen in der Ufersiedlung Hornstaad-Hörnle I*.

Liese-Kleiber, H. (1990) Züge der Landschafts- und Vegetationsentwicklung im Federseegebiet. Neolithikum und Bronzezeit in neuen Pollendiagrammen. *Berichte der Römisch-Germanischen Kommission* 71: 58–83.

Liese-Kleiber, H. (1993) Pollenanalysen zur Geschichte der Siedlungslandschaft des Federsees vom Neolithikum bis ins ausgehende Mittelalter. In C. Brombacher, S. Jacomet and J. N. Haas (eds) *Festschrift Zoller*: 263–278. Berlin, Stuttgart: J. Cramer.

Lotter, A. F. (1999) Late-glacial and Holocene vegetation history and dynamics as shown by pollen and plant macrofossil analyses in annually laminated sediments from Soppensee, central Switzerland. *Vegetation History and Archaeobotany* 8: 165–184.

Machatschek, M. (1999) *Nahrhafte Landschaften*. Wien, Köln, Weimar: Böhlau Verlag.

Magny, M., Arnaud, F., Billaud, Y. and Marguet, A. (2012) Lake-level fluctuations at Lake Bourget (eastern France) around 4500–3500 cal. a BP and their palaeoclimatic and archaeological implications. *Journal of Quaternary Science* 27: 494–502.

Magny, M., Galop, D., Bellintani, P., Desmet, M., Didier, J., Haas, J. N., Martinelli, N., Pedrotti, A., Scandolari, R., Stock, A. and Vannière, B. (2009a) Late-Holocene climatic variability south of the Alps as recorded by lake-level fluctuations at Lake Ledro, Trentino, Italy. *The Holocene* 19(4): 575–589.

Magny, M., Peyron, O., Gauthier, E., Roueche, Y., Bordon, A., Billaud, Y., Chapron, E., Marguet, A., Petrequin, P. and Vanniere, B. (2009b) Quantitative reconstruction of climatic variations during the Bronze and early Iron ages based on pollen and lake-level data in the NW Alps, France. *Quaternary International* 200: 102–110.

Maier, U. (1998) Der Nacktweizen aus den neolithischen Ufersiedlungen des nördlichen Alpenvorlandes und seine Bedeutung für unser Bild von der Neolithisierung Mitteleuropas. *Archäologisches Korrespondenzblatt* 28: 205–218.

Mariotti Lippi, M., Bellini, C., Mori Secci, M. and Gonnelli, T. (2009) Comparing seeds/fruits and pollen from a Middle Bronze Age pit in Florence (Italy). *Journal of Archaeological Science* 36: 1135–1141.

Mercuri, A. M., Accorsi, C. A., Bandini Mazzanti, M., Bosi, G., Cardarelli, A., Labate, D., Marchesini, M. and Grandi, G. T. (2006) Economy and environment of Bronze Age settlements – Terramaras – on the Po Plain (Northern Italy): first results from the archaeobotanical research at the Terramara di Montale. *Vegetation History and Archaeobotany* 16: 43–60.

Ollive, V., Petit, C., Garcia, J.-P., Wick, L. and Schlumbaum, A. (2009) Le paysage antique. In M. Reddé (ed.) *Oedenburg. Les fouilles françaises, allemandes et suisses à Biesheim et Kunheim, Haut-Rhin, France. Volume 1: Les camps militaires julio-claudiens*, 17–43. Mainz.

Perego, R. (in preparation) *Contribution to the development of the Bronze Age plant economy in the surrounding of the Alps: An archaeobotanical case study of two Early Bronze Age sites in Northern Italy (Lake Garda region)*. Doctoral thesis. Basel University.

Richard, H. and Gauthier, E. (2007) Bilan des données polliniques concernant l'âge du Bronze dans le Jura et le nord des Alpes. In H. Richard, M. Magny and C. Mordant (eds) *Environnements et cultures à l'âge du Bronze en Europe occidentale*: 71–81. Paris: Editions du CTHS.

Richoz, I. (1998) Etude paléoécologique du lac de Seedorf (Fribourg, Suisse). Histoire de la végétation et du milieu durant l'Holocène: le rôle de l'homme et du climat. [Palaeoecological study of the lake of Seedorf, Fribourg. The role of humans and climate in Holocene vegetation history and environment]. *Dissertationes Botanicae* 293: 1–177.

Rösch, M. (1983) Geschichte der Nussbaumer Seen (Kanton Thurgau) und ihrer Umgebung seit dem Ausgang der letzten Eiszeit aufgrund quartärbotanischer, stratigraphischer und sedimentologischer Untersuchungen. *Mitt. Thurg. Naturf. Ges.* 45: 1–110.

Rösch, M. (1985) Nussbaumer Seen – Spät- und postglaziale Umweltveränderungen einer Seengruppe im östlichen Schweizer Mittelland. In G. Lang (ed.) *Swiss lake and mire environments during the last 15000 years. Dedicated to the Memory of Max Welten (1904–1984)*: 337–379. Vaduz: J. Cramer.

Rösch, M. (1995) Geschichte des Nussbaumer Sees aus botanisch-ökologischer Sicht. *Mitteilungen der Thurgauischen Naturforschenden Gesellschaft* 53: 43–59.

Rösch, M. (2005) Spätneolithische und bronzezeitliche Landnutzung am westlichen Bodensee. Versuch einer Annäherung anhand archäobotanischer und experimenteller Daten. In P. Della Casa and M. Trachsel (eds) *WES'04. Wetland Economies and Societies. Proceedings of the International Conference Zurich, 10–13 March 2004*: 105–119. Zürich: Chronos.

Rösch, M., Fischer, E., Müller, H., Sillmann, M. and Stika, H.-P. (2008) Botanische Untersuchungen zur Eisenzeitlichen Landnutzung im südlichen Mitteleuropa. In D. Krausse (ed.) *Frühe Zentralisierungs- und Urbanisierungsprozesse: zur Genese und Entwicklung frühkeltischer Fürstensitze und ihres territorialen Umlandes: Kolloquium des DFG-Schwerpunktprogramms 1171 in Blaubeuren, 9. 015011. Oktober 2006*: 319–348. Stuttgart: Theiss.

Schibler, J., Hüster-Plogmann, H., Jacomet, S., Brombacher, C., Gross-Klee, E. and Rast-Eicher, A. (eds) (1997) *Ökonomie und Ökologie neolithischer und bronzezeitlicher Ufersiedlungen am Zürichsee*, Zürich, Egg: Fotorotar AG.

Schilperoord, P. (2012) Beitrag zur Geschichte der Kulturpflanzen. 1. Getreide – Schweiz, Nord- und Südtirol. e-book.

Schmidl, A. (2005) *Subsistence Strategies and Husbandry Regime in the Alpine Area during Bronze and Iron Age.* Dissertation, Leopold-Franzens-Universität Innsbruck.

Schmidl, A. and Oeggl, K. (2005) Subsistence strategies of two Bronze Age hill-top settlements in the eastern Alps – Friaga/Bartholomäberg (Vorarlberg, Austria) and Ganglegg/Schluderns (South Tyrol, Italy). *Vegetation History and Archaeobotany* 14: 303–312.

Stace, C. (1999) *Field flora of the British Isles.* Cambridge University Press.

Stika, H.-P. and Heiss, A. G. (2013) Plant cultivation in the Bronze Age. In H. Fokkens and A. Harding (eds) *The Oxford Handbook of European Bronze Age*: 340–361. Oxford: Oxford University Press.

Tinner, W., Lotter, A. F., Ammann, B., Conedera, M., van Leeuwen, J. F. N. and Wehrli, M. (2003) Climatic change and contemporanous land use phases north and south of the Alps 2300 BC to 800 AD. *Quaternary Science Reviews* 22: 1447–1460.

Valsecchi, V., Tinner, W., Finsinger, W. and Ammann, B. (2006) Human impact during the Bronze Age on the vegetation at Lago Lucone (northern Italy). *Vegetation History and Archaeobotany* 15: 99–113.

Welten, M. (1982) Vegetationsgeschichtliche Untersuchungen in den westlichen Schweizer Alpen: Bern-Wallis. *Denkschr. der Schweiz. Naturf. Ges.* 95: 86–91.

Wick, L. (1988) *Palynologische Untersuchungen zur Spät- und Postglazialen Vegetationsgeschichte am Greifensee bei Zürich (Mittelland).* Diplomarbeit, Universität Bern.

Wiemann, P., Kühn, M., Heitz-Weniger, A., Stopp, B., Jennings, B., Rentzel, P. and Menotti, F. (2012) Zurich-Alpenquai: a multidisciplinary approach to the chronological development of a Late Bronze Age lakeside settlement in the northern Circum-Alpine Region. *Journal of Wetland Archaeology* 12: 58–85.

Zech-Matterne, V. and Leconte, L. (2010) New archaeobotanical finds of *Isatis tinctoria* L. (woad) from Iron Age Gaul and a discussion of the importance of woad in ancient time. *Vegetation History and Archaeobotany* 19: 137–142.

Zoller, H. and Erny-Rodman, C. (1994) Epochen der Landschaftsentwicklung im Unterengadin. In A. F. Lotter and B. Ammann (eds) *Festschrift Gerhard Lang. Beiträge zur Systematik und Evolution, Floristik und Geobotanik, Vegetationsgeschichte und Paläoökologie*: 565–581. Berlin, Stuttgart: J. Cramer.

Chapter 7

Animal husbandry and hunting activities in the Late Bronze Age Circum-Alpine region

Barbara Stopp

Introduction

One of the most obvious innovations of the Bronze Age compared to the preceding Neolithic was the use of metal, which had now become a regular occurrence (*e.g.* Hochuli *et al.* 1998). The extraction of copper from a number of locations throughout the Alps led to new areas being opened and settled that had previously been only rarely frequented. However, the tin required to produce bronze could only be found in a few European regions, which led to an increase in the exchange and trade of goods between far-flung areas. The question might be raised, therefore, as to whether the economic changes and the resulting societal changes also had an impact on a much more essential area of life: farming. This chapter examines this question in terms of animal husbandry and hunting in the Circum-Alpine region between the Middle Bronze Age and the Early Iron Age. The following specific topics will be examined:

a) palaeo-economy and subsistence
b) aspects of animal husbandry: were environmental and cultural factors responsible for a specific type of animal husbandry being used? What were the changes in the breeding of livestock and the explanations for these changes, for instance the increased exploitation of secondary products (milk and work) and influences from outside the region (trade)?
c) changes and adaptations over space and time

Overviews of the state of research concerning archaeozoological studies in the Circum-Alpine region in the Bronze Age and Iron Age have been published for Switzerland, Italy, and Austria (Switzerland: Schibler and Studer 1998; Schibler *et al.* 1999. Italy: de Grossi Mazzorin *et al.* 2004; Petrucci 2007. Austria: Pucher 1994; Marti-Grädel *et al.* 2012). This chapter attempts to examine the various aspects of research across these countries, as well as south-eastern France and southern Germany. In addition to the range of animal species (which is usually studied) and the animal sizes, we also include information on the sex and age of the domestic animals. With a few exceptions, all the data have been taken from published archaeological and archaeozoological studies.

Figure 7.1. Map of sites with regions (red circles) referred to in the text.

Sites dating from the Middle Bronze Age to the early and Middle Iron Ages were included in the investigation. Focus was placed on the Late Bronze Age because this period has yielded the highest number of sites where archaeozoological analyses have been carried out. The data gathered were from both wetland settlements on the lake shores and dry-land settlements. This not only allowed comparison of sites with different preservation conditions but also inclusion of peripheral regions that were only settled some time during the Middle Bronze Age, such as the Alps (*e.g.* Curdy and Chaix 2009: 107; Della Casa 2002: 20; Walser 2012: 208). For the purposes of this study, the term 'wetland sites' includes lacustrine, riverine, and marshland sites. The general term 'dry-land sites' is divided further into actual dry-land sites (terrestrial sites excluding upland sites), upland sites (dry-land sites situated on promontories, ridges, or in other elevated locations), and caves/rock shelters.

The data gathered came from 79 sites (Fig. 7.1; Table 7.1); in order to be included in the study, a site had to have at least 50 identified bones. Because some of the sites yielded finds from more than one of the periods examined, the database eventually consisted of 90 archaeological units (AU), from the sites. The sites are located in five countries within the Circum-Alpine region: Switzerland (35 AU), northern Italy (32 AU), Austria (11 AU), south-eastern France (7 AU), and southern Germany (5 AU). This distribution shows that the final conclusions are most reliable for northern Italy and Switzerland because the data for the other areas are fairly scarce. The archaeozoological information included the number of fragments and weights in respect of all animal species or groups, as well as a rough age distribution, the sex ratio, and height at withers of the domestic animals – wherever possible, the state of preservation of the material was also noted.

As most of the data were gathered from published sources, it seems appropriate to add a few statements on those sources. Unfortunately, there are still very few standards that archaeozoologists generally adhere to; this refers not only to classification criteria but also to the choice of the criteria that are actually studied. While the range of species identified at different sites by different archaeozoologists can be compared without issue, this cannot necessarily be said for the determination of the age and sex of the animals. The selection of bones can also pose problems, for instance if not all the bones recovered were analysed or if only certain bones were selected for recovery during the excavation. Moreover, there are archaeological problems, such as how the results can be assessed if the excavated areas were of different sizes. In other words, can the contents of a single pit in one settlement be compared to the finds recovered from half the settlement area of another site? While there are no solutions to these problems, they must be borne in mind when interpreting the data.

Subsistence and economy

Hunting

Two phases of climate deterioration occurred during the northern Alpine Bronze Age: the first lasted from the Middle Bronze Age to the beginning of the Late Bronze Age, while the second took place towards the end of the Late Bronze Age and the beginning of the Iron Age. The deterioration of the climate was also noticeable south of the Alps; however, it had a somewhat different impact on settlement activity (Magny *et al.* 1998; Magny 2013; see also Chapter 4, this volume). During the Neolithic, such climate deteriorations led to more intense hunting activity (*e.g.* Schibler and Jacomet 2010; Menotti 2009: 64) – did the same happen in the Bronze Age?

As the presence of very small species is highly dependent on excavation methods (i.e. wet sieving) as well as the type of site, for this study, it was necessary to take into account only wild mammals larger than squirrels and small birds. As a result, comparative analyses between different sites are not fully reliable for the smaller species.

In total, 23 different wild mammals and 24 bird species were identified – most of the species identified prefer forest-rich habitats. This notion fits in well with the Bronze Age landscape throughout vast areas of Europe. However, only deer and boar were found at more than 50% of the sites, while most of the other wild animal species were identified at less than 10% of the sites. Interestingly, only a very small number of the 47 species were hunted regularly, highlighting the existence of a relatively purposeful hunting strategy.

The proportion of wild animals in the individual AU varied greatly (between 0% and 74.8%), with the average value being 5.9% and the median even lower at 2.4%. Both values, particularly the latter, show that the majority of the sites yielded only very small amounts of wild animals throughout all the periods studied. Therefore, despite the climate deteriorations, the average proportion of hunted animals was much lower than it had been during the Neolithic (Schibler and Studer 1998: 188), which suggests that farming conditions were relatively stable (Benecke 1998: 67; Schibler and Jacomet 2005: 31). This was due to the fact that crop cultivation improved greatly during the Bronze Age and was

Country	Site	Period (1)	Site type	n det. (2)	Archaeozoological literature
Austria	Bludenz-Montikel, Sch. IV	LBA	dry-land	773	Amschler 1937a
	Brixlegg-Mariahilfbergl – Plateau E, Quadrant I, Schichten 5–9	LBA	upland	1460	Boschin/Riedel 2011
	Brixlegg-Radfeld – Mauken A	LBA	upland	1525	Schibler et al. 2009
	Brixlegg-Radfeld – Mauken D	LBA	upland	1073	Schibler et al. 2009
	Drösing – Testgrabung 1994	LBA	marsh	258	Riedel 2007
	Fliess-Silberplan	MBA	dry-land	1762	Stopp unpubl. a
	Kitzbühel-Kelchalm – Scheidehalde Nr. 23	LBA	upland	3997	Amschler 1937b
	Kleinklein-Burgstallkogel	LBA–EIA	upland	1293	Peters/Smolnik 1994
	Unterhautzenthal-Leimgrube	MBA	dry-land	430	Pucher 2001
	Viehhofen-Wirtsalm – Scheidehalde 10	LBA(–EIA?)	upland	490	Stopp unpubl. b
France	Besançon – Saint-Paul	LBA	dry-land	487	Chaix 1979, Borello/Chaix 1983
	Blois-sur-Seille – Abri supérieur	LBA	rock shelter	94	Pétrequin/Vuaillat 1968
	Epervans-Vauvretin	LBA	dry-land	628	Bonnamour/Poulain 1973
	Jons-Batailles	LBA	dry-land	290	Hénon et al. 2002
	La Baume des Anges	LBA	cave	51	Chaix 1986b
	Les Planches-près-Arbois, Sch. D2-B	LBA	cave	136	Chaix 1985
	Ouroux-s-Saône – Curtil Brenot	LBA–EIA	dry-land	388	Bonnamour/Poulain 1973, Poulain 1973
	Am Hascherkeller	LBA	dry-land	235	Benefit 1983
	Breisach-Münsterberg – Schanno u. St-Laurentiusheim	LBA	dry-land	70	Arbinger-Vogt 1978
	Heidelberg-Bergheim	LBA	dry-land	56	Stephan 2007
	Hundersingen-Heuneburg, Ph. V–VII	MBA–LBA	dry-land	520	v. d. Driesch/Boessneck 1989
	Ladenburg-Ziegelscheuer	LBA	dry-land	225	Feller 2002
Italy	Bovolone	MBA–LBA	dry-land	1030	Catagnano 2008
	Brixen-Sarns – Albanbühel, Hütte A + E	MBA	upland	10392	Riedel/Rizzi 1995
	Brixen-Elvas	LBA	upland	295	Boschin 2006
	Concordia Sagittaria	EIA	dry-land	1163	Pino Uria/Tagliacozzo 2001
	Eppan-Gamberoni (aka Eppan-St Pauls – Siechenhaus)	LBA	dry-land	1416	Riedel 1985a
	Laion-Wasserbühel, Sektor F	MBA–LBA	dry-land	905	Tecchiati et al. 2011
	Legnago-Fondo Paviani	LBA	dry-land	283	Riedel 1979
	Monte Leoni	MBA	upland	347	Ammerman et al. 1978
	Noceto	MBA	marsh	648	de Grossi Mazzorin 2009

Country	Site	Period (1)	Site type	n det. (2)	Archaeozoological literature
	Nogarole Rocca – I Camponi	MBA	dry-land	1282	Riedel 1992
	Oppeano-Feniletto	LBA	marsh	97	Riedel 1982b
	Peschiera del Garda-Setteponti	MBA–LBA	lacustrine	393	Riedel 1982a
	Pfatten/Vadena-Stadlhof, Ph. III	LBA–EIA	dry-land	588	Riedel 2002, Petrucci 2007
	Pfatten/Vadena-Stadlhof, Ph. II	EIA	dry-land	1710	
	Pfatten/Vadena-Stadlhof, Ph. I	EIA–MIA	dry-land	1463	
	Pilastri-I Verri, Schnitt B + C	MBA(–LBA)	riverine	493	Farello 1995
	Poggio Rusco – Boccazzola Vechia	MBA	dry-land	196	Catalani 1984
	Poviglio – Santa Rosa-Villagio Piccolo, strati basali	MBA	marsh	2165	Riedel 2004
	Pozzuolo-Braida Roggia	LBA	dry-land	229	Riedel 1981, Petrucci 1994
	Pozzuolo-Ciastei/Castelliere	(LBA–)EIA (–MIA)	dry-land	2052	Riedel 1984b, Petrucci 1998
	Sabbionara di Veronella, untere Grubenverfüllung	LBA	dry-land	1113	Riedel 1993
	Sabbionara di Veronella, oberste Grubenverfüllung	LBA	dry-land	110	
	San Pietro di Morubio-Cavalzara	LBA	dry-land	164	Riedel 1979
	Schluderns – Ganglegg, G16-19	MBA	upland	4586	Schmitzberger 2007
	Schluderns – Ganglegg, G15	LBA	upland	947	
	Schluderns – Ganglegg, G11-13	LBA	upland	456	
	Schluderns – Ganglegg, 'Hahnhütterbödele'	LBA(–EIA)	upland	484	
	Sonnenburg, Horizont 4	MBA	dry-land	208	Riedel 1984a
	Sotćiastel, Schnitte A, B, C, E	MBA(–LBA)	upland	9088	Salvagno/Tecchiati 2011
	Tabina di Magreta, Grabung 1985	MBA	marsh	535	De Grossi Mazzorin 1989
	Tires/Tiers-Thalerbühel	EIA	upland	248	Marconi/Tecchiati 2006
	Volta Mantovana-Isolone della Prevaldesca	MBA–LBA	riverine	3147	Riedel 1975, Riedel 1977
Switzerland	Ayent-le Château, Sch. 3/4	LBA	upland	155	Chaix 1990a
	Bavois-en-Raillon, Sch. 3–6	LBA	dry-land	109	Chaix 1984
	Brig-Glis/Waldmatte, Ph. I.3	EIA	dry-land	671	Sidi Maamar/Gillioz 1995, Sidi Maamar 1997
	Cornol – Mont Terri, Schnitt 6	MBA	upland	252	Morel 1988
	Cortaillod-Est	LBA	lacustrine	3819	Chaix 1986a

Table 7.1. List of sites used in the study. (1): MBA: Middle Bronze Age, LBA: Late Bronze Age, EIA: early Iron Age, MIA: middle Iron Age. (2): all bones determinable to species or genus level, without mammals smaller than squirrels, fish, molluscs and reptiles. *Continued on p. 184.*

Country	Site	Period (1)	Site type	n det. (2)	Archaeozoological literature
	Cazis – Cresta, Planum 10-12 (Felder 14–16 zentrale Felsspalte)	MBA	upland	2300	Plüss 2011
	Cazis – Cresta, Planum 14 (Felder 14–16 zentrale Felsspalte)	LBA	upland	1595	
	Fällanden-Rietspitz	LBA	lacustrine	92	Schibler unpubl. a
	Flums-Gräpplang, Rebberg Ost	LBA	upland	1163	Kanelutti 1994
	Frasses 'Praz au Doux'	EIA	riverine	215	Mauvilly et al. 1997
	Genève – Eaux-Vives	LBA	lacustrine	1101	Revilliod/Reverdin 1927
	Greifensee-Böschen	LBA	lacustrine	319	Veszeli 2007
	Haldenstein 'Auf dem Stein'	EIA	dry-land	258	Rehazek unpubl.
	Hallwil-Rostbau (Seengen-Riesi)	LBA	lacustrine	403	Steinmann 1923, Steinmann 1925
	Hauterive – Champréveyres, Sch. 3	LBA	lacustrine	4288	Studer 1991
	Ipsach – Räberain, hpts. Sch. 3	LBA	dry-land	124	Ramstein et al. 2005
	Le Landeron-Les Marais	LBA	riverine	142	Borello/Chaix 1983
	Marin-Le Chalvaire	MBA	dry-land	66	Studer 1998
	Meilen-Schellen	LBA	lacustrine	631	Schibler unpubl. b
	Möriken-Kestenberg	LBA	upland	2754	Schmid 1952, Schmid 1955
	Nunningen-Portiflue	LBA	upland	395	Gutzwiller et al 1996
	Pieterlen – Under-Siedebrunne 3, Fundschicht 27/4	LBA	dry-land	98	Ramstein/Deschler-Erb 2005
	Savognin – Padnal, Horizont C, Felder 1 + 3	MBA	upland	4402	Bopp unpubl.
	Savognin – Padnal, Horizont B, Felder 1 + 3	LBA	upland	10792	
	Scuol – Munt Baselgia, Horizont I–III	MBA–LBA	upland	2417	Kaufmann/Stampfli 1983
	Scuol – Munt Baselgia, Horizont III–V	LBA–EIA	upland	714	
	Stanstad – Loppburg, Zone ZI, Sch. 21 und 22	LBA	upland	102	Stopp 2007
	Ürschhausen/Hüttwilen – Horn	LBA	marsh	284	Markert unpubl.
	Vex-le-Château	LBA	upland	233	Chaix 1990b
	Vinelz-Ländti	LBA	lacustrine	482	Stampfli unpubl.
	Visp – In Albon, Salle 1 + 3	LBA	cave	51	Chaix 1987
	Wittnau – Wittnauerhorn, Sonderung 4, Schicht 3b + 3a	LBA	upland	128	Berger et al. 1996
	Zug-Sumpf	LBA	lacustrine	898	Reverdin 1927, Reverdin 1928, Schibler/Veszeli 1996
	Zürich-Alpenquai, Grabungen 1916, 1919, 1970.024, 1999.186	LBA	lacustrine	6775	Wettstein 1924, Wiemann et al. 2013
	Zürich-Grosser Hafner	LBA	lacustrine	462	Schibler unpubl. c

Table 7.1. List of sites used in the study, continued

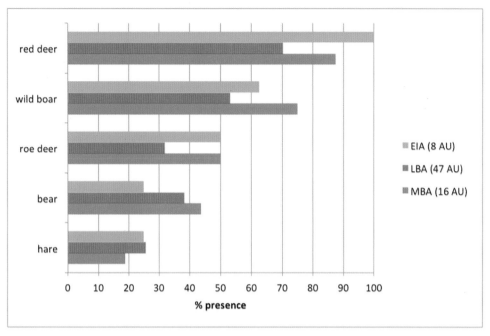

Figure 7.2. Presence of the most common wild animals. MBA: Middle Bronze Age, LBA: Late Bronze Age, EIA: early Iron Age, AU: archaeological unit.

thus more crisis resistant (see Kühn and Heitz-Weniger, Chapter 6, this volume; Schibler and Studer 1998: 174; Schibler and Jacomet 2005: 31) – only on rare occasions was it necessary, therefore, to enhance one's diet by hunting.

Based on the small percentages of wild animal species, only presence-absence analyses have been carried out in respect of the species most commonly found (*i.e.* deer, boar, roe deer, hare, and bear) for the period from the Middle Bronze Age to the early Iron Age. The presence values for the three hunted species of deer, boar, and roe deer were more regular during phases of climate deterioration in the Middle Bronze Age and early Iron Age than during the Late Bronze Age (Fig. 7.2). This, quite probably, is a reaction to the deterioration in farming conditions. Hunting, however, was pursued in a targeted manner: species that provide more meat were preferred, which is reflected in the fact that the presence of bear bones in the settlements decreased during the same period. Bones of hares were more prevalent during the Late Bronze Age and early Iron Age than before. This reflects the fact that the landscape was opened up, providing better living conditions for hares. The phase of reforestation at the end of the Late Bronze Age and the beginning of the Iron Age, which has been confirmed by pollen analyses (see Chapter 6), was therefore not very pronounced.

We know from Neolithic research that the type of site has an impact on the proportion of wild animal species: wetland sites always yield higher proportions of wild animals than dry-land sites – this phenomenon cannot, however, be satisfyingly explained only in terms of preservation (Schibler and Studer 1998: 174). Our study showed that the type of site only had an impact on the numbers of wild animals insofar as the upland sites in northern Italy and Switzerland had significantly lower proportions of wild animals than the lowland sites, irrespective of whether they were situated on wet or dry land. While the wetland sites yielded more wild animals on average than the dry-land sites and their proportions were much more heterogeneous, the differences were statistically irrelevant. The upland settlements were special in that they often served a particular function, which might in many cases explain the lower numbers or absence of wild animals. Some of these places were linked to mining; the settlements were constructed for a quite specific purpose, which obviously did not include hunting. Moreover, not all mining settlements would have been occupied all year round. This fact alone explains the lack of hunting, which was time-consuming; the limited period of time available had to be used more productively. Recent investigations carried out in the Silvretta area (Grisons, Switzerland) have suggested that Alpine pastures were used, perhaps on a seasonal basis (Reitmaier *et al.* 2013). As there is no evidence in the area to suggest mining activities, the most likely scenario is that there was an early form of Alpine farming (Walser 2012: 208). This was also an occupation that probably left very little time for hunting. Other upland sites were places of refuge, which means that hunting was not an option or that the sites were only occupied for relatively short periods of time. Based on the results obtained, the function of a site appears to have had more of an impact on the amount of hunting than climate conditions or the date of the site.

The comparison between the different regions in northern Italy in regard to the proportion of wild animals shows decreasing values from the southern to the northern Po Valley (Po Plain) and into the Alpine region; there are also marked differences between some of the Swiss areas (Fig. 7.3). While the three mountain regions of the Grisons, northern Jura, and Valais have yielded very low values (as mentioned above), central and eastern Switzerland have rather high numbers of wild animal species – the values in western Switzerland lie somewhere between the two. The same differences between eastern and western Switzerland already existed during the Neolithic, quite probably due to different environmental conditions.

The identification of regional differences in regard to the presence of wild animal species has also been attempted; the values presented here are for the various regions of northern Italy, where wild animal species were present at more than 10% of the sites (Fig. 7.4). It is immediately apparent that the wild species at the Alpine sites were quite dissimilar to those in the other regions. The difference was that the usual species of deer, roe deer, and boar were hunted less, while other wild species were hunted more often. Similar observations have been made in regard to Switzerland, although the differences are not quite as pronounced. In principle, less hunting took place in mountain sites in both countries, and hunters focused less on the usual triumvirate of deer-boar-roe deer. This can be partially explained by the fact that the three species were not quite as numerous in mountainous regions as in the lowlands. It could also reflect the result of less purposeful hunting, which was not motivated by the amount of meat to be gained. The driving force behind hunting expeditions in the uplands may have been different to that in the lowlands.

Based on the findings discussed above, it can be concluded that the amount of hunting depended on the function of a settlement on the one hand and the region it was located in on the other, not on the date of the settlement or the climate conditions.

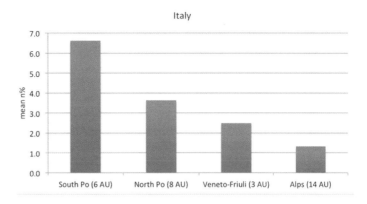

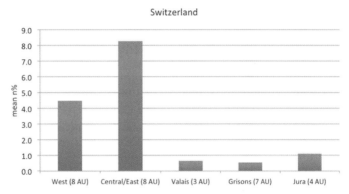

Figure 7.3. Regional differences of the proportion of wild animals in Italy and Switzerland. AU: archaeological unit.

Diet and animal husbandry

The prevalent domestic animals in the Bronze Age were cattle, sheep, goats, pigs, and dogs, as had already been the case in the Neolithic throughout Europe (Manning *et al.* 2013). Although present as a domestic animal by the end of the Neolithic, horses began to be more consistently used from the Bronze Age onwards (Benecke 1998: 61; Schibler and Studer 1998: 177). As it is often impossible to distinguish between sheep and goat bones, in our study the two species have been grouped together – this approach has become established in archaeozoological research.

Diet

As in the Neolithic, meat would have played a much smaller role in the daily diet of the Bronze Age population than fruit and vegetable produce (*e.g.* Ebersbach 2003). Meat was definitely a welcome and important part of the diet, but, in the long run, successful plant agriculture would have been much more important for the survival of the settlers. The farming situation also decided whether a settlement could continue in its chosen location or not. Because the weight of the bones is proportional to the weight of the living animals, bone weights were used to ascertain which type of meat was eaten most often. Only six AU yielded less than 50% cattle bones; therefore, beef was the main type of meat consumed in almost all the sites studied, and this appears to have been independent of period or region.

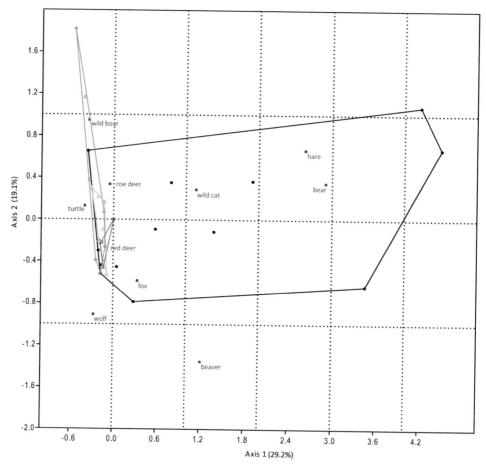

Figure 7.4. Correspondence analysis on the basis of wild animal species, which are represented in more than 10% of the Italian archaeological units. Key: black: Alps; green: North Po; light blue: South Po; red: Veneto-Friuli.

Animal husbandry

The number of bone fragments provides information about the composition of the herds and thus the focus of the animal husbandry. In general, cattle were the most common species, although in some cases sheep/goats or pigs were more numerous – or at least as common as cattle. As with the comparison between domestic and wild animals, several factors had an impact on the range of domestic species present: region/environment, date, type of site, function of the site, and (last but not least) human preference. The latter is the most interesting factor but also the most difficult to recognize – as a rule, it can only be assessed once the other factors have been excluded.

Because not all the regions and periods had the same types of site, an important task is to ascertain whether this had an impact on the range of domestic animal species present.

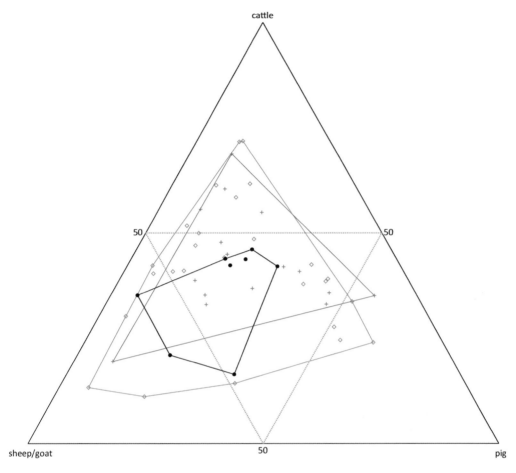

Figure 7.5. Proportions of the three main domestic species. Included are only archaeological units where the three species represent at least 90% of all animals. Key: black: wetland sites, red: dryland sites, green: upland sites.

A comparison of the three most frequent types of sites (irrespective of the countries or periods) in terms of the proportions of cattle, sheep/goat, and pig has revealed that the upland sites were the most diverse group, while the wetland sites were the most homogenous (Fig. 7.5). In mountain regions, many factors played an important role in successful farming (height above sea level, orientation of the valley, steepness of the terrain, *etc.*). The Alps, where most of the upland sites are located, are probably the landscape that offers the most diverse biotopes in the smallest possible area (Della Casa 2002: 7), which explains the diversity of animal husbandry in the upland sites. However, because the differences between the ranges of domestic animals at the different types of site are statistically irrelevant, comparative analyses are reliable.

Another factor to be considered is the dating of the sites. There is a disparity between the different countries and regions not only in regard to the types of site but also in regard to their dating. This can lead to difficulties in interpreting the results of the study. However, the problem only arises in northern Italy because this is the only region that yielded several sites dating from each of the three periods studied. The data for Switzerland is almost exclusively from the Late Bronze Age. The other countries yielded such limited numbers of sites overall that a division into chronological periods would not be significant. A correspondence analysis carried out on all the Italian sites separated by date, but not by region, did not yield any evidence to suggest that the date of the site had an impact on the range of domestic animal species present – a diachronic comparison within the region north and south of the Alps provided the same result. While the limited amounts of data do not allow us to exclude the possibility that the date of a site had an impact on its range of domestic animal species, the results do suggest that any impact would have been quite marginal. Since it seems that 'type of site' and 'date' had virtually no impact on animal husbandry differentiation, the aspects we need to consider are environmental factors and human influence.

The topographical map of the Circum-Alpine region shows that our studied area consisted of highly diverse geographical regions and thus had very different environmental conditions (Fig. 7.1). There was an important climatic divide north and south of the Alps (Primas 2009: 189; Lippert 2012: 10); even within the mountain range itself, the climate conditions in some of the valleys varied greatly (Della Casa 2002: 7; Primas 2009: 189). However, only the highest elevations in the central Alps had a tundra-like climate and vegetation and were not habitable all year round. For the purpose of this study, the Circum-Alpine region has been divided into larger regions: 'southern Alpine' (the Southern Alps or south of the Alps in general) and 'northern Alpine' (the Northern Alps, the northern foothills of the Alps, or north and west of the Alps in general). The southern Alpine region was characterised by a Mediterranean climate with usually hot, dry summers and mild, wet winters. The western and northern Alpine region, on the other hand, was influenced by a temperate, continental climate with usually warm summers, cool winters, and precipitation rates spread relatively evenly throughout the year (Lippert 2012: 10). A few northern Alpine sites in eastern Austria were located in an area influenced by a continental climate, which is drier with warm summers and cold winters. Within these large areas, further regional divisions can be made based on the climate and, above all, the environmental conditions. In our study, we decided to divide the two larger regions (north and south of the Alps) into further categories based mainly upon certain geographical aspects (Fig. 7.1).

Analyses of the range of domestic animal species show that four groups of animal spectra existed throughout the Circum-Alpine region:

a) mainly sheep/goat
b) sheep/goat and pig
c) mainly pig
d) mainly cattle. This is the largest group and could theoretically be divided further (mainly cattle, cattle/sheep/goat, and cattle/pig)

This section aims to discuss the ranges of animal species in the different areas. Firstly, we examine the conditions in the overall area of the Alps. The fact that this was a highly diversified region in terms of its environment/habitats (see above) raises the question as to whether this was reflected in the range of domestic animals. The Alps can be divided geographically into various sub-regions: the Swiss Grisons and Valais, western Austria, and the Italian Alps. The study has, interestingly, revealed that most of the sites in the Bronze Age Alpine region had quite similar ranges of domestic animals. The presence of cattle was the common factor – however, some sites yielded evidence of mainly cattle, while others exhibited a more balanced ratio between cattle and sheep/goats (Fig. 7.6), with the latter being located mainly in northern Italy.

Two regions have turned out to be quite unusual: the Valais and some sites in the Tyrolean and Salzburg Alps. Sheep/goats were clearly predominant in the Valais sites, which is a typical feature of a dry valley. The predominance of small ruminants in this area is attested from as early as the beginning of the Neolithic and continued into the Roman period (Curdy and Chaix 2009: 109). The sites located in the Tyrolean and Salzburg Alps, which yielded unusually high amounts of pig bones, were invariably mining sites – the range of domestic animal species present there was therefore directly related to the functions of the sites. An abundance of pig bones is best explained by a special exploitation of pigs, whether in the form of livestock or as prepared meat, by the miners (Schibler *et al.* 2009). Overall, one may state that animal husbandry in the Alpine valleys was quite homogenous, despite the differences in climate conditions. It was adapted or changed only in extreme conditions, as seen in the Valais, or where the function of the settlement demanded it – this result suggests that farming conditions were rather stable.

Based on their ranges of domestic animal species, the Swiss sites can be divided into three (supra-)regional groups (Fig. 7.7):

a) Valais, southern foot of the Jura Mountains: large amounts of sheep/goat
b) Northern Jura Mountains: large amounts of pig
c) Grisons, central and eastern Switzerland, and western Switzerland: large amounts of cattle or a well-balanced range

In both the warm, dry valley of the Valais and at the warm, dry, and steep southern foot of the Jura Mountains, sheep/goats were obviously the most suitable species. Given the general predominance of cattle, there must have been a good reason to prefer other species. For the cattle and sheep/goat farmers, it was thus the environs (*i.e.* the surrounding ecosystem) that determined the range of domestic animal species.

However, the fact that farmers in the northern areas of the Jura Mountains mainly kept pigs was not necessarily due to the landscape – it was more likely that the function of the settlement determined which species would be kept. The sites were all upland settlements, which were not easily accessible; in fact, some of them were even fortified and are believed to have been refuges (Schibler and Studer 1998: 185). It makes sense to use pork as part of the provisions in times of emergency, as pigs can be kept in a confined space for a short while, reproduce quickly, and are really only used as a source of meat. Another explanation would be that it was due to the cultural influence from the Upper Rhine Valley (see Chapter

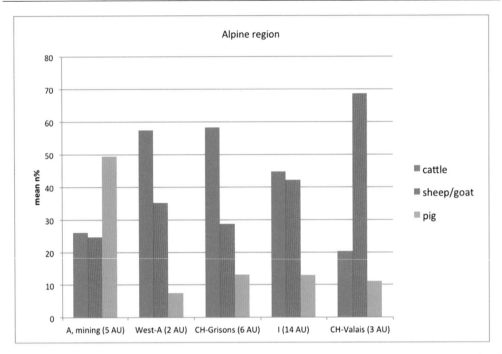

Figure 7.6. Proportions of domestic animals in the Alpine region. Key: A: Austria, CH: Switzerland, I: Italy, AU: archaeological unit.

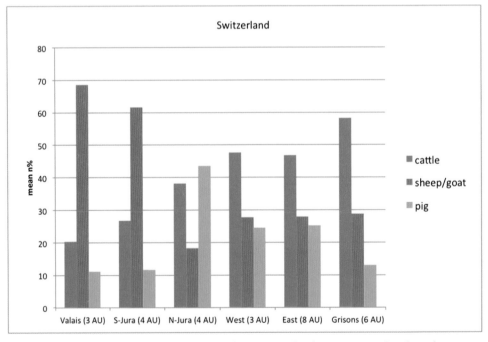

Figure 7.7. Proportions of domestic animals in Switzerland. Key: AU: archaeological unit.

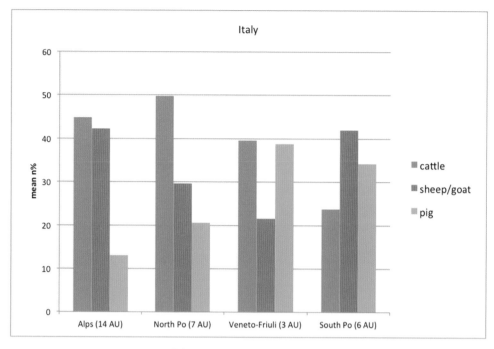

Figure 7.8. Proportions of domestic animals in Italy. Key: AU: archaeological unit.

8) in present-day Germany, where the sites also yielded large amounts of pigs. Although this is the only example known, it could show that animal husbandry in some areas may have been influenced by neighbouring regions.

The group of sites with large amounts of pig is actually the most interesting because it is the group most likely to exhibit any kind of functional or even cultural impact. The predominance of cattle and sheep/goats, on the other hand, appears to have been largely an aspect of regionality and environment. Not all sites, however, fit this trend: the Swiss site Vinelz, for example, yielded high numbers of sheep/goats, despite the fact that the settlement was not located at the southern foot of the Jura Mountains but on the eastern shore of Lake Bienne (*i.e.* in a flatter landscape). The fact that the Vinelz population kept more sheep and goats than cattle (even though the latter would in fact be more suited to the region) is surprising. This situation is also unusual because the inhabitants of the various Neolithic settlements in and around Vinelz had previously kept mostly cattle, while sheep/goats had been less numerous even than pigs (Marti and Stopp 1997). Therefore, Vinelz appears to have been one of only a few cases where the environment had less of an impact on the animal husbandry than humans did. The reasons why the Bronze Age Vinelz population kept mainly sheep and goats still remains a mystery – there may have been close contact with one of the settlements on the steep north-eastern shores of Lakes Bienne and Neuchâtel, where sheep/goats were predominantly kept; this is another possible example of the influence of nearby regions. Zurich-Grosser Hafner is another settlement that was affected by outside influence, as it yielded considerably more pig bones compared to the other sites in eastern Switzerland and also had a high proportion of wild animals. Grosser Hafner is an island in Lake Zurich that perhaps served as a sanctuary/ritual site (Primas and Ruoff 1981; Palafittes 2009), which might explain the rather unusual range of animal species.

Northern Italy can also be divided relatively clearly into three husbandry-regions, though these are less defined by just one animal species than is the case in Switzerland (Fig. 7.8):

   a) Southern Po Valley: sheep/goat and pig
   b) Veneto and Friuli: pig and cattle
   c) Northern Po Valley and Italian Alps: cattle or cattle/sheep/goat

In the case of the southern Po Valley, one could argue that the range of domestic animals might be a reflection of the chronology, as all the sites date from the Middle Bronze Age. However, because none of the contemporary sites in the other regions showed similar situations and because two of the sites in the southern Po Valley yielded a completely different range of animals than the others, it is more likely to have been the landscape that determined the composition of the animal herds. The two exceptions, Noceto and Poggio Rusco, had very similar animal husbandry to the sites from Veneto-Friuli (*i.e.* sheep/goats were replaced by cattle, while pigs were quite abundant). The question as to why these two sites had such different ranges of animals compared to the other sites in the same region cannot be answered beyond doubt. Noceto is presumed to have served a ritual purpose, which is reminiscent of the Grosser Hafner site in Switzerland mentioned above (de Grossi Mazzorin 2009: 170). Poggio Rusco was located in an area of mixed oak forest, which is ideal for pig farming. However, other influences may also have played a role. Poggio Rusco, like Noceto and Grosser Hafner, also had high numbers of wild animal bones, which is unusual for the period studied, and relatively high proportions of horse and dog bones. Consequently, Poggio Rusco may also have been a settlement with a special, perhaps ritual, function. The Italian Alpine sites were similar to those in the Grisons, though there were more settlements that, besides cattle, also kept relatively high numbers of sheep/goats. This is usually explained by the different climate conditions north and south of the Alps, with the southern regions being drier than the area north of the Alps.

Both Switzerland and northern Italy exhibited differences in terms of their range of domestic animals and their animal husbandry practices. This also supports the notion that the region, or more precisely the environment, had the biggest impact on the animal husbandry practices used at the locations studied (Benecke 1998: 62; David-Elbiali and Studer 2003: 269; Marzatico 2009b: 237–238; Petrucci 2007: 213). While the variation in domestic animal husbandry points to an economy that was very adaptable (see Riedel 1996: 74), certain preferences for a particular type of animal husbandry can be identified in some regions since the Neolithic, such as sheep/goat farming in the Valais or cattle farming in eastern Switzerland and the Grisons (Ebersbach *et al.* 2012). De Grossi Mazzorin and other Italian colleagues have reported on consistent animal husbandry practices despite changing cultural aspects (de Grossi Mazzorin *et al.* 2004: 227). Roberts' general remarks about the subsistence economy can be eloquently, and in this case very appropriately, summed up with the adage 'never change a winning horse' (Roberts 2009: 73).

Aspects of animal husbandry

Cattle, sheep/goats, and pigs were kept primarily as a source of meat. The most valuable animals were cattle because they yielded larger quantities of meat and also had more secondary uses (dairy production, traction, transport, and trade) than the other domestic animals. Cattle farming was limited by certain factors, such as dry climate conditions, steep slopes, or a lack of fodder. Sheep/goats also provided other products besides meat, such as milk and wool, with the latter, in particular, becoming more widely used over the course of the Bronze Age (Schibler and Studer 1998: 181). Riedel (2003: 210) called sheep 'stopgaps' because they can be kept anywhere, particularly in places where cattle do not thrive. Pigs only served as a source of meat but their high reproduction rate gave them an advantage over domestic ruminants – moreover, as omnivores, they were not in strong competition for food with ruminants. Pig farming only has minor limitations: pigs cannot endure the cold very well (Riedel 1996: 72) and need forests to forage in, particularly beech and oak forests; therefore, within our study area, it was really only the (high) mountains that were not suitable for pig farming.

In order to exploit the primary (meat) and secondary products (milk, dairy products, animal power, wool, *etc.*), the animals were slaughtered at different stages in their lifecycles, with male animals generally being slaughtered at a younger age than females. Therefore, age and sex determination can help ascertain the use of the animals. Animals that were used primarily as a source of meat were not kept into old age – with the exception of breeding animals – and one may expect a balanced or perhaps male-dominated sex ratio for this purpose. In order to exploit the secondary products of cattle and sheep/goats, the animals were kept longer, with a preference for female animals. The size of the animals allows us to speculate on the different breeds, the impact of the climate, and the quality of the pasture.

Another secondary use of animal husbandry that should not be underestimated is the accumulation of manure. Statements in this regard can be made by archaeological means with the discovery of animal shelters and with geoarchaeological and archaeobotanical examinations of coprolites (Marzatico 2009b: 228). The subject of manure is important because it provides information about the husbandry and use of the domestic animals in general and of individual species in particular (Akeret 2000). The lack of faeces from a particular species can highlight interesting aspects – besides providing proof of a species having been kept outside the settlement, a seasonal absence of animal remains can also be seen in the context of transhumance (see, for instance, Knipper 2005: 657; Greenfield 1999: 15). A seasonal absence of animals has both advantages and disadvantages. The advantages are that gardens, fields, and forests remain intact during phases of harvesting and gathering; also, valley meadows can recover in the absence of the domestic graminivores. The disadvantage of transhumance is, of course, a loss of secondary products.

It is also possible, however, that transhumance only concerned a certain selection of animals, for example young cattle or those animals destined for consumption. However, there is much debate among researchers as to whether transhumance was actually practised during the Bronze Age (Greenfield 1999; Marzatico 2009a: 121; Marzatico 2009b: 229; Plüss

2011: 107). On the basis of palynological studies, archaeologists have presumed that a simple form of pastoral economic activity took place as early as the (late) Neolithic (Dietre *et al.* 2012: 248; Primas 2009: 196; see also Chapter 6, this volume). However, no convincing evidence has yet been found that this type of economy existed in the Bronze Age. A basic problem with statements of this kind is that we do not know how many animals were actually kept in the settlements at any given time. Are we talking about 'herds' or were only a small number of animals kept at any one time, making transhumance unnecessary? Were animals from neighbouring settlements jointly driven to seasonal pastures?

Primary and secondary products

The best way of studying the utilisation of primary and secondary products is by determining the ages of the animals. In order to draw comparisons, the age information given in the publications was divided into three groups (mainly adult, mainly young, and no age trend).

In general, cattle and sheep/goats yielded a mainly adult or balanced age range. Because the production and utilisation of secondary products took place mainly in adulthood, this distribution was quite expected. Pigs, on the other hand, were slaughtered at younger ages, and this was also mirrored in the ratio between the three age groups.

Interestingly, regional differences are revealed when comparing the age ranges of all three domestic animal species together (Fig. 7.9). The sites in western Austria generally yielded a mainly adult range. In western Switzerland and in the Alps, the ranges tended to be younger or at least balanced, while the animals slaughtered at the central and eastern Swiss sites were mainly adult. The sites in the southern Po Valley in Italy had no species that yielded mainly young animals, as was seen in other regions. The Alpine sites, on the other hand, provided a much more balanced age range than the sites in the northern Po Valley and in Veneto-Friuli, with the latter regions yielding either more young animals or more adults.

Animal husbandry, therefore, appears to have been regionally specialised. A predominance of older animals reflects a holistic utilisation of the animals: besides meat, secondary products were also intensively used. An age range with an emphasis on young animals suggests that they were mainly used as a source of meat, which means that other possible uses were limited (whether intentionally or unintentionally). Interestingly, all three age groups were represented in the Alpine regions of Switzerland and Italy. One might expect that the entire range of possible uses would have been exploited in ecologically marginal areas such as the Alps, which would have resulted in a preponderance of adult animals in all Alpine sites. There are, however, sites where mainly young cattle and sheep/goats were slaughtered. Cheese production might have also been crucial, and it is considered a potential interpretation for the use of cattle in Sotciastel (Salvagno and Tecchiati 2011: 73) – the same has been suggested for Brixen-Albanbühel (Riedel and Tecchiati 2001: 109). Calves and lambs/kids were slaughtered for the extraction of rennet from their stomachs, which was used to coagulate the milk in the production of cheese. However, it is not known when rennet was first used for this purpose. Plant products can also aid the coagulation of milk. Cleavers (*Galium* sp.) have been found at some northern Italian Bronze Age settlements, though not at any Alpine sites (Marzatico

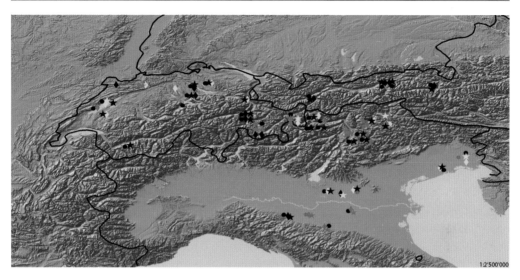

Figure 7.9. Distribution of age groups in Italy, Switzerland and western Austria. Key: circle: cattle, star: sheep/goat, diamond: pig; yellow: mainly young, black: mainly adults; pink: no trend.

2009a: 126; Marzatico 2009b: 228). Swiss sites have also yielded cleavers (Jacomet and Karg 1996). Another possible explanation for the predominance of young animals in a settlement, both in the Alps and in the lowlands, is trade. Young animals may have been used as a form of currency to pay for transport services or commodities – Hauterive-Champréveyres (Switzerland) can be cited as a possible example.

Besides young animals in general, there is also the special category of 'foetal/neonate animals', whose presence has also been recorded. Only a very limited number of sites yielded bones of such young animals, which could be due to taphonomic processes. It is nevertheless interesting to see that this age category in cattle was almost solely present in Middle Bronze Age sites, even though there were many more Late Bronze Age sites. The chances of finding them in the later period should therefore be greater. Did cattle-breeding methods improve from the Middle to the Late Bronze Age to such a degree that fewer animals died at birth? Is this a reflection of changes in animal husbandry practices because cattle, including cows in calf, were more rarely kept in the settlements themselves? Cattle generally give birth in late spring or early summer. If, for instance, transhumance was indeed practised, the pregnant animals would no longer have been in the settlements by the time they were ready to give birth (Greenfield 1999: 19). Therefore, the more frequent absence of new-born calves in the Late Bronze Age settlements might actually point to an increase in transhumance.

Although sites with mainly adult sheep/goats or with balanced age ranges were generally predominant, more AU have yielded large numbers of young animals than was the case concerning cattle. As mentioned earlier, a change took place from mainly using flax in the Neolithic to using wool in the Bronze Age. Perhaps this intensified use of wool had not yet occurred everywhere so that the animals were still being used purely as a source of meat at many sites. Interestingly, the Swiss sites with mainly young animals or with balanced age ranges were all located in the Jura Mountains and in the Alps. This at least points to a difference in the utilisation of sheep (and goats) between mountainous regions and the lowlands; in the uplands, the animals were mainly used for meat, whereas wool production was more important in the lowlands. This difference could not be identified in northern Italy.

Regarding pig farming, the production of meat was the priority. In settlements that mainly yielded adult animals, we might assume that these were the so-called producer sites, where adult animals were mainly kept for breeding and some of the young animals were traded. Settlements yielding mainly young animals would consequently be consumer sites, which were supplied with younger animals. Sites with a balanced age range can be considered independent in the sense that they kept animals for their own use. Good examples of possible consumer sites are the three Austrian mining sites of Brixlegg-Mauken, Brixlegg-Mariahilfbergl, and Viehhofen (Schibler *et al.* 2011). In these cases, it is most likely that, besides possibly keeping pigs at the site, meat was brought in from the outside, to augment the existing supplies or even as an exclusive source of meat (either in the form of live animals or as cured cuts of meat). The data from Viehhofen actually shows that most of the animals were sub-adult and young-adult males; in other words, they were animals at an ideal slaughter age and surplus to breeding requirements (Stopp, unpublished). The site therefore quite accurately corresponds with the notion of a settlement that was supplied with pork – the same can be said with reference to Brixlegg-Mariahilfbergl, where researchers found mainly young-adult animals (Riedel 2003: 246). The balanced sex ratio can probably be explained by sow-dominated pig farming at the site augmented by an outside supply of (possibly younger) male animals. The same interpretation can be offered for the age range in Brixlegg-Mauken; the site yielded the added aspect of a selection of skeletal parts suggesting that cured cuts of meat were supplied from the outside or brought in by inhabitants (Schibler *et al.* 2009, 2011). Another example is the Swiss lakeside settlement of Hauterive-Champréveyres, which is the only settlement where most of the pigs were slaughtered in their first year. Champréveyres was a settlement centre where a lot of craft-working and trading took place (see Chapter 8). Were these young pigs used as a form of currency to pay for goods? Archaeozoological studies were carried out in the commercial areas of Pozzuolo-Ciastiei and Concordia Sagittaria, which are two relatively large settlements in northern Italy. Both data sets yielded mainly young animals. This fits with the statement made above that pig farming, or in this case the consumption of pork, was linked to the function of the settlement.

Traction, transport, and trade

Trade and the associated transportation of goods such as amber and metal objects have long been known to have existed in the Bronze Age (Jennings 2014; see also Chapter 8, this volume). Bellintani (2013: 790) claims that a system of down-the-line trading/short-distance exchange seems to have prevailed during the Early and Middle Bronze Ages; in other words, trade largely took place on a regional scale. Large-scale or long-distance trading systems only evolved during the Late Bronze Age. Part of the reason for this was probably the rapid development of copper-mining activities in the central and eastern Alps; in this context, trans-Alpine trade also increased (Della Casa 2002: 72).

Besides animals and people, carts and boats were used to transport goods. The latter were probably a particularly important means of conveyance, as Haughey (2013: 385) states: 'Rivers and lakes are often seen as barriers when in fact they are major route ways within the landscape'. While roads were actually being built to transport goods by cart (Brunning and McDermott 2013), by far the largest proportion of goods would probably have been transported by water or, particularly in the Alps, on foot or with pack animals.

According to David-Elbiali and Studer (2003: 267), subsistence goods (*e.g.* foodstuffs) were not part of an organised system of exchange, at least not in terms of long-distance trade, although there is evidence to suggest that miners were in some cases supplied with goods from outside (Boschin and Riedel 2011: 591; Schibler *et al.* 2011: 1274; Marti-Grädel *et al.* 2012: 95). However, this trade probably took place only over short distances and would have originated where the miners had come from, probably the settlements in the valleys. It is very difficult or almost impossible to gain evidence of the trade in animals or animal products solely on the basis of the morphology of the animal bones. Genetic and isotope analyses would be a suitable means, but no such studies have as yet been carried out in the area and period studied.

Another possibility of formulating thoughts on the subject is sex determinations. The premise is that female animals were mainly required in the form of animal husbandry that was geared towards agriculture and breeding. A predominance of male animals in a particular settlement, whether bulls or oxen, calls for an explanation of such animals. Oxen are regularly found and sometimes even in larger numbers than bulls; because oxen are slightly lower maintenance than bulls but grow to be bigger and stronger, we may assume that they would have served as draught or transport animals.

Cattle are known to have been used to pull ploughs and carts in the Bronze Age, and clear evidence of this can be found in the petroglyphs from the northern Italian Val Camonica (Schibler/Studer 1998: 179). Moreover, deformed horn cores show that cattle were fitted with yokes (Schibler and Studer 1998: 179). While horses are also mentioned in this context (Benecke 1998: 65; Falkenstein 2009: 157, 163), their low numbers among settlement finds make it seem rather unlikely that they were used for transporting goods. They were probably too valuable to be used in such a way (Schibler and Studer 1998: 178; David-Elbiali and Studer 2003: 271). Even sheep are mentioned as possible beasts of burden (Marzatico 2009a: 123).

For the following part of our study, the settlements were divided into three groups based on the predominance or balance of the sexes (Fig. 7.10). The northern Italian sites that yielded mainly male animals were all located in the lowlands; the fact, however, that Alpine sites may have also had a male-dominated range is attested to by Savognin-Padnal (Switzerland) and Brixlegg-Mariahilfbergl (Austria). As far as one can tell from the information available, oxen appear to have been more numerous in the Alpine areas of Italy, whereas the lowland sites yielded either more male or more female animals – a balanced ratio was rarely found.

Figure 7.10. Gender group-distribution of cattle. Included are all sites with specifications on gender. Key: red: mainly females, green: mainly males, yellow: no trend.

A possible explanation would be that Alpine farming was characterised by suckler cow husbandry, while oxen were used as draught or working animals. The two aforementioned Alpine sites that yielded more male animals are interesting in this context. Brixlegg, for instance, was a mining settlement, and the male animals were almost exclusively oxen – were they used to transport the raw copper extracted or copper ingots produced on site, or were they meat supplies for the miners (Riedel 2003: 212)? The Padnal site (near Savognin) can also be associated with mining, copper smelting, and trans-Alpine trade (Lippert 2012: 60); here too, the male animals were possibly used for the transportation of goods.

The lowland sites appear to have been more specialised, resulting in fewer sites yielding a balanced sex ratio. An interesting fact in this context is that those sites in the northern Po Valley that were located closer to Lake Garda and the gateway into the large Alpine valley formed by the River Adige yielded mainly male animals, while the sites further east mainly contained remains of females. Is this a reflection of animals being used for transportation? Goods from the Alps, perhaps mainly copper, were taken from the Alpine areas either by water, by people, or by animal power and then distributed to regions further afield. Is it possible, therefore, that the sites that yielded predominantly male animals were linked with transportation, while those that contained mainly cows were farming settlements?

However, there may also be a completely different explanation for the predominance of male animals, as shown by the two north-eastern Italian sites Concordia Sagittaria and Ciastiei-Pozzuolo del Friuli (Udine) – bone working is attested in both of these early Iron Age settlements. The larger and more solid bones of male animals were better suited to the manufacture of bone artefacts, so it comes as no surprise that both sites yielded larger numbers of male animals. The bulls and oxen were most certainly bought in, whether as live animals or as processed parts.

Breeds

The sizes of the animals allow us, on the one hand, to draw conclusions about the environment because the quality and amount of feed has an impact on animals' growth (Herre and Röhrs 1990: 218); on the other hand, they also provide information about how the animals were used and, as a consequence, on the need for their sizes to change. Having larger animals, for instance, was not necessarily an advantage – while they provided more meat and working power, they also required more space and needed more food, which could have led to problems during the winter months. Another interesting question is whether a change in the animals' sizes reflects an arrival or emergence of new breeds.

During the Middle and Late Bronze Age, both cattle and sheep north of the Alps were larger than south of the Alps. In northern Italy and Austria, the size development can be observed diachronically; in fact, over the course of the Bronze Age, cattle decreased in size in both regions (Boschin and Riedel 2011: 608; Pucher 2001: 72). It was not until the early Iron Age in some areas of northern Italy that they once again began to increase in size considerably (De Grossi Mazzorin and Riedel 1997: 447ff.; De Grossi Mazzorin *et al.* 2004: 227f.; Riedel 1993: 83). The sizes of the sheep developed slightly differently in that they grew larger over the course of the Bronze Age and early Iron Age but with more pronounced regional variation compared to cattle (Riedel and Tecchiati 2001: 108; Marzatico 2009b: 225). In the southern Po Valley, for example, the sheep always remained small (De Grossi Mazzorin and Riedel 1997: 447ff.). In northern Italy, a diachronic development can be traced for cows and bulls/oxen separately. Cows' average sizes increased between the Middle Bronze Age and the early Iron Age, with the greatest spur of growth occurring at the transition from the Bronze Age to the Iron Age. Bulls and oxen also increased in size from the Middle to the Late Bronze Age but then the development ceased.

The question is how this disparity in size should be interpreted. Natural reasons such as the climate or the environment appear to be unlikely explanations, particularly for a large-scale comparison between north and south of the Alps, because this lumps together highly diverse areas with considerable differences in the abundance of food available. It is also rather unlikely that the utilisation of cattle and sheep was fundamentally different north and south of the Alps. This leads us to the obvious conclusion that the disparity in size was because different breeds existed in the two regions. Riedel mentions the possibility of new breeds having come into northern Italy, possibly from southern or south-eastern Europe (Riedel 1985b: 123). Besides the change in size, a new type of cattle has been identified that had different horns (Riedel 1996: 73).

Conclusions: change and adaptation through space and time

A number of interesting aspects have been highlighted in relation to the subsistence economy and the different characteristics of animal husbandry in the Circum-Alpine region in the

Bronze Age and early Iron Age. Thanks to significantly improved farming methods, hunting became more or less redundant. If hunting did take place, it generally targeted the most abundant and meat-rich animals, making the strategy very sound economically. The Alpine region was an exception to this rule in that hunting took place in a rather uncoordinated manner. Hunting was either carried out for different reasons than in the lowlands or the environmental conditions made the usual strategies impractical. Hunting also appears to have been linked with the function of the settlement; upland settlements that had a mining connection or were used as refuges generally yielded significantly smaller amounts of wild animals. In principle, one may state that the function of a site and the environment in the form of mountains apparently had major impacts on the hunting activities of the settlers.

Cattle were the most common animals and the predominant species kept in most of the regions. Neither the date nor the type of site had any significant impact on the animal husbandry practised in a settlement. It rather depended on the region or, in other words, the environmental conditions. This is reflected by the fact that, in many regions, husbandry practices did not change from the Neolithic to the Bronze Age, and no major changes can be identified in the early Iron Age. In some cases, the function of a settlement (for mining, as a refuge, or as a ritual site) did have an impact on animal husbandry. We may therefore conclude that the location and function of a settlement were the biggest catalysts for a particular type of animal husbandry.

Besides being kept for meat, cattle and sheep/goats were mainly kept for their secondary products – working power, milk, dairy products, and wool – whereas pigs were kept almost solely for their meat. Regional differences in the age ranges of the domestic animals suggest that there were differences in how the animals were used. Cattle were mainly slaughtered as adults because they were too valuable not to exploit all their possible uses. Sheep/goats were also mainly slaughtered in adulthood, but more settlements actually exhibited a preponderance of young animals. In Switzerland, these sites were mainly located in mountainous regions, suggesting that the animals were predominantly used for meat in the elevated areas but for wool and milk in the lowlands. Cheese production is another possible explanation for the presence of young cattle and sheep/goats.

The concept that young animals were perhaps used as a form of currency is yet another interesting thought. Because pigs were kept purely for their meat, one would expect to find fairly low slaughter ages. The fact that a variety of age ranges was actually found is best explained by the existence of consumer and producer sites and also self-sufficient settlements. Examples of consumer sites include the Austrian mining settlements, where pigs were mainly kept and/or delivered at the optimum slaughter age. Transhumance as an economic system has been debated by researchers, though its existence has yet to be proven. However, the almost complete absence of neonate cattle in the Late Bronze Age compared to the Middle Bronze Age could be one of the missing pieces of evidence that researchers have been seeking.

Cattle were crucial within the economic system: trade and transport, when not on waterways, were almost exclusively carried out with the help of cattle. Their bone remains help us to understand the function of a settlement (*e.g.* through the study of sex ratios). Cows and, at least in Italy, oxen were mainly kept in the Alps; as a result, suckler cow and draught animal husbandry probably dominated in many of the Alpine settlements. The northern Italian sites around the gateway to the Adige Valley all yielded predominantly male animals, which suggests that these settlements were trading or distribution sites. The sites to the east of the Adige Valley, on the other hand, contained more cows, which probably means that those sites were farming settlements. It is possible that the latter sent the surplus male animals to Lake Garda. The disparity in the animal sizes between the areas north and south of the Alps is best explained by the presence of various breeds, which started to spread and mix more significantly towards the end of the Late Bronze Age.

In conclusion, one can state that there was very little change, if any, in the animal husbandry practices in the Circum-Alpine region from the Middle Bronze Age to the early Iron Age. However, regional and functional differences can be identified in the hunting activities and in the husbandry and utilisation of domestic animals, some of which had a long-standing tradition.

References

Akeret, Ö. (2000) *Analyse pflanzlicher Grossreste im Kot von jungsteinzeitlichen Rindern, Schafen und Ziegen: ein Beitrag zur Erforschung vorgeschichtlicher Viehwirtschaftssysteme.* PhD, Universität Basel.

Ammerman, A. J., Butler, J. J., Diamond, G., Menozzi, P., Pals, J. P., Sevink, J., Smit, A. and Voorrips, A. (1978) Report on the excavations at Monte Leoni, a Bronze Age settlement in the Parma Valley. *Helinium* XVIII: 126–164.

Amschler, W. (1937a) Vorgeschichtliche Tierreste aus den Grabungen von Bludenz. *Mitteilungen der Prähistorischen Komission der Akademie der Wissenschaften* 3: 217–242.

Amschler, W. (1937b) Die Haustierreste von der Kelchalpe bei Kitzbühel, Tirol. *Mitteilungen der Prähistorischen Komission der Akademie der Wissenschaften* 3: 96–120.

Arbinger-Vogt, H. (1978) *Vorgeschichtliche Tierknochenfunde aus Breisach am Rhein.* PhD, Ludwig-Maximilians-Universität München.

Bellintani, P. (2013) Long-distance trade routes linked to wetland settlements. In F. Menotti and A. O'Sullivan (eds) *The Oxford Handbook of Wetland Archaeology*: 779–794. Oxford: Oxford University Press.

Benecke, N. (1998) Haustierhaltung, Jagd und Kult mit Tieren im bronzezeitlichen Mitteleuropa. In B. Hänsel (ed.) *Mensch und Umwelt in der Bronzezeit Europas – Man and Environment in European Bronze Age*: 61–75. Kiel: Oetker-Voges Verlag.

Benefit, B. R. (1983) The Faunal Remains. In P. S. Wells (ed.) *Rural economy in the early Iron Age: excavations at Hascherkeller, 1978–1981*: 95–108. Cambridge, Mass.: Harvard University Press.

Berger, L., Brianza, M., Gutzwiller, P., Joos, M., Peter, M., Rentzel, P., Schibler, J. and Stern, W. B. (1996) *Sondierungen auf dem Wittnauer Horn 1980–1982.* Solothurn: Habegger.

Bonnamour, L. and Poulain, T. (1973) Fouille d'un habitat de la fin de l'âge de Bronze à Epervans (Saône-et-Loire). *Revue Archéologique de l'Est et du Centre-Est* 24: 69–113.

Bopp-Ito, M. (unpubl.) *Archäozoologische Untersuchungen der Tierknochen aus Savognin-Padnal (GR) und ihre Bedeutung für die Umwelt-, Ernährungs- und Wirtschaftsgeschichte während der alpinen Bronzezeit (Arbeitstitel).* PhD thesis, Universität Basel.

Borello, M. A. and Chaix, L. (1983) Etude de la faune de Hauterive-Champréveyres (Neuchâtel) (Bronze final) (1979–1980). *Bulletin de la Société neuchâteloise des Sciences naturelles* 106: 159–169.

Boschin, F. (2006) La fauna protostorica del sito di Bressanone-Elvas (BZ). In U. Tecchiati and B. Sala (eds) *Studi di archeozoologia / Archäozoologische Studien / Archaeozoological studies: in onore di / zu Ehren von / in honour of Alfredo Riedel*: 131–142. Bolzano: Ripartizione Beni Culturali, Ufficio Beni Archeologici.

Boschin, F. and Riedel, A. (2011) Ein spätbronzezeitlicher Tierknochenfundkomplex aus der Kupferbergbausiedlung Brixlegg-Mariahilfbergl (Tirol). *Annalen des Naturhistorischen Museums Wien* 113: 598–618.

Brunning, R. and McDermott, C. (2013) Trackways and roads across the wetlands. In F. Menotti and A. O'Sullivan (eds) *The Oxford Handbook of Wetland Archaeology*: 359–384. Oxford: Oxford University Press.

Catagnano, V. (2008) La gestione delle risorse animali in un sito del Bronzo Medio-Recente del bacino del Garda: il caso di Bovolone (VR). In D. Bassi, S. Capitani, C. Peretto and G. Zini (eds) *Annali dell'Università di Ferrara, Sezione Museologia Scientifica e Naturalistica, Volume speciale*: 49–54. Ferrara: Cartografica Artigiana snc.

Catalani, P. (1984) Poggio Rusco (MN): la fauna. *Preistoria Alpina* 20: 203–210.

Chaix, L. (1979) Etude de la faune. In D. Baudais, A. Billamboz, A. M. Grosjean, P. Passard, P. Pétrequin, C. Tournier, J.-L. Voruz and D. Vuaillat (eds) *Le gisement néolithique et protohistorique de Besançon – Saint-Paul (Doubs)*: 157–173. Paris: Les Belles Lettres.

Chaix, L. (1984) Les restes de vertébrés du site de Bavois-en-Raillon (Vaud, Suisse) (Bronze final). In J. Vital and J.-L. Voruz (eds) *L'habitat protohistorique de Bavois-en-Raillon (Vaud)*: 79–80. Lausanne: Bibliothèque historique vaudoise.

Chaix, L. (1985) La faune de la Grotte des Planches-près-Arbois (Jura, France) (du Néolithique ancien à l'âge du Fer). In P. Pétrequin, L. Chaix, A.-M. Pétrequin and J.-F. Piningre (eds) *La Grotte des Planches-près-Arbois (Jura). Proto Cortaillod et âge du Bronze final*: 3–34. Paris: Editions de la Maison des Sciences de l'Homme.

Chaix, L. (1986a) La faune. In M. A. Borello, J. L. Brochier, L. Chaix and P. Hadorn (eds) *Cortaillod-Est, un village du Bronze final 4: Nature et environnement*: 47–73. Saint-Blaise: Eds du Ruau.

Chaix, L. (1986b) La faune de la Baume des Anges (Drôme, France) (Bronze final). *Bulletin de la Société préhistorique française* 83: 28–29.

Chaix, L. (1987) Rapport sur la faune d'une grotte de l'âge du Bronze récent/final en Haut-Valais. *Jahrbuch der Schweizerischen Gesellschaft für Ur- und Frühgeschichte* 70: 73.

Chaix, L. (1990a) La faune d'Ayent-le-Château (Valais, Suisse; Bronze ancien et Bronze final). *Jahrbuch der Schweizerischen Gesellschaft für Ur- und Frühgeschichte* 73: 44–46.

Chaix, L. (1990b) La faune de Vex-le-Château (Valais, Suisse; du Néolithique moyen au Bronze final). *Jahrbuch der Schweizerischen Gesellschaft für Ur- und Frühgeschichte* 73: 47–50.

Curdy, P. and Chaix, L. (2009) Les premiers pasteurs du Valais. *Le Globe* 149: 93–116.

David-Elbiali, M. and Studer, J. (2003) Réflexion sur l'économie à l'âge du Bronze en Suisse: autarcie vivrière et échange de biens de prestige? In M. Besse, L.-I. Stahl Gretsch and P. Curdy (eds) *ConstellaSion. Hommage à Alain Gallay*: 267–272. Lausanne: Cahiers d'archéologie romande.

De Grossi Mazzorin, J. (1989) Nota preliminare sulla fauna dell'insediamento della media età del Bronzo. In A. Cardarelli, I. Pulini and C. Zanasi (eds) *Modena dalle origini all'anno Mille. Studi di archeologia e storia*: 225–228. Modena: Editione Panini.

De Grossi Mazzorin, J. (2009) Fauna ed economia animale. In M. Bernabo Brèa and M. Cremaschi (eds) *Acqua e civiltà nelle terramare. La vasca votiva di Noceto*: 170–174. Milano: Skirà.

De Grossi Mazzorin, J. and Riedel, A. (1997) La fauna delle terramare. In M. Bernabo Brèa, A. Cardarelli and M. Cremaschi (eds) *Le terramare la più antica civiltà padana*: 475–480 and Bibliographie. Milano: Electa.

De Grossi Mazzorin, J., Riedel, A. and Tagliacozzo, A. (2004) L'evoluzione delle popolazioni animali e dell'economia nell'età del Bronzo Recente. In D. Cocchi Genick (ed.) *L'età del Bronzo Recente in Italia. Atti del Congresso Nazionale di Lido di Camaiore, 26–29 ottobre 2000*: 227–232. Viareggio (Lucca): M. Baroni.

Della Casa, P. (2002) *Landschaften, Siedlungen, Resourcen. Langzeitszenarien menschlicher Aktivität in ausgewählten alpinen Gebieten der Schweiz, Italiens und Frankreichs.* Montagnac: éditions monique mergoil.

Dietre, B., Anich, I., Reidl, D., Kappelmeyer, T. and Haas, J. N. (2012) Erste Hirten und Bauern der Silvretta. Palynologie und Ethnobotanik im Fimbertal und Paznaun. In T. Reitmaier (ed.) *Letzte Jäger, erste Hirten. Hochalpine Archäologie in der Silvretta*: 237–256. Chur: Amt für Kultur, Archäologischer Dienst Graubünden.

Ebersbach, R. (2003) Paleoecological Reconstruction and Calculation of Calorie Requirements at lake Zurich. In J. Kunow and J. Müller (eds) *Archäoprognose Brandenburg I. Landschaftsarchäologie und geographische Informationssysteme. Prognosekarten, Besiedlungsdynamik und prähistorische Raumordnungen.*: 69–88. Wünsdorf: Brandenburgisches Landesamt f. Denkmalpflege

Ebersbach, R., Kühn, M., Stopp, B. and Schibler, J. (2012) Die Nutzung neuer Lebensräume in der Schweiz und angrenzenden Gebieten im 5. Jtsd. v.Chr. – Siedlungs- und wirschaftsarchäologische Aspekte. *Jahrbuch Archäologie Schweiz* 95: 7–34.

Falkenstein, F. (2009) Zur Subsistenzwirtschaft der Bronzezeit in Mittel- und Südosteuropa. In M. Bartelheim and H. Stäuble (eds) *Die wirtschaftlichen Grundlagen der Bronzezeit Europas / The Economic Foundations of the European Bronze Age*: 147–176. Rahden/Westf.: Leidorf.

Farello, P. (1995) Fauna dell'età del Bronzo dal sito di Pilastri. In P. Desantis and G. Steffè (eds) *L'insediamento terramaricolo di Pilastri (Bondeno-Ferrara): prime fasi di una ricerca. Catalogo della Mostra*: 98–104. Firenze: All'Insegna del Giglio.

Feller, A. M. (2002) Untersuchungen an Knochenfunden vom Siedlungsplatz Ladenburg 'Ziegelscheuer'. In G. Lenz-Bernhard (ed.) *Lopodunum. Die neckarswebische Siedlung und Villa rustica im Gewann 'Ziegelacker'. Eine Untersuchung zur Besiedlungsgeschichte der Oberrheingermanen. Mit Beiträgen von A. Feller, W. Frey, R. Gogräfe und G. Schneider.*: 497–589. Stuttgart: Theiss.

Greenfield, H. J. (1999) The advent of transhumant pastoralism in the temperate southeast Europe: a zooarchaeological perspective from the Central Balkans. In L. Bartosiewicz and H. J. Greenfield (eds) *Transhumant Pastoralism in Southern Europe. Recent Perspectives from Archaeology, History and Ethnology*: 15–36. Budapest: Archaeolingua Alapítvány.

Gutzwiller, P., Marti, R., Schibler, J., Sedlmeier, J. and Veszeli, M. (1996) Zufluchtsort in unsicherer Zeit. Die Portiflue als markanter Zeuge früher Besiedlung. In H. Hänggi (ed.) *Nunningen*: 75–84. Nunningen: Kulturkommission.

Haughey, F. (2013) Rivers and lakes. A network of wetland highways. In F. Menotti and A. O'Sullivan (eds) *The Oxford Handbook of Wetland Archaeology*: 385–397. Oxford: Oxford University Press.

Hénon, P., Joly, J.-L. and Lalai, D. (2002) Le site Bronze final I/IIA des 'Batailles' à Jons (Rhône). *Revue Archéologique de l'Est et du Centre-Est* 51: 45–116.

Herre, W. and Röhrs, M. (1990) *Haustiere – zoologisch gesehen.* Stuttgart–New York: Gustav Fischer.

Hochuli, S., Niffeler, U. and Rychner, V. (eds) 1998. *Die Schweiz vom Paläolithikum bis zum frühen Mittelalter (SPM) III: Bronzezeit,* Basel: Reinhardt AG.

Jacomet, S. and Karg, S. (1996) Ackerbau und Umwelt der Seeufersiedlungen von Zug-Sumpf im Rahmen der mitteleuropäischen Spätbronzezeit – Ergebnisse archäobotanischer Untersuchungen. In D. Hartmann (ed.) *Die spätbronzezeitlichen Ufersiedlungen von Zug-Sumpf, Band 1: Die Dorfgeschichte*: 198–303 und 365–368. Zug: Kantonales Museum für Urgeschichte Zug.

Jennings, B. (2014). *Travelling Objects: Changing Values. Incorporation of the northern Alpine lake-dwelling communities in exchange and communication networks during the Late Bronze Age.* Oxford: Archaeopress.

Kanelutti, E. (1994) Tierknochen Rebberg Ost. In W. Neubauer (ed.) *Flums-Gräpplang. Eine spätbronzezeitliche Siedlung in der Schweiz. Band 1: Rebberg Ost, Grabung 1967–1982*: 89–102. Buchs: BuchsDruck.

Kaufmann, B. and Stampfli, H. R. (1983) Die Skelettreste von Scuol-Munt Baselgia. In L. Stauffer-Isenring (ed.) *Die Siedlungsreste von Scuol-Munt Baselgia (Unterengadin GR). Ein Beitrag zur inneralpinen Bronze- und Eisenzeit*: 164–179. Basel: Schweizerische Gesellschaft für Ur- und Frühgeschichte.

Knipper, C. (2005) Die Strontiumisotopenanalyse: eine naturwissenschaftliche Methode zur Erfassung von Mobilität in der Ur- und Frühgeschichte. *Jahrbuch des Römisch-Germanischen Zentralmuseums Mainz* 51. Jahrgang 2004, Teil 2: 589–685.

Lippert, A. (2012) Wirtschaft und Handel in den Alpen. Von Ötzi bis zu den Kelten. *Archäologie in Deutschland* Jahrgang 2 / Sonderheft 2/2013: 110.

Magny, M. (2013) Palaeoclimatology and archaeology in the wetlands. In F. Menotti and A. O'Sullivan (eds) *The Oxford Handbook of Wetland Archaeology*: 585–597. Oxford: Oxford University Press.

Magny, M., Maise, C., Jacomet, S. and Burga, C. A. (1998) Klimaschwankungen im Verlauf der Bronzezeit. In S. Hochuli, U. Niffeler and V. Rychner (eds) *Die Schweiz vom Paläolithikum bis zum frühen Mittelalter (SPM) III: Bronzezeit*: 135–140. Basel: Verlag Schweizerische Gesellschaft für Ur- und Frühgeschichte.

Manning, K., Stopp, B., Colledge, S., Downey, S., Conolly, J., Dobney, K. and Shennan, S. (2013) Animal Exploitation in the Early Neolithic of the Balkans and Central Europe. In S. Colledge, J. Conolly, K. Dobney, K. Manning and S. Shennan (eds) *The Origins and Spread of Domestic Animals in Southwest Asia and Europe*: 237–252. Walnut Creek: Left Coast Press.

Marconi, S. and Tecchiati, U. (2006) La fauna del villaggio della prima età del Ferro del Thalerbühel di Tires (BZ). Economia, uso del territorio e strategie insediative tra II e I millenio a.C. In A. Curci and D. Vitali (eds) *Animali tra uomini e dei. Archeozoologia del mondo preromano. Atti del Convegno Internazionale 8–9 novembre 2002*: 11–26. Bologna: Ante Quem.

Markert, D. (unpubl.). Nussbaumersee + Uerschhausen Horn, unpubl. Artenliste Stand 1992.

Marti-Grädel, E. and Stopp, B. (1997) Late Neolithic Economy at Lakeside Settlements in Western Switzerland. *Anthropozoologica* 25/26: 495–504.

Marti-Grädel, E., Stopp, B., Deschler-Erb, S., Hüster Plogmann, H. and Schibler, J. (2012) Überlegungen zur Fleischversorgung der Tiroler Bergleute in der Bronzezeit. In K. Oeggl and V. Schaffer (eds) *Die Geschichte der Bergbaus in Tirol und seinen angrenzenden Gebieten. Proceedings zum 6. Milestone-Meeting des SFB HiMAT vom 3.–5.11.2011 in Klausen/Südtirol*: 90–97. Innsbruck: Innsbruck University Press.

Marzatico, F. (2009a) Le plus ancien pastoralisme en 'territoires extremes' des Alpes italiennes centre-orientales. *Le Globe* 149: 117–136.

Marzatico, F. (2009b) Le basi economiche dell'età del Bronzo in Italia settentrionale. In M. Bartelheim and H. Stäuble (eds) *Die wirtschaftlichen Grundlagen der Bronzezeit Europas / The Economic Foundations of the European Bronze Age*: 213–252. Rahden/Westf.: Leidorf.

Mauvilly, M., Olive, C., Studer, J. and Brombacher, C. (1997) Frasses 'Praz au Doux' (FR), un site du Hallstatt ancien en bordure de rivière. *Archäologie Schweiz* 20: 112–125.

Menotti, F. (2009) Climate variations in the Circum-Alpine region and their influence on the Neolithic – Bronze Age lacustrine communities: displacement and/or cultural adaptation. *Documenta Praehistorica* 36: 61–66.

Morel, P. (1988) Kommentar zu den Tierknochen aus Schnitt 6 'Schichtpaket'. *Jahrbuch der Schweizerischen Gesellschaft für Ur- und Frühgeschichte* 71: 28–29.

Peters, J. and Smolnik, R. (1994) Fauna und Landschaft des Burgstallkogels bei Kleinklein (Steiermark) im Spiegel der Tierknochenfunde. In R. Smolnik (ed.) *Der Burgstallkogel bei Kleinklein II. Die Keramik der vorgeschichtlichen Siedlung.*: 147–158. Marburg: LIT.

Pétrequin, P. and Vuaillat, D. (1968) La grotte de Blois-sur-Seille (Jura) et la reculée de voiteur à l'Age du Bronze final. *Revue Archéologique de l'Est et du Centre-Est* 19: 99–112.

Petrucci, G. (1994) Appendice II: La Fauna. In P. Càssola Guida and E. Borgna (eds) *Pozzuolo del Friuli – I: I resti della tarda età del Bronzo in località Braida Roggia (con appendici di G. Boschian, A. Candussio, G. Petrucci)*: 199–227. Roma: Quasar di Severino Tognon.

Petrucci, G. (1998) Pozzuolo del Friuli: I dati dell'archeozoologia. In P. Càssola Guida, S. Pettarin, G. Petrucci and A. Giumlia-Mair (eds) *Pozzuoli del Friuli – II, 2: La prima età del ferro nel settore meridionale del castelliere. Le attività produttive e i resti faunistici.*: 127–138. Roma: Quasar di Severino Tognon.

Petrucci, G. (2007) Lo sfruttamento delle risorse faunistiche dell'Italia nord-orientale dell'età del ferro: archeozoologia, economia e ambiente. *Origini* 29: 183–220.

Pino Uria, B. and Tagliacozzo, A. (2001) Studio archeozoologico dei livelli protostorici del quartiere Nord-Ovest di Concordia Sagittaria (Venezia) del quadro delle faune dell'Italia Nord-Orientale. *Quaderni di Archeologia del Veneto* 17: 141–157.

Plüss, P. (2011) *Die bronzezeitliche Siedlung Cresta bei Cazis (GR): Die Tierknochen*. Zürich: Chronos Verlag.

Poulain, T. (1973) Comparaison entre deux gisements de Saône-et-Loire, 'Curtil Brenot' à Ourourx-sur-Saône et 'Vauvretin' à Epervans. *Revue Archéologique de l'Est et du Centre-Est* 24: 124–127.

Primas, M. (2009) Nicht nur Kupfer und Salz: die Alpen im wirtschaftlichen und sozialen Umfeld des 2. Jahrtausends. In M. Bartelheim and H. Stäuble (eds) *Die wirtschaftlichen Grundlagen der Bronzezeit Europas / The Economic Foundations of the European Bronze Age*: 189–211. Rahden/Westf.: Leidorf.

Primas, M. and Ruoff, U. (1981) Die urnenfelderzeitliche Inselsiedlung 'Grosser Hafner' im Zürichsee (Schweiz). Tauchgrabung 1978–1979. *Germania* 59: 31–50.

Pucher, E. (1994) Eine Gegenüberstellung prähistorischer Tierknochenfundkomplexe des Ostalpenraums – Verbindungen und Gegensätze. In M. Kokabi and J. Wahl (eds) *Beiträge zur Archäozoologie und Prähistorischen Anthropologie. 8. Arbeitstreffen der Osteologen Konstanz 1993 im Andenken an Joachim Boessneck*: 231–249. Stuttgart: Kommissionsverlag Konrad Theiss Verlag.

Pucher, E. (2001) Die Tierknochenfunde aus dem bronzezeitlichen Siedlungsplatz Unterhautzenthal in Niederösterreich. In E. Lauermann, E. Pucher and M. Schmitzberger (eds) *Unterhautzenthal und Michelberg. Beiträge zum Siedlungswesen der frühbronzezeitlichen Aunjetitz-Kultur m nördlichen Niederösterreich*: 64–103; 164–169. St. Pölten: Selbstverlag des NÖ Institutes für Landeskunde.

Ramstein, M., Büttiker-Schumacher, E. and Brombacher, C. (2005) Ipsach – Räberain. Spätbronzezeitliche Siedlungen und römischer Gutshof. *Archäologie im Kanton Bern* 6: 569–614.

Ramstein, M. and Deschler-Erb, S. (2005) Pieterlen, Under-Siedebrunne 3. Rettungsgrabung 1998: prähistorische Siedlungsreste. *Archäologie im Kanton Bern* 6: 102–109.

Rehazek, A. (unpubl.). Die Tierknochen von Haldenstein.

Reitmaier, T., Lambers, K., Walser, C., Zingman, I., Haas, J. N., Dietre, B., Reidl, D., Hajdas, I., Nicolussi, K., Kathrein, Y., Naef, L. and Kaiser, T. (2013) Alpine Archäologie in der Silvretta. *Archäologie Schweiz* 36: 4–15.

Reverdin, L. (1927) Etude faunistique de la station du Sumpf, Zoug, âge du Bronze. *Société de Physique et d'Histoire naturelle de Genève, Supplément aux Archives des Sciences physiques et naturelles* 44: 63–66.

Reverdin, L. (1928) Etude faunistique de la station du Sumpf, Zoug, âge du Bronze. 2me note. *Société de Physique et d'Histoire naturelle de Genève, Supplément aux Archives des Sciences physiques et naturelles* 45: 155–157.

Revilliod, P. and Reverdin, L. (1927) Les ossements d'animaux de la station lacustre des Eaux-Vives (Genève). *Verhandlungen der Schweizerischen Naturforschenden Gesellschaft* 240.

Riedel, A. (1975) La fauna del villagio preistorico di Isolone della Prevaldesca. *Bollettino del Museo Civico di Storia Naturale di Verona* 2: 355–414.

Riedel, A. (1977) The Fauna of Four Prehistoric Settlements in Northern Italy. *Atti del Museo Civico di Storia Naturale Trieste* 30–1: 65–122.

Riedel, A. (1979) La fauna di alcuni insediamenti preistorici del territorio veronese. *Atti del Museo Civico di Storia Naturale Trieste* 31–1: 41–73.

Riedel, A. (1981) La fauna di Braida Roggia a Pozzuolo del Friuli. *Atti dei Civici Musei di Storia ed Arte di Trieste* 12: 121–131.

Riedel, A. (1982a) Die Fauna einer bronzezeitlichen Siedlung bei Peschiera am Gardasee. *Rivista di Archeologia* 6: 23–27.

Riedel, A. (1982b) Die Fauna von Feniletto (Verona). *Rivista di Archeologia* 6: 28–30.

Riedel, A. (1984a) Die Fauna der Sonnenburger Ausgrabungen. *Preistoria Alpina* 20: 261–280.

Riedel, A. (1984b) The fauna of the excavations of Pozzuolo del Friuli (1980–1983) (Castelliere dei Ciastiei – Trench1). *Atti dei Civici Musei di Storia ed Arte di Trieste* 14: 215–276.

Riedel, A. (1985a) Die Fauna einer bronzezeitlichen Siedlung bei Eppan (Südtirol). *Rivista di Archeologia* 9: 9–25.

Riedel, A. (1985b) Ergebnisse der Untersuchung einiger Südtiroler Faunen. *Preistoria Alpina* 21: 113–177.

Riedel, A. (1992) The Bronze Age animal bone deposit of Nogarole Rocca I Camponi (Veneto). *Padusa* XXVIII Nouva Serie: 87–104.

Riedel, A. (1993) La fauna di Sabbionara di Veronella (Verona). In L. Salzani (ed.) *L'abitato e la necropoli di Sabbionara a Veronella. Prime ricerche*: 79–85 and 10 Tab. Comunità Adige-Guà: Editrice Ambrosini.

Riedel, A. (1996) Archaeozoological investigations in North-eastern Italy: the exploitation of animals since the Neolithic. *Preistoria Alpina* 30: 43–94.

Riedel, A. (2002) *La fauna dell'insediamento protostorico di Vadena / Die Fauna der vorgeschichtlichen Siedlung von Pfatten*. Rovereto: Ed. Osiride.

Riedel, A. (2003) Die frühbronzezeitliche Fauna von Brixlegg in Tirol. *Atti della Accademia Roveretana degli Agiati / B* Ser. VIII, vol. III, B: 197–281.

Riedel, A. (2004) La fauna. In M. Bernabo Breà and M. Cremaschi (eds) *Il villaggio piccolo della terramara di S. Rosa di Poviglio (Scavi 1987/1992)*: 743–777. Firenze: Istituto italiano di preistoria e protostoria.

Riedel, A. (2007) Ein spätantiker Tierknochenfundkomplex aus Drösing an der March (Niederösterreich). *Annalen des Naturhistorischen Museums Wien* 109: 29–72.

Riedel, A. and Rizzi, J. (1995) The middle Bronze Age fauna of Albanbühel. In R. Peretto (ed.) *Atti del 1º Convegno nazionale di Archeozoologia. Rovigo – Accademia dei Concordi 5–7 Marzo 1993*: 171–183. Rovigo: Centro polesano di studi storici, archeologici ed etnografici.

Riedel, A. and Tecchiati, U. (2001) Settlements and economy in the Bronze and Iron Age in Trentino-South Tyrol. Notes for an archaeozoological model. *Preistoria Alpina* 35:

Roberts, B. (2009) Subsistence, structures and craftworking: analysing economic dynamics in Britain 2500–800 BC. In M. Bartelheim and H. Stäuble (eds) *Die wirtschaftlichen Grundlagen der Bronzezeit Europas / The economic foundations of the European Bronze Age*: 65–83. Rahden/Westf.: Leidorf.

Salvagno, L. and Tecchiati, U. (2011) *I resti faunistici del villaggio dell'età del Bronzo di Sotciastel. Economia e vita di una comunità protostorica alpina (c. XVII–XIV sec. a.C.)*. San Martin de Tor: Istitut ladin 'Micurà de Rü'.

Schibler, J. (unpubl. a). Die Tierknochen von Fällanden-Rietspitz.

Schibler, J. (unpubl. b). Die Tierknochen von Meilen-Schellen.

Schibler, J. (unpubl. c). Die Tierknochen von Zürich-Grosser Hafner.

Schibler, J., Breitenlechner, E., Deschler-Erb, S., Goldenberg, G., Hanke, K., Hiebel, G., Hüster Plogmann, H., Nicolussi, K., Marti-Grädel, E., Pichler, S., Schmidl, A., Schwarz, S., Stopp, B. and Oeggl, K. (2011) Miners and mining in the Late Bronze Age: a multidisciplinary study from Austria. *Antiquity* 85: 1–20.

Schibler, J., Hüster Plogmann, H., Deschler-Erb, S., Pöllath, N. and Stopp, B. (2009) Fleischversorgung in Fundstellen des bronzezeitlichen Bergbaus: Beispiele aus dem HiMAT-Projekt. In K. Oeggl and M. Prast (eds) *Die Geschichte des Bergbaus in Tirol und seinen angrenzenden Gebieten. Proceedings zum 3. Milestone-Meeting des SFB HiMAT vom 23.–26.10.2008 in Silbertal.*: 91–107. Innsbruck: Innsbruck University Press.

Schibler, J. and Jacomet, S. (2010) Short climatic fluctuations and their impact on human economies and societies: the potential of the Neolithic lake shore settlements in the Alpine foreland. *Environmental Archaeology* 15: 173–178.

Schibler, J., Stopp, B. and Studer, J. (1999) Haustierhaltung und Jagd. In F. Müller, G. Kaenel and G. Lüscher (eds) *Die Schweiz vom Paläolithikum bis zum frühen Mittelalter (SPM) IV: Eisenzeit*: 116–136. Basel: Verlag Schweizerische Gesellschaft für Ur- und Frühgeschichte.

Schibler, J. and Studer, J. (1998) Haustierhaltung und Jagd während der Bronzezeit der Schweiz. In S. Hochuli, U. Niffeler and V. Rychner (eds) *Die Schweiz vom Paläolithikum bis zum frühen Mittelalter (SPM) III: Bronzezeit*: 171–191. Basel: Verlag Schweizerische Gesellschaft für Ur- und Frühgeschichte.

Schibler, J. and Veszeli, M. (1996) Die Tierknochen der Seeufersiedlungen von Zug-Sumpf und ihre Bedeutung im Rahmen der bronzezeitlichen Wirtschaft im nördlichen Alpenvorland. In D. Hartmann (ed.) *Die spätbronzezeitlichen Ufersiedlungen von Zug-Sumpf. Band 1: Die Dorf-Geschichte*: 305–343 u. 368–369. Zug: Kantonales Museum für Urgeschichte Zug.

Schmid, E. (1952) Die Tierknochen vom Kestenberg, Grabung 1951. *Ur-Schweiz* Jahrgang XVI: 96.

Schmid, E. (1955) Die Tierknochen der Grabung 1952. *Ur-Schweiz* Jahrgang XIX: 31–32.

Schmitzberger, M. (2007) Archäozoologische Untersuchungen an den bronze-, eisen- und römerzeitlichen Tierknochen vom Ganglegg und vom Tartscher Bichl. In H. Steiner (ed.) *Die befestigte Siedlung am Ganglegg im Vinschgau – Südtirol. Ergebnisse der Ausgrabungen 1997–2001 (Bronze-/Urnenfelderzeit) und naturwissenschaftliche Beiträge.*: 619–742. Bozen: Amt für Bodendenkmäler.

Sidi Maamar, H. (1997) Des poubelles aux bestiaires: essai d'interprétation archéozoologique d'un espace villageois alpin du premier âge du Fer (Brig-Glis/Waldmatte, Valais, Suisse). In A. Bocquet (ed.) *Espaces physiques espaces sociaux dans l'analyse interne des sites du Néolithique à l'Âge du Fer. Actes du colloque l'analyse spatiale des sites du Néolithique à l'Âge du Fer. 119e Congrès national des sociétés historiques et scientifiques, Amiens, 26–30 octobre 1994*: 423–439. Paris: Editions du CTHS.

Sidi Maamar, H. and Gillioz, P.-A. (1995) Pour une archéozoologie de la maisonnée: espaces des déchets et modes de subsistance d'une communauté villageoise alpine du 1er Âge du Fer (Brig-Glis/Waldmatte, Valais, Suisse): essai critique et résultats préliminaires. *Anthropozoologica* 21: 171–187.

Stampfli, H. R. (unpubl.). Die Tierknochenfunde der spätbronzezeitlichen Siedlung Vinelz-Ländti in Gegenüberstellung zu denjenigen der cortaillodzeitlichen Station Port-Stüdeli (Bielersee, Schweiz).

Steinmann, P. (1923) Ueber die Fauna der Pfahlbauten im Hallwiler See. *Mitteilungen der Aargauischen Naturforschenden Gesellschaft* XVI./16. Heft: 59–63.

Steinmann, P. (1925) Weitere Knochenreste vom broncezeitlichen Rostbau bei Hallwil. *Mitteilungen der Aargauischen Naturforschenden Gesellschaft* XVII./17. Heft: 184–186.

Stephan, E. (2007) Tierknochenfunde aus einer urnenfelderzeitlichen Grube in Heidelberg-Bergheim. *Fundberichte aus Baden-Württemberg* 29: 107–116.

Stopp, B. (2007) Tierknochen, Zahn- und Geweihfragmente. In J. Obrecht and P. Gutzwiller (eds) *Die Loppburg – eine befestigte Höhensiedlung. Resultate der Ausgrabungen von 2001 in einer vermeintlich mittelalterlichen Burg*: 119–122. Basel: Reinhardt Druck AG.

Stopp, B. (unpubl. a). Die Tierknochen von Fliess-Silberplan.

Stopp, B. (unpubl. b). Die Tierknochen von Viehhofen-Wirtsalm.

Studer, J. (1991) *La faune de l'âge du Bronze final du site d'Hauterive-Champréveyres (Neuchâtel, Suisse). Synthèse de la faune des sites littoraux contemporaines.* PhD, Université de Genève.

Studer, J. (1998) Restes fauniques de Marin NE-Le Chalvaire, couches 4 et 5. *Jahrbuch der Schweizerischen Gesellschaft für Ur- und Frühgeschichte* 81: 95–97.

Suter, P. J. and Schlichtherle, H. (eds) 2009. *Pfahlbauten: UNESCO Welterbe-Kandidatur 'Prähistorische Pfahlbauten rund um die Alpen' / Palafittes: candidature au Patrimonie mondial de l'UNESCO 'Sites palafittiques préhistoriques autour des Alpes' / Palafitte: candidatura a patrimonio mondiale dell'UNESCO 'Siti palafitticoli preistorici dell'arco alpino'* (in Zusammenarbeit mit Béat Arnold et al.), Bern: Palafittes, Archäologischer Dienst des Kantons Bern.

Tecchiati, U., Fontana, A. and Marconi, S. (2011) Indagini archeozoologiche sui resti faunistici della media-recente età del Bronzo di Laion-Wasserbühel (BZ). *Annali del Museo Civico di Rovereto* 26: 105–131.

Veszeli, M. (2007) Die Tierknochen (mit einem Beitrag von H. Hüster-Plogmann). In B. Eberschweiler, P. Riethmann and U. Ruoff (eds) *Das spätbronzezeitliche Dorf von Greifensee-Böschen. Dorfgeschichte, Hausstrukturen und Fundmaterial*: 232–234. Zürich und Egg: Neue Medien.

von den Driesch, A. and Boessneck, J. (1989) Abschlussbericht über die zooarchäologischen Untersuchungen an Tierknochenfunden von der Heuneburg. In E. Gersbach (ed.) *Ausgrabungsmethodik und Stratigraphie der Heuneburg*: 131–157. Mainz: Philipp von Zabern.

Walser, C. (2012) Kalt – Warm. Klima und Besiedlungsdynamik in der Silvretta. In T. Reitmaier (ed.) *Letzte Jäger, erste Hirten. Hochalpine Archäologie in der Silvretta*: 205–218. Chur: Amt für Kultur, Archäologischer Dienst Graubünden.

Wettstein, E. (1924) Die Tierreste aus dem Pfahlbau am Alpenquai in Zürich. *Vierteljahresschrift der Naturforschenden Gesellschaft in Zürich* 69: 78–127.

Wiemann, P., Kühn, M., Heitz-Weniger, A., Stopp, B., Jennings, B., Rentzel, P. and Menotti, F. (2012) The end of a lake-dwelling: a multidisciplinary approach to the Late Bronze Age lakeside settlement of Zurich-Alpenquai. *Journal of Wetland Archaeology* 12: 58–85.

Chapter 8

Bronze Age trade and exchange through the Alps: influencing cultural variability?

Benjamin Jennings

Introduction

Trade and exchange in prehistory revolved around more than simply the circulation of goods; it was about social communication, the maintenance of intra-community relationships, the transmission of technology, ideas and manufacturing processes, and the generation of social power and prestige. In this respect the Circum-Alpine region has been considered as a 'buffer' or 'interaction' zone between northern Europe and the Mediterranean, linking northern European cultures with those of the southern Alpine slopes and the Italian peninsula (Della Casa 2002; Primas and Schmid-Sikimić 1997). Utilising the theoretical concepts of *relational theory*, *object biographies* and *cultural object translation* provides an opportunity to interpret the changing social values of objects as they travelled between different regions, and illuminate the cultural effects of involvement in exchange networks on communities that participated in them. Before considering the biography of objects it is necessary to identify which objects were circulated through the Alps, where they came from, and the routes along which they flowed.

Long and short-distance trade routes through the Alps and beyond

Recent programmes of archaeological survey have helped to identify routes along which trade and communication may have flowed through the Alps, utilising Alpine valleys to connect northern Italy, Switzerland, Austria, and eastern France, in addition to the exploitation of highland resources (*e.g.* Della Casa 2002; Suter *et al.* 2006). Artefacts found during such surveys indicate that the routes were used over successive time periods, which is reasonable to expect given that the possible routes are restricted by the landscape topography and few other options were available. However, while the surveys show that the Alps were not an insurmountable barrier between the regions north and south of the mountain range, they do not provide indications of where material was being transported from, or to where it may have been destined. Considering these factors highlights one of the frequently mentioned fallacies of communication across the Alps, particularly with

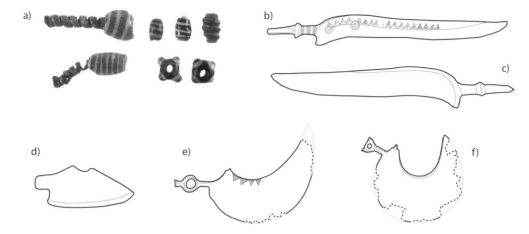

Figure 8.1. a) Pfahlbauperlen, left two shown at twice the scale of remainder (after: Rychner-Farragi 1993; reproduced with permission of Latenium, Archaeology Park and Museum, Neuchâtel); b) LBA knife from Mörigen (redrawn from Bernatzky-Goetze 1987); c) Herrnbaumgarten knife from Hadersdorf am Kamp, Austria (redrawn from Rihovosky 1972); d) Auvernier razor from Mörigen (redrawn from Jockenhovel 1971); e) Herrnbaumgarten razor from Herrnbaumgarten, Austria (redrawn from Jockenhovel 1971); f) Villanovan razor from Mörigen (redrawn from Bernatzky-Goetze 1987).

reference to later prehistory and the Iron Age: that trade, exchange and communication relationships primarily concerned the flow of goods and information from the 'advanced Mediterranean' to the 'barbarian north'. A key factor influencing such statements is the general 'invisibility' of objects which may have travelled from north to south, such as furs, pelts, and leather, when compared to those durable manufactured objects which may have moved in the opposite direction, such as glass, metalwork, and, particularly during the Iron Age, ceramics (Nash Briggs 2003).

A significant exception to these 'invisible' objects from the north is Baltic amber (succinite), sourced from along the Baltic coast and inland deposits in Latvia, Lithuania, and Poland, but also occurring as far away as eastern England. Fortunately for the archaeologist, amber is relatively durable in the archaeological record, and also definable through archaeometric analysis, allowing us to understand whether it originated from the Baltic or other regional European deposits (*e.g.* Beck and Shennan 1991, Murillo-Barroso and Martinón-Torres 2012; Angelini and Bellintani 2005). One of the earliest attempts to chart trade routes connecting northern Europe to the Italian peninsula utilised amber as the main object of focus, identifying find locations, categorising them by period, and essentially 'joining the dots' to suggest paths along which goods were transported (De Navarro 1925). While recent contributions have updated the find catalogue (*e.g.* Stahl 2006) and included areas of Europe not covered by De Navarro (*e.g.* Palavestra 2007), the overall distribution pattern of amber artefacts in Europe north of the Alps has changed little.

Objects circulated in the opposite direction (*i.e.* south to north) travelled just as far as

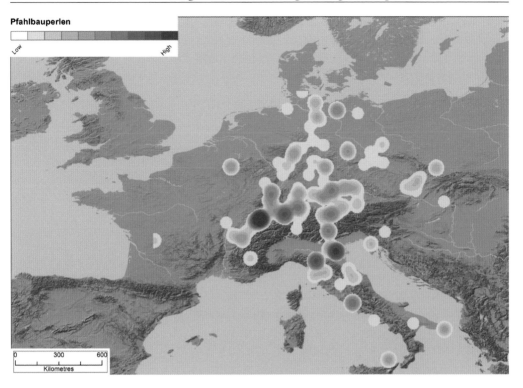

Figure 8.2. Density distribution of Pfahlbauperlen (after: Jennings 2014b).

amber. One of the best examples are the so-called *Pfahlbauperlen*: small blue and white glass beads (Fig. 8.1.a) relating to the Late Bronze Age (*c.* 1100–800 BC), found in varying quantities between the Italian peninsula and northern Germany/Denmark (Fig. 8.2). These beads were initially named due to their presence in the lake-settlements of the northern Circum-Alpine region (see Haevernick 1978), but the discovery and excavation of Frattesina (Po Plain, Italy) during the late 20th century, produced the only direct evidence for the manufacture of these beads in Europe (Angelini *et al.* 2004; Angelini *et al.* 2009; Bellintani and Stefan 2009). Archaeometric analysis has confirmed that many of these beads from northern Europe are of the glass composition known from Frattesina (Henderson 1993; Bauer *et al.* 2004; Mildner *et al.* 2013), and it is therefore assumed/hypothesised that they were produced at Frattesina and traded northwards.

It is not possible to envisage a direct or commercial trade connection between northern Europe and the Italian peninsula; rather a series of short distance interactions between communities circulating a range of items in regional exchange systems should be postulated. Such a 'down-the-line' (see Renfrew and Bahn 2012) system would, partially, explain the decreasing occurrence of the *Pfahlbauperlen* with greater distance from their production centre in the Po Plain (Fig. 8.2) (Jennings 2014b). Whether the participants at either extent of the distribution knew of the primary origin of the objects or their ultimate destination

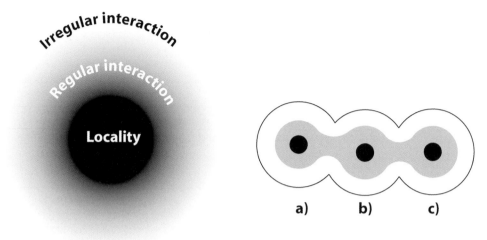

Figure 8.3. Knowledge of distant regions and communities was transmitted through communication networks, expanding the knowledge base of communities with regard to other regions (A–B), but with diminishing accuracy as distances, and number of involved regions, increases (A–C) (after: Jennings 2014b).

is unclear, but some indications are provided by the ancient Greek belief that amber originated from the Electride Islands – attributed by some authors to be in the northern Adriatic and connected to the Po Plain (Palavestra 2007; Braccesi 2004); *i.e.* the region of Frattesina and Grignano amber processing sites (Bellintani 2002; Bellintani 1997; Salzani 2009). A community's knowledge of items' origins diminished as objects travelled further away from their source, and individuals/communities participating in their circulation assimilated information of distant places acquired through communication with 'traders' into local spheres of significance and mental maps. This expanded their knowledge and perception of both local and distant environments, but also led to a mixing of fact with myth (Fig. 8.3).

In contrast to the circulation of *Pfahlbauperlen* and amber between northern and southern Europe, some objects travelled over much smaller distances, and possibly indicate quasi commercial exchange networks. For instance, the use, exchange, and deposition of regularised sickle fragments has previously been interpreted as a form of 'proto-currency' (Sommerfeld 1994; Primas 1986), potentially used in immediate return (commercial or bargaining) exchange relationships. A brief review of sickle typology of the Late Bronze Age (*e.g.* Primas 1986) indicates that sickle types and variants were primarily exchanged over *intra-* (short) rather than *inter-* (long) regional networks (Fig. 8.4). If sickle fragments were utilised as a basic unit of exchange, they did not travel long distances, raising questions as to the method by which objects travelled over larger areas. Objects circulated over short-distance networks may have travelled as *commodities*: items which have a prescribed value

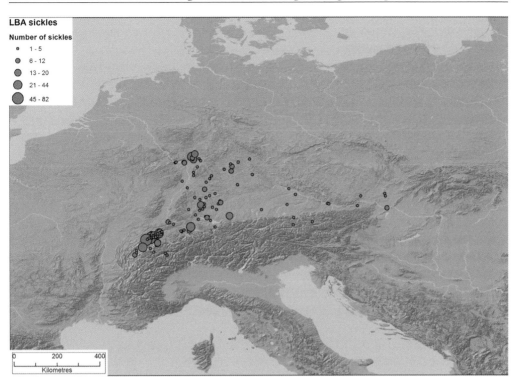

Figure 8.4. Distribution of Late Bronze Age sickles of types found in the lake-dwellings of Switzerland. Primary distribution is evident around Lake Neuchâtel, with some spread into southern Germany (data from: Primas 1986; after: Jennings 2014b).

based on their production and potential use, for example intact sickles, and primarily stay within a 'cultural region'. Glass beads, travelling over long-distance networks, are more likely to have circulated as prestige items, possibly made as gifts between elite members of communities, as they moved northwards through Europe (see Sharples 2010). However, they need not travel the entire distance as prestige gift objects; in their region of manufacture glass beads were likely treated as a commodity, only attaining a prestige value as they left their production zone. Such a pattern of value change is also recorded for amber in northern Europe/Denmark, where it was relatively absent in prestige burials of the Late Bronze Age, but instead was collected for exchange with the south (Beck and Shennan 1991).

Trade and exchange in lacustrine settlements: identifying objects

Aside from the *Pfahlbauperlen* and amber, a range of imported objects can be seen in the lake-dwellings of the northern Circum-Alpine region. These are not only confined to the Late Bronze Age, but also include the Neolithic (*e.g.* ceramics at Arbon-Bleiche 3 (Leuzinger 2000)) and the Early Bronze Age (*e.g.* loaf-of-bread idols at Bodman-Schachen I (Köninger and Schlichtherle 2001)). Although it is possible to identify some 'foreign' ceramics in

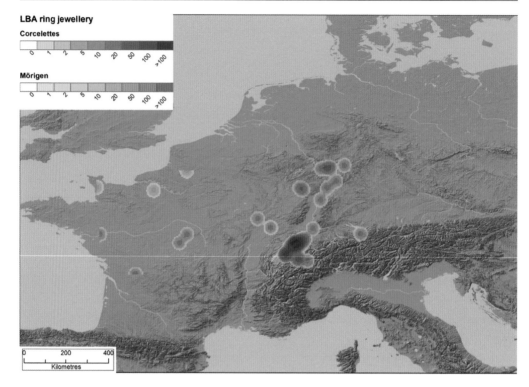

Figure 8.5. Density distribution of Late Bronze Age arm- and leg-rings of the Corcelettes and Mörigen types (after: Jennings 2014b).

the Late Bronze Age material recovered from lake settlements (*e.g.* Bernatzky-Goetze 1987; Mäder 2001b), the metalwork assemblages provide a greater opportunity to observe intra- and inter-regional connections, particularly as artefacts from many areas of Europe have been published in typological catalogues under the *Prähistorische Bronzefunde* series. The use of such catalogues and artefact distribution maps as a method of demonstrating inter-cultural communication largely fell out of fashion during the Post-Processual turn in archaeological theory; however, if combined with a sound theoretical background these catalogues and distribution plots can provide new insights to the trade and exchange routes utilised during the Late Bronze Age.

Some metalwork objects show clear distribution concentrations, and either inferred or proven (through moulds and half-fabricated pieces) manufacture in the lake settlements of western Switzerland. For instance, many styles of arm- and leg-ring are seen in high concentrations around Lake Neuchâtel, with moulds and half-fabricated objects known from Hauterive-Champréveyres (HaA-HaB) (Rychner-Faraggi 1993) and Mörigen (HaB3) (Bernatzky-Goetze, 1987). Many of these types of ring jewellery, for example *Auvernier* and *Sion*, show limited circulation within western Switzerland (Pászthory 1985). Other forms, for instance types *Homburg* and *Balingen*, are widely distributed throughout Switzerland, southern Germany, the Middle Rhine Valley, and central France (Pászthory 1985; Richter

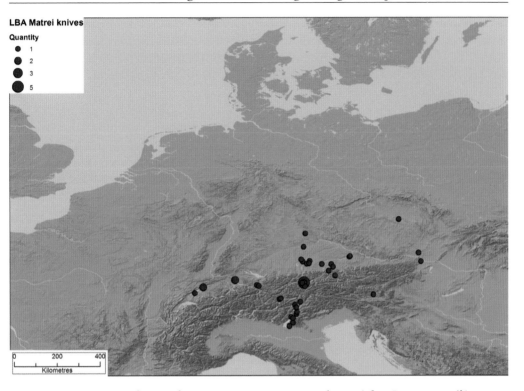

Figure 8.6. Distribution of Late Bronze Age Matrei type knives (after: Jennings 2014b).

1970), and it is possible that they were manufactured in multiple locations. Two forms, which were evidently manufactured in the west of Switzerland (given their high density) and that travelled as far as northern and western France, are the *Corcelettes* and *Mörigen* rings (Fig. 8.5). Although the apparent reduced density of amber in Late Bronze Age burial or hoard contexts from Denmark, where it was primarily used as an exchange object (see Beck and Shennan 1991), provides a caution against interpreting high density areas of specific objects as production zones, ring jewellery (and other bronzework) is not naturally occurring; these objects have to be physically manufactured and higher occurrence can be anticipated in their area of manufacture. Therefore, it is likely that high densities of manufactured objects in specific regions suggest possible production zones.

In contrast to the apparent 'export' of ring jewellery from the lake-dwelling communities, relatively few pieces seem to have been 'imported'. A few *Vénat* type rings, synonymous with the large metalwork hoard at Vénat (Saint Yrieix, France (Coffyn *et al.* 1981)) are recorded from western Switzerland (Pászthory 1985), including at the lake-dwellings of Geneva-Eaux Vives (Lake Geneva) and Nidau (Lake Biel). *Auvernier, Corcelettes* and *Balingen* rings in the hoard at Vénat suggest that these sites, and others in western Switzerland, were connected in a far reaching east-west exchange system (Coffyn *et al.* 1981).

Other forms of bronzework show a similar involvement of the lake-dwelling communities in exporting a large quantity of objects, but importing relatively few. For example, the so-called *Pfahlbaulanzen* ('lake-dwelling spears') are, as their name suggests, recorded extensively within the lake-dwellings of Switzerland (Jacob-Friesen 1967; Tarot 2000), but are also well represented in Denmark and northern Germany (Jacob-Friesen 1967; Kristiansen 1998). In contrast, few 'foreign' spearheads are recorded from the lake-dwellings, with two exceptions being a *West-Baltic* type from Grandson-Corcelettes (HaB) and a *Vénat* type from Auvernier-Bréna (HaB1) (Tarot 2000).

Knives have been classified under different typological schemes in Switzerland compared to other regions of Europe (*e.g.* Rychner 1979; Bauer *et al.* 2004), which makes a direct comparison more difficult than for other forms of bronzework. Many of the spiked- and tanged-handle forms from Switzerland show similarities to others found across Europe, particularly the *Baumgarten* type (Hohlbein 2008; Prüssing 1982; Říhovský 1972) (Fig. 8.1.b, c). Some forms are classified in the same typological systems, such as socketed knives (*Tüllenmesser*), 'Fantasy handle' knives (*Phantasiemesser*), and the *Matrei* type, illustrating the involvement of the lake-dwellings in both intra- and inter-regional exchange systems. *Matrei* type knives from Estavayer-le-Lac (Vogt 1952; Bernatzky-Goetze 1987) and Zurich-Alpenquai (Mäder 2001a) are further indications that these settlements were connected to an intra-regional exchange system, linking east and west Switzerland to northern Italy, Austria, and southern Germany (Fig. 8.6) during the early LBA (BzD-HaA) (Hohlbein 2008; Bianco Peroni 1976; Říhovský 1972). Socketed and *Phantasie* knives of the later LBA show a dominant distribution in the lake-dwelling region of western Switzerland and eastern France (particularly Lake Bourget) and in the north of Europe. However, the routes that these two knife types may have travelled appear significantly different, with socketed knives, found frequently in the Netherlands (where local manufacture may also have occurred (see Butler *et al.* 2012)), following a more westerly route than the *Phantasie* type, which is found more frequently in eastern central Europe (Fig. 8.7) (Hohlbein 2008; see Jockenhövel and Smolla 1975).

The knife varieties found in the northern Alpine region lake-dwellings show a similar pattern to that seen in other material culture, *e.g.* amber and glass beads, ring jewellery and spearheads, with some interaction and exchange links to northern Italy, but more prominent links to central Europe. Interaction with northern Italy is further suggested through the occurrence of several fibula types, for example *Mörigen* and *Wollishofen* and simple torsion arch fibulae, at Mörigen, Zurich-Wollishofen and Zug-Sumpf respectively, which show good comparison to many Late Bronze Age fibulae in the Po Plain and southern Alpine valleys (Betzler 1974; Eles Masi 1986). A single *Platten* (plate) fibula from Grandson-Corcelettes lies well outside of their main distribution in northern Europe, and when combined with the *West Baltic* spearhead and a *hanging vessel*/belt box decorated with Nordic style motifs from the same lake-settlement (Sprockhoff 1966; Sprockhoff and Höckmann 1979), provides a strong indication of communication routes extending to northern Europe.

In opposition to these objects which travelled over long distances, razors evidently circulated across short distances during the Bronze Age, with specific styles (based on shape and handle attachment) being common in various regions (Jockenhövel 1980; Jockenhövel 1971; Bianco Peroni 1979; Henniing 1986). The majority of LBA (HaB) razors recorded from the northern

Circum-Alpine region are single-sided, trapezoid and half-moon in shape, with tangs or spikes for handle attachment; quite different from '*Villanovan*' lunate razors with cast handle or eastern European quasi-lunate razors with handle, such as the *Herrnbaumgarten* type (Fig. 8.1.d, e, f). Both *Villanovan* style and *Herrnbaumgarten* razors are recorded from the lake-dwelling region, the former at Mörigen (Pászthory 1985) and the latter not in a lake-settlement, but a burial from the Alpine Rhône valley at Chelin/Lens (Jockenhövel 1971).

Finally, unique or unusual objects in the lake-dwellings attest to further sporadic interaction with both northern Europe and northern Italy. For example a horse-shaped cheek piece (part of a horse harness) from Zurich-Alpenquai (Mäder 2001a) has most affinities with horse-gear from the Italian peninsula (see Von Hase 1969), and fragments of sheet bronze vessels and funnel-like needles (*Stangentrichter*) from Zurich-Wollishofen and Zurich-Alpenquai are similar to objects found in southern Germany and the Carpathian Basin (Mäder 2001a; Primas 2004). The sheet bronze pieces may indicate the movement of fragmentary bronzework on a commodity basis as material of prime value and recyclability, but the *Stangentrichter* and horse-shaped cheek piece appear to have been circulated as objects, and dismantled prior to deposition (assuming that the cheek piece had actually been used as harness equipment).

Detecting cultural variations

The use of distribution and density maps indicates objects which travelled across Bronze Age Europe in systems of long- and short-distance exchange networks, but they do not provide evidence of the cultural and social effects of participation in such exchange networks. To attempt an understanding of such cultural variations a theoretical approach linking objects and exchange interaction to cultural change and development is required. Three principles can be used to address these issues: 1) Relational Theory; 2) Cultural and Object Translation; 3) The Biography of Objects.

Relational theory

Combing the principles of relational theory (see Strathern 1988; Watts 2013) and systems theory, it is possible to consider societies as the culmination of a number of factors, and how they interact (Fig. 8.8). One of the factors to be considered as a formative component of the cultural composition of communities is their interaction with other communities through exchange relationships (Jennings 2014b). The loss or establishment of such relationships may have significant impacts upon the composition of society, especially if they were used as a part of social legitimisation practices (see Helms 1988). If the ability to participate in exchange relationships, and the knowledge of foreign regions and access to products that this would provide, were used as methods of supporting, legitimising, and perpetuating the social status of community members, a change to such interaction practices would require modification of other social structures to fulfil such functions. For example, a loss of trade partnerships and the social status that they provided, potentially hereditary based on the transfer of knowledge between generations, could have been replaced by an expansion of the burial ritual to express

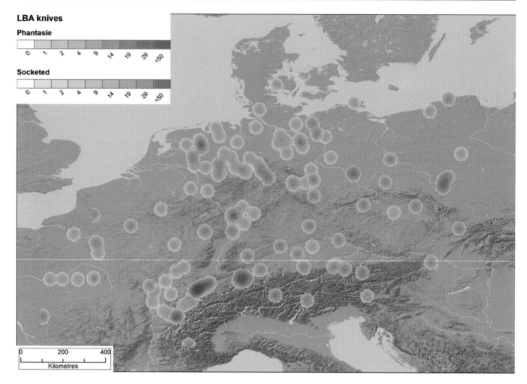

Figure 8.7. Density distribution of Socketed and Phantasie handle knives (after: Jennings 2014b).

hereditary links and ancestral rights. Of course, the opposite situation could also induce social changes, with new interaction routes and exchange goods creating opportunities for social display, but in this situation the exchange objects may have been directly appropriated by the elite members of society involved in trade partnerships.

It is also possible to follow the more traditional object focus of Strathern's (1988) and Gell's (1998) approach, under which artefacts and humans can be seen as becoming intertwined through their use and circulation. This may have resulted in the circulation of objects as *gifts* between elite members of communities, with the exchange act becoming a significant part of an object's value. Such practices are hinted at through the circulation of '*Brotlaibidole*' during the Early Bronze Age (mainly found in northern Italy, Croatia, and Austria, but several examples from Lake Constance (Köninger and Schlichtherle 2001)) which have been interpreted as a form of trade marker, with the object deliberately fragmented at the conclusion of an exchange partnership (Trnka 1992).

Cultural and object translation

The acceptance of new or 'foreign' styles of material culture was dependent upon the successful translation of objects into their new cultural setting (see Maran 2013). This could

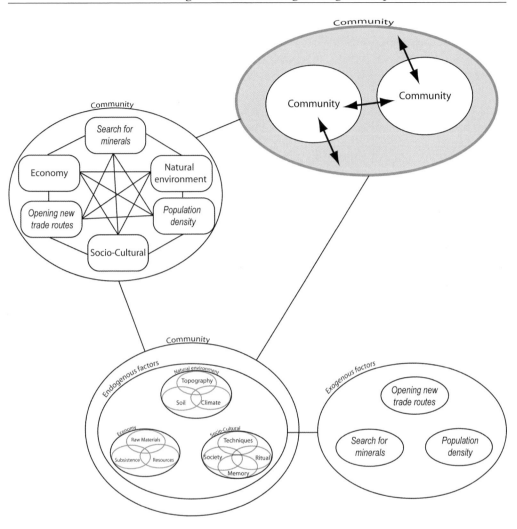

Figure 8.8. A relational model of communities. The cultural composition of communities can be seen not only as the composite of multiple endogenous and exogenous factors (lower section), but also the result of the interaction of those factors (middle sphere), and the interaction of communities with each other (upper sphere) (after: Jennings 2012).

have been achieved either through 'importive translation', where the individuals responsible for trade and exchange interaction – usually seen as elite members of society (see Helms 1988) – used their position to generate locally specific meaning for imported objects, or by 'productive translation' under which objects were given meanings through replication and emulation in new locales (see Jennings 2014b).

There are many examples of successful object translation throughout Europe and the lake-dwelling region – as indicated by the occurrence of quantities of 'foreign' objects in various regions – and a good example is the *Pfahlbauperlen* ranging from the Italian peninsula to northern Germany but with different value associations (see below). However, the northern Alpine region also shows indications of failed translation or object rejection. At two sites, Hauterive-Champréveyres and Montlingerberg (hilltop settlement in the Rhine Valley, Canton St Gallen, Switzerland), *Allumiere* type amber beads have been recovered. These beads are primarily recorded in the Mediterranean region and the Italian peninsula, with the two sites north of the Alps being distinct outliers in the distribution (Negroni Catacchio 1999; Rychner-Faraggi 1993; Steinhauser and Primas 1987; Jennings 2014b). Both of these settlements show other indications of involvement in exchange networks with northern Italy, particularly the *Pfahlbauperlen* at Hauterive-Champréveyres and inner Alpine ceramics at Montlingerberg. Despite these connections, and the apparent ready translation and acceptance of the *Pfahlbauperlen*, the *Allumiere* beads (which were also manufactured in the Po Plain at Frattesina and Gignano (Negroni Catacchio 1999; Salzani 2009)) were not widely incorporated into society, or passed on to other communities north of the Alps. If there was sufficient desire in these settlements to utilise the *Allumiere* form, more could have been imported (as many *Pfahlbauperlen* were) or even manufactured locally from amber being circulated towards northern Italy. The fact that neither of these occurred indicates the failure to translate these objects into local relevance north of the Alps.

The biography of objects

One way to observe the changes that occured in a society as a result of a re-organisation of various factors is through a broad study of material culture – not only the traditional interpretation as portable objects, but as immoveable features such as settlement form, construction techniques and funerary practices. Observing changes in the treatment of objects – or reconstructing an objects biography – illuminates changing cultural attitudes towards the value and significance of specific forms of material culture (*e.g.* Appadurai 1986; Gosden and Marshall 1999). This comparison can occur across both time and space, with changing value associations observed between different regions as objects were circulated, or within a specific region over successive time periods. A good example of the changing status of a single category of object can be seen in the use of amber in Denmark during the Neolithic and Bronze Age; initially used as a status indicator in burials, the material subsequently became a trade commodity used to acquire other prestige objects (bronzework) from the south (see Beck and Shennan 1991).

The biographical approach can be used to address both groups of objects/artefacts, for example amber as a material or arm-rings as an object class, to observe an 'idealised biography', or specific and 'individualised' objects which have been removed from the normal biographical cycle and diverted into new value regimes (Kopytoff 1986); for example several razors manufactured from arm-rings known from Switzerland (Jennings 2014a). In the case of 'idealised biographies', object groups are treated as a whole and the changing value of objects is generalised from multiple sources of evidence. For example, the social biography of arm-/leg-rings could be seen as a general progression from bronze stock commodity, to production of the ring-jewellery as either commodity or social object, to probable use as social identifier and display object during specific social events, before

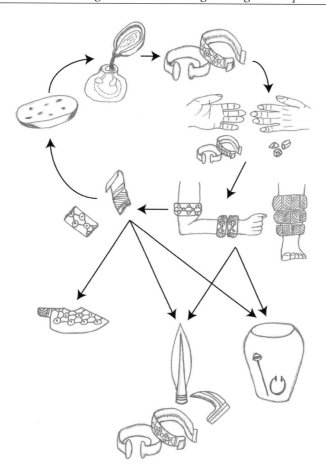

Figure 8.9. Hypothesized biography of Late Bronze Age arm- and leg-rings in the northern Circum-Alpine region. Initial production of the ring began with a bronze ingot, which was melted and cast as a piece of ring-jewellery. This would have effectively represented a commodity to the bronze worker who could 'sell' or exchange it with the commissioner or customer. It could then be further exchanged as a commodity of gift, but would eventually end up being worn and used as a social and status identifier during daily life or special events. Some rings were effectively retained by their owner during death, with their inclusion in the burial ceremony affirming their use as personal identity or status identifiers. Other rings were deposited in hoards, and might represent more communal identities. Finally, some rings were intentionally broken, and some of the fragments from this process may have been recycled by bronze smiths, but other parts may have been directly converted to new objects and used as mnemonic devices in a process related to the biography and social identity of their owners.

deposition in burial or hoard assemblages. In contrast, 'individualised' biographies address the biography of specific objects, observing how they were manipulated and extracted from the standard pathway for their object class – for example the ring-razors were diverted from the normal deposition practice for arm-rings and converted into new objects, extending their use life and diverting them into new value associations (Fig. 8.9).

The significance of exchanged goods

How imported objects were valued, and the significance that they assumed in their new cultural locales may be demonstrated by the contexts in which they were deposited. Of course, single items deposited in locations significantly removed from their main area of distribution may indicate the movement of individual people rather than the gift or commodity exchange of objects (see Jockenhövel 1991). For instance, the single *Herrnbaumgarten* razor from Chelin/Lens has been interpreted as the burial of a migrant individual (Nicolas 2003), and the small collection of Nordic style objects (*Platten* fibula, *West Baltic* spearhead, hanging vessel) from Grandson-Corcelettes may be the result of specific relocation. However, the placement of the *Herrnbaumgarten* razor in a burial is a significant divergence from the local deposition trends for razors, with very few being recorded from such contexts in Switzerland (see Jockenhövel 1971). This suggests that either other (surviving) members of the community knew of the practice for depositing *Herrnbaumgarten* razors with the deceased owner (typical practice in their main area of distribution in east-central Europe and also northern Italy (Jockenhövel 1971; Weber 1996; Gedl 1981; Bianco Peroni 1979)) and carried out such deposition, or that the placement of the razor in the burial with the 'migrant' was a convenient way of removing a 'foreign' object from the local cultural milieu.

When objects were repeatedly incorporated into the material culture assemblage of new cultural locales, it may be possible to observe changing value associations and social functions for the imported objects through their deposition contexts and associated items. The use of Multiple Correspondence Analysis (MCA) (Shennan 2006) privileges an insight to how values associated with specific objects changed as they were used in different regions, through visualizing how similar/dissimilar collections are based upon the categories of objects included (see Jennings 2014b). Unfortunately, this is not always possible with material recorded from lake-dwellings, as many objects are simply documented as coming from a 'lake settlement' without further contextual information. However, excavations in the latter half of 20th century recognised structured hoard deposits within these settlements, *e.g.* at Auvernier-Nord (Rychner 1987), and recently many objects from western Switzerland have also been re-assessed in an attempt to observe deposition patterns (Fischer 2012). A minority of the material culture finds recorded from the lake-dwelling areas of the northern Alpine region are known from burial contexts, which provides an opportunity to compare directly the deposition contexts of goods circulated between different regions of Europe.

One of the best objects to perform such analysis is the *Pfahlbauperlen*, found in burials from the Italian peninsula to northern Germany (Fig. 8.10). Burials containing these beads in Italy replicated the same associations many times, indicating a consistent deposition assemblage and value association in what are typically interpreted as female burials (*e.g.* Osteria dell'Osa (*e.g.* Bietti Sestieri 1992)). Moving north of the Alps, in burials at Le Boiron (Beeching, 1977) and Vidy Chavannes, these beads (possible fragments at Vidy) are associated with few other objects, but at Vidy occur in the cremation of a male individual (Kaenel and Klausener 1990; Moinat and David-Elbiali 2003). Travelling further north through Europe the beads were often deposited in both hoard and burial assemblages,

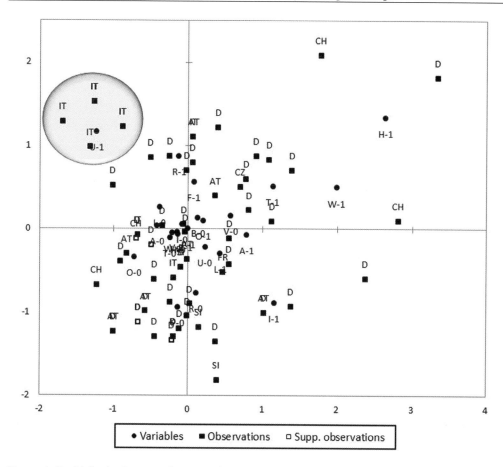

Figure 8.10. Multiple Correspondence Analysis (MCA) plot of assemblages (Observations) containing Pfahlbauperlen from different areas of Europe. A cluster of assemblages from Italy is clearly evident in the upper left, indicating that the assemblage are relatively similar in composition (based on other objects found in the assemblages; Variables). Other regions show less clustering reflecting a rather diverse deposition practice, but distinctly different from that employed in Italy. Observations labels: AT = Austria; CH = Switzerland; CZ = Czech Republic; D = Germany; FR = France; IT = Italy; SI = Slovenia (data after: Jennings 2014b).

frequently with large ring jewellery and needles, but rarely with weapons or domestic production objects, such as spindle whorls. The cultural translation of these beads into areas north of the Alps resulted in their conversion from foreign objects with typically female associations, to high status objects of mixed gender symbolism, for deposition in locally specific manners: the beads' value did not travel with them, but was recreated and re-contextualised at various points along the exchange route (Jennings 2014b).

The *Pfahlbau* and *West Baltic* type spearheads also provide a good opportunity to observe changing value associations. Again, direct comparison with the lake-dwelling region is difficult because few of the spearheads are recorded with associated objects, but it is possible to compare both forms in regions of northern Europe. It is evident from these depositions that the *West Baltic* and *Pfahlbau* spearhead were, to some extent, used interchangeably: sometimes the imported form was used in place of a local type, for example in hoard assemblages at Spelvik, and Ekes (both in Sweden) and Kølpengård (Denmark) (Jacob-Friesen 1967). A number of the *West Baltic* spearheads in northern Europe are placed in hoards containing hanging vessels and/or *Platten* fibula (*e.g.* Grönhult (Sweden), Hindenburg (Germany), Hyldtoft (Denmark) (Jacob-Friesen 1967)), and it is interesting to note that the hanging vessel assemblage from Grandson-Corcelettes contained a local *Pfahlbau* type spearhead (Fischer 2012), even though a *West Baltic* type is known from the same settlement. These objects were successfully translated to the extent that they became interchangeable despite different production zones (Jennings 2014b).

How significant the exchanged objects became in their new cultural setting is uncertain; once objects were successfully translated into the material culture assemblage of the importing regions they were assigned significance through their incorporation. Whether or not the objects continued to retain 'foreign' associations is somewhat irrelevant because they had become a local product through use and assimilation, even though their 'foreignness' may have been exploited as symbols of prestige and resulted in restriction of use through forms of sumptuary laws (see Helms 1988). Furthermore, the incorporation of 'foreign' objects did not necessarily equate to the adoption of cultural aspects along with material culture, as clearly demonstrated by the deposition practices for, and value associations of, *Pfahlbauperlen* in their region of manufacture compared to regions of import. The process of translation created new meanings, values, and use practices for material culture objects as they travelled between regions, incorporating them into existing cultural settings rather than importing objects with a 'cultural package'.

The adoption of social attitudes along with objects, as opposed to cultural translation, is suggested by several weights from LBA (HaA and HaB period) lake-dwellings in the northern Alpine forelands (for instance Auvernier, Grandson-Corcelettes, Mörigen, Zurich-Alpenquai and Zurich-Wollishofen) directly related to those used in settlements of the Po Plain. Some of these weights have been classified as *terramare* type and others as *Pfahlbau* type depending upon their mass (and divisions/multiplications thereof), which ranges between 0.1 and 1.0 kilos with a cluster at *c.* 0.7–0.8 kg (Pare 1999). It is not clear what these objects were used to weigh, but given their relatively low mass, it is possible that they were used for the exchange of objects rather than in manufacturing processes (Pare 1999). More significantly, the occurrence of *terramare* type weights in both the Po Plain and lake-dwellings north of the Alps may indicate a transfer of trade concepts between the two regions, with an increasing commoditisation of exchange relationships (Pare 2013, see also Renfrew 2005). It is important to note that these are not the first or only weights recorded from Europe north of the Alps, and there are instances known relating to early LBA (BzD) contexts, for example from a cemetery at Wangen an der Aare (Switzerland) (Pare 1999). However, the later examples are significantly heavier than the earlier ones (*e.g.* Wangen an der Aare = 0.013 kg), indicating that they were intended for use with larger quantities of, or heavier, objects. Assuming a pragmatic trade function rather than a symbolic one, it is possible to suggest that attitudes towards object value and commoditisation were directly transformed in the lake-dwelling communities due to their trade and communication relationships with settlements in the Po Plain.

Such direct indications for social development as a result of exchange relationships are relatively rare, and of greater concern to the consideration of cultural change is the significance that involvement in trade and exchange relationships had on communities. Under the Relational model proposed above, the involvement (or not) of communities in exchange partnerships may have influenced the cultural constitution of those societies. When participation in exchange networks remained stable, cultural variations would have been initiated through other social aspects and would have been largely unaffected by the trading activities. Exchange objects, varying over time, would have been translated and incorporated for use in social functions, and may have been used in manners of social expression different to their production use. However, changing participation in trade and exchange practices could have led to significant social disruption, especially if the ability to participate in exchange, and to acquire the materials that circulated, was used as a method of social stratification, status identification, and/or legitimisation.

Indications for social change during the Late Bronze Age as a result of trade and interaction are possibly seen in the occurrence of a number of 'keys' at lake-settlements (*e.g.* Mörigen, Zurich-Alpenquai, Zurich-Wollishofen), and also at a 'highland' settlement (Montlingerberg) on the north-south trade route. Although it is not proven that these objects were definitely 'keys', it is generally accepted that this is one of the most likely functions for the objects, and iconographic representation from ancient Greek ceramics shows similar items in use (Speck 1981). It is unclear whether these objects are directly related to the involvement of the settlements in exchange relationships, but it is evident that they are only recorded from sites supposedly incorporated into long-distance trade routes. Several of these keys have plastic bird decoration, which has led to suggestions that they were 'ritual' equipment (Van Willigen, 2011), but more interesting is the termination of many of them in rings, which suggests that they were intended to be displayed, possibly hung from clothing or belts. In this context keys could have been used to symbolise, and demonstrate through display, the ability to control access to structures and the contents stored therein.

The distribution of various forms of Late Bronze Age and early Iron Age material culture in Switzerland, eastern France and southern Germany indicate a slight reorganisation of the trade routes flowing through the northern Alpine forelands during the 9th century BC (HaB3). The distribution of various types of Late Bronze Age swords, particularly *Mörigen* but also *Tarquinia*, *Tachlovice*, and *Weltenburg* swords, demonstrate the dominance of the lake-dwellings in the vicinity of Lake Neuchâtel in the circulation of these items, and an extension of their use into the Rhône valley (Fig. 8.11). The *Gündlingen* type sword, relating to the beginning of early Iron Age (early 8th century BC; HaC) circulated shortly after *Mörigen* type, but is extremely uncommon in the region of Lake Neuchâtel, and Switzerland in general, with only two examples recorded (at Font and Sion (Cowen 1968)). However, elsewhere in Europe, particularly southern Germany and the Rhône valley, these swords show a similar distribution pattern to the *Mörigen* type (Fig. 8.11).

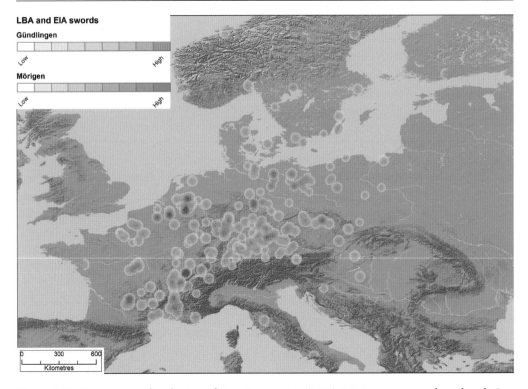

Figure 8.11. Comparative distribution of Late Bronze Age (LBA) Mörigen type swords and early Iron Age (EIA) Gündlingen type swords. The two types are relatively similar in their distribution, except for a distinct density reduction in the region of Lake Neuchâtel, representing the reduced involvement of the region in long-distance exchange networks during the early Iron Age (after: Jennings 2014b).

This reduced involvement of the former lake-dwelling regions in inter-regional exchange networks of the early Iron Age is indicated through other objects, particularly arm- and leg-ring jewellery. Instead of continuing as the significant manufacturing centre that it had been during the Late Bronze Age (as suggested by the distribution of, amongst other objects, arm-/leg-ring and knife types), western Switzerland appears to have been relatively restricted in the circulation of these goods during the early Iron Age (see Schmid-Sikimić 1996). During the short period of time between the decline of the circulation of *Mörigen* swords (HaB3) and height of use of *Gündlingen* swords (early HaC (see Harding 2000; Fontijn 2002)), the region was apparently disassociated from the main trade and exchange networks that linked southern Germany to the Rhône valley. For later stages of the Iron Age (*e.g.* HaD) the region appears to have been re-integrated to wider exchange networks with southern Germany, eastern France, and northern Italy, as evidenced by wider distributions of daggers (Sievers 1982), ring jewellery (Schmid-Sikimić 1996), fibulae (Primas 1970; Lüscher 1991), and later ceramics (Guggisberg 2011).

The significance of these objects is not as great as the significance of the involvement of the region in exchange networks, and the changes that may have been induced by restricted access to those networks. It is unclear whether the lake-dwellings were abandoned before the movement of trade routes away from Lake Neuchâtel to a more westerly Rhône-Saône route or vice-versa, but it is clear that by the time *Gündlingen* swords were widely utilised the region was largely circumvented. This may have led to a re-organisation of social structures to provide new arenas of elite legitimisation, potentially including a return to significant emphasis on the burial rite as an expression of social status (see Lüscher 1993; Lüscher and Müller 1999), and the establishment and occupation of settlements in visible hilltop locations to provide a visible presence in the landscape, and as an overt display of the ability to consume labour, resources, and coordinate the construction of such settlements. The beginning of the Iron Age was defined by cultural changes and social developments across a wide area of Europe, but the impetus for change should not be seen as universal. In the northern Alpine region, the Iron Age Hallstatt period can be seen as a development of the preceding Urnfield tradition (see Cunliffe 2008), but different influences for cultural variation would have occurred even within this zone; particularly in the former lake-dwelling region where the burial practice of the lake-dwellers remains largely unknown.

Cultural contact or just travelling objects … or both?

From the above discussion it clear that during the Bronze Age exchanged goods were never just *travelling objects*, or solely about the movement of goods and materials from one region to another. Cultural contact was an inherent part of the exchange practices, and resulted in the transfer of ideas, techniques, beliefs and practices along with the material goods. However, it was only through the process of *translation* and a redefinition of social value that any objects, or co-travelling aspects, were incorporated into new cultural locales. By the time *translation* had occurred, the socially relevant acts had already taken place: cultural contact had already happened, exchange partnerships had been created, objects had been re-contextualised to a local setting, and social changes may already have been initiated.

The occurrence of weights can provide direct indications of cultural changes related to the involvement of communities with exchange networks. These changes were not related to the modification of social structures, but to the valuation of objects and basic concept of trade. Instead of circulating objects on a gift basis or as fragmented bronze stock (*e.g.* sickles), it was possible to equivalate items to each other based on their mass; objects became commoditised with exchange values based upon weight or volume rather than social values based on concepts of prestige or biographies (see Renfrew 2005). Furthermore, the move to commoditisation and exchange of objects by mass suggests that trade was conducted on the basis of immediate return, with interactions being commenced and completed on a single occasion. This would liberate exchange participation from the domain of selected individuals possessing the correct trading partners to a more 'freelance' basis, under which traders were able to interact with various regions and communities, and also remove the need for exchange-partnership markers such as the *Brotlaibidole*. Such a development could have been of great benefit to the lake-dwelling communities, which evidently formed a significant manufacturing centre circulating objects to other parts of central Europe (for example ring jewellery, spearheads and knives), in that the items they produced could be easily exchanged with communities in both short- and long-distance interactions.

Keys provide further indications of changing social structures at some of the sites involved with long-distance exchange relationships in the northern Alpine forelands. These objects may have been utilised as indicators of social status and the ability of individuals to control access to specific buildings within settlements. Their status as 'key holders' may have been generated or legitimised through the control and manipulation of exchange relationships to bring exotic and mundane goods into the community, but also reflects an increasing hierarchisation of society during the LBA based on a principle of access, and a social need to secure specific buildings. The fact that many keys (26 items from 8 sites (Jennings 2014b; Speck 1981)) are known from lake-settlements is interesting because these sites typically show no social stratification based on structure size, orientation, or position, and the burial practices of these communities remain relatively unknown. Involvement in exchange networks may have been one of the factors influencing social status, and also provided the means of expressing that status through the display of 'foreign' objects or equipment.

The distribution of many forms of material culture demonstrates that the lake-dwelling communities, especially of western Switzerland and eastern France, were well connected to those of southern and western Germany, and particularly the region around Mainz and Frankfurt. Exchange relationships between the lake-dwellings and northern Italy are observed through several types of object, including jewellery beads and fibulae, but their connection does not appear to have been as intense as that to northern Europe. Furthermore, items were not universally translated and accepted into the material culture repertoire of the northern Alpine communities, as demonstrated by the limited distribution of the *Allumiere* amber beads. For translation to occur there needed to be a combination of desire for the objects, a function for them to fulfil in social practices, and a relevance to the existing cultural milieu; the *Pfahlbauperlen* as novel objects and symbols of foreign connections fulfilled these criteria, whereas the *Allumiere* amber beads, being made of a material already present in society which could have been worked locally, and already symbolising foreign connections to the north of Europe, did not.

The circulation of various material culture objects not only moved the objects themselves, but also ideas and techniques. Yet, the cultural contact required to initiate the movement of goods did not result in the 'diffusion' of culture from one participant region to the other through traditional interpretations of 'acculturation'. Rather, communities translated, re-contextualised, and incorporated sections of the material culture and social practices that they desired to form specific functions in their cultural model. The incorporation of travelling objects was not as significant for cultural variation as the actual cultural contact and participation (or not) in exchange networks which permitted the movement of those objects. Not because of 'acculturation' processes, but expanding or reducing contact and exchange relationships may have induced endogenous social and cultural change related to the control of resources, access to materials, and, ultimately, expressions of social status.

References

Angelini, I., Artioli, G., Bellintani, P., Diella, V., Gemmi, M., Polla, A. and Rossi, A. (2004) Chemical analyses of Bronze Age glasses from Frattesina di Rovigo, Northern Italy. *Journal of Archaeological Science* 31: 1175–1184.

Angelini, I. and Bellintani, P. (2005) Archaeological ambers from Northern Italy: An FTIR-Drift study of provenance by comparison with the Geological Amber Database. *Archaeometry* 47: 441–454.

Angelini, I., Polla, A., Giussani, B., Bellintani, P. and Artioli, G. (2009) Final Bronze-Age glass in Northern and Central Italy: is Frattesina the only glass production centre? In J.-F. Moreau, R. Auger, J. Chabot and A. Herzog, (eds) *Proceedings of the 36th International Symposium on Archaeometry, 2006 Quebec City*: 329–337. Quebec: CELAT.

Appadurai, A. (ed.) (1986) *The social life of things: commodities in cultural perspective*, Cambridge: Cambridge University Press.

Bauer, I., Ruckstuhl, B. and Speck, J. (2004) *Zug-Sumpf: Die Funde der Grabungen 1923–37*. Zug: Kantonales Museum für Urgeschichte.

Beck, C. W. and Shennan, S. J. (1991) *Amber in prehistoric Britain*. Oxford: Oxbow Monograph.

Beeching, A. (1977) *Le Boiron: une nécropole du bronze final près de Morges (Vaud, Suisse)*. Lausanne: Musée d'archéologie et d'histoire.

Bellintani, P. (1997) Frattesina: l'ambra e la produzione vitrea nel contesto delle relazioni transalpina. In L. Endrizzi and F. Marzatico (eds) *Ori delle Alpi*: 117–129. Trento: Servizio beni culturali Provinica autonoma di Trento.

Bellintani, P. (2002) Bernsteinstraßen, Glasstraßen. In G. Schnekenburger (ed.) *Über die Alpen: Menschen – Wege – Waren*: 39–48. Stuttgart: Theiss.

Bellintani, P. and Stefan, L. (2009) Nuovi dati sul primo vetro Europeo: il caso di Frattesina. *In* A. Magna, (ed.) *Atti del primo convegino interdiciplinare sul vetro nei beni culturali e nell'arte di ieri e di oggi, 2008 Parma*: 71–86. Parma: Belling Anti Publisher.

Bernatzky-Goetze, M. (1987) *Mörigen: die spätbronzezeitlichen Funde*. Basel: Verlag Schweizerische Gesellschaft für Ur- und Frühgeschichte.

Betzler, P. (1974) *Die Fibeln in Süddeutschland, Österreich und der Schweiz I: (urnenfelderzeitliche Typen)*. Prähistorische Bronzefunde: 14/3. München: Beck.

Bianco Peroni, V. (1976) *Die Messer in Italien*. Prähistorische Bronzefunde: 7/2. München: Beck.

Bianco Peroni, V. (1979) *I rasoi nell'Italia continentale*. Prähistorische Bronzefunde: 8/2. München: Beck.

Bietti Sestieri, A. M. (ed.) (1992) *La necropoli laziale di Osteria dell'Osa*, Roma: Quasar.

Braccesi, L. (2004) The Greeks on the Venetian lagoon. In K. Lomas and B. B. Shefton (eds) *Greek identity in the western Mediterranean papers in honour of Brian Shefton*: 349–361. Leiden: Brill.

Butler, J. J., Arnoldussen, S. and Steegstra, H. (2012) Single-edged socketed Urnfield knives in the Netherlands and western Europe. *Palaeohistoria* 2011/2012: 65–107.

Coffyn, A., Gomez, J. and Mohen, J.-P. (1981) *L'apogée du bronze atlantique: le dépôt de Vénat*. Paris: Picard.

Cowen, J. D. (1968) The Hallstatt Sword of Bronze: on the Continent and in Britain. *Proceedings of the Prehistoric Society* 33: 377–454.

Cunliffe, B. W. (2008) *Europe between the oceans: themes and variations 9000 BC-AD 1000*. New Haven: Yale University Press.

De Navarro, J. M. (1925) Prehistoric Routes between Northern Europe and Italy Defined by the Amber Trade. *The Geographical Journal* 66: 481–503.

Della Casa, P. (2002) *Landschaften, Siedlungen, Ressourcen: Langzeitszenarien menschlicher Aktivität in ausgewählten alpinen Gebieten der Schweiz, Italiens und Frankreichs*. Montagnac: Monique Mergoil.

Eles Masi, P. v. (1986) *Le fibule dell'Italia settentrionale*. Prähistorische Bronzefunde: 14/5. München: Beck.

Fischer, V. (2012) *Les bronzes en contexte palafittique sur les rives du Léman et des Trois-Lacs (Suisse occidentale)*. Lausanne: Musée cantonal d'archéologie et d'histoire.

Fontijn, D. R. (2002) *Sacrificial landscapes: cultural biographies of persons, objects and 'natural' places in the Bronze Age of the southern Netherlands, c. 2300–600 BC*. Leiden: University of Leiden.

Gedl, M. (1981) *Die Rasiermesser in Polen*. Prähistorische Bronzefunde: 8/4. München: Beck.

Gell, A. (1998) *Art and agency: an anthropological theory*. Oxford: Clarendon Press.

Gosden, C. and Marshall, Y. (1999) *The cultural biography of objects*. London: Routledge.

Guggisberg, M. (2011) La ceramica greca a nord delle Alpi. Contesto e fuzione. In F. Marzatico, R. Gebhard and P. Gleirscher (eds) *Le grandi vie delle civiltà: relazioni e scambi fra Mediterraneo e il centro Europa dalla preistoria alla romanità*: 227–228. Trento: Castello del Buonconsiglio.

Haevernick, T. E. (1978) Urnenfelderzeitliche Glasperlen. *Zeitschrift für Schweizerische Archäologie und Kunstgeschichte* 35: 145–157.

Harding, A. F. (2000) *European societies in the Bronze Age*. Cambridge: Cambridge University Press.

Helms, M. W. (1988) *Ulysses' sail: an ethnographic odyssey of power, knowledge, and geographical distance*. Princeton: Princeton University Press.

Henderson, J. (1993) Chemical analyses of the glass and faience from Hauterive-Champréveyres, Switzerland. In A.-M. Rychner-Faraggi (ed.) *Hauterive-Champréveyres 9: Métal et parure au Bronze final*: 111–117. Neuchâtel: Musée cantonal d'archéologie.

Hennig, H. (1986) Einige Bemerkungen zu den Urnenfeldern im Regensburger Raum, *Archäologisches Korrespondenzblatt*, 16(3): 289–301.

Hohlbein, M. (2008) *Die spätbronze- und urnenfelderzeitlichen Bronzemesser im mittleren und südlichen Westdeutschland I*. Doctor of Philosophy, Westfälische Wilhelms-Universität zu Münster.

Jacob-Friesen, G. (1967) *Bronzezeitliche Lanzenspitzen Norddeutschlands und Skandinaviens*. Hildesheim: August Lax.

Jennings, B. (2012) When the Going Gets Tough...? Climatic or Cultural Influences for the LBA Abandonment of Circum-Alpine Lake-Dwellings. In J. Kniesel, W. Kirleis, M. Dal Corso, N. Taylor and V. Tiedtke (eds) *Collapse or Continuity? Environment and Development of Bronze Age Human Landscapes. Proceedings of the International Workshop 'Socio-Environmental Dynamics over the Last 12,000 Years: The Creation of Landscapes II'*: 85–99. Kiel: Rudolf Habelt.

Jennings, B. (2014a) Repair, Recycle or Re-use? Creating mnemonic devices through the modification of object biographies. *Cambridge Archaeological Journal* 24: 163–176.

Jennings, B. (2014b) *Travelling Objects: Changing Values. The role of northern Alpine lake-dwelling communities in exchange and communication networks during the Late Bronze Age*. Oxford: Archaeopress.

Jockenhövel, A. (1971) *Die Rasiermesser in Mitteleuropa (Süddeutschland, Tschechoslowakei, Österreich, Schweiz)*. Prähistorische Bronzefunde: 8/1. München: Beck

Jockenhövel, A. (1980) *Die Rasiermesser in Westeuropa (Westdeutschland, Niederlande, Belgien, Luxemburg, Frankreich, Grossbritannien und Irland)*. Prähistorische Bronzefunde: 8/3. München: Beck.

Jockenhövel, A. (1991) Räumliche Mobilität von Personen in der mittleren Bronzezeit des westlichen Mitteleuropa. *Germania* 69: 49–62.

Jockenhövel, A. and Smolla, G. (1975) Le dépôt de Juvincourt-Damary (Aisne). *Gallia Préhistoire* 18: 290–313.

Kaenel, G. and Klausener, M. (1990) Quelques tombes à incinération du Bronze final (Xe siècle av. J.-C.) à Vidy (Lausanne VD). *Jahrbuch der Schweizerischen Gesellschaft für Ur- und Frühgeschichte* 73: 51–82

Köninger, J. and Schlichtherle, H. (2001) Foreign Elements in South-West German Lake Dwellings: transalpine Relations in the Late Neolithic and Early Bronze Ages. *Preistoria Alpina* 35: 43–53.

Kopytoff, I. (1986) The Cultural biography of things: commoditization as process. In A. Appadurai (ed.) *The social life of things: commodities in cultural perspective*: 64–91. Cambridge: Cambridge University Press.

Kristiansen, K. (1998) *Europe before history*. Cambridge: Cambridge University Press.

Leuzinger, U. (2000) *Die jungsteinzeitliche Seeufersiedlung Arbon-Bleiche 3. Befunde*. Frauenfeld: Departement für Erziehung und Kultur des Kantons Thurgau.

Lüscher, G. (1991) Frühkeltische 'Fürstensitze' in der Schweiz. *Archäologie der Schweiz* 14: 68–74.

Lüscher, G. (1993) *Unterlunkhofen und die hallstattzeitliche Grabkeramik in der Schweiz*. Basel: Verlag Schweizerische Gesellschaft für Ur- und Frühgeschichte.

Lüscher, G. and Müller, F. (1999) Gräber und Kult. In F. Müller, G. Kaenel and G. Lüscher (eds) *Eisenzeit: Die Schweiz vom Paläolithikum bis zum frühen Mittelalter*: 249–282. Basel: Verlag Schweizerische Gesellschaft für Ur- und Frühgeschichte.

Mäder, A. (2001a) *Die spätbronzezeitliche Seeufersiedlung Zürich-Alpenquai 1: Die Metallfunde: Baggerungen von 1916–1919*. Zürich: Baudirektion Kanton Zürich, Hochbauamt.

Mäder, A. (2001b) *Zürich-Alpenquai 2: Die Schultergefässe und Kugelbecher: Baggerungen von 1916 und 1919*. Zürich: Baudirektion Kanton Zürich, Hochbauamt.

Maran, J. (2013) Bright as the sun: The appropriation of amber objects in Mycenaean Greece. In H. P. Hahn and H. Weiss (eds) *Mobility, Meaning and Transformations of Things: shifting contexts of material culture through time and space*: 147–169. Oxford: Oxbow Books.

Mildner, S., Schüssler, U., Falkenstein, F. and Brätz, H. (2013) Bronzezeitliches Glas zwischen Alpenkamm und Ostsee – erste Ergenisse einer archäometrischen Bestansaufnahme. In A. Hauptmann, O. Mecking and M. Prange (eds) *Archäometrie und Denkmalpflege* (Metalla 6, special edition): 246–250. Bochum: Deutsches Bergbau-Museum

Moinat, P. and David-Elbiali, M. (2003) *Défunts, bûchers et céramiques: la nécropole de Lausanne-Vidy (VD) et les pratiques funéraires sur le Plateau suisse du XIe au VIIIe s.av.J.-C.* Lausanne: Cahiers d'archéologie romande.

Murillo-Barroso, M. and Martinón-Torres, M. (2012) Amber Sources and Trade in the Prehistory of the Iberian Peninsula. *European Journal of Archaeology* 15: 187–216.

Nash Briggs, D. (2003) Metals, Salt, and Slaves: Economic Links Between Gaul and Italy From the Eighth to the Late Sixth Centuries BC. *Oxford Journal of Archaeology* 22: 243–259.

Negroni Catacchio, N. (1999) Produzione e commercio dei vaghi d'ambra tipo Tirinto e tipo Allumiere alla luce delle recenti scoperte. In O. Paoletti, (ed.) *Protostoria e Storia del 'Venetorum Angulus' Atti del XX Convegno di Studi Etruschi ed Italici, 1996 Este*: 241–265. Pisa: Instituti editoriali e poligrafici internazionali.

Nicolas, I. (2003) Au fil du rasoir: étude des rasoirs métalliques de l'âge du Bronze jusqu'a haut Moyen Age en Suisse. In M. Besse, L.-I. Stahl Gretsch and P. Curdy (eds) *ConstellaSion. Hommage à Alain Gallay*: 273–289. Lausanne: Cahiers d'archéologie romande.

Palavestra, A. (2007) Was there an amber route? In I. Galanaki, H. Tomas, Y. Galanakis and R. Laffineur, (eds) *Between the Aegean and Baltic seas: prehistory across borders, 2005 Zagreb*. 349–356. Liège: Université de Liège.

Pare, C. F. E. (1999) Weights and Weighing in Bronze Age Central Europe. In R.-G. Z. M. Kolloquium, (ed.) *Eliten in der Bronzezeit*: 421–514. Bonn: Habelt.

Pare, C. F. E. (2013) Weighing, commodification, and money. In H. Fokkens and A. F. Harding (eds) *The Oxford handbook of the European Bronze Age*: 508–527. Oxford: Oxford University Press.

Pászthory, K. (1985) *Der bronzezeitliche Arm- und Beinschmuck in der Schweiz*. Prähistorische Bronzefunde: 10/3. München: Beck.

Primas, M. (1970) *Die südschweizerischen Grabfunde der älteren Eisenzeit und ihre Chronologie.* Basel: Birkhäuser.

Primas, M. (1986) *Die Sicheln in Mitteleuropa I (Österreich, Schweiz, Süddeutschland).* Prähistorische Bronzefunde: 18/2. München: Beck.

Primas, M. (2004) Wirtschaft und Gessellschaft urnenfelderzeitlicher Seeufersiedlungen – eine Aktualisierung. In B. Hänsel (ed.) *Parerga Praehistorica: Jubiläumsschrift zur Prähistorischen Archäologie: 15 Jahre UPA*: 113–133. Bonn: R. Habelt.

Primas, M. and Schmid-Sikimić, B. (1997) Interaction Across the Alps. In Istituto Italiano di Preistoria e Protostoria, (ed.) *La Valle D'Aosta nel quadro della preistoria e protostoria dell'arco alpino centro-occidentale, 1994 Courmayeur.* Firenze: Istituto Italiano di Preistoria e Protostoria.

Prüssing, P. (1982) *Die Messer im nördlichen Westdeutschland (Schleswig-Holstein, Hamburg und Niedersachsen).* Prähistorische Bronzefunde: 7/3. München: Beck.

Renfrew, C. (2005) Archaeology and commodification: the role of things in societal transformation. In W. M. J. v. Binsbergen and P. Geschiere (eds) *Commodification: Things, Agency, and Identities: (The Social Life of Things Revisited)*: 85–97. Münster: Lit.

Renfrew, C. and Bahn, P. G. (2012) *Archaeology: theories, methods and practice.* London: Thames & Hudson.

Richter, I. (1970) *Der Arm- und Beinschmuck der Bronze- und Urnefelderzeit in Hessen und Rheinhessen.* Prähistorische Bronzefunde: 10/1. München: Beck.

Říhovský, J. (1972) *Das Messer in Mähren und dem Ostalpengebiet.* Prähistorische Bronzefunde: 7/1. München: Beck.

Rychner-Faraggi, A.-M. (1993) *Hauterive-Champréveyres 9: Métal et parure au Bronze final.* Neuchâtel: Musée cantonal d'archéologie.

Rychner, V. (1979) *L'âge du bronze final à Auvernier (Lac de Neuchâtel, Suisse): typologie et chronologie des anciennes collections conservées en Suisse.* Lausanne: Bibliothèque historique vaudoise.

Rychner, V. (1987) *Auvernier 1968–1975, le mobilier métallique du Bronze final: formes et techniques.* Lausanne: Bibliothèque historique vaudoise.

Salzani, L. (2009) Rovigo. Notizie preliminari sulle ricerche nel sito dell'età del Bronzo di Grignano Polesine. *Quaderni di archeologia del Veneto* 25: 37–39.

Schmid-Sikimić, B. (1996) *Der Arm- und Beinschmuck der Hallstattzeit in der Schweiz: mit einem Anhang der Gürtelhaken und Gürtelgehänge der Hallstattzeit im Schweizerischen Mittelland, Jura und Wallis.* Prähistorische Bronzefunde: 10/5. Stuttgart: Franz Steiner Verlag.

Sharples, N. M. (2010) *Social relations in later prehistory: Wessex in the first millennium BC.* Oxford: Oxford University Press.

Shennan, S. J. (2006) *Quantifying archaeology.* Iowa City: University of Iowa Press.

Sievers, S. (1982) *Die mitteleuropäischen Hallstattdolche.* Prähistorische Bronzefunde: 6/6. München: Beck.

Sommerfeld, C. (1994) *Gerätegeld Sichel: Studien zur monetären Struktur bronzezeitlicher Horte im nördlichen Mitteleuropa.* Berlin: Walter de Gruyter.

Speck, J. (1981) Schloss und Schlüssel zur späten Pfahlbauzeit. *Helvetia Archaeologica* 45/48: 230–241.

Sprockhoff, E. (1966) Ein Geschenk aus dem Norden. In R. Degen, W. Drack and R. Wyss (eds) *Helvetia antiqua: Festschrift Emil Vogt: Beiträge zur Prähistorie und Archäologie der Schweiz*: 101–110. Zürich: Conzett und Huber.

Sprockhoff, E. and Höckmann, O. (1979) *Die gegossenen Bronzebecken der jüngeren nordischen Bronzezeit.* Mainz: Römisch-Germanisches Zentralmuseum Mainz.

Stahl, C. (2006) *Mitteleuropäische Bernsteinfunde von der Frühbronze- bis zur Frühlatènezeit: ihre Verbreitung, Formgebung, Zeitstellung und Herkunft.* Dettelbach: J. H. Röll.

Steinhauser, R. A. and Primas, M. (1987) Der Bernsteinfund vom Montlingerberg (Kt. St Gallen, Schweiz). *Germania* 65: 203–214.

Strathern, M. (1988) *The gender of the gift: problems with women and problems with society in Melanesia.* Berkeley: University of California Press.

Suter, P. J., Hafner, A. and Glauser, K. (2006) Lenk – Schnidejoch. Funde aus dem Eis – ein vor- und frühgesichtlicher Passübergang. *Archäoloie im Kanton Bern* 6: 499–522

Tarot, J. (2000) *Die bronzezeitlichen Lanzenspitzen der Schweiz: unter Einbeziehung von Liechtenstein und Vorarlberg.* Bonn: Habelt.

Trnka, G. (1992) Neues zu den 'Brotlaibidolen'. In A. Lippert and A. Spindler (eds) *Festschrift zum 50jährigen Bestehen des Institutes für Ur- und Frühgeschichte der Leopold-Franzens-Universität Innsbruck*: 615–622. Bonn: Habelt.

Van Willigen, S. (2011) 3.48. Chiave. In F. Marzatico, R. Gebhard and P. Gleirscher (eds) *Le grandi vie delle civiltà: relazioni e scambi fra Mediterraneo e il centro Europa dalla preistoria alla romanità*: 476. Trento: Castello del Buonconsiglio.

Vogt, E. (1952) Der Zierstil der späten Pfahlbaubronzen. *Zeitschrift für Schweizerische Archäologie und Kunstgeschichte* 4: 193–206.

Von Hase, F. W. (1969) *Die Trensen der Früheisenzeit in Italien*. Prähistorische Bronzefunde: 16/1. München: Beck.

Watts, C. (ed.) (2013) *Relation Archaeologies: humans, animals, things,* Abingdon: Routledge.

Weber, C. (1996) *Die Rasiermesser in Südosteuropa*. Prähistorische Bronzefunde: 8/5. Stuttgart: Franz Steiner Verlag.

Chapter 9

The 3500-year-long lake-dwelling tradition comes to an end: what is to blame?

Francesco Menotti

Introduction

When we look at the chronological history of occupation of the lake-dwellings around the Circum-Alpine region, we cannot help but wonder why and how such a long tradition (more than three and a half millennia) 'suddenly' came to an end. If we consider all the variables involved in answering such seemingly straightforward questions, it is perhaps not surprising that a single straight answer may not be possible. We are however pleased to state that, although involving some degree of complexity, a plausible explanation has indeed been found. Not only does this final chapter draw the conclusions of an edited book, but it sums up the result of a four-year project carried out specifically to shed some light on the above-mentioned fascinating mystery. Within the project (and for this volume), the Bronze Age Circum-Alpine region has been studied inside out; from its cultural geography, climate and internal/external influence (trade, exchange and movement of people), to its economy (including people's subsistence). The effectiveness of a multidisciplinary approach to research (see Chapters 3–8) is that it offers the possibility to identify all of the interactive factors which make up a socio-economic and environmental system, subsequently allowing us to 'test' them against each other, to prove (or disprove) their validity. It is then by joining the various dots together that plausible explanations to our initial question can be found.

Circum-Alpine region's Bronze Age cultural geography

As often stressed throughout the volume, the Circum-Alpine region (see also Note 1 in Chapter 1, for definition) consists of a myriad of environments, which, in addition to the majestic mountain ranges, include also fertile plains and, within them, a fairly large number of lakes (see Fig. 1.1 in Chapter 1). This diverse setting has not only contributed to shape the relationships between the various Bronze Age cultural groups, but also their formation and development. Considering the relatively short duration of the Bronze Age (24th to 9th century BC – even shorter if we take into account only the lacustrine settlements, see Fig. 2.1 in Chapter 2) and the considerable lengths in lake-dwelling occupational hiatuses

(Menotti 2001), it is perhaps not surprising that the number of 'cultural' groups within the region (especially in the northern parts of the Alps) is lower than that of the Neolithic.

The Bronze Age of the Circum Alpine region is usually divided into three main periods, namely Early (EBA), Middle (MBA) and Late Bronze Age (LBA), which themselves have different sub-divisions and terminology according to the different areas/countries. In most of the northern Alpine region German-speaking areas, the three periods are called *Frübronzezeit* (EBA), *Mittelbronzezeit* (MBA) and *Spätbronzezeit* (LBA), and it is the Reinecke system that still prevails; but as we move west (especially eastern France) the terminology changes into *Bronze ancien* (BA I–II), *Bronze moyen* (BM I–III) and *Bronze final* (BF I–III). South of the Alps (mainly northern Italy) the division *Bronzo Antico*, *Bronzo Medio*, *Bronzo Recente* and *Bronzo Finale* (the latter corresponding to the *Proto-Golasecca* I–III) also seem to follow Reinecke's system (see Chapter 2, and in particular Fig. 2.1).

In terms of cultural entities occupying the northern Circum-Alpine region during the Early Bronze age, two main groups stand out, namely the *Bodenseegruppe* (including the *Singen* and *Arbon* groups), and the *Rhône* group. The former encompasses the Lake Constance and Lake Zurich areas, and in the very southern part of Germany it also includes the *Neckar*, *Straubing* and *Oberrhein* sub-groups (Krause 1988). The latter (*Rhône* group), on the other hand, is well represented only in the Valais, Bernese Oberland and of course in the Lake Geneva region, extending northwards to the French Jura (Hafner 1995). Although not clearly defined, the eastern Alpine region of Switzerland shows different cultural influences, which started to develop (and continued also during the MBA – see below) into the so-called *Inner Alpine* group, extending (but again with different characteristics) to part of the Ticino. Still remaining in the northern slops of the Alpine region, but moving east towards south-eastern Germany and Austria, the prevailing EBA groups were the *Straubing* A2 group and the *Unterwülbling/Veteřov* groups respectively (Strahm, 1997). South of the Alps, the *Litzen* and *Encrusted* ceramic groups occupied present-day Slovenia, whereas the *Polada* culture and the *Ledro* group (in the east), and the *Monate/Mercurago* groups (in the west) dominated the northern Italian scenario (Fasani 1994; De Marinis 2010).

The Middle Bronze Age northern Circum-Alpine region experienced an expansion of the so-called *Tumuli* culture, although in the far-western regions (namely eastern France and western Switzerland), the influence of the *Rhône* group still persisted. The *Inner Alpine* group and the *Ticino/Mesolcina* group in the central-southern part of Switzerland did not change considerably from the EBA, but a new group (though strongly influenced by the *Tumuli* culture), the *Valais* group, began to emerge, but resulted in being relatively short-lived (Rychner *et al.* 1998). The *Encrusted* ceramic group dominated the entire MBA in Slovenia, whereas for northern Italy, in addition to the significant development of the *terramare* (Bernabó Brea and Cardarelli 1997), the cultural aspect is more localised with influential settlements such as Lavagnone and Fiavé in the east, and Mercurago, Viverone and Scamozzina in the west (De Marinis 2010).

In the Late Bronze Age, despite the fairly homogeneous influence of the *Urnfield* culture in most of the northern Circum-Alpine region (Strahm 1997), some areas, such as Switzerland for instance, experienced the development of distinct regional groups. The geographical distribution of these groups was rather complex, and although they can certainly be distinguished from each other, they show signs of significant contact. The west of the country was dominated by the western group of the *RSFO* (Rhin-Suisse-France-Oriental) culture, whereas the east by the *RSFO's* central/eastern group. Interestingly, the two areas were separated by a narrow strip of 'neutral' influence exercised by the original *RSFO* group, which was more linked to the original eastern France *RSFO* group. The very eastern part of the Swiss Alpine areas (on the border with Austria) was occupied by the *Laugen-Melaun* culture, whereas more to the west (but still in the mountainous areas) there was a mix between local *RSFO* groups and the surrounding *Main-Swabia* and *Laugen-Melaun* groups. The southern part of Switzerland was influenced by the developing *Proto-Golasecca* group of north-western Italy (Rychner *et al.* 1998; Hochuli *et al.* 1998). South of the Alps, while Slovenia was mostly influenced by the *Urnfield* culture, two major groups characterised the LBA of northern Italy; the *Proto-Golasecca* group in the west, and the *Proto-Villanova* group in the east (Nicolis 2013). The western area also includes the *Pont-Valperga* group (influenced by both the *Proto-Golasecca* and the *RSFO*) and the *Canegrate* culture, whereas the LBA of the east (mainly the Po Plain) dealt primarily with the latest stage of the *terramare* (De Marinis 2010; Rubat Borel 2009).

Regardless of their geographical location and/or the their chronological period, all the above-mentioned cultural groups were, in one way or another, fairly well connected to a well-developed short-/long-distance trade network. While it is difficult to tell how exactly the trade took place, and/or how to reconstruct the exact trade routes, we can certainly monitor the intensity and directions of traded goods. As a result, it is interesting to notice a significant development of trade networks and circulation of goods during the Late Bronze Age. This intensification of circulated goods as well as movement of people might have brought prosperity to some regions, but it also triggered inevitable socio-cultural changes with significant repercussions on long-lasting traditions (see below).

Climate change in the Bronze Age Circum-Alpine region

Because of its geographical location (sandwiched between a wetter/cooler central European continental environment in the north, and a drier/temperate Mediterranean one in the south) and its highly irregular topography, the Circum-Alpine region climate is one of the most variable and unpredictable in Europe. This accentuated variability is not obviously only an issue of the present, but it has been recorded throughout prehistoric times, and the lake-dwelling period (42nd–7th centuries BC) is no exception. In fact, if we take a close look at palaeoclimatological charts of the past six millennia, we notice a constant oscillation from cold/wet to warm/dry conditions, or vice versa. (Magny 2013; Magny *et al.* 2009; Maise 2005). It is of course understood that these climatic fluctuations do not follow a regular pattern, nor are they of the same length – there were sometimes long periods of favourable climate alternated with short periods of adverse one, or vice versa. It is interesting to notice though, that at least in the northern Circum-Alpine region these climatic variations coincide with the majority of lake-dwelling occupational patterns: good climate equals settlements on the lake; bad climate equals abandonment. Furthermore, because climatic conditions are very much linked to the environmental hydrology (of *e.g.* lakes, rivers, marshes and other water basins), cold and wet also means an increase in water levels, which, in turn, may affect the lacustrine settlements directly (if the settlements are in proximity to the water), or indirectly (*e.g.* subsistence and economy) (Schibler *et al.* 1997a; Menotti 2003, 2001).

The Bronze Age climate of the northern Circum-Alpine region was anything but clement with the lacustrine populations. Although it started with a phase of reasonably good conditions, the climate briefly worsened right at the end of the 25th century BC. It then improved in the 24th century, but again, this period was followed by a few centuries of unstable conditions (see Chapter 4 and Fig. 4.2). It has to be pointed out though that during this time (*c.* 2300–1800 BC), despite the lake levels being higher than usual, climatic conditions were not always bad – some palaeoclimatological charts (see fig. 3 in Suter *et al.* 2005) even describe it as a fairly warm period, and in fact the absence (with a few exceptions) of lacustrine sites north of the Alps is often regarded as cultural. In general, climate became more favourable from the 18th century onwards and the lake shores were more frequently occupied until the next degradation at the beginning of the 15th century BC. The MBA lake-dwelling occupational hiatus (*c.* 15th–12th centuries BC) was almost certainly caused by climatic conditions, although, once triggered, cultural factors have also greatly contributed to it (Menotti 2003). Favourable conditions started again in the 12th century BC, and with them, a new wave of lacustrine settlements appeared along the lake shores. Although widespread, this last phase of occupation was not as intense as the previous ones (especially in the Neolithic) – settlements were built in various ways and in some cases became quite large (see Chapter 2), but there was already a sort of 'change' in the air (see Jennings, Chapter 8 this volume; and below). However, the lacustrine occupational patterns were, once again, disturbed by a, yet another, significant climate deterioration towards the end of the 9th century BC. Responsible for this was the so-called 'Göschenen I' cold and wet phase, which lasted for about two centuries (see fig. 8 in Pétrequin *et al.* 2005; see also Fig. 2.1 this volume), but in some regions the repercussions (*e.g.* high lake levels) were felt for longer (see Magny, Chapter 4 this volume). Despite this climatic crisis, sporadic attempts to repopulate the lake shores occurred here and there around the northern Circum-Alpine region (Gollnisch-Moos 1999; Köninger 2002; Schlitzer 2009), but they were all short-lived.

Surprisingly enough, palaeoclimatological charts south of the Alps (*e.g.* northern Italy) show similar climatic tendencies to those in the north, with comparable patterns of favourable/unfavourable climatic conditions (Magny *et al.* 2012; Vannière *et al.* 2013; Magny *et al.* 2013). However, what is even more surprising, is that the occupational patterns do not seem to coincide – in fact, not only do we have a rather continuous (although not fully supported by dendrochronology) occupation from the Early to the Late Bronze Age, but lacustrine/wetland settlements seem to have thrived and reached their maximum expansion exactly during the MBA occupational hiatus of the northern Circum-Alpine region (Magny and Peyron 2008; Martinelli 2005; Marzatico 2004; Perini 1987; Menotti 2001). This is also confirmed by the *terramare*, whose maximum development also coincided with the above-mentioned period; and ironically, their disappearance is possibly linked to an increase of drier climatic conditions in the 12th century BC (Cremaschi *et al.* 2006).

As previously mentioned, the climate was certainly not very gentle with the BA lacustrine groups, and this is reflected by their occupational patterns and their resilience against environmental threat (Menotti *et al.* 2014), especially in the northern slopes of the Alps. In the south, on the other hand, people seemed to have coped better with the climate, but the final lake-dwelling abandonment occurred even earlier. Climate variability certainly affected the lacustrine populations, but, given their exceptional adaptability (*e.g.* see Chapter 6), something more unexpected, perhaps even wanted, must have happened to give up a tradition that had shaped their lives for more than 3500 years.

Trade and exchange influence on lacustrine settlements

Despite incorrect preconceptions of isolation, the Bronze Age, and, in particular, the Late Bronze Age Circum-Alpine region lake-dwelling communities were very much involved and incorporated in trade and exchange networks stretching from the Mediterranean and northern Italy, to northern Europe/Scandinavia. The circulated goods were mainly made of imperishable materials, ranging from amber, glass beads, pottery, bronze artefacts (swords, knives, sickles, razors, pins, spearheads, daggers, arm/leg-rings, *etc.*) to other less common artefacts (weights, keys, horse harness cheek pieces, *etc.*). It is understood that although the objects might have come from very long distances, the exchange system was mainly based upon the so-called 'down-the-line' exchange scheme, whereby people exchanging those goods did not travel too far. As a result, also perishable goods (*i.e.* food, animals, *etc.*) could have been moved within this 'short-distance' travelling.

We all know that once communities/groups are involved in, or part of, a complex exchange network, their success in maintaining vital links depends upon a myriad of internal/external factors, whose repercussions could be as unexpected as detrimental to some groups, but, depending on the cultural context, also beneficial to others. According to Jennings (2014b), these ammensalistic/commensalistic (and rarely mutualistic) processes of exchange and cultural contact/variations are better understood by adopting a combination of theoretical approaches often used in material culture studies, namely the 'relational theory' (Strathern 1988; Gell 1998), 'cultural object translation' (Hahn and Weiss 2013), and object biographies (Gosden and Marshall 1999).

Following the principle of the 'relational theory' in association with 'system theory', societies are considered as the culmination of a number of interacting factors, of which exchange relationships play a crucial role (Jennings 2012). As a result, modification of the latter may have repercussions on the entire social structure of one or more social groups involved in the exchange network(s). The acceptance of the circulated goods depends upon the 'cultural translation' of the various objects (Maran 2013), which, in itself (the translation), could be either 'importive' or 'productive'. With the former, people involved in the exchange use their position to achieve particular meaning(s) for imported objects; whereas with the latter, artefacts are given 'new' meanings by replicating them in 'new' social contexts (Jennings 2014b). In his study of the LBA trade and exchange systems in the Circum-Alpine region, Jennings (2013; Chapter 8 this volume) provides eloquent examples of both successful (*e.g.* the *Pfahlbauperlen*), and failed (*e.g. Allumiere* amber beads) translations of imported artefacts into new cultural locales of the northern Circum-Alpine region. Finally, observing how objects change as they travel through space and time may provide us with vital clues as to how those artefacts acquire/lose cultural significance in specific new cultural environments (Gosden and Marshall 1999). Reconstructed 'object biographies' can be even more informative in case of 'idealised' or 'individualised' biographical accounts (Kopytoff 1986). In the first case, object groups are considered as a whole and their changing value is obtained from multiple sources; whereas the 'individualised' biographies consider specific objects and how they are totally extracted from a specific context/meaning, modified, and re-associated to new socio-cultural values (see the exampe of arm/leg-ring conversion/recycling into razors in Jennings 2014a).

Another crucial aspect of studying exchanged (or travelling) goods over space and time is to identify their significance once they are re-fitted into a new cultural milieu – the best way to do so is to analyse the context(s) in which the objects were re-deposited. The deposition of objects at significant distances from the artefacts original source may indicate movement of people rather than simply object transfer/exchange; a good example is the *Herrnbaumgarten* razor found at Chelin-Lens (Switzerland) (Nicolas 2003). Changing value associations and social functions may be observed where artefacts are recurrently integrated into object assemblages in new cultural contexts. In doing so, a great help comes from Multiple Correspondence Analysis (MCA), which allows spotting how values of specific objects change as they are used in different geographical areas (Shennan 2006). One of the best examples of this analysis is the lake-dwelling glass beads found in three different areas: northern Italy (area of origin), the northern Alpine foreland, and further north in northern Europe/Scandinavia. It is interesting to notice the translation of these *Pfahlbauperlen* as they crossed the Alps, changing from typical female association to high status artefacts mixed with gender symbolism (Jennings 2013, 2014b; see also Chapter 8 this volume). Other good examples of changing value associations are provided by the *Pfahlbau* and *West Baltic* spearheads. Despite the fact that the former were more largely imported into northern Europe (from the Circum-Alpine region) than the latter were imported into the northern Alpine foreland, both became 'interchangeable', *e.g.* used in place of a local type (Jennings 2014b). What is important to notice in both the above-mentioned examples is that the objects did not travel with their original value, but the value was re-contextualised along the exchange route. In other words, the process of translation 'coined' new meanings and values as the artefacts travelled between regions, thus incorporating them, as Jennings (this volume: p. 226) clearly argues, 'into existing cultural settings, rather than importing them with a cultural package'. It should be noted however that in some cases, instead of cultural translation, there was simply the adoption of social attitudes along with artefacts, as proven by the several weights found throughout the Circum-Alpine region. The occurrence of these weights in different regions (*e.g.* from the Po Plain *terramare* area, to north of the Alps) may also signify transfer of trade concepts between regions as a result of an increase of commoditisation of exchange relationships (Jennings 2014b; Pare 2013). Indication of social change linked to exchange interactions is also accentuated by the number of (door) keys, which started to be used at a few lacustrine settlements such as ZH-Alpenquai, ZH-Wollishofen and Mörigen, as well as at inland sites, namely Montlingerberg, during the Late Bronze Age (Jennings 2013; Speck 1981).

From the concept of 'relational theory' discussed above, it is evident that the cultural shaping of the various communities would have been strictly linked to their involvement in any given exchange system. As a result, any slight re-organisation of trade routes would have also influenced the cultural setting of all the communities involved (note for instance the LBA/early Iron Age lake-dwelling exclusion from the inter-regional trade of the *Gündlingen* swords – see below). If accentuated instability had prevailed, it would have triggered specific socio-cultural changes, which, to a certain degree, would have no longer been avoidable.

Bronze Age subsistence and economy around the Alps: 'stability' or change?

As tempting as it might be, speaking of a ubiquitous BA Circum-Alpine region economy is certainly not feasible. The highly diverse environmental and cultural contexts will make it impossible to draw an average picture of the various economies and subsistence strategies. Moreover, the marked differences in taphonomic site formation processes between inland and lacustrine settlements/sites would certainly obscure any plausible conclusion. Instead, we will simply highlight crucial aspects linked to both subsistence and economy which are crucial for identifying signs of change/instability that might have contributed (along with goods/people circulation) to significant cultural variation, hence causing (or not) the demise of the lake-dwelling tradition in the Circum-Alpine region. One of the best ways to achieve this goal is to take a geographically 'zoomed-out' approach by paradoxically zooming-in to specific sites. It is then by joining the various dots that a larger and more detailed picture will emerge. Within our project (see Note 10 in Chapter 1), this ambitious exercise has been achieved by synergetic work between archaeobotany (Chapter 6) and archaeozoology (Chapter 7), with, at times, the invaluable help from geoarchaeolgy (Chapter 5), dendrochronology/dendrotypology (Chapter 3), palaeoclimatology (Chapter 4), and material culture studies (Chapter 8). Archaeobotany, along with palynology, is an ideal tool to study the interaction between people and the environment. In fact, not only are plant gathering, cereal cultivation and agriculture in general crucial for identifying changes in people's subsistence and economy, but they also provide valuable insights into climate and environmental variability. This relationship (people-environment) sometimes does confirm the norm (*e.g.* unfavourable climatic conditions = economic/subsistence crisis, and vice versa), but other times it reveals the unexpected.

Despite the fact that plant economy (including cereal cultivation and agriculture) and animal husbandry are usually studied separately by archaeobotany and archaeozoology respectively, it is astonishing to notice how remarkably interwoven and dependent on one another the two entities are. Both of them are for instance very much linked to climate and environmental conditions, but it is by combining the two together that extreme situations (*e.g.* economic/subsistence crisis) are avoided. One of the typical examples in the Circum-Alpine region Bronze Age is the insignificant (if any at all) increase of hunting activity during periods of unfavourable climate conditions. In fact, contrary to the Neolithic, when worsened climate usually triggered a higher hunting activity (to the extent that some species risked extinction – see Schibler 2004; Schibler *et al.* 1997b), in the Bronze Age, bad climate did not have this repercussion on Alpine and pre-Alpine communities (including the lake-dwellers). The reason why that did not happen is fairly straightforward: the adoption of a greater diversity in the spectrum of cultivated plants (especially those more resistant to climatic variations) kept harvest losses to a minimum (see Kreuz and Schäfer 2008; and Chapter 6 this volume), hence reducing the necessity of alternative subsistence strategies (*i.e.* hunting). Diversity in crop cultivation was indeed one of the main 'technological' developments in agricultural activity in the Circum-Alpine region during the Late Bronze Age/early Iron Age. The philosophy was: 'if you cannot beat it (the climate) then adapt to it'. It therefore became crucial to find which crop suited best the surrounding environment, and with which other crop (cereal) it would match better for a combined/risk-free cultivation. For instance, although barley and millet were the two most ubiquitous and less-demanding crops, they were employed differently in the northern and southern slopes of the Alpine region (Jacomet *et al.* 1989). Because of its suitability for low-quality soil, short growing season and resistance to drought, the former (barley) was cultivated more in the north, and would fit perfectly with emmer, spelt, einkorn and, sometimes, millet (depending on the area); whereas millet, because of its vulnerability to lower temperatures, was more used in the south (*e.g.* northern Italy/southern Switzerland), where, on the other hand, barely was not extremely popular (see Kühn and Heitz-Weniger, this volume; Brombacher 2008).

Although to a lesser degree, also animal husbandry depended upon environmental factors. Cattle were the most common animals and they were kept just about everywhere in the Alpine region, but some areas were certainly more suitable for other species such as sheep and goats (see Stopp, Chapter 7 this volume). Pigs were also extremely common though because of their susceptibility to very cold climate, they were not the best candidates for Alpine (high-altitude) locations (Riedel 1996). It is also interesting to notice that the function of the site/settlement also played an important role in establishing the type of animal husbandry (and perhaps even vice-versa). Different characteristics of animal husbandry, along with the determination of sex and age of slaughtering can also give us useful insights on the site function, external influence and/or regional/supra regional contact. For instance, more male cattle in northern Italy's Late Bronze Age settlements of the Adige Valley suggest a form of distribution/trading posts; whereas the prevalence of female animals (cows) in the eastern part of the valley hints to farming agglomerates. Moreover, the high number of young pig slaughtered at Hauterive-Champréveyres (Switzerland), Pozzuolo-Ciastiei and Concordia Sagittaria (Italy) might support the idea of animals used as a form of currency (see Stopp, this volume); and, the absence of new-born calves in Late Bronze Age settlements (as opposed to some examples in MBA sites) might actually point to an increase in transhumance. Finally, even the absence of the above-mentioned rules of thumb could point to an atypical function of the settlement as is the case of Poggio Rusco and Noceto (Italy) and Zurich-Grosser Hafner (Switzerland), where a large variety of bones (unusually including wild animals) may suggest ritual activities (de Grossi Mazzorin 2009 and Stopp, Chapter 7 this volume).

As highlighted above and throughout Chapters 6 and 7, despite the influence from both the climate and the various exchange networks (including contact and people movement), the Late Bronze Age/early Iron Age was not a period of radical transformations concerning the subsistence economy of the Circum-Alpine region communities. Instead, there was a series of rather clever processes of technological (in both crop cultivation and animal husbandry) adaptations to internal/external influence; these 'adjustments' depended upon cultural as well as environmental factors, and they were not the same in all geographical regions. Yet, notwithstanding this apparent and deceiving 'continuity/stability', something major was happening: a radical socio-cultural change that would transform and eventually diminish a millennia-long living tradition.

Late Bronze Age in the Alpine region: a multitude of interacting factors

Contrary to what the economic subsistence elements may hint towards, the Late Bronze Age/early Iron Age period in the Circum-Alpine region was anything but stagnant. Directly or indirectly, a multitude of interacting factors did indeed stretch the apparent stability and resilience to change of the Alpine-foreland lake-dwellings to the limit. From an environmental point of view, those lacustrine communities were under attack by drastic climatic deteriorations (Magny *et al.* 2013; Magny and Peyron 2008; Magny *et al.* 2009; see also Chapter 4, this volume), against which they showed remarkable resilience (Menotti *et al.* 2014), although alas in many cases unsuccessful. Colder and wetter climatic conditions accompanied by abrupt lake level fluctuations did not only threaten the settlements, but they also jeopardized the subsistence and production economy. Fortunately, the adoption of innovative advances in agriculture (*e.g.* greater diversity in the spectrum of cultivated plants, and the combined cultivation of one or more particular species of cereals) reduced the damage significantly (see Chapter 6), avoiding drastic measures, *i.e.* increase of hunting activities, as had happened previously in the Neolithic (Schibler *et al.* 1997b – see also Chapter 7 this volume). The cultural threat was even more 'severe', but, as usual, difficult to become aware of until the 'damage' was done. As shown by the development of trade centres such as Hauterive-Champréveyres, the increased exchange activities as well as the movement of peoples and ideas linked to the LBA long-distance trade networks was initially welcomed by the lacustrine groups (especially in the northern Alpine foreland). However, excessive protective measures (*i.e.* more export than import) and/or a series of 'failed object translations' (Jennings 2014b) limited their involvement in inter-regional trade and exchange networks. One of the best examples is the re-organisation of the LBA trade routes in the region of the Three-Lakes (Lake Neuchâtel, Lake Biel and Lake Murten) in north-western Switzerland, immediately following the trade connections of the *Mörigen* swords. The well-established trade route (with *Mörigen* swords), linking central Europe to southern France via the Rhône and Middle Rhine Valley, became peripheral during the subsequent circulation of the *Gündlingen* type swords (i.e. immediately after [early Iron Age – HaC] the *Mörigen* swords), excluding important nodal points of a large portion of the north-western Circum-Alpine region lake-dwelling areas. A process of re-integration into vital network systems seemed to have occurred at the later stage of the Iron Age (HaD), but by then, most of the lake-dwellings had disappeared (Jennings 2013; see also Jennings, Chapter 8 this volume).

It is clearly understood that trade networks do not only, and/or simply, involve the circulation of goods, but, most importantly, also the movement of people, ideas, and even cultural traits. For instance, the change in burial practices from flat graves to tumuli in the latest phase of the Late Bronze Age and in the Iron Age (Jennings 2013) stresses the shift of emphasis from the dividual/community to the individual, with the 'new' (or renewed) importance of demonstrating social status through the display of material culture as well as landmarks (including settlements) in the cultural landscape. This process of transformation is not only noticeable with the construction of the above-mentioned tumuli, but also with the deposition (in burial and hoards) of particular objects, such as keys, highly decorated (with iron inlays) sword handles, and even symbolically-charged artefacts such razors re-manufactured from arm/leg rings, possibly signifying the attainment of a particular social status at a certain stage of an individual's life (Jennings 2014a). Settlements were also part of that particular physical display in the landscape – becoming 'visible' was not only a matter of 'showing off', but also part of being accepted into a socio-economic network of prestige. A typical example of this is the development of the so-called *Fürstensitze*, high-status hilltop settlements that acted as regional manufacturing and exchange centres, often located in strategic nodal points of well-established trade networks (Jennings 2014b).

Through the concept of 'relational theory' we have clearly seen how all the above-mentioned interacting factors influence each other, and the various repercussions of events (either positive of negative) do not spare anyone/anything involved in any given interacting network.

We have seen for instance how the climate influences people; people affect the environment; the environment has an impact on subsistence and economy, which, in turn, may contribute to shaping people's socio-cultural development … and so on and so forth. However, we have also noticed that this 'processual' series of events is not always as straightforward as it might seem. People's conscious, sometimes even 'irrational', decisions may lead to unexpected outcomes, whose repercussions may be inconceivable (see for example the clever crop cultivation strategy to fight climate change discussed above, and in Chapter 6). At this stage though, an obvious question arises: can the above-mentioned interacting series of events be considered separately, in order for us to identify the culprit (the cause for the demise of the lake-dwelling tradition)? And, if we are lucky enough to 'find' it, will it be a 'solo felon', or are we, once again, faced with a series of 'offenders' supported by a number of accomplices?

Lake-dwelling tradition: why the end?

After four years of research, painstaking analyses, and the consideration of a large number of candidates, our project team finally selected four possible suspects: climate, economic crisis, long-distance trade, and cultural change. At the beginning, the strongest suspect was, and always had been, the climate; it had started bothering those poor lacustrine communities since they decided to settle the northern Circum-Alpine region in the late part of the fifth millennium BC, forcing them to abandon the lake shores several times throughout the three and a half millennia of lake-dwelling tradition. Their resilience and determination did however always drive them back to the lake shores (Magny 2013; Magny *et al.* 2005; Magny *et al.* 2013; Magny and Peyron 2008; Vannière *et al.* 2008; Schlichtherle 1997; Menotti

2009, 2003, 2004, 2001, 2012; Hafner 2002). Since a drastic climate change did also occur during the Late Bronze Age, especially in the northern Circum-Alpine region, and it did indeed influence the lacustrine communities significantly (Menotti *et al.* 2014) with yet another lake-shore abandonment in the 9th century BC, it would have been obvious to hold the climate responsible. However, it was indeed our second suspect (economic crisis) that let it off the hook. In fact, despite the lake-dwelling subsistence and economy (especially considering agriculture) being affected by colder and wetter climate conditions, people were able to take the right precautions (*i.e.* greater diversity in the spectrum of cultivated crops – see above, and Chapter 6) and limit the damage considerably. Therefore, our first two suspects were discharged, although the former (climate) did cause a lot of trouble.

The third suspect (long-distance trade) had also been under serious scrutiny, as, along with the climate, it was thought to have played a crucial role in the final disappearance of the lake-dwellings. As repeatedly discussed throughout the volume, trade and exchange is not simply circulation of objects through space and time, and, as Jennings (see Chapter 8) argues exchanged goods are not just 'travelling objects', but they involve cultural contact, transfer of ideas, beliefs and practices. As the exchanged object reaches the 'new' destination, it is through a process of 'translation' and 'redefinition' of social value that the object itself, and the various aspects that travel with it, becomes incorporated in the new cultural setting. The lake-dwellers initially welcomed the impetus brought by the LBA movement of goods and people, but then, they subsequently adopted a 'defensive' attitude towards it, and got temporarily excluded from it. In the meantime, social transformations such as change in funerary practices (*e.g.* from flat graves to tumuli), more emphasis on identity and status, and the need to be more 'visible' in the landscape began to spread and become integrated into the Alpine foreland local communities' cultural makeup. At that time (*e.g.* the very end of the Late Bronze Age/beginning of the Iron Age – *c.* 8th century BC), the lake-dwellings had already disappeared and been replaced by a number of thriving inland settlements – in particular the well-visible high-status *Fürstensitze*. It is difficult to pinpoint whether the disappearance occurred during or after the aforementioned trade network exclusion in the early Iron Age, but, at this point, it is completely irrelevant as the disappearance was not a consequence of that trade shift, but the result of an undergoing cultural change that had started well before. This statement leads us to our final verdict: it was not the long-distance trade that forced the lake-dwellers to abandon the lake shores; it was their processes of adapting to the various cultural variations brought along with it that did it. As undramatic as it may seem, the lake-dwellers did not probably know that their 3500-year-long lacustrine way of life was under threat...all the choices that they made during that cultural transformation were, almost certainly, voluntarily.

As we might expect, there were indeed a couple of nostalgic attempts to repopulate the lake shores after the demise (see for instance Ürschhausen-Horn (Gollnisch-Moos 1999), and a few more examples later), but they were very sporadic and short-lived. By then, a number of socio-cultural aspects, funerary practices, beliefs and even the cultural landscape had changed to the extent that living on the lake was no longer viable. The lake-dwellers needed to adapt to fast-changing social dynamics, and re-fit into a more sustainable social context. It might seem sad that three-and-a-half-millennia of lake-dwelling tradition 'suddenly' came to an end, but perhaps it was time for a 'temporary' change – in fact, judging from today's numerous lacustrine resorts/villages/towns of the Circum-Alpine region, we have indeed returned to the lake after all.

References

Bernabó Brea, M. and Cardarelli, A. (1997) Le terramare nel tempo. In M. Bernabó Brea, A. Cardarelli and M. Cremaschi (eds) *Le terramare: La più antica civiltà padana*: 295–378. Milan: Electa.

Brombacher, C. (2008) Unpublished data from Bronze Age and Iron Age Roveredo GR San Fedele Valasc. Basel University.

Cremaschi, M., Pizzi, C. and Valsecchi, V. (2006) Water management and land use in the terramare and a possible climatic co-factor in their abandonment: The case study of the terramare of Poviglio Santa Rosa (northern Italy). *Quaternary International* 151: 87–98.

De Marinis, R. C. (2010) Continuity and discontinuity in northern Italy from the recent to the final Bronze Age: a view from north-western Italy. In Scienze dell'Antichità (ed.) *Le ragioni del cambiamento/Reasons for Change*: 535–45. Roma: Edizioni Quasar.

Fasani, L. (1994) Il Calcolitico e l'etá del Bronzo nell'Italia settentrionale. *Bullettino di Paletnologia Italiana* 85: 245–59.

Gell, A. (1998) *Art and Agency*. Oxford: Clarendon Press.

Gollnisch-Moos, H. (1999) *Ürschhausen-Horn: Haus- und Siedlungsstrukturen der spätestbronzezeitlichen Siedlung*. Frauenfeld: Departement für Erziehung und Kultur des Kantons Thurgau.

Gosden, C. and Marshall, Y. (1999) The cultural biography of objects. *World Archaeology* 31(2): 169–78.

Hafner, A. (1995) *Die Frühe Bronzezeit in der Westschweiz: Funde und Befunde aus Siedlungen, Gräern und Horten der entwickelten Frühbronzezeit*. Bern: Staatlicher Lehrmittelverlag.

Hafner, A. (2002) Vom Spät- zum Endneolithikum. Wandel und Kontinuität um 2700 v. Chr. in der Schweiz. *Archäologisches Korrespondenzblatt* 32(4): 517–31.

Hahn, H. P. and Weiss, H. (eds) (2013) *Mobility, Meaning and the Transformation of Things: shifting contexts of material culture through time and space*. Oxford: Oxbow Books.

Hochuli, S., Niffeler, U. and Rychner, V. (eds) (1998) *Die Schweiz vom Paläolithikum bis zum frühen Mittelalter: SPM III Bronzezeit*. Basel: Schweizerische Gesellschaft für Ur- und Frühgeschichte.

Jacomet, S., Brombacher, C. and Dick, M. (1989) *Archäobotanik am Zürichsee*. Zürich: Orell Füssli Verlag.

Jennings, B. (2012) When the Going Gets Tough…? Climatic or Cultural Influences for the LBA Abandonment of Circum-Alpine Lake-Dwellings. In J. Kniesel, W. Kirleis, M. Dal Corso, N. Taylor and V. Tiedtke (eds) *Collapse or Continuity? Environment and Development of Bronze Age Human Landscapes. Proceedings of the International Workshop 'Socio-Environmental Dynamics over the Last 12,000 Years: The Creation of Landscapes II'*: 85–99. Kiel: Rudolf Habelt.

Jennings, B. (2013) Travelling Objects: Changing Values. Trade, exchange and cultural influences for the decline of the lake-dwelling tradition in the northern Circum-Alpine region during the Late Bronze Age. *Fakultät Philosophisch-Naturwissenschaft*. Universität Basel.

Jennings, B. (2014a) Repair, Recycle or Re-use? Creating mnemonic devices through the modification of object biographies. *Cambridge Archaeological Journal* 24(1): 163–76.

Jennings, B. (2014b) *Travelling Objects: Changing Values. The role of northern Alpine lake-dwelling communities in exchange and communication networks during the Late Bronze Age*. Oxford: Archaeopress.

Köninger, J. (2002) Oggelshausen-Bruckgraben – Funde und Befunde aus einer eisenzeitlichen

Fischfanglage im suedlichen Federseeried, Gemainde Oggelshausen, Kreis Biberach. *Heimat- und Altertumsverein Heidenheim an der Brenz* 2001–2002: 34–56.

Kopytoff, I. (1986) The cultural biography of things: commoditization as process. In A. Appadurai (ed.) *The social life of things: Commodities in cultural perspective*: 64–91. Cambridge: Cambridge University Press.

Krause, R. (1988) *Die endneolithischen und frühbronzezeitlichen Grabfunde auf der Nordstadtterrasse von Singen am Hohentwiel*. Stuttgart: Konrad Theiss.

Kreuz, A. and Schäfer, E. (2008) Archaeobotanical considerations of the development of Pre-Roman Iron Age crop growing in the region of Hesse, Germany, and the question of agricultural production and consumption at hillfort sites and open settlements. *Vegetation History and Archaeobotany* 17(1): 159–179.

Magny, M. (2013) Palaeoclimatology and archaeology in the wetlands. In F. Menotti and A. O'Sullivan (eds) *The Oxford Handbook of Wetland Archaeology*: 585–97. Oxford: Oxford University Press.

Magny, M., Bégeot, C., Peyron, O., Richoz, I., Marguet, A. and Billaud, Y. (2005) Habitats littoraux et histoire des premières communautés agricoles au Néolithique et à l'Âge du Bronze: une mise en perspective paléoclimatique. In P. Della Casa and M. Trachsel (eds) *WES'04: Wetland economies and societies*: 133–42. Zurich: Chronos Verlag.

Magny, M., Combourieu-Nebout, N., De Beaulieu, J. L., Bout-Roumazeilles, V., Colombaroli, D., Desprat, S., Francke, A., Joannin, S., Ortu, E., Peyron, O., Revel, M., Sadori, L., Siani, L., Sicre, M. A., Samartin, S., Simonneau, A., Tinner, W., Vannière, B., Wagner, B., Zanchetta, G., Anselmetti, F., Brugiapaglia, E., Chapron, E., Debret, M., Desmet, M., Didier, J., Essallami, L., Galop, D., Gilli, A., Haas, J. N., Kallel, N., Millet, L., Stock, A., Turon, J. L. and Wirth, S. (2013) North–south palaeohydrological contrasts in the central Mediterranean during the Holocene: tentative synthesis and working hypotheses. *Climate of the Past* 9: 2043–71.

Magny, M., Joannin, S., Galop, D., Vannière, B., Haas, J. N., Bassetti, M., Bellintani, P., Scandolari, R. and Desmet, M. (2012) Holocene palaeohydrological changes in the northern Mediterranean borderlands as reflected by the lake-level record of Lake Ledro, northeastern Italy. *Quaternary Research* 77: 382–96.

Magny, M. and Peyron, O. (2008) Variations climatiques et histoire des sociétés à l'Age du Bronze au nord et au sud des Alpes. In J. Guilaine (ed.) *Villes, villages, campagnes de l'Age du Bronze*. Paris: Editions Errance.

Magny, M., Peyron, O., Gauthier, E., Rouèche, H., Bordon, A., Billaud, Y., Chapron, E., Marguet, A., Pétrequin, P. and Vannière, B. (2009) Quantitative reconstruction of climatic variations during the Bronze and early Iron Ages, based on pollen and lake-level data in the NW Alps, France. *Quaternary International* 200: 102–10.

Maise, C. (2005) Archäoklimatologie neolithischer Seeufersiedlungen. In D. Gronenborn (ed.) *Klimaveränderung udn Kulturwandel in neolithischen Gesellschaften Mitteleuropas, 6700–2200 v. Chr.* Mainz: Verlag des Römisch-Germanischen Zentralmuseums.

Maran, J. (2013) Bright as the sun: The appropriation of amber objects in Mycenaean Greece. In H. P. Hahn and H. Weiss (eds) *Mobility, Meaning and Transformations of Things: shifting contexts of material culture through time and space*: 147–69. Oxford: Oxbow Books.

Martinelli, N. (2005) Dendrocronologia e archaeologia: situazione e prospettive della ricerca in Italia. In P. Attema, A. Nijboer and A. Zifferero (eds) *Communities and settlements from the Neolithic to the Early Medieval Periods*: 347–448. Oxford: BAR International Series 1452.

Marzatico, F. (2004) 150 years of lake-dwelling research in Northern Italy. In F. Menotti (ed.) *Living on the lake in prehistoric Europe: 150 years of lake-dwelling research*: 83–97. London: Routledge.

Menotti, F. (2001) *'The missing period': Middle Bronze Age lake-dwellings in the Alps*. Oxford: Archaeopress.

Menotti, F. (2003) Cultural response to environmental change in the Alpine lacustrine regions: the displacement model. *Oxford Journal of Archaeology* 22(4): 375–96.

Menotti, F. (ed.) (2004) *Living on the lake in prehistoric Europe.* London: Routledge.

Menotti, F. (2009) Climate variations in the Circum-Alpine region and their influence on the Neolithic – Bronze Age lacustrine communities: displacement and/or cultural adaptation. *Documenta Praehistorica* 36: 61–66.

Menotti, F. (2012) *Wetland Archaeology and Beyond: Theory and Practice.* Oxford: Oxford University Press.

Menotti, F., Jennings, B. and Gollnisch-Moos, H. (2014) 'Gifts for the Gods': lake-dwellers' macabre remedies against floods in central Europe Bronze Age. *Antiquity* 88(340): 456–69.

Nicolas, I. (2003) Au fil du rasoir: étude des rasoirs métalliques de l'âge du Bronze jusqu'a haut Moyen Age en Suisse. In M. Besse, L.-I. Stahl Gretsch and P. Curdy (eds) *ConstellaSion. Hommage à Alain Gallay*: 273–89. Lausanne: Cahiers d'archéologie romande.

Nicolis, F. (2013) Northern Italy. In H. Fokkens and A. F. Harding (eds) *The Oxford handbook of the European Bronze Age*: 692–705. Oxford: Oxford University Press.

Pare, C. F. E. (2013) Weighing, commodification, and money. In H. Fokkens and A. F. Harding (eds) *The Oxford handbook of the European Bronze Age*: 508–27. Oxford: Oxford University Press.

Perini, R. (1987) *Scavi archeologici nella zona palafitticola di Fiavè-Carera.* Trento: Servizio Beni culturali della Provincia di Trento.

Pétrequin, P., Magny, M. and Bailly, M. (2005) Habitat lacustre, densité de population et climat. L'exemple du Jura français. In P. Della Casa and M. Trachsel (eds) *WES'04: Wetland economies and societies*: 143–68. Zurich: Chronos Verlag.

Riedel, A. (1996) Archaeozoological investigations in North-eastern Italy: the exploitation of animals since the Neolithic. *Preistoria Alpina* 30: 43–94.

Rubat Borel, F. (2009) Entre Italie et Gaule: la transition âge du Bronze / âge du Fer dans le Piémont nord-occidental et la Vallée d'Aoste. In M. J. Roulière-Lambert, A. Daubigney, P.-Y. Milcent, M. Talon and J. Vital (eds) *De l'âge du Bronze à l'âge du Fer en France et en Europe occidentale (Xe–VIIe siècle av. J.-C.). Actes du XXXe colloque international de l'A.F.E.A.F., thème spécialisé co-organisé avec l'A.P.R.A.B (Saint-Romain-en-Gal, 26–28 mai 2006)*: 237–52. Dijon: Revue Archéologique de l'Est, supplément 27.

Rychner, V., Bolliger Schreyer, S., Carazzetti, R., David-Elbiali, M., Hafner, A., Hochuli, S., Janke, R., Rageth, J. and Seifert, M. (1998) Geschichte und Kulturen der Bronzezeit in der Schweiz. In Schweizerische Gesellschaft für Ur- und Frühgeschichte (ed.) *Die Schweiz vom Paläolithikum bis zum frühen Mittelalter: SPM Bronzezeit*: 103–33. Basel: Schweizerische Gesellschaft für Ur- und Frühgeschichte.

Schibler, J. (2004) Bones as a key for reconstructing the environment, nutrition and economy of the lake-dwelling societies. In F. Menotti (ed.) *Living on the lake in prehistoric Europe: 150 years of lake-dwelling research*: 144–61. London: Routledge.

Schibler, J., Hüster-Plogmann, H., Jacomet, S., Brombacher, C., Gross-Klee, E. and Rast-Eicher, A. (eds) (1997a) *Ökonomie und Ökologie neolithischer und bronzezeitlicher Ufersiedlungen am Zürichsee.* Zurich: Direktion der öffentlichen Bauten des Kantons Zürich.

Schibler, J., Jacomet, S., Hüster-Plogmann, H. and Brombacher, C. (1997b) Economic crash in the 37th and 36th century BC cal in Neolithic lake shore sites in Switzerland. *Anthropozoologica* 25–26: 553–70.

Schlichtherle, H. (1997) Pfahlbauten rund um die Alpen. In H. Schlichtherle (ed.) *Pfahlbauten rund um die Alpen*: 7–14. Stuttgart: Konrad Theiss Verlag GmbH.

Schlitzer, U. (2009) Seeufersiedlungen in Bayern. Die Roseninsel im Starnberger See und das Problem der bayerischen Lücke. In J. M. Bagley and C. Eggl (eds) *Alpen, Kult und Eisenzeit*: 493–504. Rahden: Studia honoraria.

Shennan, S. (2006) *Quantifying archaeology.* Iowa City: University of Iowa Press.

Speck, J. (1981) Schloss und Schlüssel zur späten Pfahlbauzeit. *Helvetia Archaeologica* 45/48: 230–41.

Strahm, C. (1997) Chronologie der Pfahlbauten. In H. Schlichtherle (ed.) *Pfahlbauten rund um die Alpen*: 124–26. Stuttgart: Konrad Theiss Verlag GmbH.

Strathern, M. (1988) *Gender of the Gift.* Berkeley: University of California Press.

Suter, P. J., Hafner, A. and Glauser, K. (2005) Prähistorishe und frügeschichtliche Funde aus dem Eis – der wiederentdeckte Pass über das Schnidejoch. *Archäologie Schweiz* 28: 16–23.

Vannière, B., Colombaroli, D., Chapron, E., Leroux, A., Tinner, W. and Magny, M. (2008) Climate versus human-driven fire regimes in Mediterranean landscapes: the Holocene record of Lago dell'Accesa (Tuscany, Italy). *Quaternary Science Reviews* 27: 1181–96.

Vannière, B., Magny, M., Joannin, S., Simonneau, A., Wirth, S., Hamann, Y., Chapron, E., Gilli, A., Desmet, M. and Anselmetti, F. (2013) Orbital changes, variations in solar activity and increased anthropogenic activities: controls on the Holocene flood frequency in the Lake Ledro area, Northern Italy. *Climate of the Past* 9: 1193–209.